Making the New Middle East

Contemporary Issues in the Middle East
Mehran Kamrava, *Series Editor*

Select Titles in Contemporary Issues in the Middle East

Colonial Jerusalem: The Spatial Construction of Identity and Difference in a City of Myth, 1948–2012
Thomas Philip Abowd

Democracy and the Nature of American Influence in Iran, 1941–1979
David R. Collier

In the Wake of the Poetic: Palestinian Artists after Darwish
Najat Rahman

Iraqi Migrants in Syria: The Crisis before the Storm
Sophia Hoffmann

Islam, Arabs, and the Intelligent World of the Jinn
Amira El-Zein

Making Do in Damascus: Navigating a Generation of Change in Family and Work
Sally K. Gallagher

The Mizrahi Era of Rebellion: Israel's Forgotten Civil Rights Struggle, 1948–1966
Bryan K. Roby

Shahaama: Five Egyptian Men Tell Their Stories
Nayra Atiya

Making the New Middle East

Politics, Culture, and Human Rights

Edited by Valerie J. Hoffman

Syracuse University Press

Syracuse, New York 13244-5290

First Edition 2019

19 20 21 22 23 24   6 5 4 3 2 1

∞ The paper used in this publication meets the minimum requirements of the American National Standard for Information Sciences—Permanence of Paper for Printed Library Materials, ANSI Z39.48-1992.

For a listing of books published and distributed by Syracuse University Press, visit www.SyracuseUniversityPress.syr.edu.

ISBN: 978-0-8156-3606-9 (hardcover)
978-0-8156-3612-0 (paperback)
978-0-8156-5457-5 (e-book)

Library of Congress Cataloging-in-Publication Number: 2018053056

Manufactured in the United States of America

Contents

Illustrations and Tables

Illustrations

Tables

Acknowledgments

This book has its origins in a conference titled "The New Middle East: Social and Political Change in the Twenty-First Century," sponsored by the Center for South Asian and Middle Eastern Studies at the University of Illinois at Urbana–Champaign on October 18–20, 2012. Taking place in the middle of the Arab Spring uprisings, the conference brought together twenty-seven scholars for an exciting conversation across disciplines, ending with a joint discussion on the future of democracy in the Middle East. Among the many conferences that took place on the Arab Spring at this time, this one stood out for its broad perspective beyond the events that grab headlines and for the way it brought together experts from such diverse disciplines as political science, anthropology, sociology, media studies, and comparative literature. The organizers decided that the conference afforded an opportunity to create a uniquely broad narrative on the contemporary Middle East that ought to find expression in a published text. Although many books were rapidly produced on the Arab Spring in 2011 and 2012, there was a dearth of up-to-date books on the broader cultural and social issues of the contemporary Middle East. It was decided to translate the momentum provided by the conference into a book that would be interesting and insightful for the informed public and usable as a textbook in undergraduate and graduate classes on the Middle East.

Many of the conference speakers had already committed their papers to other publications, so other contributors were brought into the project in order to cover the major issues at stake in the struggle for justice in the Middle East. None of the authors were compensated for their contributions; I owe each of them a debt of thanks. Work on this book was delayed because of a plethora of other commitments, and the authors responded by updating their contributions to reflect changes on the ground. For this, too, I thank them. During the period of final revisions, one of the authors, Cheryl Ann Rubenberg, passed away. I am grateful that, even in her final illness, she remained deeply committed to this project. While writing a memorial notice for the *Review of Middle East Studies*, I learned of the extent of her dedication to the cause of Palestinian human rights and her personal involvement in helping several Palestinians study in North America; she modeled the combined pursuit of meticulous scholarship and humanitarian advocacy.

The conference in 2012 was funded by a Hewlett International Conference Grant from International Programs and Studies at the University of Illinois, with additional funding from the US Department of Education's Undergraduate International Studies and Foreign Language Program. The UISFL grant also provided me with summer salary in 2013 to enable me to devote time to this book. The following units at the University of Illinois cosponsored the conference: the Center for Advanced Study; the College of Liberal Arts and Sciences; the School of Literatures, Cultures, and Linguistics; the European Union Center; the Departments of Anthropology, History, Media and Cinema Studies, Political Science, Religion, and Sociology; the Programs in Comparative and World Literature, Jewish Culture and Society, and Women and Gender in Global Perspectives; and the Global Crossroads Living and Learning Community. I thank all of them for their participation in this exciting gathering of scholars.

Asaf Volanski of B'Tselem was extraordinarily helpful in preparing the maps for figures 1 and 2; I am very grateful to him and to Roy Yellin of B'Tselem for granting permission to use them. I would also like to thank Dr. Brendan McKay for providing me with the photograph used for figure 3 and the United Nations Office for the Coordination of Humanitarian Affairs for providing me with the map used in figure 4.

I would also like to express my appreciation to Alison M. Shay, former acquisitions editor at Syracuse University Press, for all her patience, persistence, and assistance in helping bring this project to fruition, and Fred Wellner for designing the book cover.

Finally, I thank my husband, Kirk Hauser, for his constant support of my work.

Making the New Middle East

Introduction

VALERIE J. HOFFMAN

No one can doubt that the Middle East is a region of pivotal importance in the world today. The source of much of the world's oil reserves and the site of many conflicts, it is a focus of heightened interest among policy makers and others concerned with global security. Less attention has been paid to the rampant abuse of human rights in the region; both residents and analysts assumed the durability of entrenched authoritarian regimes and the hopelessness of active struggle for justice. In recent years, however, there were signs that the populace was becoming less resigned to the status quo, beginning with the April 6 Youth Movement founded in Egypt in 2008 and followed by the spontaneous protests of Iran's "Green Movement" following the 2009 presidential elections. Neither of these movements had any notable success, and the latter was brutally suppressed. But protests launched in Tunisia in December 2010 brought down the government in January 2011 and inspired a series of "Arab Spring" uprisings in 2011–12, catalyzed by demands for democracy, dignity, and human rights in states ruled for a half century by military strongmen and other types of authoritarian regimes. These events captured the world's imagination and inspired popular protests in Europe and the United States. The whole world watched as new regimes were formed in Tunisia, Egypt, Yemen, and Libya; international alliances shifted; and creative spirits produced bold new visions of society in art, music, and literature.

It was in this context that many people began to speak of a "new Middle East." This term had been used earlier with different references: Shimon Peres used it to refer to politics after the Oslo Accords

(1993), former US secretary of state Condoleezza Rice used it in 2006 to express a hope that the bloodshed occurring in Iraq and Lebanon represented "creative chaos" and the "birth pangs of a New Middle East" (Harnden 2006; Kamal 2015), and the president of the Council on Foreign Affairs, writing that same year, used the term to refer to the demise of the United States' power and prestige in the region after the invasion of Iraq in 2003 (Haass 2006). However, the term gained new traction during the Arab Spring as analysts expressed unprecedented optimism concerning the possibility of democracy in the Arab world and pondered the implications of unfolding events. The currency of the term is reflected in the large number of recently published books with "the new Middle East" in their titles.

Six years later, the Middle East remains unstable and authoritarianism's hold has barely been loosened—indeed, it has been strengthened in Egypt and Turkey, while Syria, Libya, and Yemen remain in the grip of civil war. This book examines the struggles for justice in today's Middle East from the perspective of multiple disciplines by analyzing the dynamics and outcomes of the upheavals, the status of human rights and gender relations, the prospects for democracy, and popular aspirations for dignity and justice as expressed through literature, media, and the arts. For the purposes of this book, the Middle East includes all of the countries on North Africa's Mediterranean coast (Morocco, Algeria, Tunisia, Libya, and Egypt), Sudan, and the countries east of the Mediterranean, from Turkey in the north to the southern tip of the Arabian Peninsula, and east to Afghanistan.

True justice, entailing the rule of law, equality before the law, and guarantees of personal security and freedoms, is a challenging goal in any region or context, but it has been vexingly absent in the Middle East. An understanding of why this is so requires a review of some of the region's most important attributes.

Demographic and Economic Characteristics

The relative aridity of the Middle East makes water management and control of water resources significant economic and political

Table 1
Population, GDP, and average individual income

Country	*Population*	*GDP*	*Average income*
Afghanistan	32,564,342	$61.69 billion	2,000
Algeria	39,542,166	$552.6 billion	14,300
Bahrain	1,346,613	$61.56 billion	51,400
Egypt	88,487,396	$945.4 billion	11,100
Iran	81,824,270	$1.284 trillion	16,500
Iraq	37,056,169	$505.4 billion	14,100
Israel	8,049,314	$268.3 billion	33,400
Jordan	8,117,564	$79.77 billion	11,900
Kuwait	2,788,534	$283.9 billion	71,000
Lebanon	6,184,701	$80.51 billion	17,900
Libya	6,411,776	$103.3 billion	16,600
Morocco	33,322,699	$254.4 billion	7,700
Oman	4,092,000	$163.6 billion	44,100
Palestine—Gaza Strip	1,816,379	$1.3 billion	876
Palestine—West Bank	2,731,052	$5.4 billion	1,924
Qatar	2,194,817	$323.2 billion	144,400
Saudi Arabia	27,752,316	$1.616 trillion	52,800
Sudan	36,108,853	$159.5 billion	4,500
Syria	17,064,854	$107.6 billion[a]	5,100
Tunisia	11,037,225	$125.1 billion	11,400
Turkey	79,414,269	$1.515 trillion	19,600
United Arab Emirates	5,779,760 (CIA est.) 9,445,624 (UN est.)	$605 billion	65,000
Yemen	26,737,317	$106 billion	3,900
	Comparison countries		
China	1,367,485,388	$17.63 trillion	12,900
Germany	80,854,408	$3.613 trillion	44,700
India	1,251,695,584	$7.277 trillion	5,800
Indonesia	255,993,674	$2.554 trillion	10,200
Kenya	45,925,301	$134.7 billion	3,100
Malaysia	30,513,848	$746.8 billion	24,500
Mexico	121,736,809	$2.143 trillion	17,900
Russia	142,423,773	$3.568 trillion	24,800
United States	321,368,864	$17.46 trillion	54,800

Source: Statistics from CIA World Handbook. Population estimates are generally for 2015; GDP estimates are generally for 2014.
[a] Estimate for 2011.

issues, but such concerns are often forced into the background by the dominance of oil in the region's economy and by intense, often violent struggles over power and ideology. Home to some of the wealthiest countries in the world as well as some of the poorest, the Middle East is marked by extreme contrasts of wealth and poverty.

Over the past century, the Middle East underwent extremely rapid social and political change, including independence struggles, the founding of nation-states, the birth of new political ideologies, the adoption of modern technologies, and the institution of mass education. Improvements in public health led to a dramatic decrease in child mortality, a corresponding rise in population, and, because of the region's high birthrate, a demographic shift toward societies that are disproportionately young (Moghadam 2013, 291–95). The inability of rural areas to sustain their growing population led many thousands to migrate to the cities; despite the images of deserts and nomads that often spring to Western minds at the mention of the Middle East, about 73 percent of the region's population lived in cities in 2010—up from 24 percent in 1950 (Moghadam 2013, 288). Despite the perdurance of some aspects of Middle Eastern culture, the impact of urbanization and globalization on lifeways and values can scarcely be overestimated.

Religion

Although its significance has often been overstated, religion has a strong influence on social and political life in the Middle East. Many of the chapters in this book address, in one form or other, the role of religion, particularly Islam, in politics and the struggle for justice in the Middle East. The overwhelming majority of the inhabitants of the Middle East, almost 95 percent, are Muslim, of whom approximately 74 percent are Sunnis. The Muslims of North Africa, Palestine, and Jordan are almost entirely Sunni, but much of the rest of the Middle East has significant Shi'ite minorities, and most of the Muslims in the Sultanate of Oman belong to the tiny Ibadi sect (Hoffman 2015). The significance of these sectarian splits, which originated in disputes over political leadership in the early Muslim community, was largely subordinated to an impulse toward Islamic unity during the struggle against European colonialism in the late nineteenth and early twentieth centuries and to Pan-Arabism during the heyday of Arab socialism in the 1950s and 1960s. This subordination of sectarianism does not mean that sect-based discrimination was absent during these years: Iraq was dominated by Sunni Arabs, who constituted only 17 percent of the population; Syria was dominated by Alawites, who constituted only 18 percent of the population of that country; Bahrain was ruled by Sunnis, although the Shi'a are demographically dominant; Saudi Arabia discriminated against its Shi'i minority; and Libya discriminated against its Ibadi minority. Nonetheless, sectarian differences did not arouse the virulent hatreds we see today in many places.

Even the emergence of Islamism as a prominent political ideology in the 1970s did not immediately arouse sectarian sentiments; the Shi'ite-dominated Islamic revolution of Iran was initially regarded with enthusiasm by many Sunnis, who saw it as proving the viability of an Islamic political ideology and took pride in the humiliation of the Americans and the US-backed government of the shah. The Saudis, however, were alarmed by the Iranian revolution, and the rise of Saudi influence in the Muslim world, especially since its involvement in the Afghan war in the 1980s, led to the reemergence of violent anti-Shi'ite sentiment among radical Sunni Islamists. The dominance of the long-suppressed Shi'a in the Iraqi government after the removal of Saddam Hussein from power sparked rampant sectarian violence in that country. In recent decades there has been a spike in bombings of Shi'ite shrines in the Middle East and Pakistan. In the wake of the US-led invasion of Iraq in 2003 and the Arab Spring uprisings of 2011–12, sectarianism has contributed to the region's volatility. Chapter 1 examines the role of religion in the politics of the Arab Spring and its aftermath.

Christians are the largest non-Muslim religious group in the Middle East, numbering approximately 16 million, although there are no reliable statistics. Egypt has the largest number of Christians, with estimates ranging from 4.6 to 17 million, or 5 to 20 percent of the population; most sources estimate the percentage of Christians at 10 percent, or 9 million (Tadros 2013, 30–35). Most Egyptian Christians belong to the Coptic Orthodox Church of Alexandria, which has its own pope, currently Tawadros II. Although Copts did not enjoy the same rights as Muslims under the government of Gamal Abdel Nasser (Hasan 2003), the rise of Islamism in the 1970s led to violent attacks against the Copts, who were perceived as an obstacle to the achievement of an Islamic state (Kepel 1984, 195–201). The regimes of Anwar Sadat (1970–81) and Hosni Mubarak (1981–2011) made strategic concessions to the Islamists in an effort to co-opt their message, while at the same time suppressing independent Islamist groups. The Copts felt forced to accept an authoritarian government that often failed to protect them, for fear of the inevitably worse Islamist alternative. Similar dynamics have kept Syria's 1.7 million Christians loyal to the regime of Bashar al-Assad. But the lethal bombing of a Coptic church in Alexandria on December 31, 2010, provided, for many Copts, evidence of the government's failure to protect them; many threw in their lot with the January 25 revolutionaries. The fall of Mubarak in 2011, however, led, as feared, to a rise in violent attacks against Copts, as Mariz Tadros discusses in chapter 7 of this book. The removal of a military strongman from power in 2003 likewise made Iraq's Christians vulnerable to attacks on churches on such a scale that very few Christians remain in that country.

The eastern part of Anatolia was home to as many as 2 million Armenian Christians before the Ottoman Empire ordered the deportation and killing of between 0.9 and 1.2 million Armenians in 1915–16. Only 50,000–70,000 Armenians remain in Turkey today, mostly in Istanbul and its environs. Ironically, the founding of the secular Republic of Turkey after World War I was accompanied by a massive transfer of Christians from Turkey to Greece and of Muslims from Greece to Turkey (Shields 2013), making the Republic of Turkey nearly entire Muslim. In chapter 4 of this book, Joshua D. Hendrick reviews Turkey's struggles to define its identity vis-à-vis Islam.

The only Middle Eastern country where Christians have a substantial share of power is Lebanon, a state carved out of greater Syria in 1920 by the French in order to create a Middle Eastern state with a Christian majority. Lebanon is dominated by a "confessional system" in which religious affiliation plays an important role in structuring social life: one normally marries within one's own religious group, attends a school belonging to one's religious group, and finds a job through connections among one's kin and religious group, and one's ultimate loyalty belongs to one's kin and religious group. Lebanon's power-sharing system is also based on this confessional system, conforming to the relative size of religious groups at the time of the 1932 census. According to this unwritten "National Covenant," government offices are distributed on a ratio of six to five in favor of the Christians. The president is a Maronite Christian, the prime minister a Sunni, and the Speaker of the Chamber of Deputies is Shi'ite. Non-Christians in Lebanon came to resent this arrangement as, over time, the share of Christians in the population shrank to approximately 39 percent. The relative strength of the confessional system and the weakness of the state led to civil war from 1975 to 1989, when the Charter of National Reconciliation, also known as the Ta'if Agreement, transferred much of the president's authority to the cabinet and increased Muslim representation. Nonetheless, Lebanon remained a weak state, occupied by Syrian forces from 1976 to 2005 and bombed and invaded numerous times by Israel. The fragility of the government is exemplified by the fact that the office of president remained vacant from May 25, 2014, until October 31, 2016.

Although there were small but significant Jewish communities in many Arab countries, such as Morocco, Egypt, Algeria, Yemen,

Tunisia, Syria, and Iraq, in the first half of the twentieth century, political tensions caused by the establishment of Israel as a Jewish state in Arab Palestine in 1948 led most Jews in Arab countries to migrate to Israel or to the West. Jews constitute approximately 75 percent of Israel's population, nearly 6 million people. Today, Morocco is the only Arab country with a Jewish population that rises above 1,000, but at 2,500 to 6,500 it is but a shadow of its former size, which was estimated at 250,000 to 350,000 in 1948. Even in Iran, a non-Arab country, it is estimated that one-third of the Jewish population migrated to Israel between 1948 and 1952 (Sanasarian 2000, 47); today, estimates of the Jewish population of Iran range from 9,000 to 25,000. The horrors of the Holocaust prompted the United Nations to endorse the founding of the state of Israel as a homeland for Jews in Palestine in 1947. The war that established the state of Israel forced some 720,000 Palestinians off their land and into exile, setting the stage for decades of war and conflict in the region. Israel's capture of the West Bank and Gaza Strip in the 1967 war also produced new and persistent human rights violations, as described by Cheryl A. Rubenberg in chapter 8.

Other religious minorities in the Middle East include the Alevis of Turkey and the Druze of Lebanon, Israel, and Jordan, offshoots of Shiʿism that diverge significantly enough from mainstream Islam that often they are not considered Muslims, although Alevis are included among the Shiʿa in table 2; the Yazidis, a Kurdish group numbering approximately 500,000 in Iraq and 50,000 in Syria, followers of an ancient, syncretic monotheistic religion with beliefs that include both Zoroastrian and Islamic elements; the Baha'is of Iran, whose persecution is discussed in chapter 6; and Hindus, who live in the Gulf countries as migrant laborers, where they lack the rights of citizens and have been granted the freedom to practice their faith only in Oman and the United Arab Emirates. All of these groups have suffered from various degrees of discrimination, and sometimes even persecution, as discussed in chapter 6 of this book.

Table 2
Religion in the Middle East

Regional Estimates[a] *Total Middle East population: 560,424,386*		
Religion	*Population*	*Percentage*
Muslims	530,921,966	94.74% of total
Sunnis	394,912,796	74.38% of Muslims
Shi'a	132,639,335	24.98% of Muslims
Twelvers	113,782,740	85.69% of Shi'a
Zaydis	9,273,838	6.99% of Shi'a
Alevis	6,340,435	4.78% of Shi'a
Alawites	3,071,674	2.32% of Shi'a
Isma'ilis	170,648	0.13% of Shi'a
Ibadis	3,369,835	0.63% of Muslims
Christians	16,494,787	2.94% of total
Jews	6,536,781	1.17% of total
Hindus	1,531,266	0.27% of total
Druze	997,078	0.18% of total

Country Estimates

Country	*Population*	*Percentage estimates*
Afghanistan	32,564,342	Sunni Muslim 80%; Shi'a Muslim 19%; other 1%
Algeria	39,542,166	Nearly 100% Sunni Muslim
Bahrain	1,346,613	Muslim 70.3% (60% Shi'a, 40% Sunni); Christian 14.5%; Hindu 9.8%; Buddhist 2.5%; 35 Jews; folk religion <.1%; unaffiliated 1.9%; other 0.2% (2010 est.)
Egypt	88,487,396	Muslim (nearly entirely Sunni) 90%; Christian 10% (mostly Coptic Orthodox; others include Armenian Apostolic, Catholic, Maronite, Orthodox, and Anglican)
Iran	81,824,270	Muslim 99.4% (Shi'a 90–95%; Sunni 5–10%); other 0.3% (Zoroastrian, Jewish, Christian, Baha'i); unspecified 0.4%

[a] There are no reliable statistics on religious affiliation in the Middle East. These estimates are derived from the CIA World Factbook, *Encyclopaedia Britannica*, and various Internet sources.

Table 2 (*Cont.*)
Religion in the Middle East

Country	*Population*	*Percentage estimates*
Iraq	37,056,169	Muslim 99% (Shi'a 60–65%; Sunni 32–37%); Yazidi 1.75%; Christian 0.5–1.2%; Hindu <0.1%; Buddhist <0.1%; Jewish <0.1%; folk religion <0.1%; unaffiliated 0.1%; other <0.1%
Israel	8,049,314	Jewish 75%; Muslim 17.5%; Christian 2%; Druze 1.6%; other 3.9%
Jordan	8,117,564	Muslim 97.2% (predominantly Sunni); Christian 2.2% (majority Greek Orthodox, but some Greek and Roman Catholics, Syrian Orthodox, Coptic Orthodox, Armenian Orthodox, and Protestant); Buddhist 0.4%; Hindu 0.1%; Jewish <0.1%; folk religion <0.1%; unaffiliated <0.1%; other <0.1%
Kuwait	2,788,534	Muslim 76.7% (39% Shi'a); Christian 17.3%; other and unspecified 5.9%
Lebanon	6,184,701	Muslim 54% (50% Sunni; 50% Shi'a); Christian 40.5% (59% Maronite Catholic; 19.75% Greek Orthodox; 12.35% Greek Catholic; 9% other); Druze 5.6%; very small numbers of Jews, Baha'is, Buddhists, Hindus, and Mormons
Libya	6,411,776	Muslim 96.6% (nearly all Sunni; Ibadis are <1%); Christian 2.7%; Buddhist 0.3%; Hindu <0.1%; Jewish <0.1%; folk religion <0.1%; unaffiliated 0.2%; other <0.1%
Morocco	33,322,699	Sunni Muslim 99%; other 1% (Christian, Jewish, Baha'i); about 6,000 Jews

Table 2 (*Cont.*)
Religion in the Middle East

Country	*Population*	*Percentage estimates*
Oman	4,092,000	Muslim 85.9% (75% Ibadi; others Sunni and Shi'a); Christian 6.5%; Hindu 5.5%; Buddhist 0.8%; Jewish <0.1%; other 1%; unaffiliated 0.2%
Palestine—Gaza Strip	1,816,379	Sunni Muslim 98.7%, Christian 0.7%, Jewish 0.6%
Palestine—West Bank	2,731,052	Sunni Muslim 75%; Jewish 17% Christian and other 8%
Qatar	2,194,817	Sunni Muslim 77.5%; Christian 8.5%; other 14% (mainly Hindu and other Indian religions)
Saudi Arabia	27,752,316	Saudi citizens are 85–90% Sunni Muslim; 10–15% Shi'a Muslim; no statistics on non-Saudi residents
Sudan	36,108,853	Sunni Muslim 97%; Christian 1.5%; traditional African 1.5%
Syria	17,064,854	Sunni Muslim 74%; Alawites 18%; Christian 12% (Orthodox, Uniate, and Nestorian); Twelver Shi'a 3%; Druze 3%; Isma'ili Shi'a 1%; Yazidi 0.3%; Jewish <0.1%
Tunisia	11,037,225	Sunni Muslim 99.1%; other 1% (Christian, Jewish, Shi'a, Baha'i)
Turkey	79,414,269	Muslim 99.8% (Sunni 90%; Alevi 8%; Twelver Shi'a 1%); Christian 0.2%
United Arab Emirates	5,779,760 (CIA est.)	All Emirati citizens are Muslim (85% Sunni; 15% Shi'a); among entire population, Muslim 70% (Sunni, Shi'a, Isma'ili, Bohra, Ahmadi); Hindu 15%; Christian 9%; Buddhist 5%; other <1% (Parsi, Baha'i, Druze, Sikh, Jewish)
Yemen	26,737,317	Muslim 99.1% (Sunni 65%; Zaydi Shi'a 35%); other 0.9% (Jewish, Baha'i, Hindu, Christian)

Language and Ethnicity

Arabs are the dominant ethnic group in all countries of the Middle East except Iran, Turkey, Afghanistan, and Israel. Although "Arab" is often understood as an ethnicity, the Arab League defines it linguistically: anyone whose native tongue is Arabic is an Arab, regardless of physical appearance. Arabic is the national language of eighteen Middle Eastern countries: Algeria, Bahrain, Egypt, Iraq, Jordan, Kuwait, Lebanon, Libya, Morocco, Oman, Palestine, Qatar, Saudi Arabia, Sudan, Syria, Tunisia, the United Arab Emirates, and Yemen. Israel recognizes both Hebrew and Arabic as official languages. Persians, Turks, Kurds, Armenians, Azeris, Berbers, Baluchis, Turkomans, Pashtuns, Tajiks, Hazaras, Uzbeks, and non-Arab Israelis are some of the more important non-Arab groups of the Middle East. Iran's official language is Persian (Farsi), that of Turkey is Turkish, and Afghanistan has two official languages, Persian (Dari) and Pashto. The politics of language can be contentious: in Turkey it was illegal to speak Kurdish until 1991, although it is the language of between 18 and 20 percent of the population, and it still may not be used as a language of instruction in schools. As a result of protests during the Arab Spring, the government of Morocco in 2011 acknowledged Tamazight (a Berber language) as an official language, in addition to Arabic (Aslan 2014). There are some 17 million speakers of Berber languages in Morocco, 14 million in Algeria, 50,000–90,000 in Tunisia, and 300,000–550,000 in Libya.

The most persistent ethnic conflict in the Middle East stems from the Kurds' frustrated desire for a state of their own. In 1997 McDowall estimated that the Kurds numbered 24 to 27 million, about half of whom lived in Turkey (McDowall 1996, 3). After the Ottoman Empire's defeat in the First World War, Kurdistan was partitioned between Turkey, Iraq, Iran, and Syria. Kurds joined Turks in armed resistance to the European occupation of Anatolia and the creation of an independent republic. In the years before international recognition of the Republic of Turkey, Atatürk and other nationalist leaders spoke of the Kurds and Turks as a single people. But the government formed in 1923 imposed harsh measures in an effort to create a homogenous nation. Kurdish schools, newspapers, and associations were forcibly shut down (McDowall 1992, 36), and the Kurdish language, dress, and names were banned. These measures met with vigorous resistance; Kurds initiated sixteen of the eighteen revolts that broke out in the early republican period (Aslan 2011, 76; McDowall 1996, 184–213). Although the Constitution of 1961 allowed the Kurds freedom of expression, the press, and association, the 1964 Political Parties Act criminalized Kurdish political parties and any reference to diverse languages and ethnicities in Turkey. Following the military coup of 1980, any use of the Kurdish language became a criminal offense for which many were imprisoned (Aslan 2014).

In 1984 the Kurdish Workers Party launched a guerrilla insurgency against the republic that lasted until 2013 and claimed nearly 40,000 lives (Kayaoğlu 2013). The leader of the PKK, Abdullah Öcalan, has been in prison since 1999. In 2009 the government announced what has been called the "Kurdish opening": that it would ease the remaining bans on Kurdish broadcasting, allow the use of Kurdish names for villages, and establish departments of Kurdish language and literature in universities (*Economist* 2009). In 2012, Prime Minister Recep Tayyip Erdoğan announced that the Kurdish language could be taught in all schools (Mirenzi 2012), although it cannot be used as a primary language of instruction. However, Kayaoğlu charges, "Instead of giving the 'opening' substance and direction, Erdogan's Justice and Development Party (AKP) has wobbled between two extremes: at times, the prime minister and his subordinates embraced Kurds as fellow Muslims. At other times, however, Erdogan catered to the basest forms of ultra-nationalism—going so far as to threaten to restore capital punishment—which would have been used against Abdullah Öcalan, the PKK's imprisoned leader. Despite the recent lull and claims that the PKK would lay down its arms in the near future, the conflict could re-escalate any time" (2013).

Turkey allowed 130,000 Kurdish refugees from the ISIS-besieged city of Kobani in northern Syria to flood into Turkey, but the government failed to come to the aid of the city against an Islamist movement from which Turkey had formerly purchased oil. In an unprecedented move, the government allowed Kurdish fighters affiliated with the PKK to travel through Turkey in October 2014 to Kobani's rescue (Chulov, Letsch, and Hawramy 2014). In July 2015, however, the Turkish government launched air strikes against Kurds in northern Iraq whom the United States regarded as key to the fight against ISIS. The government said this move was in retaliation for a Kurdish attack that killed two Turkish policemen; analysts attributed it to Kurdish defections from the ruling AKP party, which cost the party its majority in Parliament, or the perceived threat posed by the Kurds' rapid territorial gains in northern Syria. In response to the aerial campaign against its cohorts, the PKK declared an end to the fragile cease-fire. In October the Turkish government also struck Kurdish forces in northern Syria. In January 2016 more than 1,000 academics from ninety Turkish universities signed a public statement calling on the government to end the "deliberate massacre" of Kurds caught in clashes between Turkish security forces and militants of the PKK. The government responded by arresting prominent signatories. After a failed coup attempt in July 2016, the government ushered in a wide crackdown and purge of political opponents and, some charge, a new attempt to eradicate Kurdish language and culture (Kingsley 2017a).

In Iraq the government of Saddam Hussein responded brutally to Kurdish demands for autonomy. In 1988 it massacred between 50,000 and 200,000 Kurds in the Anfal campaign, which included the systematic destruction of villages, mass deportations, executions, and chemical warfare. The most notorious attack was on the city of Halabja on March 16, 1988, when a chemical attack led to the deaths of approximately 5,000 people; those individuals who survived suffered from horrible injuries, including skin eruptions, blindness, severe neurological damage, cancer, infertility, and congenital diseases (al-Ali and Pratt 2009, 43). The Iraqi regime also forced populations to relocate in order to Arabize the oil-rich Kurdish

Table 3
Ethnic groups in the Middle East

Country	*Population*	*Ethnic group population estimates*
Afghanistan	32,564,342	Pashtun 42%; Tajik 27%; Hazara 9%; Uzbek 9%; Aimaq 4%; Turkmen 3%; Baloch 2%; remaining 4% are Nuristani, Pamiri, Arab, Gujar, Brahui, Qizilbash, Pashai, and Kyrghyz
Algeria	39,542,166	Arabic speakers of Berber origin 85%; Berbers 15%
Bahrain	1,346,613	Bahraini Arabs 46%; South Asians 45.5%; other Arabs 4.7%; African 1.6%; European 1%; other 1.2%
Egypt	88,487,396	Egyptian Arabs 99.6%
Iran	81,824,270	Persian 61%; Azeri 16%; Kurd 10%; Lur 6%; Baloch 2%; Arab 2%; Turkmen and Turkic tribes 2%; other 1%
Iraq	37,056,169	Arab 75%–80%; Kurdish 15%–20%; Turkoman, Assyrian, or other 5%
Israel	8,049,314	Jewish 75% (of which Israel-born 74.4%; Europe/America/Oceania-born 17.4%; Africa-born 5.1%; Asia-born 3.1%); non-Jewish 25% (mostly Arab)
Jordan	8,117,564	Arab 98%; Circassian 1%; Armenian 1%
Kuwait	2,788,534	Kuwaiti Arabs 31.3%; other Arabs 27.9%; South Asians 37.8%; Africans 1.9%; other 1.1% (European, North American, South American, Australian)
Lebanon	6,184,701	Arab 95%; Armenian 4%; other 1%
Libya	6,411,776	Libyan Arabs 87.5%; Libyan Berbers 9.5%; other 3% (includes Greeks, Maltese, Italians, Egyptians, Pakistanis, Turks, Indians, and Tunisians)
Morocco	33,322,699	Arabs of Berber origin 66%; Berbers 33%; other 1%
Oman	4,092,000	Omani Arabs 56.3%; expatriates 43.7% (mainly South Asian)

Table 3 (*Cont.*)
Ethnic groups in the Middle East

Country	*Population*	*Ethnic group population estimates*
Palestine—Gaza Strip	1,816,379	Palestinian Arab 98.7%
Palestine—West Bank	2,731,052	Palestinian Arab 83%; Israeli Jews 17%
Qatar	2,194,817	Arab 40%; Indian 18%; Pakistani 18%; Iranian 10%; other 14%
Saudi Arabia	27,752,316	Saudi Arabs 69%; other Arabs 21%; South Asians and Africans 10%
Sudan	36,108,853	Sudanese Arabs 70%; Fur 2.5%; Beja 3.3%, Nuba 2.8%, Fallata 10%
Syria	17,064,854	Arab 90.3%; Kurds, Armenians, and other 9.7%
Tunisia	11,037,225	Arab 98%; European 1%; Jewish and other 1%
Turkey	79,414,269	Turks 70–75%; Kurds 18%; other minorities 7–12%
United Arab Emirates	5,779,760 (CIA est.) 9,445,624 (UN est.)	Emirati Arabs 19%; other Arabs and Iranians 23%; South Asian 50%; other expatriates (includes Westerners and East Asians) 8%
Yemen	26,737,317	Yemeni Arabs 99%

Sources: Statistics are derived from various sources, including the CIA World Factbook, *Encyclopaedia Britannica*, and various Internet sources.

region of Kirkuk. After the Gulf War of 1990–91, the United States and the United Kingdom imposed a no-fly zone over the Kurdish areas of northern Iraq, granting the region de facto autonomy. Following the fall of Saddam Hussein, one of two rival Kurdish leaders, Jalal Talabani, served as president of Iraq from 2005 to 2014.

Western Impingement and Islamic Reform Movements

Because the Qur'an mandates the imposition of God's law and appears to guarantee victory over non-Muslims as long as Muslims are faithful to God, economic setbacks and military defeats have sometimes been interpreted as indications that Muslims have strayed from God's straight path. The economic impact of the rise of the West and European voyages of discovery that allowed merchants to circumvent the Middle East prompted various types of Islamic reform movements even in areas that were not in direct contact with European powers. The most famous of these movements, as well as the most radical and impactful, is the Wahhabi movement, which arose in the Arabian Peninsula in the eighteenth century. Although some have rejected the application of the word *fundamentalism* to Islam, from the vantage point of the comparative study of religion Wahhabism can be characterized as "fundamentalist" because its proponents insist on the need to "return" to a literal application of the Qur'an and Sunna; they reject Muslim scholarship that had developed over more than a millennium and seek to recover what they perceive as the original, pure faith. The movement's founder, Muhammad ibn 'Abd al-Wahhab (1703–92), rejected Sufism, theology, and other aspects of tradition and recognized as Muslims only his own followers. After Ibn Sa'ud entered into an alliance with him in 1744, their followers seized much of Arabia, massacring the inhabitants of the southern Iraqi Shi'ite holy city Karbala in 1802 and the men of Ta'if, Arabia, in 1803. This first Saudi state was defeated by an expedition sent on behalf of the Ottomans by Muhammad Ali Pasha of Egypt in 1818.

More than a century later, a new Saudi military campaign led to the establishment of the Kingdom of Saudi Arabia in 1932. Saudi Arabia has an outsize global influence, as it has used its oil wealth to propagate its rigid and austere version of Islam around the world. The United States' reliance on Saudi oil has led to a close alliance between the two countries. The United States worked with Saudi Arabia to support the Mujahideen in the fight against the Soviets in the 1980s, and the Saudis promoted Wahhabi education in schools for Afghan refugees in Pakistan. The international terrorist organization al-Qaeda emerged out of that conflict, and from it emerged the so-called Islamic State (IS, ISIL, or ISIS). Despite al-Qaeda's ideological ties to Saudi Arabia, the latter's alliance with the United States led to political estrangement, so that al-Qaeda regards the Saudi government as its enemy, even as Saudis close to the government are major funders of the terrorist organization. The Saudi impact on global Islam was also extended by offering scholarships to Muslim students in poorer countries, especially in sub-Saharan Africa, to study in Saudi universities (Dorsey 2017). Upon returning to their home countries, many of those students vehemently denounced local Islamic practices and promoted Wahhabi ideology. The challenge Wahhabism and other Islamist ideologies pose to human rights is explored in chapter 6.

In colonized Muslim lands, Europeans founded new schools that often used European languages as a medium of instruction, leading to the emergence of an elite that was trained in the sciences and languages of Europe and held the traditionally educated ulema in contempt. The ulema, in turn, distrusted customs and disciplines imported from Europe and regarded Islamic tradition as capable of providing all the guidance necessary for life. Some scholars who were educated in both Islamic tradition and the modern sciences sought to bridge the gap between the two. "Islamic modernists," such as Sayyid Ahmad Khan of India (1817–98), Jamal al-Din al-Afghani of Iran (1839–97), and Muhammad 'Abduh of Egypt (1849–1905), argued that there is no contradiction between Islam and modern science and that Islamic education needed to be reformed in order to enable it to meet the needs of modern society. They denounced aspects of Islamic tradition that they felt impeded the moral, social, political, and economic development of Muslim societies, such as polygamy, the seclusion of women, the veneration of saints, and authoritarian rule. None of these things, they argued, was really Islamic; they were harmful customs that had developed under premodern social conditions and should now be cast aside. While Khan wrote that British rule was beneficial to the Muslims of India, Afghani and 'Abduh strongly disagreed. Afghani, who spent several years in Egypt and was a major influence on 'Abduh, felt that European imperialism was an evil that could be overthrown only if Muslims acquired the things that made the Europeans strong: scientific thought and nationalism. Afghani, 'Abduh, and other reformers in the late nineteenth and early twentieth centuries also emphasized the ideal of Muslim unity across regions, even as they encouraged the development of nationalisms that would unite Muslims and non-Muslims in the struggle for freedom. Although ʿAbduh's struggle to reform al-Azhar University was unsuccessful in his own time, his ideas became increasingly popular and have had an enduring impact. No one needs to argue anymore for the necessity of universal and modern scientific education; that battle has been won. Other battles initiated by the modernists, such as the need to reinterpret Islamic law, especially regarding women's rights, and the promotion of democracy, have had uneven results. Popular movements in Turkey and Iran led to important constitutional reforms in the early twentieth century, but in both cases these positive developments were temporary.

Postcolonial Politics

Most of the leaders of independence movements in the Middle East in the early to mid-twentieth century sought to establish Western-style parliamentary democracies. Although Islam was often an aspect of national identity, for none of the leaders of the newly independent states did it feature as the nation's primary source of national identity or political ideology. Atatürk opted for a secularism that entirely subordinated Islam and eliminated the influence of the sharia in all aspects of life. In most countries the domain of the sharia had become gradually reduced to personal status matters: marriage, divorce, and inheritance. By adopting the Swiss Civil Code for personal status law, outlawing traditional garb, adopting the Gregorian calendar and metric system, and mandating use of the Latin alphabet for Turkish, Turkey fully embraced the European model for modernity. Joshua D. Hendrick explores the long-term implications of this legacy in chapter 4. Other states in the Middle East continued to apply the sharia to family law, often with some concessions to modernist goals, such as setting a minimum age for marriage (usually younger for women than for men) in order to eliminate child marriage, and instituting some restrictions on polygamy, such as requiring official permission or at least the notification of the first wife before a man could contract an additional marriage. Tunisia's personal status code, promulgated in the year of its independence, 1956, under the presidency of Habib Bourguiba, implemented the most radical reforms by banning polygamy and granting women significant new rights in marriage and divorce; what Turkey had done by eliminating the sharia, Tunisia had accomplished through a modernist reinterpretation of the sharia.

After the Russian Revolution of 1917, Iran became an arena of struggle between Russia and Britain. With British support, Reza Khan led a coup d'état in 1921 and in 1925 was crowned shah (king) of Iran, adopting the name Reza Shah Pahlavi. Reza Shah visited Turkey in 1934 and greatly admired Atatürk's modernization. In 1936 he decreed the mandatory unveiling of women, for which he was allegedly inspired by what he saw in Turkey (Kashani-Sabet 2011, 156). Reza's aim was to modernize Iran by updating its economic and communications infrastructure, limiting the influence of religious scholars, and establishing schools patterned after the ones in Europe. Women were to be an integral part of the modernization project (Abrahamian 1982, 140).

While Western-style modernity proved seductive for many Muslims, it alienated others, who believed that Islam offered the only sound basis for social and political organization. The Muslim Brotherhood, founded in Egypt in 1928, contrasted Western materialism with the moral perfection of Islam, which alone could restore global preeminence to Egypt and other Muslim nations (Euben and Zaman 2009, 49–78). By planting cells in towns and villages all over Egypt and providing basic social services for the poor, the Muslim Brotherhood grew into a massive grassroots movement and became an important force in Egyptian politics. Branches and offshoots of the Muslim Brotherhood were established in other Arab countries as well.

Disaffection with Europe, and especially with Western support for Israel, led many to turn away from Western-style government and embrace socialism in the 1940s, 1950s, and 1960s. Arabism's combination of Pan-Arabism and socialism underlies the Ba'ath military regimes of Syria and Iraq, the 1952 revolution of Nasser's "Free

Officers," Algeria's National Liberation Front, the Egypt-sponsored government that came to power in northern Yemen in 1968, and the military regimes of Ja'far al-Numayri's Sudan (May 1969) and Mu'ammar al-Qaddafi's Libya (September 1969). An even more radical Marxist government came to power in South Yemen in 1969. Socialist governments provided public health systems, free education, and subsidies on basic foods and housing; some also promised jobs to university graduates. Nasser became a hero to many in the Arab world and the Third World generally when he nationalized the Suez Canal in 1956, defying the combined forces of Britain, France, and Israel. The Pan-Arab nationalist project inspired Egypt and Syria to unite in 1958 as the United Arab Republic, which lasted until 1961. Libya's Qaddafi pursued many unification schemes with various Arab governments, but none was successful.

Nasser may have been popular, but he was ruthless with his opponents. His regime was particularly harsh in its crackdown on the Muslim Brotherhood after a Muslim Brother allegedly tried to assassinate him in 1954. Six Brotherhood leaders were hanged, and thousands were arrested and tortured in prison. An alleged Brotherhood plot to overthrow the government led to further arrests and the hanging of Sayyid Qutb, the most popular writer of the Muslim Brotherhood, in 1966.[1]

The Islamist Turn

The devastating defeat of Egypt, Syria, and Jordan in the Six-Day War of June 1967, in which Israel occupied the West Bank, the Golan Heights, the Gaza Strip, and the Sinai Peninsula, undermined Nasser's prestige and led some to question the soundness of his policies. Many Arabs, both Muslim and Christian, turned toward religion. The Islamic resurgence of the 1970s was marked by increased

1. For the perspective of a member of the Brotherhood on these events, see Hoffman 1985 or Euben and Zaman 2009, 288–301.

attendance at mosques and religious lessons, new interest in reading popular Islamic literature, the creation of new styles of "Islamic" dress (especially for women), and an increase in the number of Islamic charitable associations. The idea that Islam might offer a better solution for Arab socioeconomic problems than either capitalism or socialism gained traction in the 1970s and emerged as the distinct political ideology known as Islamism, which holds that the sharia must form the basis of society and politics.

Anwar Sadat, president of Egypt from 1970 to 1981, freed the Muslim Brothers from prison and encouraged Islamist activity on university campuses, partly to counter the strength of Nasserists. He adopted public symbols of piety, calling himself "the believing President Muhammad Anwar Sadat" and having his attendance at Friday prayer filmed for state television. Although the Muslim Brotherhood remained illegal and the government remained authoritarian, Sadat allowed its members to run for parliament. Formerly socialist leaders, such as Qaddafi of Libya and Numayri of Sudan, also now embraced Islam as a central part of their political platforms.

Egypt's October 1973 surprise attack on the Israeli line of defense in the Sinai Peninsula was filled with religious symbolism: the operation, code-named Badr, was launched during the Jewish fasting day of Yom Kippur and the holy Muslim month of Ramadan. Egyptian narratives include visions of angels helping the soldiers and of the Prophet holding a banner over their heads. Although the Israelis rapidly recuperated and launched a counteroffensive, which was halted only through international intervention, Arabs generally regard the war as an Arab victory, whereas the Israelis were psychologically shaken from their assumption of invincibility. It was therefore from a vantage point of strength that Sadat was able to pursue a peace strategy with Israel in late 1977, culminating in the treaty officiated by US president Jimmy Carter in March 1979. In return for making peace with Israel, the United States dramatically increased its economic and military support for Egypt (Sowa 2013). Not only did this aid help entrench the power of Egypt's authoritarian regime, but the military extended its control of certain sectors of the economy (Noll 2017, 2).

Sadat's pursuit of peace with Israel was partly for economic gain. Socialist projects had become unsustainable; in the 1970s, Arab countries borrowed money from the World Bank and the International Monetary Fund, which forced them to privatize their economies and open them to foreign investment. While doing so brought some advantages, it also re-created the socioeconomic inequalities that had made socialism appealing in the first place. Government cutbacks on subsidies on basic foodstuffs prompted "bread riots" in Egypt (1977, 1984, 1986, 1989), Morocco (1981, 1984, 1990), Tunisia (1983–84), Algeria (1988), and Jordan (1989, 1996). The number of people in the Middle East living in poverty increased from 60 million in 1985 to 73 million in 1990—from 30.6 percent of the population to 33.1 percent (Moghadam 2013, 303). The rising population of university graduates with expectations of attaining careers and a middle-class lifestyle soon exceeded available resources, leading to widespread resentment and frustration. Furthermore, Egypt paid a costly political price for its peace with Israel: it became a pariah in the Arab world; the Arab League moved its headquarters from Cairo to Tunis. Islamists felt the peace treaty was a betrayal of Islam, as well as of the Arab cause.

Radical Islamists in Egypt felt that the Muslim Brotherhood had abandoned the goals of Islamism by participating in the political process. Islamists who rejected participation in mainstream politics often did not hesitate to employ violence. A number of such groups emerged in the 1970s and attracted adherents among disaffected young people, even in the army. The rise of radical Islamism led to attacks on Copts, whom Islamists regarded as an obstacle to the imposition of Islamic rule in Egypt. After months of such violence in 1981, Sadat responded with a broad crackdown on Islamists, Coptic leaders, and other political opponents; some 1,600 were arrested on September 3, 1981 (Ibrahim 1996, 212). At a parade commemorating Operation Badr on October 6, 1981, radical Islamist soldiers sprayed the viewing stand with bullets, killing Sadat and 11 other people.

During the 1980s and 1990s, under the rule of Sadat's successor, Hosni Mubarak, militant Islamists attacked Copts, government officials, banks, and government buildings. In the towns of Minya and Asyut (152 miles and 243 south of Cairo, respectively), they waged street battles with police and security forces. Islamists controlled university campuses, moved into Cairo's slums, and spread their influence in southern towns and villages, offering social services and imposing their own moral code. "By the early 1990s, they virtually ruled the southern towns and had established their 'Islamic Republic of Imbaba' in the heart of the capital city" (Bayat 2007, 137).

In the 1990s, the government cracked down so harshly on radical Islamists that imprisoned leaders of al-Jama'a 'l-Islamiyya (sometimes referred to as the "Islamic Group") unilaterally renounced violence in July 1997. Some group members rejected the cease-fire and responded with a shocking attack on tourists at an ancient temple in Qurna, across the Nile from Luxor, killing 62 people. The government also took steps to limit the ability of the moderate Muslim Brotherhood to operate legitimately in the public sphere. At the same time, the government granted strategic concessions to the increasingly religiously oriented public, appropriating the language of religion, censoring publications for offenses against religion, promoting conservative sexual mores, and allowing personal vendettas to take the form of court cases accusing human rights advocates of apostasy (Bayat 2007, 168–79)—although apostasy is not a criminal offense in Egypt (March 2009, 8; Weaver 2000, 245–46). Weaver notes the cultural poverty produced by the combined pressures of Islamism and government authoritarianism, commenting, "Egypt produced better and freer cinema in the 1930s than it does now" (2000, 237).

By 1980 Islamists dominated the student unions of universities across the Arab world. In 1981 Ja'far al-Numayri, the president of Sudan who had come to power through a Nasser-style military coup in 1969, allied himself with the Muslim Brotherhood. In 1983 he announced the imposition of Islamic law, alienating the non-Muslim south and provoking a second civil war, which ended only in 2005. In 1985, in an effort to prove his Islamist credentials, he executed Mahmoud Mohamed Taha, leader of the Republican Brothers, a Sufi-oriented group that advocated gender equality, religious pluralism, and human rights. This strategy backfired for Numayri, who was overthrown later that year. In 1989, however, a military coup brought a new Islamist regime to power in Sudan under Colonel Omar al-Bashir, who remains in power and has been charged with human rights violations by the International Criminal Court because of his complicity in genocide in Darfur.

The Palestinian liberation movement, formerly dominated by secularists, came increasingly to be dominated by Islamists after the founding of the Muslim Brotherhood affiliate Hamas in 1988. The secular Palestinian National Authority, led by the Fatah party, refused to recognize Hamas's electoral victory in 2006, leading to armed conflict between the two factions and the division of Palestine between Gaza, ruled by Hamas, and the West Bank, ruled by Fatah.

In Algeria President Chadli Benjadid responded to social unrest in 1988 by allowing the formation of opposition parties. The Islamic Salvation Front (Front Islamique de Salut) won provincial elections in June 1990 and the first round of national elections in December 1991. Two days before the second round of elections scheduled to take place on January 13, 1992, the army staged a coup, canceled the elections, and brought in Mohammed Boudiaf, an exiled leader of the liberation struggle against the French, to serve as president. Boudiaf's assassination in June 1992 led to massive arrests of Islamists, the formation of radical militant groups, and the outbreak of a bloody civil war that lasted until 2002.

Islamists were also active outside the Arab world. Pakistan was formed when India was granted independence in 1947, under leaders who desired a secular democracy in which Muslims would be a majority. Originally composed of eastern and western wings, Pakistan was rent asunder by civil war in 1971, when East Pakistan declared its independence and became Bangladesh. The civil war led to a political and psychological crisis whose impact in the remaining western wing has been compared to that of the Six-Day War on the Arab world. Throughout the 1970s, even secular politicians such as Zulfikar Ali Bhutto (ruled 1971–77) felt pressured to affirm Islamic values. In 1977 Bhutto was overthrown by a military coup led by General Muhammad Zia-ul-Haq. In 1979 Zia proclaimed an "Islamic System" (*Nizam-e Mustafa*) and implemented broad and widely unpopular measures: censorship, new taxes, restrictions on women's dress and right to testify in court, and the harsh penalties (*hudud*) prescribed by classical Islamic law for adultery, slander, theft, blasphemy, apostasy, and intoxication. The law against slander is based on Qur'an 24:4, which orders flogging with eighty stripes those individuals who charge women with adultery without producing four witnesses to the offense. The verse was meant to protect women against unwarranted charges, but in Pakistan it was broadly applied against women's interests. Women's testimony is inadmissible as evidence in charges of crimes punishable by *hudud*, and the requirement of four eyewitnesses was interpreted as meaning four adult men who witnessed the actual act of penetration. On the one hand, it makes charges of adultery very hard to prove, but, on the other hand, it also makes it impossible for women or girls to prove allegations of rape, which is often used as a political weapon in Pakistan (Haeri 1995).[2] The political difficulty of repealing allegedly Islamic laws is indicated by the fact that Benazir Bhutto, an outspoken supporter of women's rights elected prime minister after Zia's death in 1988, was unable to overturn the law. It was only with the passing of the Women's Protection Bill in 2006 under the military dictatorship of Pervez Musharraf that rape cases were moved from Islamic courts to criminal courts, eliminating the need for four male witnesses to the act and allowing other types of forensic evidence.

In Iran Ayatollah Khomeini, a religious scholar exiled in 1963 for fomenting opposition to the regime of Muhammad Reza Shah Pahlavi, became a powerful symbol among a wide range of opponents to the shah's despotic rule. Khomeini proclaimed the illegitimacy of monarchy and advocated the direct rule of religious scholars (*velayat-e faqih*)—a major innovation in Islamic thought. After a popular

2. For an excellent sociological study and analysis of the impact of the Hudood Ordinance on women and children, see Khan 2006.

revolution overthrew the Shah in 1978–79, Khomeini returned to Iran in February 1979 and was recognized as supreme leader. Bayat argues that, contrary to common assumptions, the Iranian revolution was not the result of a strong Islamic movement; rather, the ulema became leaders of the revolution only late in its course, few Iranians were aware of Khomeini's ideology, and secular and Islamist tendencies were growing simultaneously (Bayat 2007, 29–32). It was the writings of 'Ali Shari'ati, who strongly opposed the ulema and radically reinterpreted Shi'ism in a Marxist fashion, that captivated young intellectuals. Many of the revolutionaries were not Islamists and were dismayed by the imposition of conservative sharia law and the rollback of women's rights in the Islamic Republic. The Pahlavi regime had been extremely despotic, but the new Islamic regime was no less so; tens of thousands were executed in the new republic's early years. The outbreak of regional independence movements led some to speculate that the regime would not endure, but Saddam Hussein's attack on Iran in September 1980 prompted the population to rally behind the Islamic regime. During the Iran-Iraq War, which lasted until April 1988, the Iranian government called on volunteers to embrace martyrdom on the front lines; hundreds of thousands died in this protracted conflict. Through Iran's sponsorship of Hezbollah in Lebanon, the strategy of suicide operations entered into the Arab–Israeli conflict and was later adopted by Sunnis in that conflict and others, most spectacularly in al-Qaeda's attacks on the World Trade Center and the Pentagon on September 11, 2001.

The Impact of Foreign Intervention

The Soviet invasion of Afghanistan in December 1979 had repercussions throughout the Muslim world. The battle against the Soviets in Afghanistan was cast as a jihad that drew thousands from other Muslim countries; estimates of the number of volunteers range from twenty to thirty-five thousand. The United States and Saudi Arabia funneled billions of dollars through the Pakistani secret services to train and equip guerrilla fighters, known as the Mujahideen, during the Soviet-Afghan War, which lasted until February 1989. The "Afghan Arabs" included Osama bin Laden and others who formed al-Qaeda, the global militant Islamist organization. The departure of the Soviets was followed by a civil war between different Mujahideen factions that paved the way for the takeover of Afghanistan by the brutal and ultraconservative Taliban, whose misogyny was denounced even by the Iranian regime (Sciolino 1996). The Taliban were removed from power by the US invasion after al-Qaeda's attacks on New York and Washington on September 11, 2001, because the Taliban had sheltered al-Qaeda and refused to turn over bin Laden to the United States.

US assistance to the Mujahideen and the invasion of Afghanistan were only the latest in a series of often controversial interventions in the affairs of Middle Eastern nations, of which perhaps the most notorious is the 1953 Central Intelligence Agency–sponsored military coup that overthrew Iran's popular, nationalist prime minister, Mohammed Mossadeq, and restored the shah to the throne. Over the next twenty-five years the United States supported the increasingly repressive and megalomaniacal shah, the United States's "policeman of the Gulf." Many Iranians saw the United States as complicit in the shah's crimes against humanity and were outraged when he was admitted to the United States for medical treatment after the 1979 revolution. Student protesters seized the US Embassy in Tehran and held hostage fifty-two American diplomats and other citizens from November 4, 1979, to January 20, 1981; the slogan "Death to America" became a rallying cry in demonstrations.

Although Eisenhower refused to take part in the joint attack on Egypt by Britain, France, and Israel during the Suez Canal Crisis of 1956, the United States has been a crucial ally of Israel, the recipient of the largest amount of US foreign aid, and has done little to stop Israeli aggression in Palestine and Lebanon. The United States has typically allied itself with monarchs and strongmen who served its strategic and economic interests, regardless of ideological compatibility or human rights violations: the shah of Iran; the kings of Saudi

Arabia, Jordan, and Morocco; Presidents Sadat, Mubarak, and Sisi of Egypt; and President Ben Ali of Tunisia.

Because the United States regarded the Islamic Republic of Iran as a threat to the stability of the Middle East and to US interests, Presidents Ronald Reagan and George H. W. Bush provided financial, technological, intelligence, and military support to assist Saddam Hussein's assault on Iran during the bloody Iran-Iraq War (1980–88) (Timmerman 1991; Friedman 1994). However, after Iraq invaded and annexed Kuwait on August 2, 1990, the United States and Great Britain pressured the United Nations to impose harsh economic sanctions against Iraq that led to widespread malnutrition and disease and are blamed for the death of a half-million children (Center for Economic and Social Rights 1996; Rieff 2003). In response to fears that Iraq would attack Saudi Arabia, a key US ally, President Bush sent US troops into that country on August 7, 1990. After the failure of a negotiated settlement, a US-led coalition of thirty-four nations on January 17, 1991, launched a campaign of aerial bombardment and ground attacks known as Operation Desert Storm. Iraq withdrew from Kuwait on February 27, and the following day Bush declared the end of hostilities. The United States tacitly encouraged Iraqi discontents, particularly the Kurds and the Shi'a, to finish the job by overthrowing Saddam Hussein. Although the United States, Britain, and France established "no-fly zones" over northern Iraq to protect the Kurds and over southern Iraq to protect the Shi'a and an autonomous Kurdish republic was established in northern Iraq, the Iraqi government engaged in bloody mass reprisals, especially in the south, resulting in tens of thousands of deaths and the displacement of 1.8 million refugees. UN sanctions against Iraq were not lifted until May 2003.

The presence of US troops in Saudi Arabia, US aggression against Iraq, and US support for Israel were the major complaints of Osama bin Laden, the "Afghan Arab" and wealthy Saudi founder of al-Qaeda, in his "Declaration of War against the Americans occupying the Land of the Two Holy Places." He charged that "the people of Islam have suffered from the aggression, iniquity, and injustice imposed on them by the Zionist–Crusader alliance and their collaborators, to the point where Muslim blood has become the cheapest and their wealth as loot in the hands of their enemies. . . . All false claims and propaganda about 'human rights' have been exposed and discredited by the massacres of Muslims that have taken place in every part of the world" (Euben and Zaman 2009, 436–37). His words indicate that he regarded al-Qaeda's attacks on American targets, including the US embassies in Nairobi and Dar Es Salaam on August 7, 1998; the USS *Cole* on October 12, 2000; and the World Trade Center and Pentagon on September 11, 2001, as responses to US aggression, not as unprovoked violence against innocent targets, as they are viewed in the West.

The shock of the attacks of September 11, 2001, induced Congress the following month to pass the USA PATRIOT Act (Uniting and Strengthening America by Providing Appropriate Tools Required to Intercept and Obstruct Terrorism), which authorized indefinite detention of immigrants, the search of homes and businesses without the owners' or occupants' consent or knowledge, and unprecedented government access to telephone, e-mail, and financial records. On October 7, 2001, the United States and Great Britain launched a military campaign against Afghanistan, Operation Enduring Freedom. Combat operations in Afghanistan, taken over by NATO in August 2003, formally ended only on December 28, 2014.

President George W. Bush's invasion of Iraq, launched in March 2003, was preceded by a long campaign, conducted through the United Nations and the media, that argued that Iraq possessed weapons of mass destruction, supported al-Qaeda, and constituted a threat to security in the Middle East (Isikoff and Corn 2007; Institute for Public Accuracy 2002; Hayes 2003). However, searches for weapons of mass destruction after the invasion produced no results, and Saddam Hussein had little tolerance for power cells of any sort, including al-Qaeda. On the other hand, the removal of Saddam Hussein from power, the sweeping dissolution of the army, the illegalization of the Ba'ath Party, and the establishment of a

Shi'ite-dominated government alienated many Sunnis, who could not find employment and felt persecuted by the new regime. Not all Shi'a approved of the foreign invasion: Muqtada al-Sadr's Mahdi Army harried British and American troops, and some US military leaders worried that Iran was fighting American troops through a proxy war in Iraq (Weiss and Hassan 2015, 50–57). The US invasion and the power vacuum it created turned Iraq into a prime arena for jihad; Muslims came from other countries to engage in what they believed to be a fight for Islam against the infidel aggressor (Ali and Eedle 2007), a perception exacerbated by the revelation in April 2004 of abuse of Iraqi prisoners by US personnel at Abu Ghraib prison. Abu Mus'ab al-Zarqawi, a Jordanian militant, pledged allegiance to bin Laden in 2004 and led al-Qaeda in Iraq, horrifying the world with video releases of his gruesome beheadings of foreigners. Even more ominous for Iraq's future was his hatred for the Shi'a, who bore the brunt of the organization's brutality. In a letter to bin Laden, Zarqawi denounced the Shi'a as "a sect of treachery and betrayal" (Aaron 2008, 239), "the lurking snake, the crafty and malicious scorpion" (V. Nasr 2006, 205). Bin Laden's lieutenant Ayman al-Zawahiri cautioned Zarqawi against targeting the Shi'a rather than focusing on the United States (Weiss and Hassan 2015, 59), but to no avail. In 2005–6, even as Iraqis elected a transitional government and approved a new constitution, the country devolved into sectarian war. After Zarqawi was killed by American forces in June 2006, bin Laden changed course and encouraged Sunni attacks on the Shi'a in Iraq (O. Nasr 2006). US troops withdrew from Iraq in December 2011, but the emergence of the Islamic State in Iraq and Syria (ISIS), also known as Da'esh and as the Islamic State in Iraq and the Levant (ISIL), the successor to al-Qaeda in Iraq, led to a resumption of US air operations in June 2014.

Democratic Aspirations and Political Upheaval

In the twenty-first century the processes of globalization were intensified through the spread of satellite television, the Internet, and the use of social media. People all over the world now partake of a common global pop culture. More important, democracy and human rights have become widely accepted norms and aspirations, even among the Muslim Brotherhood, which had formerly rejected democracy and human rights as Western inventions that violate the tenets of Islam. In the 2000s educated youth in the Middle East became increasingly unwilling to accept entrenched patterns of authoritarianism and corruption. The influence of global media can be seen in the adoption by members of Egypt's April 6 Youth Movement, founded in 2008, of the symbol of Serbia's "Otpor!" civic protest movement of 1998–2004 (Cushing 2015). When Mahmoud Ahmadinejad was proclaimed winner of Iran's presidential election in 2009, regime opponents accused the government of falsifying election results and took to the streets in protest, in what is known as the Green Movement (Bayat 2013, 170; Rezai 2013; Dabashi 2010; Cross 2010), which was brutally crushed.

In 2011 the world was enthralled by the eruption of the "Arab Spring" revolts. Tunisia, Egypt, Yemen, Syria, and Libya experienced revolutionary upheavals launched by demands for democratic freedoms. More limited protests shook several of the Arab monarchies—Jordan, Morocco, Oman, and Bahrain—leading to government concessions in the first three and a brutal crackdown in the last. The Arab uprisings raised an enormous challenge to the status quo and created new international alliances in the region. In Turkey the 2013 Gezi Park protests against the authoritarianism of Prime Minister Recep Tayyip Erdoğan did not prevent his election as president in 2014. After an attempted coup on July 15, 2016, failed to oust Erdoğan, he introduced a state of emergency and conducted a broad purge of people who are critical of his regime; some 50,000 people have been arrested, including more than 170 journalists and over a dozen lawmakers, and more than 140,000 regime opponents in government, education, and the media have been fired or suspended from their jobs. In June–July 2017 thousands participated in a 250-mile March for Justice from Ankara to Istanbul (Kingsley 2017b).

Of the five states that experienced revolutionary upheavals in the Arab Spring, only Tunisia has attained a significantly more democratic political atmosphere with relative stability. In Egypt Islamists captured the major elected positions after the revolution of 2011 but were subsequently removed by the military. Both Islamists and advocates of secular democracy have been imprisoned under the regime of President Abdel Fattah el-Sisi, whose heavy-handed methods surpass even Nasser's in their suppression of all opposition; there are over 60,000 political prisoners in Egypt's expanded prison system (Bar'el 2016). The Syrian uprising rapidly devolved into a bloody civil war that continues unabated, and Yemen and Libya have collapsed into chaos. Violent extremists linked to ISIS conquered large swaths of Iraq and Syria and claim responsibility for terrorist acts in Libya, Yemen, Tunisia, Egypt, Germany, Britain, Pakistan, the United States, and elsewhere. Aspirations for democracy and human rights have rarely led to genuine democratization; they have sometimes resulted in a reemergence of strongman politics and other times in political chaos that has been exploited by radical Islamist groups that are decidedly undemocratic.

We can discern several ideological phases in the postcolonial politics of Middle Eastern states. From the 1920s to the 1950s, newly independent states sought to emulate the political models of western Europe by creating parliamentary democracies or constitutional monarchies. In the 1950s and 1960s, socialism and Pan-Arabism gained currency in many Arab countries, often as the result of military coups (for example, Egypt, Syria, Iraq, Libya, Sudan). From the 1970s through the 1990s, Islamists became important in the politics of the Middle East, sometimes in violent opposition to existing regimes, sometimes in opposition parties in authoritarian states, and in two instances (Iran and Afghanistan) seizing power as a result of a popular uprising (in Iran against the Shah, in Afghanistan against the Soviets). In the 2000s democracy became a widespread aspiration, although in most cases authoritarian regimes and extremist groups alike militate against its realization. The Middle East is a region that suffers a severe democracy deficit.

Table 4

Democracy index and regime types in the Middle East

Country	*Democracy index score and category*[a]	*Regime type*[b]	*Polity IV category*[c]	*Notes*
Afghanistan	2.77 authoritarian	Islamic republic	failed/occupied[d]	The Taliban were removed from power and there is an elected government, but the country is plagued by corruption, nepotism, and widespread insecurity; ethnicity plays a major role in elections.
Algeria	3.83 authoritarian	Presidential republic	Open anocracy[e]	Influence of the military and intelligence services limits democracy. Nineteen-year state of emergency was lifted in 2011.
Bahrain	2.87 authoritarian	Constitutional monarchy	autocracy[f]	Although calling itself a constitutional monarchy, most analysts see it as an absolute monarchy.

[a] Data based on the *Economist* Intelligence Unit's *Democracy Index 2014: Democracy and Its Discontents*, http://www.eiu.com/public/thankyou_download.aspx?activity=download&campaignid=Democracy0115.

[b] Regime type is according to the CIA World Factbook, with the further specification, for democracies, of whether it is a presidential or a parliamentary democracy. The Factbook does not provide a government type for Palestine.

[c] Polity IV Project: Political Regime Characteristics and Transitions, 1800–2013, http://systemicpeace.org/polity/polity4x.htm.

[d] This description is from 2013, before the withdrawal of NATO troops.

[e] Polity IV uses "anocracy" to describe a regime characterized by a mix of democratic and autocratic traits and practices and political instability and ineffectiveness. "Open anocracy" means the country has democratic elections, but not very free, and there are limitations on human rights.

[f] An autocracy is a regime in which supreme power is concentrated in the hands of one person, whose decisions are subject to neither external legal restraints nor regularized mechanisms of popular control.

Table 4 (*Cont.*)

Democracy index and regime types in the Middle East

Country	*Democracy index score and category*[a]	*Regime type*[b]	*Polity IV category*[c]	*Notes*
Egypt	3.16 authoritarian	Presidential republic	Closed anocracy	General Abdel Fattah el-Sisi, elected president in 2014, has harshly suppressed all political opposition.
Iran	1.98 authoritarian	Theocratic republic	autocracy	The president is elected, but candidates are vetted by a council of religious scholars. An unelected religious leader, Ayatollah Khamenei, holds supreme authority.
Iraq	4.23 hybrid regime	Parliamentary democracy	Open anocracy	An insecure, Shiʿite-dominated government deals harshly with Sunnis, facilitating the rise of the ISIS, which controls large swaths of territory.
Israel	7.53 flawed democracy	Parliamentary democracy	Full democracy	Laws and policies that discriminate against Arabs detract from the overall democratic culture.
Jordan	3.76 authoritarian	Constitutional monarchy	Closed anocracy	
Kuwait	3.78 authoritarian	Parliamentary democracy	autocracy	
Lebanon	5.12 hybrid regime	Parliamentary republic	Open anocracy	
Libya	3.80 authoritarian	Transitional government	failed/occupied	Independent militias have undermined the effectiveness of the transitional government.

Table 4 (*Cont.*)

Democracy index and regime types in the Middle East

Country	*Democracy index score and category*[a]	*Regime type*[b]	*Polity IV category*[c]	*Notes*
Morocco	4.00 authoritarian	Constitutional monarchy	Closed anocracy	
Oman	3.15 authoritarian	Monarchy	autocracy	
Palestine (West Bank)	4.72 hybrid regime	Presidential republic	none given	The Palestine Authority rejected Hamas's 2006 parliamentary victory, leading to fighting and a split between the Fatah-dominated West Bank and Hamas-dominated Gaza.
Qatar	3.18 authoritarian	Emirate	autocracy	
Saudi Arabia	1.82 authoritarian	Absolute monarchy	autocracy	
Sudan	2.54 authoritarian	Republic under military dictatorship	closed anocracy	
Syria	1.74 authoritarian	Republic under an authoritarian regime	autocracy	Civil war since 2012 has failed to bring down the regime of Bashar al-Asad, though parts of Syria are ruled by ISIS and other opposition groups. Almost half the population has been displaced.
Tunisia	6.31 flawed democracy	Presidential republic	Open anocracy	

Table 4 (*Cont.*)

Democracy index and regime types in the Middle East

Country	*Democracy index score and category*[a]	*Regime type*[b]	*Polity IV category*[c]	*Notes*
Turkey	5.12 hybrid regime	Republican parliamentary democracy	democracy	The elected government secured its hold on power vis-à-vis the military, but became more authoritarian under Recep Tayyip Erdoğan (prime minister, 2003–14, then president).
United Arab Emirates	2.64 authoritarian	Federation of emirates	autocracy	
Yemen	2.79 authoritarian	Presidential republic	open anocracy	The country is currently in a state of civil war, with the president in exile, the Houthis fighting with both the Saudi-supported government and a southern rebellion, and the Saudis engaging in a brutal bombing campaign.

Plan of the Book

This book, which explores different aspects of the struggle for justice in the Middle East, comprises four parts. Part one deals with religion, politics, and major social trends. In chapter 1, I examine the role of religion in what is undoubtedly the most prominent expression of the struggle for justice in the new Middle East, the Arab Spring, and in its often dismaying aftermath. In chapter 2, Behrooz Ghamari-Tabrizi describes the ideological development of the Islamic Republic of Iran since the 1979 revolution. Although the revolution was an expression of outrage over the injustices of the shah's regime, the Islamic regime established under Khomeini was no less despotic and unjust. The stages of the republic's development since then demonstrate a continual process of self-definition that has included disparate articulations of the goals of the regime with regard to justice and human rights. Frustrated struggles for democracy and human rights were particularly evident in the landslide election of reformist Mohammad Khatami to the presidency in 1997 and 2001 and in the brutally crushed Green Movement of 2009. In chapter 3, Feisal G. Mohamed describes how the goals of the Egyptian revolution of 2011 were lost in the bitter struggle between the Islamists and the military that followed. In chapter 4, Joshua D. Hendrick chronicles Turkish protests and struggles for democracy amid that country's public battles over the articulation of its national identity and the increasing repression of the Erdoğan regime. In chapter 5, Ramazan Erdağ points out that the Arab Spring's demands for freedom, justice, and government accountability were aimed in particular at the security sector, but the failure to attain a democratic transition after the Arab Spring uprisings in North Africa caused new levels of insecurity, including the rise of uncontrolled militias, that led to continued violations of human rights.

Part two explores the problems of minority human rights in the Middle East. In chapter 6, I discuss the meaning of human rights, arguments over their universality, various "Islamic" approaches to human rights, their implications for the rights of non-Muslims, and the realities on the ground for various non-Muslim minorities. In chapter 7, Mariz Tadros presents data on and analyzes the implications of violent attacks against Copts in Egypt since the fall of Hosni Mubarak. In chapter 8, Cheryl A. Rubenberg discusses the ongoing denial of justice for Palestinians through a detailed analysis of Israeli policies toward Palestinians in Israel, the West Bank, and Gaza.

Writers on the Middle East have long decried the violation of women's rights in the region. The situation on the ground, however, has become ever more complex and resists broad generalizations. Part three explores the changing gender dynamics in the Middle East. In chapter 9, I look at various analyses of the persistent gender inequalities in the region; the ways that legal reforms, the rise of Islamism, and social change have impacted gender norms; and different Muslim approaches toward attaining gender equality and justice. In chapter 10, Gül Aldıkaçtı Marshall discusses the political dimensions of the ongoing struggle for gender justice in Turkey, a nation that made the promotion of women's rights part of its national identity in the early republic. In chapter 11, Haideh Moghissi discusses the meaning of the Arab Spring for women in light of the experience of women in Iran, where women's participation in the 1979 revolution did not prevent the imposition of new, draconian restrictions on women in its aftermath. Her chapter is both a word of caution and a call for renewed determination to protect women's rights and demand gender equality.

Part four is devoted to expressions of the struggle for justice in the media and the arts. In chapter 12, Niki Akhavan analyzes the media and culture wars in Iran as one aspect of the struggle for justice in that country. In chapter 13, Roger Allen discusses the ways that Moroccan authors in the years before the Arab Spring expressed a longing for justice and human rights through literary depictions of political power and corruption. The book ends with Ted Swedenburg's presentation of the role of music in the Egyptian uprising and the way that music expresses Egyptian aspirations for freedom, dignity, and human rights.

Each of these areas—religiopolitical dynamics, minority rights, gender relations, and popular culture—is an arena in which the struggle for justice, dignity, and human rights is being waged. It is hoped that this book will serve as a record and analysis of the state of this struggle in the Middle East at this point in time.

Sources Cited

Aaron, David. 2008. *In Their Own Words: Voices of Jihad—Compilation and Commentary*. New York: RAND.

Abrahamian, Ervand. 1982. *Iran between Two Revolutions*. Princeton, NJ: Princeton Univ. Press.

Ali, Huda, and Paul Eedle. 2007. "Jihad TV: Mass Media and Terrorism." Documentary film. Princeton, NJ: Films for the Humanities and Sciences.

al-Ali, Nadje, and Nicola Pratt. 2009. *What Kind of Liberation? Women and the Occupation of Iraq*. Berkeley: Univ. of California Press.

Aslan, Senem. 2011. "Everyday Forms of State Power and the Kurds in the Early Turkish Republic." *International Journal of Middle East Studies* 43: 75–93.

———. 2014. *Nation-Building in Turkey and Morocco: Governing Kurdish and Berber Dissent*. Cambridge: Cambridge Univ. Press.

Bar'el, Zvi. 2016. "60,000 Political Prisoners and 1,250 Missing: Welcome to the New Egypt." *Ha'aretz*, Sept. 11. http://www.haaretz.com/middle-east-news/.premium-1.741178.

Bayat, Asef. 2007. *Making Islam Democratic: Social Movements and the Post-Islamist Turn*. Stanford, CA: Stanford Univ. Press.

———. 2013. *Life as Politics: How Ordinary People Change the Middle East*. 2nd ed. Stanford, CA: Stanford Univ. Press.

Center for Economic and Social Rights. 1996. "Unsanctioned Suffering: A Human Rights Assessment of United Nations Sanctions on Iraq." http://cesr.org/downloads/Unsanctioned%20Suffering%201996.pdf.

Chulov, Martin, Costanze Letsch, and Fazel Hawramy. 2014. "Turkey to Allow Kurdish Peshmerga across Its Territory to Fight in Kobani." *Guardian*, Oct. 20. https://www.theguardian.com/world/2014/oct/20/turkey-allows-peshmerga-forces-to-travel-to-kobani.

Cross, Kevin. 2010. "Why Iran's Green Movement Faltered: The Limits of Information Technology in a Rentier State." *SAIS Review of International Affairs* 30 (2): 169–87.

Cushing, Lincoln. 2015. "A Brief History of the 'Clenched Fist' Image." Docs Populi. http://www.docspopuli.org/articles/Fist.html.

Dabashi, Hamid. 2010. *Iran, the Green Movement and the USA: The Fox and the Paradox*. London: Zed Books.

Dorsey, James M. 2017. "Creating Frankenstein: Saudi Arabia's Ultra-conservative Footprint in Africa." Jan. 21. https://mideastsoccer.blogspot.my/2017/01/creatingfrankenstein-saudi-arabias.html.

Economist. 2009. "Turkey and the Kurds: Peace Time?" Aug. 27. http://www.economist.com/node/14313719.

Euben, Roxanne L., and Muhammad Qasim Zaman, eds. 2009. *Princeton Readings in Islamist Thought: Texts and Contexts from al-Banna to Bin Laden*. Princeton, NJ: Princeton Univ. Press.

Friedman, Alan. 1994. *Spider's Web: The Secret History of How the White House Illegally Armed Iraq*. New York: Bantam Books.

Haass, Richard N. 2006. "The New Middle East." *Foreign Affairs* (Nov.–Dec.) https://www.foreignaffairs.com/articles/middle-east/2006-11-01/new-middle-east.

Haeri, Shahla. 1995. "The Politics of Dishonor: Rape and Power in Pakistan." In *Faith and Freedom: Women's Human Rights in the Muslim World*, edited by Mahnaz Afkhami, 161–74. Syracuse, NY: Syracuse Univ. Press.

Harnden, Toby. 2006. "Death and Despair amid US Pursuit of 'New Middle East.'" *Telegraph*, July 30. http://www.telegraph.co.uk/news/1525200/Death-and-despair-amid-US-pursuit-of-new-Middle-East.html.

Hasan, Sana S. 2003. *Christians versus Muslims in Modern Egypt: The Century-Long Struggle for Coptic Equality*. Oxford: Oxford Univ. Press.

Hayes, Stephen F. 2003. "Saddam's al Qaeda Connection." *Weekly Standard*. http://www.weeklystandard.com/article/4277.

Hoffman, Valerie J. 1985. "An Islamic Activist: Zaynab al-Ghazali." In *Women and the Family in the Middle East: New Voices of Change*, edited by Elizabeth W. Fernea, 233–54. Austin: Univ. of Texas Press.

———. 2015. "Ibadism: History, Doctrines and Recent Scholarship." *Religion Compass* 9: 297–307.

Ibrahim, Saad Eddin. 1996. *Egypt, Islam and Democracy: Twelve Critical Essays*. Cairo: American Univ. in Cairo Press.

Institute for Public Accuracy. 2002. "Detailed Analysis of October 7, 2002 Speech by Bush on Iraq." http://www.accuracy.org/1029-detailed-analysis-of-october-7-2002-speech-by-bush-on-iraq/#more-1029.

Isikoff, Michael, and David Corn. 2007. *Hubris: The Inside Story of Spin, Scandal, and the Selling of the Iraq War.* New York: Random House.

Kamal, Baher. 2015. "Silence, Please! A New Middle East Is in the Making." *Inter Press Service*, Dec. 14. http://www.ipsnews.net/2015/12/silence-please-a-new-middle-east-is-in-the-making/.

Kashani-Sabet, Firoozeh. 2011. *Conceiving Citizens: Women and the Politics of Motherhood in Iran.* New York: Oxford Univ. Press.

Kayaoğlu, Barin. 2013. "Turkey's Missed Opportunities." *Al-Monitor*, July 30. http://www.al-monitor.com/pulse/originals/2013/07/turkey-erdogan-missed-opportunities-kurds.html?utm_source=&utm_medium=email&utm_campaign=7886#ixzz2adnk7Z5G.

Kepel, Gilles. 1984. *Le Prophète et Pharaon: Les mouvements islamistes dans l'Egypte contemporaine.* Paris: La Découverte.

Khan, Shahnaz. 2006. *Zina, Transnational Feminism, and the Moral Regulation of Pakistani Women.* Vancouver and Toronto: UBC Press.

Kingsley, Patrick. 2017a. "Amid Turkish Purge, a Renewed Attack on Turkish Culture." *New York Times*, June 29.

———. 2017b. "On the Road with Protesters Marching across Turkey to Condemn Erdogan's Purge." *New York Times*, July 2.

March, Andrew F. 2009. *Islam and Liberal Citizenship: The Search for an Overlapping Consensus.* Oxford: Oxford Univ. Press.

McDowall, David. 1992. *The Kurds: A Nation Denied.* London: Minority Rights Group.

———. 1996. *A Modern History of the Kurds.* New York: I. B. Tauris.

Mirenzi, Nicola. 2012. "Progress on the Kurdish Question." Translated by Francesca Simmons. *ResetDoc*, June 20. http://www.resetdoc.org/story/00000022009.

Moghadam, Valentine N. 2013. "Population Growth, Urbanization, and Unemployment." In *Understanding the Contemporary Middle East*, edited by Jillian Schwedler, 287–314. 4th ed. Boulder, CO: Lynne Rienner.

Nasr, Octavia. 2006. "Bin Laden Tells Sunnis to Fight Shiites in Iraq." CNN, July 2. http://edition.cnn.com/2006/WORLD/meast/07/02/binladen.message/.

Nasr, Vali. 2006. *The Shia Revival: How Conflicts within Islam Will Shape the Future.* New York: W. W. Norton.

Noll, Jessica. 2017. "Egypt's Armed Forces Cement Economic Power." *SWP Comments*, no. 5 (Feb.). Berlin: Stiftung, Wissenschaft und Politik.

Peres, Shimon. 1993. *The New Middle East.* New York: Henry Holt.

Rezai, Hamid. 2013. "Green Movement in Iran." In *The Wiley Encyclopedia of Social and Political Movements.* Chichester, West Sussex: Wiley-Blackwell. http://onlinelibrary.wiley.com/doi/10.1002/9780470674871.wbespm468/full.

Rieff, David. 2003. "Were Sanctions Right?" *New York Times*, July 27. http://www.nytimes.com/2003/07/27/magazine/27SANCTIONS.html.

Sanasarian, Eliz. 2000. *Religious Minorities in Iran.* Cambridge: Cambridge Univ. Press.

Sciolino, Elaine. 1996. "The Many Faces of Islamic Law." *New York Times*, Oct. 13. http://www.nytimes.com/1996/10/13/weekinreview/the-many-faces-of-islamic-law.html.

Shields, Sarah. 2013. "The Greek–Turkish Population Exchange." *Middle East Report and Information Project*, no. 267. http://www.merip.org/mer/mer267/greek-turkish-population-exchange.

Sowa, Alexis. 2013. "Aid to Egypt by the Numbers." Center for Global Development, July 19. https://www.cgdev.org/blog/aid-egypt-numbers.

Tadros, Mariz. 2013. *Copts at the Crossroads: The Challenges of Building Inclusive Democracy in Egypt.* Cairo: American Univ. in Cairo Press.

Timmerman, Kenneth R. 1991. *The Death Lobby: How the West Armed Iraq.* New York: Houghton Mifflin.

Weaver, Mary Anne. 2000. *A Portrait of Egypt: A Journey through the World of Militant Islam.* New York: Farrar, Straus and Giroux.

Weiss, Michael, and Hassan, Hassan. 2015. *ISIS: Inside the Army of Terror.* New York: Regan Arts.

Part One

Religion, Politics, and Society in the Middle East

1

Religion and Politics in the Arab Spring and Its Aftermath

VALERIE J. HOFFMAN

It is often claimed that there is no separation between religion and politics in Islam. Although this point has also been disputed, scholars continue to argue that there is something distinctive about Islam's relationship to politics (Hamid 2016, 5). This is not to say that Islam in any way determines the politics of the Middle East but that a significant number of the inhabitants of the Middle East believe that Islam provides the best foundation for justice, and therefore for political legitimacy. To some extent, each of the chapters in this part of the book deals with aspects of the relationship between religion and politics in the contemporary Middle East—in the Arab uprisings and their aftermath, the Islamic Republic of Iran, the power struggles in Egypt during the writing of two new constitutions, the struggle for political identity in Turkey today, and security challenges in North Africa.

Religion was largely absent in the language of the Arab Spring protests. Protesters demanded democracy, freedom, dignity, and an end to corruption, without reference to religion. The protests that began in the working-class towns of Sidi Bouzid and Kasserine in Tunisia were spontaneous expressions of outrage by ordinary workers, prompted by the abuse, humiliation, and sheer desperation that led Mohammed Bouazizi to set himself on fire on December 17, 2010. The bloggers in Tunis who learned via Facebook of the protests and their brutal suppression by the police were educated, middle class, and largely secular young people who organized protests in the capital in support of the regional workers' protests. They were motivated by sympathy for the plight of the protesting workers to the south and by hatred for a deeply corrupt regime. Their cries were for freedom, democracy, and, ultimately, the fall of the regime. Their wish was granted when President Zine El Abidine Ben Ali fled the country on January 14, 2011, and other members of his government trying to flee were arrested.

The unexpected success of the massive demonstrations, thanks mainly to the Tunisian army's unwillingness to shoot at the protesters, motivated a similar demographic in Egypt—young, educated, and technologically savvy—to organize protests in Cairo's Tahrir Square. In 2008 Facebook had already been used by the April 6 youth movement to support the demands for a living wage by striking workers in the industrial town of El-Mahalla El-Kubra. For years, the Egyptian regime had been unable to provide the government jobs earlier guaranteed for university graduates—a policy that had resulted in a bloated, inefficient government bureaucracy—and the rate of unemployment among Egyptian college graduates was ten times the rate of those individuals who did not go to college (LaGraffe 2012, 73). Furthermore, the neoliberal policies implemented since Sadat's "Open Door Policy" in the mid-1970s had led to a sharp rise in prices, far outstripping the capacity of civil service jobs to provide for families and forcing many people to work two or three jobs.

Low police salaries encouraged the growth of a pervasively corrupt system that fed on bribes, routinely tortured suspects, and acted with impunity. Most of the victims of these human rights abuses were Islamists, whose plight did not concern the secular youth. That situation changed when two policemen seized one of their own, a young man named Khaled Saeed, from a cyber café in Alexandria on June 6, 2010, and brutally beat him to death in a nearby alley (Danahar 2015, 91). Saeed's brother managed to photograph the mangled corpse; the circulated photograph prompted street protests against police brutality. Wa'el Ghonim, an Egyptian marketing executive for Google in Dubai, established a Facebook group called "We Are All

Khaled Saeed." By January 2011, the group had five thousand members (Danahar 2015, 91). But no one expected anything to change—until the Tunisians forced the ouster of Zine El Abidine Ben Ali.

The Egyptian protests were scheduled for January 25, 2011, National Police Day, in order to protest police brutality and demand the ouster of Interior Minster Habib al-Adly and an end to the decades-old emergency law that gave police broad powers of arrest, suspended constitutional rights, and curbed nongovernmental political activity. Had the activists targeted only their own demographic, the protests would have rapidly fizzled out. But they cleverly raised slogans against high prices, low wages, unemployment, and corruption in Cairo's lower-class neighborhoods and led marches from multiple directions that converged on Tahrir Square. The police and security forces responded to the protests with characteristic brutality. The "Day of Rage" protests of January 28 attracted an even larger and more diverse crowd of men and women, young and old, poor and middle class, educated and illiterate, and—for the first time—significant numbers of Islamists.

In a blatant sign of the irrelevance of religion in the first days of the protests, the leaders of Egypt's largest Islamist organization, the Muslim Brotherhood, declined to take part in the January 25 protests; some young Brothers defied that order, but they made it clear that they participated as Egyptians demanding justice and freedom, not as Islamists advocating an Islamic state. But "in response to the impressive, organic mobilisation of ordinary Egyptians, the Brotherhood leadership decided to change their original stance of disassociation from the protests, and formally called for their members to mobilise by the evening of Jan. 27" (Hellyer 2014). The Muslim Brotherhood lent its enormous organizational skills and its devoted followers to the cause of democracy. Without their leadership, the uprising might not have succeeded.

Pope Shenouda III of the Coptic Orthodox Church "officially declared his support of President Hosni Mubarak and the legitimacy he represented, asking Copts to boycott the demonstrations" (Guirguis 2012, 512). Nonetheless, many Copts were among the estimated

11 percent of all Egyptians who participated in the protests, and on February 11, the day that Mubarak resigned, the pope issued a statement that "the Coptic church salutes the honorable youth of Egypt, the youth of January 25, who led Egypt in a strong, white revolution and sacrificed for this cause precious blood, the blood of the nation's martyrs" (513).

In the catharsis of a united goal and shared passion, the protesters emphasized the unity of Egyptian Muslims and Copts: on Friday, February 4, Coptic protesters formed a protective circle around Muslims performing the noon prayer in the square, to keep the police from attacking them. The following Sunday, the Muslims returned the favor, as the Copts celebrated Mass in the square. The extraordinary spectacle of the cross raised in the center of the city, protected by Muslims, must have brought tears to the eyes of many Christians, accustomed as they were to institutionalized restrictions on public display of Christian symbols and public expression of the Christian faith. The protests were marked by ecstatic demonstrations of interfaith unity and were represented in the spectacular art that appeared on formerly blank walls all over the city. When the army forced Hosni Mubarak to resign on February 11, 2011, the influential Muslim Brotherhood member and al-Azhar–trained scholar Yusuf al-Qaradawi returned to Egypt from Qatar, where he had lived in exile for fifty years. Asked the day after Mubarak's resignation whether it was now time to establish the sharia in Egypt, he replied, "Preserving the people's freedom is more important than setting up a system of Shari'a" (*Egypt Independent* 2011). In a sermon during Friday prayer in Tahrir Square on February 18, he explicitly addressed both Muslims and Copts (Kirkpatrick 2011) and declared sectarianism to have died in Tahrir Square (Murphy 2011).

The only Arab Spring uprising that took on a sectarian hue early on was in the tiny island nation of Bahrain, where an oppressive Sunni monarchy rules a population in which the Shi'a constitute a majority. Initially, Sunnis joined Shi'a in the protests, and the demands were for democratic reform, freedom of expression, and an end to corruption—the same demands made in all the Arab Spring uprisings.

As Noueihed and Warren note, "The divides in Bahrain were not religious in nature—they revolved around universal calls for the Al Khalifa family to relinquish some political power to the people, to empower the elected parliament, to boost transparency and to end discrimination—but by the close of the year divisions were being couched in increasingly sectarian terms. . . . Sunnis who began 2011 believing reform could resolve political tensions, ended it believing the Shi'ites would only be satisfied with the overthrow of the monarchy. Shi'ites who began 2011 believing reform was enough, ended it believing the Al Khalifa monarchy had to go" (2013, 136). But, as Noueihed and Warren point out, Bahrain was spared an armed conflict, despite the harshness of the government's response to protests, because the people were unarmed (161). Unlike in Libya and Syria, where Qatar and Saudi Arabia armed rebel groups, in Bahrain Saudi Arabia and the United Arab Emirates assisted the government in crushing the protests.

Perhaps it was inevitable that religious tensions and divisions would manifest themselves as a result of the Arab Spring uprisings, but not, as is commonly believed, because of innate hostility between Sunnis and Shi'a or between Muslims and Christians. The dictators and strongmen of the Middle East warned that if they were removed from power, Islamists would seize the reins of the government. That warning played well in the United States, where President Obama's government was slow to express support for the democratic uprisings. This fear was not unwarranted; in a politically repressive context that disallowed the development of political parties capable of contesting the regime's stranglehold on power, the strongest and most organized political opposition was in the mosques and Islamic organizations. The oldest, largest, and best-organized Islamist organization in the region, Egypt's Muslim Brotherhood, had spawned similar groups in other countries throughout the Sunni Middle East. In Egypt, where religious parties were not allowed, the Muslim Brothers joined other political parties and successfully ran for seats in parliament during the reign of Mubarak. In Morocco they formed the Justice and Development Party and in Jordan the Islamic Action

Front; these groups enjoyed variable success according to the mood of the ruling monarch. In Yemen the Islamist Islah (Reform) party constituted the strongest opposition to President Ali Abdullah Saleh. The first electoral success of an Islamist party in the Middle East was in Turkey, the one state in the Middle East that was founded on an explicitly secular basis. The Justice and Development Party (Adalet ve Kalkınma Partisi) came to power in 2002 and remains in power to this day. The Bush administration's "Freedom Agenda" promoted democracy, but Hamas's victory in Palestinian parliamentary elections in 2006 symbolized to many the pitfalls of democratic processes in the absence of liberal democratic values.

Rached Ghannouchi, leader of the long-repressed Ennahda (Resurrection) party, established in 1989 by Tunisia's Islamic Tendency Movement, returned from nearly twenty-three years in exile to a tumultuous welcome on January 30, 2011. The first elections in Tunisia after the uprising were held on October 23, 2011, for the Constituent Assembly, to elect those individuals who would write a new constitution for the republic. Predictably, Ennahda won the largest share of the votes. The strength of Tunisia's secular tradition was such that efforts to overturn the rights given to women in the Personal Status Code of 1956 were rapidly squelched, as were attempts to speak of women as "complements" to men, rather than their equals. But nothing could stop the assassination of two leading secular politicians in 2013, crimes likely committed by Salafis.

In light of Tunisia's strong secular tradition, it was a shock to see the sudden appearance of Salafis on the streets of Tunisia, the men wearing the characteristic untrimmed beards and robes of Salafis across the Middle East, the women wearing face veils and the heavy, full dresses and head coverings of Salafis in Egypt and elsewhere, a far cry from the traditional sheer *safsari* that had, in any case, long been abandoned by the middle class. "Salafism," a term based on the notion of following the ways of the earliest Muslims—the *salaf*—was a label originally applied to the relatively liberal, modernist reform movement of Muhammad 'Abduh (1849–1905) and Rashid Rida (1865–1935), who wanted to revive the dynamism of early Islam but not to follow the specific manners and rulings of the early Muslims. But in recent years, Salafism has come to mean the most rigid, literalist Islamists, who may properly be called fundamentalists, since they seek to restore what they believe to be the original, pure version of Islam and to apply the letter of traditional interpretations of the sharia. The Salafis sent shivers down the spines of Tunisia's secular elite with their demands for an Islamic state, raising the black flag of al-Qaeda. The Tunisian revolution was followed by Salafi destruction of the tombs of *marabouts*, holy men and women for whom reverence is deeply embedded in Tunisian culture. Throughout the Muslim world, veneration for God's special "friends" (often translated into English as "saints") prompts pilgrimages to their tombs, where the pious seek God's favor by virtue of their blessedness and holiness. Ibn Taymiyya of Damascus (1265–1328) decried these practices as idolatry, but the popularity of the saints and the Sufi orders that they founded were such that Ibn Taymiyya spent his final years in prison. His evident lack of success at the time was demonstrated by the fact that, when he died in prison, he was buried in a Sufi cemetery, where his tomb received the same veneration he had long decried. But Ibn Taymiyya's ideas inspired the militant Wahhabi movement of the eighteenth century, the ideology behind the formation of three Saudi successive states, including the current Kingdom of Saudi Arabia, which was established in 1932. The Saudis have destroyed saints' tombs and other important religious sites, and other Salafis have emulated this practice across the Muslim world. The removal of strongmen in Iraq, Tunisia, Egypt, and Libya allowed Salafis to destroy holy sites they deemed offensive, an aggression that has gone largely unchallenged. Egypt's highest religious officials, the sheikh of al-Azhar and the grand mufti, both members of Sufi orders, responded with outrage at Salafi destruction of Sufi shrines (El-Kashef 2011). The Sufi orders in Egypt play important roles in Egyptian culture and have long been apolitical. In response to the Salafi attacks, however, some Sufis announced the formation of political parties (Islamopedia Online 2011; Parties and Movements 2011), but thus far these groups have proved largely ineffective (El Masry 2012; Ammar 2013).

The uprising in Egypt was rapidly followed by numerous bombings of Coptic churches throughout Egypt. The Supreme Council of Armed Forces (SCAF), which assumed control of the transitional government after Mubarak's resignation, proved singularly unwilling to protect the churches or do anything to stop the violence. On October 9, 2011, they responded with shocking brutality to a Coptic protest in front of the radio and television building in a part of Cairo known as Maspero: they repeatedly drove enormous armored vehicles into the crowd, literally flattening some protesters, killing 27 and wounding 329. They announced on television that the Copts were attacking the army and called on people to protect their army. Some Muslims were only too ready to respond to the call and inflicted further casualties on the hapless protesters. There were numerous reports of the army preventing medical personnel from reaching the wounded. The inspiring interfaith unity evinced during the uprising had been savagely suppressed (Tadros 2011). One week later, Muslims and Christians gathered in a silent memorial of the victims, holding hands across Qasr al-Nil Bridge, in mute protest of the military's brutal denial of justice.

The Muslim Brotherhood in Egypt initially tried to allay fears of an Islamist takeover of the country by saying it would not form a political party or field a candidate in presidential elections. It went back on both those promises, forming the Freedom and Justice Party and fielding candidates. Salafis in Egypt had traditionally refused to participate in electoral politics, but they too changed their minds. A number of Salafi parties were formed, the most important of which was al-Nour. Their success in the first round of parliamentary elections in November and December 2011—and the crippling failure of secular parties—was a deep shock to the secular activists who had initiated the January 25 uprising. As Feisal Mohamed recounts in his contribution to this volume, the presidential elections of spring 2012 ended in a runoff between a former general who had served as prime minister under the Mubarak regime and Mohammed Morsi, the candidate of the Freedom and Justice Party. Given a choice between a representative of the old regime and a member of the Muslim

Brotherhood, many opted for the latter as the lesser of two evils. As Mohamed points out, members of the Brotherhood carried an aura of morality that would be a welcome relief after the brutal corruption of Mubarak's regime, which was largely continued under the SCAF administration. And so the military ceded the presidency to a representative of their decades-long enemy, the Muslim Brotherhood, though they retained a significant amount of power for themselves.

Morsi proved to be an unpopular and ineffective president. Although he had won by less than 52 percent, he saw his victory as a sweeping mandate that eliminated the need to negotiate with other political parties. He did not dare attempt to impose Islamic law on Egypt's huge and complex society, but he rapidly squandered whatever goodwill the Muslim Brotherhood had acquired through its charitable works and support of the revolution and alienated vast portions of the electorate. Attacks on churches continued unabated, provoking an unusual public denunciation of the government by Coptic pope Tawadros II (Associated Press 2013).

Under Morsi's presidency, anti-Shiʿa hate speech was allowed to spread unchecked. Through his prominent, silent presence during a Salafi speech on June 15, 2013, that described the Shiʿa as "unbelievers who must be killed," he seemed to endorse the inflammatory rhetoric. The next day, four Shiʿites were murdered in Giza (Human Rights Watch 2013). The Egyptian Initiative for Personal Rights issued a report on July 21, 2016, showing that there were seventy incidents of assault against Egyptian Shiʿites during the period from January 2011 to May 2016 (Hidji 2016). The Shiʿa are a small, statistically negligible minority in Egypt, and they found themselves suddenly, terrifyingly, vulnerable.

The Egyptian populace had, undoubtedly unrealistically, expected changes for the better under the first president who came to power through a free, fair election. Morsi's arrogance and failure to form alliances with non-Islamists provoked new public protests. The minister of defense, General Abdel Fattah el-Sisi, publicly warned that the conflict "could lead to a collapse of the state"—"the sort of thing that generals like to say just before they embark on a coup"

(Danahar 2015, 118). It now appears that the military was behind the Tamarrod campaign, which demanded early presidential elections (Dreyfuss 2013; Giglio 2013). Morsi's ineptitude was such that he even managed to alienate other Islamists; the Salafis applauded the military coup that removed him from power on July 3, 2013, and subsequently labeled the Muslim Brotherhood a terrorist group, criminalizing membership in the organization. Thousands of Islamists—and other political activists—were arrested; hundreds were sentenced to death.

The immediate beneficiaries of the uprisings in Tunisia, Egypt, and Morocco were the Islamists. But in the wake of the coup in Egypt, Ennahda worried that Tunisia might follow suit. Anger over the assassination of secular politicians and fears of a military takeover ultimately forced Ennahda to allow early elections, in which secular groups formed a coalition (Nidaa Tounès) that succeeded in forcing the Islamists out of power (Beinin 2015).

The exception to the rule that Islamists would be the immediate beneficiaries of the Arab Spring uprisings was Libya. Qaddafi, who seized power in a military coup in 1969, introduced his own idiosyncratic interpretation of Islam and wrote his political philosophy in *The Green Book*, which was written, like Mao's *Red Book*, in "a simple, understandable style with many memorable slogans" (Metz 1987). Schoolchildren in Libya were taught to memorize passages from this book and chant them in a way that is comparable to the memorization and chanting of the Qur'an in other Muslim countries (Anderson 1983; Mayer 1982). Qaddafi dissolved all normal political and business establishments, announcing joint ownership by workers and residents and rule by people's committees. He had many titles for himself, including "brotherly leader and guide of the revolution" and "king of kings" of Africa. The fear and terrible exploitation in which Libyans lived under a self-aggrandizing, brutal, and hedonistic dictator are graphically depicted in the harrowing book *Gaddafi's Harem* (Cojean 2013). The ferocity of the anger of ordinary Libyans against the fallen dictator is indicated by the savage street justice he received, and the shallowness of the inculcation of Qaddafi's ideology is evident in the lack of any faction in post-Qaddafi Libyan society displaying loyalty to the self-appointed philosopher of the revolution.

Despite the deep conservatism of Libyan society, when elections were held after the collapse of the Qaddafi regime Islamists did not come to power. On the other hand, no one was able to control the entire country; hundreds of armed militias battled each other in the streets of all the major cities. Even Libya's prime minister—one of seven prime ministers in the space of four years—was kidnapped briefly in October 2013. The transitional government had to beat a retreat from the capital, Tripoli, in August 2014, when it was seized by a militia from Misrata, which set up its own cabinet and assembly. In the Benghazi region, where the uprising against Qaddafi had begun, a Salafi group attacked the American consulate on September 11, 2012, killing US ambassador J. Christopher Stevens and three other Americans. Islamist groups predominate in the eastern part of the country. After the military coup in Egypt ousted the Islamist government in that country, militants claiming affiliation with the Islamic State committed grisly murders of Egyptian workers in Libya, most famously killing twenty-one Copts on a beach near Misrata on February 15, 2015 (Wehrey and Alrababa'h 2015), prompting Egypt to launch air strikes in Libya the following day. Despite these high-profile attacks, one cannot say that the civil war in Libya is between Islamists and anti-Islamists; the conflict involves multiple groups with diverse motivations (McQuinn 2015).

Yemen was a classic weak state, which allowed al-Qaeda in the Arabian Peninsula to operate in the southeast part of the country, in the provinces of Abyan, Shabwa, al-Bayda', and Hadramawt. The uprising in Yemen succeeded in ousting President Ali Abdullah Saleh but did not succeed in overthrowing his regime. The opposition in Yemen was badly fractured, and the leading opposition party, Islah, described as "a tribal–Islamist alliance" (Noueihed and Warren 2013, 199), alienated many in the opposition by its arrogant assumption of authority over the protests (vom Bruck, Alwazir, and Wiacek 2014, 294–97). Saleh's vice president, 'Abd Rabbuh al-Hadi, assumed the presidency after Saleh's resignation. Hadi hailed originally from the southern part of the country, but in 1994 he led the suppression of a southern revolt against the domination of the northern part of the country, which had united as a single republic only in 1990. Tawakkul Karman, who shared the 2011 Nobel Peace Prize with two Liberians, President Ellen Johnson Sirleaf and peace activist Leymah Gbowee, was a prominent member of Islah. But Karman rapidly faded into the background, and Islah itself receded in significance as the National Dialogue Conference tried unsuccessfully to formulate a plan for the country that would represent the many factions in Yemeni politics over a period of ten months, from March 18, 2013, to January 24, 2014 (Thiel 2015).

One group that was consistently sidelined in Yemeni politics was the Houthis. Contrary to consistent reports that the Houthis are a branch of Twelver Shi'ism, they are, in fact, Zaydi Shi'a. The Zaydis are the third main branch of Shi'ism, the others being the Twelvers/Imamis, who predominate in Iran, Iraq, Lebanon, and Bahrain, and the Isma'ilis, who were major players on the political scene in the tenth and eleventh centuries but today are found mainly as minorities in the Indian subcontinent and among Indian expatriate communities around the world. In the tenth and eleventh centuries, there were Zaydi imamates in Morocco and central Arabia. Today, the only significant Zaydi population is in northern Yemen. A Zaydi imam ruled much of present-day Yemen until a military coup overthrew the last imam in 1962 and introduced a republic. The new republic took a hostile attitude toward the Zaydis. Although, according to Haider, "the later Zaidi imams explicitly favored Sunni scholars, they were now depicted as avid—if not fanatical—tyrants who persecuted all non-Zaidi religious groups. The revolution was thus interpreted as a victory of the larger Yemeni population over a parochial tribal Zaidism" (Haider 2015). The state persecuted conservative Zaydis and underfunded their communities, promoted Sunni proselytization in Zaydi territory, outlawed classical Zaydi teachings, and shut their educational institutions (Haider 2015). In the hostile new political environment, many Zaydis adopted Sunni doctrines. As Haider

(2015) put it, "The current atmosphere does not permit an individual to be both a Yemeni citizen and an adherent of Zaidism."

The overall sense of grievance and neglect led to the rise of the Ansar Allah movement, often referred to as "Houthis" because of the dominance of the Houthi tribe in its leadership. A Houthi uprising in 2004 was brutally suppressed. The National Dialogue Conference included only one Houthi representative, who refused to agree to the inequities built into a proposed redrawing of provincial boundaries; this representative was later assassinated (Thiel 2015). In what appears to have been a demand for inclusion in the decision-making processes, the Houthis advanced on Sana'a in September 2014 and besieged the presidential palace. Hadi dissolved parliament and fled to Saudi Arabia on September 22, leaving the capital in the hands of the Houthis, who seem never to have intended to conquer it. From there the Houthis began extending their control over the rest of the country. They encountered resistance not only from the remnants of the national army but also from southern separatist forces and al-Qaeda in the southeast. They succeeded in capturing Aden, the former capital of South Yemen and the center of southern separatism, on March 25, 2015, and engaged in battles with al-Qaeda forces elsewhere.

Enter the Saudis, who declared the Houthis a proxy army for the Saudis' archrival, Iran. Although Iran has provided a small amount of funding to the Houthis, the Houthis do not identify with Iran or its form of Shi'ism and cannot be described as proxies for Iran. On the other hand, Iran has directly intervened in the politics of post-Saddam Iraq and the civil war in Syria, where it supported the regime of Bashar al-Assad. Hence, they were an important presence on Saudi Arabia's northern border; the specter of Shi'ite domination to the south as well was more than the Saudis were willing to tolerate. Yemen, the poorest nation in the Arab world, had always been dependent on Saudi assistance, and many Yemenis have worked in Saudi Arabia. Now Saudi Arabia withheld aid from Yemen and prevented the flow into the country of oil, food, and other necessities of life. On March 26, 2015, a Saudi-led Arab coalition, which included Qatar, Bahrain, Kuwait, the United Arab Emirates, Egypt, Jordan, Morocco, and Sudan, began an intensive bombing campaign in Yemen that, while aiming at Houthi forces, devastated parts of the capital, including parts of the old city of Sana'a, a UNESCO World Heritage Site, killing hundreds of civilians (Gladstone 2015). Although the United States expressed alarm at the rising civilian casualties, it continued to arm the Saudis and provide logistical support. US-made cluster bombs, which are banned by most of the international community, have inflicted tremendous suffering on a people who were already on the brink of starvation. Intermittent peace talks organized by the United Nations have thus far failed even to get the opposing sides to meet face-to-face. By October 2016, the war's toll had reached 4,125 civilian deaths and 7,207 wounded (Cole 2016). By May 2017, two-thirds of Yemen's 26 million people lived with the reality of famine, with around 7 million already suffering from acute malnutrition. Of this number, more than 3 million people faced acute malnutrition, and cholera had killed hundreds and threatened many more (Dingli 2017).

Of all the sectarian conflicts that arose out of the Arab Spring uprisings, the most catastrophic is the Syrian. The Syrian uprising began as a nonsectarian demand for democracy and the ouster of Bashar al-Assad, but the inevitability that it would take a sectarian turn was dictated by the structure of the state itself. During the period of the French mandate (1920–46), the French employed the strategy of preventing an effective mass uprising by placing the military in the hands of a minority, the Alawites, who were only 12 percent of the population. The Alawites continue to dominate the Syrian army, from which Hafez al-Assad, himself an Alawite, seized power in 1970. The Alawites are an offshoot of Twelver Shi'ism that Sunnis deem to have gone beyond all acceptable bounds in its veneration (some would say deification) of the Prophet's young cousin and son-in-law 'Ali ibn Abi Talib, the first imam for all Shi'ite sects (Friedman 2009). Although the ruling Ba'ath party guarantees the secularity of the regime, Syria's closest ally in the region is Iran, and

Iran's proxy, Hezbollah of Lebanon, has become a key player in the civil war that has engulfed Syria since 2012. The Syrian opposition has always been divided; even the Free Syrian Army (FSA), which the United States supported and helped train, is only a coalition of ideologically divided groups. Qatar actively funded and supported the Muslim Brotherhood, while Saudi Arabia provided funds and armaments to the Nusra Front, an affiliate of al-Qaeda, which rapidly became the most important rebel group in Syria (Danahar 2015, 376). Given the dominance of jihadist groups among the rebels fighting against the Assad regime, it is no surprise that Syria's Alawites and Christians have linked their own survival to that of the regime. Any faith in the FSA's embrace of democratic ideals must be tempered by the fact that when Theo Padnos escaped from his Nusra Front captors to an FSA outpost, they returned him to Nusra (Padnos 2014). US support for the FSA amounted to an unintended alliance between the United States and al-Qaeda in trying to force Assad from power.

President Obama stated repeatedly that Bashar al-Assad must step aside. But as the Islamic State of Iraq and Syria (ISIS) became the greatest threat to US interests in the Middle East, the removal of Assad faded as a priority. The United States had failed to intervene when the Syrian army tortured and murdered children, bombed civilians, or destroyed the city of Hama. On August 20, 2012, Obama declared that if the government used chemical weapons against civilians, that would be "a red line for us" that could force US intervention. But when the Syrian army launched a major chemical attack on August 21, 2013, Obama decided to defer to Congress, which refused to support an attack on Syria. When Secretary of State John Kerry said, in response to a question, that the threat of a US attack on Syria could be removed if the government allowed an international team to dismantle its chemical weapons, Russia seized upon these words, and the process of removing and dismantling the weapons began (Danahar 2015, 403–5).

Al-Qaeda in Iraq, which had captured headlines through its barbaric executions until its leader Abu Mus'ab al-Zarqawi was killed by US forces in 2006, had retreated across the porous Syria-Iraq border.

In Syria it adopted the name the "Islamic Call in Iraq and Syria" (al-Da'wa 'l-Islamiyya bi-'l-'Iraq wa-'l-Sham), known by the acronym "Da'esh." As the authority of the Iraqi government was challenged by a Sunni uprising in Ramadi in December 2013, Da'esh reentered that country and began to raise revenues by capturing oil refineries and abducting foreign journalists and aid workers, whom it would release in exchange for multimillion-dollar ransoms. American and British captives, whose governments were unwilling to pay for their release, were executed in grisly fashion, their beheadings filmed in increasingly sophisticated fashion and broadcast on the Internet. They also massacred non-Sunni men and enslaved non-Muslim women, especially Yazidis, holding open-air markets where women were displayed in chains, bearing price tags. In June 2014 Da'esh captured the northern Iraqi city of Mosul, where their leader Abu Bakr al-Baghdadi mounted the pulpit in the main mosque and proclaimed the establishment of the Islamic State of Iraq and the Levant, later renamed the Islamic State of Iraq and Syria, and finally just the Islamic State. Al-Baghdadi adopted the religiously symbolic title of caliph.

The last time a ruler had adopted the title of caliph was under the Ottoman empire; Atatürk abolished that caliphate in 1924. The proclamation of a caliphate made ISIS more than a terrorist group like al-Qaeda; it resonated with many Muslims around the world as an overturning of all the humiliations brought upon the Muslims by European colonialism, US imperialism, and the establishment of the state of Israel in the heart of the Arab world. Tens of thousands of alienated young Muslims flocked to join ISIS from countries as geographically separated as the United States and Indonesia. The largest number went from little Tunisia;[1] the second largest went from Saudi Arabia, whose Wahhabi ideology had spawned al-Qaeda in the first place (Hashim 2014). Al-Qaeda and ISIS are both sworn enemies of the kingdom, which, they feel, has abandoned its original militant

1. This fact seems shocking, given Tunisia's long tradition of secularism. For an attempt to make sense of this, see Hamid 2016, chap. 7.

ideology by allying itself with the United States, but that enmity in no way contradicts the fact that the religious ideas of Saudi Arabia and of al-Qaeda are fundamentally alike. It is no wonder, therefore, that Saudis have funded al-Qaeda and its affiliates and that Saudis have constituted the second-largest national component of the armed forces of the "Islamic State." While the world gazed in horror at the mass executions, crucifixions, and beheadings of men and the enslavement and mass rapes of women, and could not fathom the source of the attraction to its youth of such a brutal army, the alienated and humiliated continued to set out for Syria to join up. ISIS soon extended its domain into Syria, making the northern city of Raqqa its capital in that country. ISIS's leaders declared they would wipe out the colonial border between the two countries.

The entry of ISIS onto the playing field of Syria's civil war prompted some startling shifts in tactics and alliances. As ISIS forces threatened to capture the city of Kobani on the Turkish border in October 2014, the Turkish government, which had supported Islamist rebel forces in Syria and had purchased oil from ISIS, caved in to American pressure and, in an unprecedented gesture, allowed Kurdish Workers Party forces, which until recently had long been at war with the Turkish government, to pass through Turkey to Kobani to defend the city against ISIS (Parkinson 2014). As the United States and France began to bomb ISIS targets in Syria, they tacitly cooperated with Hezbollah and the Syrian army. In September 2015, Putin announced that Russia would join the bombing campaign against ISIS, but of the hundreds of known Russian bombing strikes in Syria, few were on ISIS-controlled targets; most targeted Syrian rebels, who were a much more direct threat to Assad's hold on power—the FSA and Nusra. As Maxim Trudolyubov noted, Russia seemed to label all anti-Assad forces in Syria "ISIS" (Trudolyubov 2015). Putin's campaign in Syria enjoyed strong support from the Russian public, as it affirmed a renewal of Russia's importance on the global stage.

The Syrian war became a catastrophe on a scale unseen since the Second World War. Half of Syria's prewar population of 23 million had been displaced; more than 4 million Syrians fled to neighboring countries, threatening the stability of its fragile neighbors, especially Lebanon. In August 2015, Europe was caught unawares when a massive wave of migrants began pouring onto its shores, many of them from Syria. By February 2016, the Syrian Center for Policy Research said 470,000 people had been killed by the conflict (Boghani 2016), including large numbers of civilians: the Syrian Network for Human Rights reported that 206,923 civilians had been killed between March 2011 and March 2017. An end to the war is nowhere in sight.

Despite the rise of sectarian conflicts in the Middle East since the collapse of the regime of Saddam Hussein, the common presumption that Sunnis and Shi'a have been at war for centuries and that any loosening of authoritarian rule is bound to produce these conflicts is incorrect. Violent conflict between Sunnis and Shi'a has not been the historical pattern and is not inevitable. The rise of sectarian conflicts in the Middle East is owing to a confluence of factors:

1. Colonial policies of divide and rule favored minority domination in Iraq (Arab Sunnis) and Syria (Alawites). This arrangement continued under authoritarian Ba'athist rule, despite the secular ideology embraced by these regimes. The distribution of power and privilege according to sectarian affiliation naturally heightens sectarian identification; the majority resents the ruling minority, and the ruling minority fears the ascendancy of the majority. Non-Muslim minorities ally themselves with the minorities in power, in a pact for their common survival in the face of a seething majority.
2. Saudi Arabia has used its oil wealth to spread Wahhabism, an often militant form of radical Islamism that has been hostile to Shi'ism and Sufism since the eighteenth century.
3. The overthrow of the shah of Iran and the establishment of a regime hostile to the United States alarmed the United States, which had relied on the shah to serve as the its policeman in the Gulf. The establishment of an Islamic republic in a predominantly Shi'ite country also alarmed Saudi Arabia, which could no longer count on being the main model of an

Islamic polity in the Middle East. Like Saudi Arabia, the Islamic Republic of Iran sought, at least initially, to spread its ideology. The rise of Hezbollah as a major player in Lebanon and in the Arab–Israeli conflict pointed to Iran's reach in the Arab world.

4. Sectarian identities were exploited on both sides of the Iran-Iraq War of 1980–88: the regime of Saddam Hussein conflated Shi'ism with Persian identity and Sunnism with Arab identity, while Iran portrayed its fight against Iraq's aggression as a fight against unbelief and tried to appeal to Shi'ite discontent in Iraq. Although the war remained mainly nationalistic and nonsectarian, in retrospect it may be seen as a signal of the impending rise of sectarianism.
5. The alliance of the United States and Saudi Arabia with Pakistan in support of the struggle of the Mujahideen against the Soviets in Afghanistan encouraged the spread of radical Salafism in South Asia and the Middle East.
6. In the aftermath of the American-British defeat of Saddam Hussein in the Gulf War of 1991, President George H. W. Bush encouraged Iraqi dissidents to overthrow Saddam Hussein but did not assist in that endeavor. The resulting massacre of as many as thirty thousand Shi'a (BBC News 2005) deepened the resentment and disaffection of Iraqi Shi'a.
7. The US-led invasion of Iraq in 2003 was another major catalyst for sectarian conflict in the region. The removal of the authoritarian minority regime and the institution of free elections in Iraq led to a government dominated by the majority sect. In the case of Iraq, the disbanding of the army, the banning of former Ba'ath party members from government employment, and the empowerment of a formerly persecuted minority was a recipe for sectarian conflict. The presence of the United States as an occupying power galvanized Muslims from many Sunni countries to join the resistance in a struggle that came to be identified as a Sunni jihad.
8. In Syria and Yemen, grievances based on political and socioeconomic injustices were sectarianized by the

involvement of Iran and Hezbollah, on one side, and Saudi Arabia, Qatar, and the United Arab Emirates, on the other. I agree with Nader Hashemi, Vali Nasr, and others who argue that the rise of sectarian conflict is owing not to the differences between Sunnism and Shiʿism but to the leveraging of sectarian identities for political purposes (Hashemi and Postel 2017).

Conclusion

The Arab Spring uprisings may have begun as nonreligious demands for democracy, freedom, dignity, and a living wage, but the removal of powerful authoritarian regimes paved the way for the opening of religious conflicts on multiple fronts: Salafis against Sufis, Salafis against secularists, militant Islamists against Christians and Yazidis, and Shiʿa against Sunnis. A region in which, fifty years ago, the political salience of religion had faded and conflict between Sunnis and Shiʿa barely existed is now boiling over with violence, often justified on the basis of religion or fears of domination by opposing religious groups. The removal or weakening of authoritarian regimes in the Middle East led to civil wars in Libya, Syria, and Yemen, in which neighboring states and nonstate actors from other countries became directly involved. It would have been naive to expect that the removal of a tyrant would necessarily lead to democracy, but the level of violence in the aftermath of the Arab Spring seems to have exceeded even the worst fears of experts in the region. The politicization of religion, a trend that had been building since the 1970s, has attained its final, horrific end.

Sources Cited

Ammar, Hassan. 2013. "Egyptian Sufis Thrive despite Attacks." *Al Arabiya English*, June 14. http://english.alarabiya.net/en/News/middle-east/2013/06/14/Egyptian-Sufis-thrive-despite-attacks.html.

Anderson, Lisa. 1983. "Qaddafi's Islam." In *Voices of Resurgent Islam*, edited by John L. Esposito, 134–49. New York: Oxford Univ. Press.

Associated Press. 2013. "Coptic Pope Tawadros II Criticizes Egypt's Islamist Leadership, New Constitution." *AhramOnline*, Feb. 5. http://english.ahram.org.eg/NewsContent/1/64/64135/Egypt/Politics-/Coptic-Pope-Tawadros-II-criticises-Egypts-Islamist.aspx.

BBC News. 2005. "Mass Grave Unearthed in Iraq City." Dec. 27. http://news.bbc.co.uk/2/hi/middle_east/4561872.stm.

Beinin, Joel. 2015. "Sanitizing the Tunisian Revolution." Oct. 13. http://stanfordpress.typepad.com/blog/2015/10/sanitizing-the-tunisian-revolution.html.

Boghani, Priyanka. 2016. "A Staggering New Death Toll for Syria's War—470,000." *Frontline*, Feb. 11. http://www.pbs.org/wgbh/frontline/article/a-staggering-new-death-toll-for-syrias-war-470000/.

Cojean, Annick. 2013. *Gaddafi's Harem: The Story of a Young Woman and the Abuses of Power in Libya.* Translated by Marjolijn de Jager. New York: Grove Press.

Cole, Juan. 2016. "The U.S. Goes to War with Houthis in Yemen (Openly)." *Informed Comment*, Oct. 13. https://www.juancole.com/2016/10/houthis-yemen-openly.html.

Danahar, Paul. 2015. *The New Middle East: The World after the Arab Spring.* Rev. ed. London and New York: Bloomsbury.

Dingli, Sophia. 2017. "Saudi–U.S. War on Yemen: No Victory, but Cholera, Famine, State Collapse." The Conversation, May 31. https://theconversation.com/after-two-years-of-war-yemenis-face-cholera-famine-and-state-collapse-77902.

Dreyfuss, Bob. 2013. "Egypt's Fake Mass 'Rebellion'?" *Nation*, July 11. https://www.thenation.com/article/egypts-fake-mass-rebellion/.

Egypt Independent. 2011. "Al-Qaradawi: Freedom Takes Priority over Islamic Law." Feb. 12.

El-Kashef, Injy. 2011. "The Shrine Affair." *Al-Ahram Weekly*, Apr. 7. http://www.masress.com/en/ahramweekly/26273.

El Masry, Sarah. 2012. "Sufi Islam in Egypt." *Daily News Egypt*, Oct. 21. http://www.dailynewsegypt.com/2012/10/21/sufi-islam-in-egypt/.

Friedman, Yaron. 2009. *The Nusayri-'Alawis: An Introduction to the Religion, History and Identity of the Leading Minority in Syria.* Leiden: Brill.

Giglio, Mike. 2013. "A Cairo Conspiracy." *Daily Beast*, July 12. http://www.thedailybeast.com/articles/2013/07/12/a-cairo-conspiracy.html.

Gladstone, Rick. 2015. "Explosion Destroys Ancient Cultural Heritage Site in Yemen Capital." *New York Times*, June 12. http://www.nytimes.com/2015/06/13/world/middleeast/yemen-sana-explosion-houthis-saudi-arabia.html?ref=world&_r=0.

Guirguis, Magdi. 2012. "The Copts and the Egyptian Revolution: Various Attitudes and Dreams." *Social Research: An International Quarterly* 79 (2): 511–30.

Haider, Najam Iftikhar. 2015. "What Do the Leaders of Yemen's Houthis Want?" *Al Jazeera*, Feb. 7. http://america.aljazeera.com/opinions/2015/2/what-do-the-leaders-of-yemens-houthis-want.html.

Hamid, Shadi. 2016. *Islamic Exceptionalism: How the Struggle over Islam Is Reshaping the World*. New York: St. Martin's Press.

Hashemi, Nader, and Danny Postel, eds. 2017. *Sectarianization: Mapping the New Politics of the Middle East*. Oxford: Oxford Univ. Press.

Hashim, Mohanad. 2014. "Iraq and Syria: Who Are the Foreign Fighters?" *BBC News*, Sept. 3. http://www.bbc.com/news/world-middle-east-29043331.

Hellyer, H. A. 2014. "Faking Egypt's Past: The Brotherhood and Jan. 25." *Al Arabiya News*, Jan. 20. http://english.alarabiya.net/en/views/news/middle-east/2014/01/20/Faking-Egypt-s-past-the-Brotherhood-and-Jan-25.html.

Hidji, Ahmed. 2016. "How Do Egypt's Official Religious Authorities View Shi'ites?" *Al-Monitor*, Aug. 12. http://www.al-monitor.com/pulse/originals/2016/08/egypt-divide-sunni-shiites-accusations-abuse-azhar.html?utm_source=Boomtrain&utm_medium=manual&utm_campaign=20160815&bt_email=vhoffman@illinois.edu&bt_ts=1471278448708.

Human Rights Watch. 2013. "Egypt: Lynching of Shia Follows Months of Hate Speech." June 27. https://www.hrw.org/news/2013/06/27/egypt-lynching-shia-follows-months-hate-speech.

Islamopedia Online. 2011. "Contested Sufi Electoral Parties: The Voice of Freedom Party and the Liberation of Egypt Party." Dec. http://www.islamopediaonline.org/country-profile/egypt/islam-and-electoral-parties/contested-sufi-electoral-parties-voice-freedom-par.

Kirkpatrick, David D. 2011. "After Long Exile, Sunni Cleric Takes Role in Egypt." *New York Times*, Feb. 18. http://www.nytimes.com/2011/02/19/world/middleeast/19egypt.html?_r=0.

LaGraffe, Daniel. 2012. "The Youth Bulge in Egypt: An Intersection of Demographics, Security, and the Arab Spring." *Journal of Strategic Security* 5 (2): 65–80.

Mayer, Ann Elizabeth. 1982. "Islamic Resurgence or New Prophethood: The Role of Islam in Qadhdhafi's Ideology." In *Islamic Resurgence in the Arab World*, edited by Ali E. Hillal Dessouki, 196–219. New York: Praeger.

McQuinn, Brian. 2015. "Debunking Three Dangerous Myths about the Conflict in Libya." The Conversation, Jan. 20. https://theconversation.com/debunking-three-dangerous-myths-about-the-conflict-in-libya-36521?utm_source=Sailthru&utm_medium=email&utm_term=*Mideast%20Brief&utm_campaign=2014_The%20Middle%20East%20Daily_1.22.15.

Metz, Helen Chapin. 1987. "The Green Book." In *Libya: A Country Study*. Washington, DC: Library of Congress. http://countrystudies.us/libya/80.htm.

Murphy, Dan. 2011. "Egypt's Revolution Unfinished, Qaradawi Tells Tahrir Masses." *Christian Science Monitor*, Feb. 18. http://www.csmonitor.com/World/Middle-East/2011/0218/Egypt-revolution-unfinished-Qaradawi-tells-Tahrir-masses.

Noueihed, Lin, and Alex Warren. 2013. *The Battle for the Arab Spring: Revolution, Counter-revolution and the Making of a New Era*. Rev. ed. New Haven, CT: Yale Univ. Press.

Padnos, Theo. 2014. "My Captivity: Theo Padnos, American Journalist, on Being Kidnapped, Tortured and Released in Syria." *New York Times Magazine*, Oct. 29. http://www.nytimes.com/2014/10/28/magazine/theo-padnos-american-journalist-on-being-kidnapped-tortured-and-released-in-syria.html?_r=0.

Parkinson, Joe. 2014. "In Reversal, Turkey to Open Passage to Kobani for Kurdish Fighters." *Wall Street Journal*, Oct. 20. http://www.wsj.com/articles/turkey-to-allow-transfer-of-iraqi-kurdish-fighters-to-kobani-1413810406.

Parties and Movements (*Al-Jadaliyya* and *Ahram Online*). 2011. "Egyptian Tahrir Party." *Al-Jadaliyya*, Dec. 13. http://www.jadaliyya.com/pages/index/3501/egyptian-tahrir-party.

Syrian Network for Human Rights. 2017. "207,000 Civilians Have Been Killed Including 24,000 Children and 23,000 Females; 94% of the

Victims Were Killed by the Syrian-Iranian-Russian Alliance." May 18. http://sn4hr.org/blog/2017/03/18/35726/.

Tadros, Mariz. 2011. "Egypt's Bloody Sunday." Middle East Research and Information Project, Oct. 13. http://www.merip.org/mero/mero101311?ip_login_no_cache=76936e7142f75b095038a71a06748dff.

Thiel, Tobias. 2015. "Yemen's Imposed Federal Boundaries." Middle East Research and Information Project, July 20. http://www.merip.org/yemens-imposed-federal-boundaries.

Trudolyubov, Maxim. 2015. "Sheikh Putin of Syria." *New York Times*, Oct. 22. http://www.nytimes.com/2015/10/23/opinion/sheikh-putin-of-syria.html?action=click&pgtype=Homepage&module=opinion-c-col-left-region®ion=opinion-c-col-left-region&WT.nav=opinion-c-col-left-region&_r=0.

vom Bruck, Gabriele, Atiaf Alwazir, and Benjamin Wiacek. 2014. "Yemen: Revolution Suspended?" In *The New Middle East: Protest and Revolution in the Arab World*, edited by Fawaz A. Gerges, 285–308. Cambridge: Cambridge Univ. Press.

Wehrey, Frederic, and Ala' Alrababa'h. 2015. "Rising Out of Chaos: The Islamic State in Libya." Carnegie Endowment for International Peace, Mar. 5. http://carnegieendowment.org/syriaincrisis/?fa=59268.

2

The Islamic Republic and the Politics of the New Middle East

BEHROOZ GHAMARI-TABRIZI

By all accounts, the Iranian revolution of 1978–79 appeared like a "thunderbolt from the blue." Only one year earlier, at a New Year's Eve state dinner in Tehran, President Jimmy Carter praised the shah of Iran for making his country "an island of stability in one of the more troubled areas of the world" (Peters and Woolley 1999–2016). Under the Pahlavi dynasty, Iran played a crucial role in maintaining a balance of power and protecting Western strategic interests in the Middle East. But the Islamic revolution under the leadership of Ayatollah Khomeini changed the political map of the region (Ramezani 1986).

Ayatollah Khomeini considered the Islamic Republic to be a regime that defended the rights of the downtrodden and the "wretched of the earth." He believed that Western powers had plundered the Middle East and had alienated Muslims from their own cultures, traditions, and beliefs. To him, being faithful to the tenets of Islam meant that Muslims had to liberate themselves from the yoke of foreign powers and establish a political order that was consistent with the teaching of Islam. Although Khomeini's message resonated with the experiences of many Muslims around the world, the internal politics of the postrevolutionary regime in Iran dampened the initial enthusiasm that the revolution had generated. The project of state building after the revolution proved to be a bloody process that led to the execution of thousands. Tens of thousands were imprisoned and exiled during the first decade of the Islamic Republic. In addition,

Saddam Hussein tried to take advantage of the inexperience of the young revolutionary regime and imposed an eight-year war on Iran that led to hundreds of thousands of casualties. Khomeini's Islamic Republic was not a model of governance that any other nation in the Middle East intended to emulate (Ghamari-Tabrizi 2008).

In the United States, the takeover of the American Embassy in Tehran in 1979 and the holding of its staff as hostages for 444 days defined what the Islamic Republic was all about: an irrational regime, hostile to the basic principles of modern life, particularly in regard to issues of liberty and equal rights for men and women. Although hostility between Iran and the United States and many European countries continues, none of the predictions that Iran would return to the Middle Ages under the Islamic Republic came true (Adib-Moghaddam 2008).

The Iranian constitution established a form of state that was unprecedented in Iranian and Islamic history. It recognized the sovereignty and will of the people as the main source of the state's legitimacy. At the same time, it established the office of the supreme leader in a political institution called *velayat-e faqih*, or the Guardianship of the Jurist. This novel political doctrine, articulated by Khomeini during his fifteen years of exile from Iran, held that, in the absence of the Shi'ite imam, the government ought to be headed by a supremely authoritative religious scholar. This duality of democratic sovereignty and religious leadership created an inherent contradiction in the sources of political authority in Iran. On the one hand, electoral processes play a major role in Iranian politics; on the other hand, many believe that the unfettered authority of the supreme leader makes elections in Iran irrelevant. But, as we shall see, this political process in Iran has also generated an unprecedented space for political participation and social change in Iran (Moslem 2002; Schirazi 1998).

By all accounts, the Iranian revolution remains an unfinished project. The intensity of factionalism in Iranian state politics and ongoing friction between the state and civil society are reflected in various domains of social and political life in Iran. While influential factions of the clergy have hampered the expansion of democratic institutions (free press, electoral politics, civil liberties), their efforts to establish a theocratic totalitarianism in Iran have also failed. The Iranian regime is neither theocratic nor totalitarian. It is not theocratic, for it does follow a constitution (albeit with contradictory assertions about the institutional sources of power), and in qualified ways it draws its legitimacy from popular political processes. It is not a totalitarian regime, because the competing interests within the polity are genuine and do not allow one faction to dominate all the instruments of power (Brumberg 2001).

Competing interests within the polity have also created a significant space in civil society for the expression of the demands of different social actors. In contrast to general perception, under the Islamic Republic a vibrant civil society and political openness have promoted considerable changes in the country. Iranian society has gone through major transformations during the first three decades of the Islamic Republic. These transformations carry within themselves contradictions similar to those that exist in the Iranian constitution. For example, while Iran has one of the most vibrant press media in the region, incomparable to the situation under the shah, it also has one of the most constraining judicial bodies, which incessantly limit the freedom of the press. While Iran has one of the highest number of female university students in the region, with women constituting 60 percent of incoming students in 2012,[1] women occupy only 20–25 percent of all jobs in the country. Although women's participation in politics and their role in civic associations are comparable to men's experiences, their basic rights, particularly in family and criminal law, remain subject to the gendered biases of the judiciary. These contradictions mark the experience of an emerging democratic society with competing social and political forces that intend, on the one

1. Only Bahrain and Qatar are higher: in 2007 the share of females in higher education in Bahrain was 68 percent and in Qatar was 64 percent (Conger and Long 2013).

Table 5
Iran's five republics

	Period	*Orientation*	*Main objective*
First Republic	1979–89	Ideological	State building
Second Republic	1989–97	Pragmatic	Institutionalizing
Third Republic	1997–2005	Reformist	Building civil society
Fourth Republic	2005–13	Populist	Second-generation consolidation
Fifth Republic	2013–present	Moderate	National reconciliation

hand, to accelerate democratization and, on the other, to contain and eventually repress it (Adelkhah 2004; Vakil 2013).

This chapter demonstrates some of the inherent complexities of the Iranian political system, in particular how the postrevolutionary regime has shown flexibility as well as rigidity in accepting or rejecting democratic institutional changes. Since the revolution in 1979, Iran has gone through five republics, in the manner of the French Revolution, each of which assumed power with a particular agenda and a dominant ideology. The table depicts the time line and main objectives of each republic.

These republics by no means constitute a rupture in the general progression of the postrevolutionary regime, and indeed they emerged to secure the continuity of the Islamic regime. However, each assumed power with a distinct ideological commitment and specific political agenda, which in significant ways contradicted its predecessor's objectives.

The First Republic (1979–1989)

This period was characterized by the project of postrevolutionary state building led by the leader of the revolution, Ayatollah Khomeini. State building is actually a euphemistic conception of the brutal processes through which the state consolidated its power by eliminating and delegitimizing competing groups. During these years, between ten and fifteen thousand people were executed in summary trials, tens of thousands were tortured and imprisoned under inhumane conditions, and more than one million Iranians were exiled.

Khomeini and his allies ridiculed the liberal nationalists who formed the Provisional Government in February 1979 for their Western propensities. The Islamists and the secular Left accused them of betraying the anti-imperialist core of the revolution and of failing to carry out radical projects of social justice. The takeover of the American Embassy in Tehran on November 4, 1979, culminated the militants' initial attempt to consolidate power. The seizure of the embassy served two purposes for the new regime: first, it forced the liberal Provisional Government of the first prime minister, Mehdi Bazargan, to resign; second, it defused the secular Left's critique of the clergy as too accommodating to Western powers. It is important here to make a crucial distinction between the embassy takeover and the hostage crisis. Rather than a carefully designed confrontation with the United States, the takeover of the American Embassy in Tehran was primarily motivated by domestic considerations of state building. The *hostage crisis* was an unintended consequence of the invasion of the embassy grounds; it put an unanticipated onus on the militant Muslim students' shoulders. The students had originally intended to salvage the revolution from secular leftist competition and what they regarded as the liberals' incompetence. However, their actions made the new regime vulnerable to American military retaliation and economic embargo. In effect, the hostage crisis and later the Iraqi invasion of Iran shaped the process of state building in Iran and made it more repressive and exclusionary.

The brutality of state building intensified when the leftist loyal opposition, which had contributed to the elimination of the liberal faction, withdrew its support and began to organize against the Islamist regime. In 1981 the new regime initiated an atrocious campaign of executions, which by the mid-1980s assured the monopolization of state power in the hands of a governing elite that was unified around its commitment to the principle of *velayat-e faqih*, or the Guardianship of the Jurist (Moslem 2002).

With the end of Iran-Iraq War in 1988, the Islamic Republic enjoyed relative stability. It was free from serious internal challenges, and Saddam Hussein, its principal foreign military threat, was kept at bay. Before his death in June 1989, Ayatollah Khomeini set the stage for the emergence of the Second Republic.

The Second Republic (1989–1997)

This period is primarily associated with the two-term presidency of Hojjat al-Islam Ali Akbar Hashemi Rafsanjani. In a decree issued in 1987, Ayatollah Khomeini laid out the main ideological foundations of this new state formation. In a pragmatic move based on the old Shi'ite notion of *maslaha* (expediency), Khomeini pronounced that the Islamic government (the elected body) "was the most important of the divine commandments and has primacy over all derivative divine commandments, . . . even over prayer, fasting and the pilgrimage to Mecca" (Ghamari-Tabrizi 2008).

Furthermore, he declared, "In order to build a road, the state is justified in demolishing a mosque." With these words, Khomeini intended to counter the dogmatic tendencies within the regime, prominently represented by the Guardian Council, the responsibility of which was to determine the constitutionality of laws passed by the Majlis (the Iranian Parliament).

In order to advance his pragmatic approach to the interests of the Islamic state, and in order to contain the veto power of the conservatives of the Guardian Council, in 1988 Khomeini ordered the establishment of the Shura-ye Tashkhis-e Maslahat-e Nizam (Council for the Discernment of the Expediency of the [Islamic] Regime, known as the Expediency Council). The Expediency Council initially consisted of thirteen members of the Majlis, the executive branch of the government, and the Guardian Council.

After the establishment of the Expediency Council, the head of the Guardian Council, Ayatollah Safi, presented his resignation to Ayatollah Khomeini. In his letter of resignation, Safi expressed his dissatisfaction with the idea of prioritizing the expediency of the

Islamic state over the injunctions of the sharia. Safi declared that he could not fulfill his duties under such a pretense. Ayatollah Safi's resignation reflected profound doctrinal differences within the Islamic Republic; it was a turning point in the institutional separation of religion and state.

Khomeini's institutionalization of the means of arbitration between different governing factions was designed in anticipation of his eventual death, which occurred in June 1989. He was conscious of the crisis that might emerge in the absence of his charismatic authority. Khomeini's decision to create an institution to determine the expediencies of the state underlined the fact that what made the regime "Islamic" was not a set of predetermined injunctions and regulations. Rather, the Islamic character of the state was to be determined through a negotiated and debated process between elected and religious sources of power. During his lifetime, Khomeini enjoyed an unparalleled authority in shaping state policies and goals, but with his demise, gone was the absolute authority of the *faqih* in informing the mandates of the state and its religious justifications.

The Second Republic was officially inaugurated with the ascension of Hojjat al-Islam Khamene'i to the office of supreme leader and the subsequent election of Rafsanjani to the presidency. Because Khomeini's religious credentials had been impeccable, he could successfully advocate the primacy of state needs over religious injunctions. Unlike Khomeini, whose authority was discretionary and pragmatic, Khamene'i could not legitimate the political needs of the Islamic state in his person. He had neither the charisma nor the religious stature to forge political consensus. Therefore, in place of the authoritative discretionary power of Khomeini, Rafsanjani pushed through a constitutional amendment in order to legitimate the political authority of the office of the leader. While Rafsanjani was aware that this amendment would limit the powers of the office of the presidency, since he played a key role in the transfer of power to Khamene'i, he was confident that the change would not limit the powers of his administration (Arjomand 2012).

In his inaugural address, Rafsanjani emphasized that with his presidency, the revolution had entered its period of "reconstruction." The country, he said, needed to recover from the economic devastation caused by the eight-year war with Iraq, US sanctions, and international isolation following the Islamic revolution. In his first term, the revolutionary rhetoric of the redistribution of wealth and social justice disappeared from Rafsanjani's political lexicon. Instead, he advocated the notion of the Islamic virtues of prosperity and economic success.

Rafsanjani intended to dilute the revolutionary core of the regime with a pragmatic policy that would encourage domestic as well as foreign investment in Iran. He attracted many technocrats to his administration and embarked on an economic reform program, albeit without a corresponding political reform. Not only did Rafsanjani use the power of his office to realize his agenda, but he also encouraged the organization of an emerging technocratic intelligentsia whose main goal was to establish support in civil society for his agenda. To a great extent, Rafsanjani played an important role in moving Iran away from its Jacobin period of state building, ushering in an era when the objectives of the revolution could be discussed again without the threats of blood and iron.

The Third Republic (1997–2005)

This period was by no means the inevitable result of the Second. Indeed, the Third Republic emerged unexpectedly as a response to the Second Republic's inability, or unwillingness, to engage institutions of civil society in its proposed agenda of reconstruction. In 1997 Mohammad Khatami defeated Nateq Nuri, the candidate of the status quo, with close to 70 percent of the popular vote. More than 85 percent of eligible voters participated in the presidential election to send Khatami, who had held the insignificant position of head of the National Library, to the office of the presidency. Khatami won the election by promising to strengthen the foundations of civil society by making the state and all ruling factions accountable to the constitution and to popular demands.

Khatami's stunning victory was made possible by a strong coalition of women and youth movements. These groups were mobilized in student and professional associations and neighborhood organizations. The strength of this movement became evident when Khatami's campaign offices were closed in Tehran only a week prior to Election Day. In the two days after the closure, women's organizations mobilized more than 250,000 women to march on the streets of Tehran in support of his candidacy. University students, although not great in numbers, also played a crucial role in mobilizing the populace to participate in the election. Students set up campaign offices even in rural and remote areas of the country in order to ensure mass participation and a landslide victory for Khatami (Tazmini 2013).

In addition to popular movements, the reform was also supported and promoted by an emerging class of Muslim intellectuals who advocated a more open interpretation of Islam. These developments have taken theological debates and issues of jurisprudence out of the closed quarters of seminaries into a large public sphere of laymen and -women. Not only did this reform movement facilitate the emergence of the Third Republic, but it also represented an unprecedented reflective understanding of Islam and its institutional presence in Iranian society. Iranians had never before been so deeply and so widely engaged in debates about democracy and culturally specific issues of rights. It is rare that controversial issues of hermeneutics and religious debates so profoundly and directly impact the everyday life of a nation. Iran is passing through such a historical moment. From the trial of a newspaper editor to custody battles in family court, from regulations of parliamentary elections to gender-segregated bus seats, all have become issues for Qur'anic exegesis and competing interpretations of Islamic canon law (Ghamari-Tabrizi 2013).

One should not overlook the significance of the fact that the leaders of the Second Republic conceded their defeat and handed over the office of the presidency to the candidate of the loyal opposition.

At the time, in 1996, the reconstructionists of the Second Republic were considering a referendum for a constitutional amendment to allow Rafsanjani to run for a third term and, in effect, turn himself into another Middle Eastern president for life. But the decision to abandon the project shows that the regime was willing and flexible enough to absorb the shocks of change of power in the hands of competing factions. It also demonstrated that the popular legitimacy of the regime continued to be a foundational element of the Islamic Republic.

Khatami's Third Republic set out to transform the regime from within by (1) increasing the power of the office of the president, (2) making the supreme leader accountable to law and the constitution, (3) containing the extrajudicial and arbitrary powers of rogue elements within the security forces, (4) implementing more permissive Islamic codes of ethics and behavior in the public sphere, and (5) advocating equal rights for men and women under family and criminal law.

The first two years of the Third Republic saw a burgeoning of new print media and the formation of interest groups in civil society. The promising first two years encouraged more participation in the electoral process and in both the municipal and Majlis elections of 1999 and 2000, respectively; close to 75 percent of the eligible voters cast their ballots. The Third Republic demonstrated that the factional politics inside the regime are genuine and that participatory politics remains an instrument for solving social problems in the country.

The terrorist attacks of September 11, 2001, on the World Trade Center and the Pentagon happened during the second term of Khatami's presidency. Iranians were the only Muslim people in the Middle East who poured into the streets of major cities and held a candlelight vigil in honor of the victims of the Twin Tower attacks. Not only did the regime refrain from interfering with the public ceremonies of mourning, but it also officially extended its sympathy and condolences to the American people. The attacks of September 11 had two significant consequences for Iranian American relations. First, the Iranian regime saw the tragedy as an opportunity to vindicate themselves from involvement in the global networks of terror. The Islamic Republic had long been hostile to the al-Qaeda terrorists and their Taliban supporters in Kabul. Second, September 11 gave another chance to the Islamic Republic to move closer to the United States through ensuring a peaceful and smooth transition in post-Taliban Afghanistan. On both fronts, Iranians were sincere. They did not oppose military action against Afghanistan and the expansion of the American military presence in Central Asia, and, furthermore, they offered combat search-and-rescue assistance to American forces operating near Iranian territories (Dobbins 2004).

In December 2001, the Iranian delegation played a crucial role in the Bonn conference that was convened to determine the composition of the interim government in Afghanistan. The Iranians forced their own ally and the former president of Afghanistan Burhanuddin Rabbani to withdraw in favor of the American candidate, Hamid Karzai. It was one of the rare moments when the Iranian president was able to assert his leadership in regard to Iran-US relations without significant resistance from his conservative opposition. Unfortunately, the Bush administration did not recognize the magnitude of the Islamic Republic's gesture. Not only did the administration fail to acknowledge the Iranians' role, but President Bush further muted the overtures emerging from Iran by lumping them with Iraq and North Korea in an "axis of evil" in his State of the Union speech in 2002.

The increasing hostility of the Bush administration and the Iranian regime's inability to deliver all its promises of social justice and civil liberties contributed to the failure of the Third Republic. In his second term, President Khatami faced a hostile parliament and found meager success against the judiciary's arbitrary exercise of power. The vast majority of the underprivileged masses felt alienated and disillusioned and looked for an alternative in the growing populist politics of a new generation of conservative politicians.

The Fourth Republic (2005–2013)

In 2003 a group of conservative technocrats, with the support of a number of influential commanders of the Revolutionary Guards, formed a coalition called E'telāf-e Abadgaran-e Iran-e Eslami (Alliance of Builders of Islamic Iran). The alliance, which became known simply as Abadgaran, followed two main objectives: first, to capture the majority in the Parliament, which was dominated by reformist parties, and to capture the office of the presidency; second, to carry out that project without relying on the old clerical guard of the revolution. Initially, the Abadgaran situated themselves in three different spheres of civil society—politics, economy, and culture—in contradistinction to three dominant factions in the Iranian polity.

Culturally, they distanced themselves from the conservatism of the ideologically committed old guard, those individuals who continued to define themselves in opposition to the reformists' promotion of civil liberties and their permissive policies in regard to the public sphere. Economically, Abadgaran intended to end the monopoly of Hezb-e Kargozaran-e Sazandegi (Party of the Executives of Construction) in the management of postwar reconstruction projects. For more than a decade, Kargozaran, the political party of former president Hashemi Rafsanjani, had acted as the only viable force for the liberalization of the Iranian state-centered economy. Abadgaran launched an anticorruption campaign against the crony capitalism that had become associated with Hashemi Rafsanjani and his political allies. Politically, they campaigned against the conciliatory posture of the reformist administration of President Khatami toward the West, particularly in regard to the liberalization of foreign investment and Iran's right to nuclear technology.

In the absence of charismatic and prominent personalities, the neoconservative Abadgaran followed the strategy of building grassroots support by focusing mostly on municipal elections, first in Tehran and then in other provinces. With only 12 percent participating in Tehran's municipal election in 2003, Abadgaran captured the majority of seats in the city council and appointed a rather unknown figure, Mahmoud

Ahmadinejad, as Tehran's mayor. Soon thereafter, in February 2004, Abadgaran formed a broader coalition of old and new conservatives under the banner of Osulgerayan (the Principlists) and seized control of the Parliament in a controversial election in which the Guardian Council had disqualified most reformist candidates from running for reelection. Through a combination of the low rate of participation and the Guardian Council's extrajudicial interventions, the reformists lost two key electoral races in less than one year.

The pace of Abadgaran's electoral victories worried many conservatives. They worried that in their haste to discredit the reformists, Abadgaran would endanger the legitimacy of the entire system. On September 29, 2004, an editorial on the front page of the conservative newspaper *Resalat* opined that many members of the old guard believed that the Abadgaran faction was leading Iran in a dangerous direction. "We had all accepted that the new parliament should be free of tension and discord, particularly with the government," the editorial remarked. "But instead, an image is being formed that sensationalism, politicking and, above all, heady radicalism and extremism are becoming the norm there."

But the Abadgaran were successful on both fronts. They discredited the Khatami administration and created doubts about the viability of his domestic and foreign policies. And, more important, they generated enough support among other conservative factions to situate themselves as a formidable force in the upcoming presidential election of 2005. In addition to their aggressive power politics and Bonapartist factional strategy, their ascendancy to power was also made possible by the Bush administration's uncompromising position against Iran and its disastrous miscalculations in Iraq. With the American quagmire in Iraq, President Bush's threats now sounded more like inane rhetoric rather than a serious deterrent to the Islamic Republic's nuclear ambitions.

Mahmoud Ahmadinejad also situated himself as the defender of the downtrodden and advocated domestic populist policies of redistribution of wealth. But these policies were also associated with a new form of crony capitalism of those who benefited immensely from the increasing tensions with the United States and European powers. Ahmadinejad's controversial statements and policies led to more international isolation and more comprehensive sanctions against Iran (Ansari 2008).

Toward the end of his first administration (2005–9), Ahmadinejad's popular support began to decline dramatically. The first and foremost reason for that decline was the rapidly rising rate of inflation and economic hardship. Furthermore, his projects to assist low-income families and deliver services to remote areas in the country were marred by corruption and inefficiency. Second, he increasingly alienated his own supporters and relied more heavily on his close advisers and a tight circle of allies.

No one expected Ahmadinejad to win a second term in 2009. With an 80 percent turnout, however, Ahmadinejad won more than 60 percent of the vote in the first round of the election. That appeared to hundreds of thousands of voters to be a sign of a rigged election. For the first time in the history of the republic, millions of people protested the result of the election by demonstrating on the streets of big cities in Iran. In Tehran millions rallied and asked for their votes to be counted. The opposition claimed victory but was later arrested and put under house arrest. For weeks, the streets of Tehran witnessed clashes between police and demonstrators. Hundreds of people were arrested, and the security forces killed at least fifty-five people during the protest movement.

In what became known as the Green Movement, the color chosen by the opposition candidate, Iranians demonstrated that they would not tolerate fraud or take the electoral process seriously. Ahmadinejad's second term began with controversy and ended in charges of more economic corruption and political incompetence (Hashemi and Postel 2011).

The Fifth Republic (2013–Present)

The Guardian Council vets the candidates for presidency and disqualifies many for not meeting the required qualifications. This process

Table 6
Main actors and events during each of Iran's five republics

	Main actors	*Main events*
First Republic (1979–89)	Clerical establishment: Ayatollah Khomeini (leader) Liberals: Mehdi Bazargan (provincial prime minister) Secular Left and Mujahideen	Invasion of American Embassy Iran-Iraq War Civil war in Kurdistan Executions and exiles Complete suppression of dissent
Second Republic (1989–97)	The president: Rafsanjani The leader: Khamenei The emerging dissident intelligentsia New social movements (youth and women)	Constitutional amendments Privatization efforts Emerging civil society
Third Republic (1997–2005)	The reformists: President Khatami abolitionists—transformationist Traditionalists and pragmatist alliance: the judiciary / security forces Office of the Leader the Guardian Council The Expediency Council Student and women's movements	1997 election and the peaceful transfer of power to the loyal opposition candidate Student riots of 1999 Burgeoning of new papers and the struggle to keep them open Stalemate of the reform September 11, 2001, and American threats
Fourth Republic (2005–13)	The principalists: new generation of technocratic conservatives The supreme leader as the main support Rising power of the Revolutionary Guards in politics and economy	The quagmire of the American invasion of Iraq Nuclear technology production and crisis Expansive sanctions Unprecedented economic crisis and inflation
Fifth Republic (2013–present)	Moderates and reformists The supreme leader, the reluctant supporter Civil society actors, women, journalists, artists	Rapprochement To be determined!

is purely political and is designed to keep those individuals whose allegiance to the Islamic Republic is questionable from running. It does not mean that the candidates who run do not have major political differences. Although in no uncertain terms the supreme leader had thrown his support behind conservative candidates, a candidate from the reformist and moderate camps was qualified and won the presidency of the republic. Hassan Rouhani was elected on a platform of reconciliation and moderation. He promised that he would reconsider all the policies of his predecessor and offered a new vision of engagement with the world and toleration at home.

Although it is too early to see whether this president will be able to carry out his promises, one thing is clear: Iranians have found multiple ways of transforming their society. They have shown that they take the electoral process seriously and are determined to advance their demands through that very institution. They have also shown that the expansion of civil society—that is, a vibrant media, nongovernmental organizations, cultural and educational groups, women's organizations, youth clubs, and the like—is the only means through which social transformations can be sustained.

Reformists versus Conservatives

Today, the dichotomy between reformists and conservatives does not capture the essence of factional politics in Iran. Neither of these camps is homogenous. There are actors in each camp that are closer to others in the opposite group than to some elements in their own. Each of these factions contains two divisions among themselves. Among the reformists there are those actors whom I call "accommodationists," in contrast to the "abolitionists," and in the conservative coalition there are "concessionists" and "autocratic abolitionists."

Hassan Rouhani's victory gave the accommodationists within the reformist camp a chance to exercise authority. The "accommodationists" led by the president intend to continue the path of

Table 7
What does each faction in Iran envision?

Faction	Subgroup	Vision
Reformists	Accommodationists:	Transforming the regime into an Islamic democratic state without abolishing *Velayat-e Faqih*.
	Abolitionists:	Leave the polity and establish a nonloyal opposition, possibly with secular oppositional forces. Democratic regime without the institutionalization of Islam.
Conservatives	Concessionists:	Maintain the status quo and tolerate a paralyzed reform movement.
	Autocratic abolitionists:	Security forces and ideological factions; the second phase of "state-building."

transformation from within. They do acknowledge sluggish progress and a failure to implement their campaign promises. However, they argue that institutional change requires time and may only be sustainable through a mass societal participation. The key to Rouhani's success is to refrain from making authoritarian use of his popularity on behalf of liberating civil society. He rightly believes that finding a solution to domestic problems in Iran depends on increasing Iran's international credibility. Resolving the nuclear crisis would eventually dry up the sources of rampant economic corruption in the country and contain the militarization of Iranian politics. The trials and tribulations of the Islamic Republic might serve as a valuable example of the transformation of a Middle Eastern nation on a sustainable and comprehensive path.

Sources Cited

Adelkhah, Fariba. 2004. *Being Modern in Iran.* New York: Columbia Univ. Press.

Adib-Moghaddam, Arshin. 2008. *Iran in World Politics: The Question of the Islamic Republic.* New York: Columbia Univ. Press.

Ansari, Ali. 2008. *Iran under Ahmadinejad: The Politics of Confrontation.* London: Routledge.

Arjomand, Said Amir. 2012. *After Khomeini: Iran under His Successors.* Oxford: Oxford Univ. Press.

Brumberg, Daniel. 2001. *Reinventing Khomeini: The Struggle for Reform in Iran.* Chicago: Univ. of Chicago Press.

Conger, Dylan, and Mark C. Long. 2013. "Women Students Dominating in Many Countries." *University World News*, Mar. 2. http://www.universityworldnews.com/article.php?story=2013022612105131.

Dobbins, James. 2004. "Time to Deal with Iran." *Washington Post* op-ed., May 6. https://www.rand.org/blog/2004/05/time-to-deal-with-iran.html

Ghamari-Tabrizi, Behrooz. 2008. *Islam and Dissent in Postrevolutionary Iran: Abdolkarim Soroush and the Religious Foundation of Democratic Reform.* London: I. B. Tauris.

———. 2013. "Women's Rights, Shari'a Law, and the Secularization of Islam in Iran." *International Journal of Culture, Politics, and Society* 26: 237–53.

Hashemi, Nader, and Danny Postel, eds. 2011. *People Reloaded: The Green Movement and the Struggle for Iran's Future.* New York: Melville House Books.

Moslem, Mehdi. 2002. *Factional Politics in Post-Khomeini Iran.* Syracuse, NY: Syracuse Univ. Press.

Peters, Gerhard, and John T. Woolley. 1999–2016. "Jimmy Carter: Tehran, Iran Toasts of the President and the Shah at a State Dinner, December 31, 1977." American Presidency Project. http://www.presidency.ucsb.edu/ws/?pid=7080.

Ramezani, R. K. 1986. *Revolutionary Iran: Challenge and Response in the Middle East.* Baltimore: Johns Hopkins Univ. Press.

Schirazi, Asghar. 1998. *The Constitution of Iran: Politics and the State in the Islamic Republic.* London: I. B. Tauris.

Tazmini, Ghoncheh. 2013. *Khatami's Iran: The Islamic Republic and the Turbulent Path to Reform*. London: I. B. Tauris.

Vakil, Sanam. 2013. *Women and Politics in the Islamic Republic of Iran: Action and Reaction*. London: Bloomsbury Academic.

3

The Military, the Islamists, and the Battle over Egypt's Constitution

FEISAL G. MOHAMED

The Egyptian Revolution of 2011 was one of history's rare feel-good moments. Undaunted by a notoriously brutal security apparatus, Egyptians took to the streets in wave after wave of nonviolent protest, toppling Hosni Mubarak's thirty-year presidency in little more than a fortnight. But this revolutionary break with the past also had conservative qualities. Had the Mubarak family achieved its dynastic aspirations, Gamal Mubarak would have been the first nonmilitary president of Egypt since the 1952 Free Officers' revolt gave rise to the republic. The 2011 revolution instead allowed the military to reassert its political influence, which had been waning as Mubarak and his party increasingly saw their rule as buttressed by security forces and the business elite. The other immediate beneficiaries of the ouster of Mubarak, of course, were the Muslim Brotherhood, who had been politically active and well organized for some time. Their internal rigidity, ossified by decades of arrest and torture, did not make them a group well suited to collaboration and compromise with broad segments of Egyptian civil society. The first postrevolutionary elections thrust them into a position of prominence in a delicate transition that they were fundamentally unqualified to lead. Even if they were qualified, the Brotherhood was unlikely to gain friends in the military and judiciary, who long ago settled into the habit of despising them. If the revolution itself seemed heaven sent, subsequent events reminded us that political transition is deeply profane, a writhing, blood-drenched cockpit where established and self-interested factions fight ruthlessly for control over the new political order.

Factionalism was fully on display during the writing of the first postrevolutionary constitution, the now defunct constitution of 2012. Feeling shut out of the drafting process, human rights activists and parties of the secular Left came increasingly, and derisively, to term this the "Brotherhood Constitution." That perception was only confirmed by the actions of President Mohammed Morsi, originally of the Brotherhood's Freedom and Justice Party (FJP), who put a precipitous stop to the drafting process and hastily brought the new constitution to a public referendum. But did the Brotherhood truly highjack the process? And even if they did, was the 2012 constitution really so bad?

Whatever our answers to these questions, that document has been consigned to the dustbin. Morsi's signal achievement as president was to become the most despised man in Egypt with remarkable celerity. The spring and summer of 2013 saw the petition to remove him circulated by Tamarrod, or the "Rebel" movement, gather twenty-two million signatures. Styling themselves the guardians of the nation, the military demanded on June 30 that Morsi respond to the will of the people within forty-eight hours by relinquishing some or all of his presidential authority. When he refused, he was forcibly removed on July 3, and the constitution he oversaw was removed with him. A new text was drafted and ratified in a referendum, to become the constitution of 2014. We will wonder if this instrument is a fuller expression of those aspirations expressed in one of the most popular chants of the 2011 revolution: "Bread, freedom, social justice."

The following pages explore two major aspects of the two postrevolutionary constitutions: the process by which they were written and the written products themselves. I will conclude by asking just how important written constitutions really are and just how much they can do to secure political and personal rights.

Process: Depose, Draft, Ratify, Repeat

When Egyptians took to the streets on January 25, 2011, one of their first actions was to set ablaze the headquarters of the ruling National Democratic Party (al-Hizb al-Watany).[1] The target of their ire was clearly not only Mubarak, but a ruling apparatus guilty of widespread graft and of exercising a stranglehold on Egypt's wealth and power. For all that it had been the source of Egypt's dictators, the army, by contrast, was viewed as a potential ally—"The army and the people are one hand," ran one revolutionary slogan. The sentiment aimed in part to forge an alliance of convenience between Tahrir Square and the military. But it also reflects the esteem in which the military is held in many segments of Egyptian society. The army, many felt, would put national interests before Mubarak's and would not train its guns on its people. That was more true in Egypt than it would be in Libya or Syria, though of course not entirely so. As the revolution proceeded, the military was most assiduous in securing its own interests. Its honeymoon with Tahrir Square was short-lived, as stories quickly emerged of the army's arrest, torture, and routine sexual assault of protesters.

These facts should be borne in mind as we approach the first phases of political life after Mubarak, the ones dominated by the Supreme Council of Armed Forces. When Mubarak stepped down, it was SCAF who assumed authority. In fact, we might see the moment of their political ascendancy as earlier still: it has been argued that it was the army leaders who pushed Mubarak out of office as much as protesters in the street. It was also SCAF who oversaw the first post-revolutionary parliamentary elections. In many ways those elections were a success. Turnout was 62 percent, high by any measure and a striking contrast to the previous round of parliamentary elections in 2010, when only 27.5 percent of eligible voters went to the polls (BBC News 2011). Clearly, Egyptians were more sanguine about the

1. For a detailed time line of events, see *New York Times*, June 23, 2014.

political process than they had been under Mubarak. Though the National Democratic Party had been excluded from officially participating, several parties identifiable as NDP offshoots did participate. The electorate had no truck with them: taken together, these parties earned 6 percent of the vote. The biggest winners in the parliamentary elections were the Islamist parties. Of 498 elected seats, 225 (45.2 percent) went to the "Democratic Alliance" led by the Muslim Brotherhood's Freedom and Justice Party, and 123 (25 percent) went to the "Islamist Alliance" led by the Salafist party al-Nour. Egypt's most historically significant liberal party, al-Wafd, earned 41 seats (8.2 percent), and the "Egyptian Bloc"—a loose collection of secular Left parties, some with relatively long histories and others arising after the revolution—earned 34 seats (6.8 percent) (Electoral Institute for Sustainable Democracy in Africa 2013).

A certain kind of observer in the West might see such results as reflecting popular desire in the Middle East for Islamic theocracy and as justifying previous support of Mubarak and other dictators. This view is misguided. There is no question that Islam is a powerful cultural influence in Egypt and that it inflects politics because it inflects the majority's sense of the good life. The same cannot be said for the principles of secular liberalism, though those principles were abundantly displayed in Tahrir Square. It is also true that the style of Islamic observance favored in the Persian Gulf has gained traction in Egypt in recent decades, as more Egyptians have migrated to the Gulf for work and tuned in to satellite television originating in Saudi Arabia and Qatar. But the strong performance of the Islamist parties does not indicate a desire to turn Egypt into a Gulf-style theocracy. Rightly or wrongly, many Egyptians felt that members of the Islamist parties would have personal integrity and thus eschew the corruption that had infected the NDP to the core. The Muslim Brotherhood was also a known quantity, particularly among the rural poor, having organized charity hospitals and schools and subsidized grocery stores. The leftists of the Egyptian Bloc, by contrast, seemed in many segments of Egyptian society to be a rabble of loquacious and disruptive Cairene intellectuals. The Brotherhood was also the party with the strongest Election Day strategy by far. They had a quasi-official Election Day presence, stationed at key intersections and drawing maps to the nearest polling stations on leaflets for their own candidates. In terms of mobilizing support on the ground, nobody else came close.

SCAF were not surprised by the outcome of the parliamentary elections of 2011–12; they were also deeply displeased with it. Antipathy to the Brotherhood is a settled fixture in the mentalité of the officer corps. With presidential elections looming, they were eager to thwart the growing power of the FJP. The solution was to throw their weight fully behind their own candidate, Ahmed Shafik, a carryover from the old regime who still enjoyed a positive reputation in some quarters (despite more than two dozen corruption charges pending against him at the time of the elections). That effort was assisted by the fact that the FJP's presidential candidate, Khairat al-Shater, had his own legal troubles: because he had been imprisoned under Mubarak, the courts declared him ineligible to run for president. The party had anticipated this turn of events and as an insurance measure placed a second candidate in the race, Mohammed Morsi, whom satirical souls branded "the spare tire." With their first choice excluded, the party machine went to work on the spare tire and made a candidate of Morsi. The field narrowed in the runoff election to Shafik and Morsi, leaving many in the electorate to feel as though they faced a choice between Scylla and Charybdis: either hand the presidency to one of Mubarak's former prime ministers and turn back the clock on the revolution, or give the Brotherhood the keys to the presidential palace. In the event, Morsi seemed the lesser evil: he was announced the winner of the presidential election on June 24, 2012, with just under 52 percent of the vote (Spencer 2012).

But a funny thing happened during the presidential elections: results of the parliamentary election were being challenged before the courts. Under election law, two-thirds of parliamentary seats were to be allocated to political parties and one-third to be held by independents. The goal of the independent seats was broader representation of Egyptian society than a straightforward party system would allow. During the 2011 elections, however, many "independents" ran as individuals but openly displayed their party affiliations and thus made the distinction between party and independent seats largely nugatory. One independent candidate who lost a race for an independent seat to someone with a clear party affiliation challenged the result in court. The case was fast-tracked to the Supreme Constitutional Court, which issued a sweeping verdict. Precedent in Egyptian law would call for the court to declare the election for the seat in question to be null, leaving parliament to administer a by-election for that seat. The court might also have declared unconstitutional the electoral law pertaining to independents, so that fresh elections might be held for one-third of parliamentary seats. Instead, they declared the electoral law governing independent seats to be unconstitutional and thus the entire parliament to be unconstitutional. Acting swiftly on this court decision, SCAF vacated parliament on June 16, 2012.

To some extent we may only conjecture as to why the court would act this way. Khaled Abou El Fadl, a legal expert who had been consulting with many in the Egyptian judiciary at the time of the decision, offers some informed hypothesis:

> The military council gave the Supreme Court a doomsday scenario. They didn't tell the court that they were backing Shafik and that he was going to win [the presidential election]. Rather, they said that there is a good chance that the Ikhwan [Muslim Brotherhood] are going to win: the elections are being observed by a lot of outside parties and the judiciary, so our hands are tied. And if the Islamists win the presidency and control the parliament, this country is going to collapse, Saudi and American investors are going to run away—and here they pointed to the stock market, which happened to lose a lot of points when it was reported that the Ikhwani person was likely to win. Egypt, they said, is in danger of becoming another Iran or worse—or, we're really worried about the Israelis invading.

It was "the military council that drafted the electoral law that turned out to be unconstitutional," Abou El Fadl points out, and the military council that evacuated parliament when the court's decision was handed down (Mohamed 2012). In this analysis, two established players on the Egyptian political scene, the army and the courts, leagued to stem the rising influence of an unwelcome newcomer. Though the court had preserved relative independence under Mubarak and his predecessors, it seems in this instance to have been swayed by the view that having the Brotherhood control parliament and the president's palace would pose a threat to Egyptian democracy of longer duration than the dissolution of a single parliament would do.

All of these political tumults bear directly on the drafting of the postrevolutionary constitution. Early in its term, the elected parliament had appointed a Constituent Assembly, charged with the drafting of a new constitution. The composition of this body directly reflected the makeup of the new parliament: sixty-six of its one hundred members were Islamists, five were Copts, and six were women. Its imbalance was challenged before the courts, which dissolved it in April 2012. One of parliament's last actions before being vacated in June 2012 was to appoint a new Constituent Assembly, this one striving more fully to represent Egyptian society. The Islamists relinquished some of their seats, though they still held a majority, and labor unions and civil society organizations were represented. The new assembly was also challenged before the courts. As the case worked its way to the Supreme Constitutional Court, now president Mohammed Morsi clearly felt that the court was set to dissolve the assembly again. That feeling animated his highly controversial constitutional declaration of November 22, 2012, and especially its fifth article: "No judicial body can dissolve the Shura Council or the Constituent Assembly" (*Ahram Online* 2012). Morsi wished to bring the drafting process to a conclusion and had no patience for meddling from the courts or from those politically liberal elements within the assembly who had stormed out during the drafting process. The Second Constituent Assembly may have begun its sitting with the promise of a reduced Islamist presence, but after everyone else stormed out in protest it became in the end a decidedly bearded affair. Having brought the drafting period to a close, Morsi precipitously called a public referendum to ratify the constitution. Though international observers were largely kept away, the referendum did take place under judicial supervision in December 2012; 63.8 percent of those voting approved the new constitution, with a turnout of 32.9 percent (BBC News 2012). Morsi had his wish of a ratified constitution, but it had come at the price of utter political isolation. The president whose first action in office had been to relinquish his membership in the FJP was left with no one outside his own party willing to give him the time of day.

That Morsi was perceived to have forced the constitution on the nation became but one of the many complaints against him. The Egyptian economy struggled, and the president's efforts to secure foreign investment, including a loan from the International Monetary Fund, seemed to come to naught. To many these failures indicated that the Brotherhood's new power had led Egypt to lose standing on the world stage. Perhaps most pressing for many Egyptians was the struggle of daily life, which had only intensified after the fall of Mubarak: rising food prices, chronic fuel shortages, regular power outages, breakdowns in law and order. The Brotherhood was increasing its control over many aspects of the state, at the national and governorate levels, oblivious to the many signs that they did not have the expertise to do so. In many parts of Egypt, their offices were routinely vandalized. Their reputation was not helped by rumors and conspiracy theories that seemed daily to proliferate: that they had fixed all the elections after Mubarak's fall, that the Americans had orchestrated their rise to power, that the Qataris had orchestrated their rise to power, that Hamas had orchestrated their rise to power, that they had a secret plot to give upper Egypt to Sudan, that they wanted to make the education of young girls illegal, and on and on.

In this climate signatures quickly accumulated on the petition of the Tamarrod campaign, which declared a lack of confidence in Morsi and called for early presidential elections. By the early summer of 2013, the movement had gathered twenty-two million signatures. In the largest protests since the revolution of 2011, millions of Egyptians took to the streets on June 30, 2013, to pressure Morsi into a response. Respond he did, with characteristic fist-shaking defiance.

Having signaled that he must bend to the will of the people, the military seized upon Morsi's recalcitrance: they forced him out of power on July 3 and installed the chief justice of the Supreme Constitutional Court, Adli Mansour, as interim president. Joining him as vice president was Mohamed ElBaradei, the Nobel peace laureate and former director general of the International Atomic Energy Agency, who had become a leading figure among an older generation of liberals. This move seemed entirely consistent with the widespread recognition that the transition to democracy must have secular and civilian leadership.

Or so it seemed. Morsi's supporters felt deeply aggrieved, taking to the streets in volatile protests that often left churches and other property ablaze in their wake. The army unleashed a ruthless crackdown, killing hundreds of protesters over the course of the summer of 2013 and jailing thousands more. Leaders of the Brotherhood, including Morsi himself, had been imprisoned. Unable to persuade the military to temper its response, ElBaradei resigned his vice presidency and left the country. It had become clear that the civilians installed on July 3 were window dressing: Mansour was carted out on special occasions, but it was the military, and especially Morsi's own appointee as minister of defense, Abdel Fattah el-Sisi, who were running the show. In what became widely touted in official news outlets as a "War on Terrorism," they rapidly moved to suppress all forms of dissent, arising not only from the Brotherhood but also from the secular Left: every prominent dissident in Egypt seemed to be arrested at least briefly, and a draconian antiprotest law passed in November 2013 ensured that public demonstrations against the military's reign could be promptly crushed. Alarmingly, the public embraced these actions as a return to order, and overnight Sisi became a national hero. It was no surprise when he was elected to the presidency in June 2014.

It is in this climate that Egypt's second postrevolutionary constitution was drafted. With the constitution of 2012 suspended, a new Constituent Assembly of fifty members was formed under the direction of Amr Moussa, a sometime Mubarakite who had ably served as secretary-general of the Arab League and, with ElBaradei and Hamdeen Sabbahi, had become one of the leaders of the secular liberal coalition party, the National Salvation Front. The new assembly gathered many of the institutions and interest groups that felt marginalized by the Islamist parties. The Brotherhood was unsurprisingly kept out of the drafting process, though the more religiously conservative Salafists did have two representatives. A draft was presented to interim president Mansour in December 2013, and a referendum was held the following month. The military knew it needed a result that would embarrass the 64 percent approval of the "Brotherhood Constitution," and, perhaps all too conveniently, that is precisely what they got: 98.1 percent of voters approved the new constitution, though with a turnout only slightly better than in 2012, with 38.6 percent of those Egyptians eligible casting a ballot (*Ahram Online* 2014). The former figure reflects the approval in many quarters of the army's actions against the Brotherhood. The latter figure reflects the widespread view that approval was a foregone conclusion. Facing insurmountable headwinds, opposition forces could not organize a "no" campaign, and many simply did not participate.

The Products: Key Provisions of the 2012 and 2014 Constitutions

It is productive, I think, to consider the process in isolation, as we have just done, before turning to the texts of these constitutions. Procedures matter in a democracy. So which procedures seem to us more legitimate, the ones producing the 2012 constitution or those producing the 2014 constitution? Each is a mixed bag. The 2012 document arose from a committee appointed by an elected assembly, but that committee was consistently accused of ignoring the wishes of large swaths of civil society. The Tamarrod movement is also a politically significant expression of popular will, so the 2014 document does not arise only from a military putsch. But we cannot ignore that a putsch did take place and that it removed an elected president. Both constitutions are ratified through popular referendum. Is one process more legitimate than the other? Even if we say that the process leading to the 2012 constitution was more democratically legitimate, how much should it matter?

If evaluating the process leaves us puzzled, we might turn to the texts themselves in answering the question of legitimacy. But in making that turn, we should recognize that we have implicitly placed a limit on democracy: turning to the texts to decide which is the better constitution tacitly acknowledges that the measure of a legal document is not only its ratification by popular vote but also its harmony with a set of supralegal norms that we recognize as just—consistency with the Universal Declaration of Human Rights, for example. Should one of those norms be the document's secularity? Those readers who would quickly say yes should note that many nations have an official state religion, including Denmark, England, Ireland, Portugal, and Spain.

Nearly every political actor outside of the Islamist parties felt frustration and dismay over the course of drafting the constitution of 2012. One notable example is the human rights activist Manal al-Tibi, who stepped down from the second Constituent Assembly on September 24, 2012, and released her letter of resignation to the press:

> I have reached a final conviction that there is no use in continuing to be a member of the Constituent Assembly, given that the final product—despite my struggle to present many suggestions for constitutional clauses that reflect freedom, social justice and human dignity for all citizens without discrimination—would never meet the expectations of the majority of Egyptians. Rather, it became clear that the constitution was being prepared to serve one particular group, entrenching the idea that the religious state might obtain power in such a manner. Eventually, the process would create a constitution that would maintain the same primary foundations of the regime that the revolution had risen up to overthrow, while only changing the personnel; not a radical change in the structure of the regime as an inevitable result of the glorious Egyptian revolution. (Sabry 2012)

There are three major prongs to al-Tibi's objections: that the constitution seeks to establish a religious state, that this state will be undemocratic, and that it will not respect citizens' rights and liberties, particularly those of women and religious minorities. In what follows, we shall explore the extent to which the final text of the constitution justifies these objections and whether the constitution of 2014 is an improvement in these regards.

The prerevolutionary constitution was passed in 1971. It stipulated a presidential term of six years, with a president being eligible for an unlimited number of terms (Mubarak's predecessors Gamal Abdel Nasser and Anwar Sadat had held the office until death) (1971 Art. 77). The 2012 constitution, by contrast, limits a presidential term to four years and bars a president from running for more than two consecutive terms (2012 Art. 133).[2] This provision remained unchanged in the 2014 constitution (2014 Art. 140). In the postrevolutionary constitutions, the president must also work more collaboratively with parliament in forming a government. The 1971 constitution had required a two-thirds parliamentary majority to dissolve the government, which was formed by presidential appointment. In the 2012 constitution, the president appoints a prime minister and cabinet from within parliament, which must approve the appointments, and parliament may dissolve this government by simple majority (2012 Arts. 126, 139). Presidential authority is limited further still in 2014 in that parliament can reject the president's appointed prime minister and the prime minister's appointed cabinet. In this event, the president must appoint the prime minister selected by the party or coalition holding the most seats in parliament (2014 Art. 146). Fresh from the experience of a failed elected president, the

2. The Comparative Constitutions Project has prepared a graphic comparing the three versions of the Egyptian Constitution (1971, 2012, and 2014), available at http://comparativeconstitutionsproject.org/comparing-the-egyptian-constitution/. Further references to these constitutions are in parentheses.

2014 constitution also grants parliament the power of impeachment: a two-thirds majority can withdraw confidence in the president and force a popular referendum to hold early presidential elections. Once that referendum is held, it may pass by simple majority (2014 Art. 161). Both 2012 and 2014 thus take significant steps toward a mixed system and away from a strongly presidential one.

The executive does nonetheless retain a good deal of power. The president is placed in charge of foreign policy and defense and is the commander in chief of the armed forces (2012 Arts. 145–47; 2014 Arts. 145–47). The 2014 constitution adds, somewhat oddly, that any peace treaty or alliance must be approved by popular referendum (2014 Art. 151). In both postrevolutionary constitutions, the president can declare a state of emergency but must have the approval of parliament to do so (2012 Art. 148; 2014 Art. 154). The 2012 constitution limits the time of a declared emergency to six months; the 2014 constitution cuts that time in half, to three months. These limits sound like appropriate brakes on a president's power to impose martial law, but we should recall that the 1971 constitution had similar provisions, and they did not prevent Mubarak from ruling under a state of emergency for his entire presidency (1971 Art. 148). Sisi declared a three-month state of emergency following the April 2017 attacks on Coptic churches in Tanta and Alexandria. The state of emergency has been repeatedly extended every three months and remains in force at the time of this writing.

The president in the 2012 text also appoints one-tenth of the upper house, or Shura Council (2012 Art. 128). Though this portion is significantly smaller than the one-third of appointees in the previous constitution (1971 Art. 196), it had been criticized for allowing the executive too much influence within the legislative branch—to offer an American parallel, imagine the expansion of executive power, and diminution of democratic representation, that would occur if a president could appoint ten members of the Senate, with the elected number being reduced to ninety. The 2014 constitution solves this problem by eliminating the upper house altogether, converting Egypt into a unicameral system. In its provisions, the powers previously held by the Shura Council are transferred to the House of Representatives.

The 1971 constitution had already declared the sharia (Islamic law) to be "the principal source" of Egyptian legislation (1971 Art. 2). Given the Islamist presence in the drafting process, that provision was not likely to be eliminated in 2012. The only real question was the extent to which the constitution's declared affinities with Islamic law would become more robust and whether those new affinities would force the secular courts to adopt religious jurisprudence. On this point the 2012 constitution is both specific and vague. Unlike its predecessor, it specifies just what it perceives the sharia to be: "The principles of Islamic law include general evidence, the foundational principles of Islamic jurisprudence (*usul al-fiqh*), and the reliable sources from among the Sunni schools of thought (*madhahib*)" (2012 Art. 219). Such remarks on the legitimate sources of the sharia were previously absent. The 2012 constitution also prescribes a new role for Cairo's al-Azhar University, the oldest seat of learning in Sunni Islam, which it not unjustly describes as a "beacon for moderate, enlightened thought" (2012 Preamble 11). The university received no mention in the previous constitution; now its senior scholars are to be consulted on matters pertaining to the sharia (2012 Art. 4). Much as these new provisions make the relationship between Egyptian law and the sharia sound more concrete, it is entirely unclear just how they might be applied. There is no mention of the sharia trumping existing national law, so that the courts are more likely to follow their existing legal resources: primarily the Civil Code penned by the great jurist al-Sanhuri in 1949, which declares that cases are to be decided first by law, next by custom, and last by the sharia. But of course activist judges or aggressive statute making by Islamist legislators could change that. And if the learned and moderate scholars of al-Azhar were to tell less learned and moderate politicians that their views of the sharia are false, the 2012 constitution did not require the latter to take heed. Al-Azhar must be consulted, but only consulted.

Just how the controversial 2012 provisions on the sharia would have affected Egyptian law will forever remain a matter of speculation, for they are removed from the 2014 text. The 2014 constitution does keep Article 2, stating, as its two predecessors had done, that the principles of the sharia are the main source of legislation (2014 Art. 2). Article 219, however, which stipulated the sources of the sharia, is eliminated, and the preamble of the constitution states that the past decisions of the Supreme Constitutional Court are the primary reference on matters pertaining to the sharia (2014 Preamble). Al-Azhar is no longer to be consulted on legal matters, a role that it never sought. Its independence is nonetheless maintained (2014 Art. 7; cf. 2012 Art. 4).

The other debates stirring controversy surrounded the rights of women and religious minorities. The following headline from Amnesty International's news page sums up widely held perceptions: "Egypt's New Constitution Limits Fundamental Freedoms and Ignores the Rights of Women" (2012). In several of its articles, the 2012 constitution guarantees freedoms of belief, of association, of the press, of creative expression, and of scientific inquiry. It declares that the press must not be censored, but also limits that provision: press censorship may be applied by court order or in times of national emergency or mobilization (2012 Arts. 43–54). But all of these provisions were in the previous constitution; they did little, especially in the context of emergency law, to ensure that any of these freedoms were respected (1971 Arts. 46–55). And the 2012 constitution added a limit on free expression that was previously absent: "It is forbidden to insult any messengers or prophets" (2012 Art. 44). That labile provision might lend itself to curtailing the speech of non-Muslims or secularists.

The 2014 constitution eliminates this provision and also adds several articles on rights and freedoms. Torture is declared unequivocally to be a crime and one with no statute of limitations; any evidence gathered through torture is inadmissible, and the accused gains the right to remain silent (2014 Arts. 52, 55). A good deal more antidiscrimination language is added, and a permanent, independent commission is formed to eliminate discrimination and hate crimes (2014 Art. 53). Any international human rights instrument that has been ratified by Egypt gains the force of law (2014 Art. 93). Here it is worthwhile to recall that this provision includes many major UN conventions and covenants, including the International Convention on the Elimination of All Forms of Racial Discrimination; the International Covenant on Civil and Political Rights; the International Covenant on Economic, Social, and Cultural Rights; the Convention on the Elimination of All Forms of Discrimination against Women; the Convention on the Rights of the Child; and the Convention on the Rights of Persons with Disabilities.

Constitutional provisions on women's rights were also contentious in drafting the 2012 text and a point on which many inside and outside of Egypt were deeply skeptical of the Islamists' intentions. Much of that controversy became focused on draft-article 68, which promised to guarantee gender equality so long as it did not violate the sharia. Secular forces and human rights activists within the Constituent Assembly naturally opposed the qualifier and wished to see gender equality affirmed in the constitution. Much as one would like to lay responsibility for the dispute on the shoulders of the Islamists, it is worthwhile to recall that the previous constitution had a nearly identical article: "The State shall guarantee harmonization between the duties of woman towards the family and her work in society, ensuring her equal status with man in fields of political, social, cultural, and economic life without violation of the rules of Islamic jurisprudence [the sharia]" (1971 Art. 11). The question before the Islamist contingent in the Constituent Assembly, then, was whether to part with one of the previous constitution's references to the sharia, which is quite different from introducing a mention de novo. For members of the secular Left, however, a fundamental equality was at stake and one close to the heart of the revolution's democratic promise. In the event, the controversial article was eliminated from the final draft.

This point was one on which the Constituent Assembly drafting the 2014 constitution could signal its distance from regressive Islamist scruples. The result is a fairly lengthy article on the rights of women, in which the following provisions are entirely new:

> The state shall ensure the achievement of equality between women and men in all civil, political, economic, social and cultural rights, in accordance with the provisions of the constitution.
>
> The state shall endeavor to take measures ensuring the adequate representation of women in parliament, as prescribed by law, and to ensure the right of women to hold public office and senior management positions in the state and to be recruited by judicial institutions without discrimination.
>
> The state is committed to the protection of women against all forms of violence, and to empower women to balance their family and work duties. (2014 Art. 11)

In their every syllable these provisions pummel the Islamists for their refusal to acknowledge gender equality and for their equivocations on violence against women. As a political blow, they are enormously effective. As a constitutional declaration of rights with practical force, they are vague and may never be effectively implemented.

And that issue, of course, is a central problem of interpreting the value of any written constitution. Some of the most wonderfully progressive constitutional texts arose in the socialist republics of the early twentieth century, guaranteeing all sorts of rights and freedoms that in the end were not respected by the state at all. Constitutions have particularly limited significance in civilian, rather than common-law, legal systems, where they are in large measure a statement of political identity rather than the primary source of rule of law—France is currently on its fifth postrevolutionary constitution, but the code has been in place since the reign of Napoleon.

As I write these pages, it looks very much as though counterrevolutionary forces have been victorious in Egypt: the prisons are chock-full of Muslim Brothers, forced disappearances of all varieties of political dissident number in the thousands, an army strongman sits in the president's palace, and an elected if also entirely acquiescent parliament eagerly bends to his will. Sisi's military-led regime is buttressed by financial support from Saudi Arabia and the Emirates and has received an enthusiastic endorsement from President Trump, who is entirely willing to partner with autocrats taking a hard line against terrorism. The most recent constitution ensures that the assertion of military authority and marginalization of the Brotherhood will be part of the political landscape in the long term: as in its 1971 predecessor, the 2014 constitution outlaws religious political parties (2014 Art. 74; cf. 1971 Art. 5); both the 2012 and 2014 constitutions allow the military to choose the minister of defense (212 Art. 195; cf. 2014 Art. 201).

The kinds of things so hotly debated during the drafting of these constitutions—equal treatment of religious minorities and women—will depend a great deal on statute writing and on the extralegal and quasi-legal transactions of everyday life, not to mention a thoroughgoing reform of such institutions as the Ministry of the Interior and police. Despite powerfully symbolic moments of confessional unity during the revolution itself, there has been little sustained effort to calm religious strife in civil society. And in fact that strife has been violent at several points since 2011, with Christians increasingly vulnerable to the attacks of terrorist groups claiming allegiance to the Islamic State—coming to mind are not only the Palm Sunday 2017 bombings in Tanta and Alexandria, but also the deadly bombing in December 2016 of Saint Mark's Coptic Cathedral in Cairo and the May 2017 attack on a bus of Coptic pilgrims in Minya Province. Despite the widespread participation of women in the revolution itself, several problems surrounding the equality of women also persist: from state-sanctioned sexual assault and widespread sexual harassment to female genital mutilation. Even if the constitutional text were to get things exactly right, fulfillment of the revolution's goals would depend on many things that the text cannot do, such as sustained development of democratic and socially progressive institutions. The existing constitution does not create obstacles to that project. It also does not, and cannot, do a great deal to advance it.

Sources Cited

Ahram Online. 2012. "English Text of Morsi's Constitutional Declaration." Nov. 22. http://english.ahram.org.eg/News/58947.aspx.

———. 2014. "Table: Official Results of Egypt's 2014 Constitutional Referendum." Jan. 19. http://english.ahram.org.eg/NewsContent/1/155/91957/Egypt/Constitution-/Table-Official-results-of-Egypts--constitutional-r.aspx.

Amnesty International. 2012. "Egypt's New Constitution Limits Fundamental Freedoms and Ignores the Rights of Women." Nov. 30. https://www.amnesty.org/en/latest/news/2012/11/egypt-s-new-constitution-limits-fundamental-freedoms-and-ignores-rights-women/.

BBC News. 2011. "Egypt Election Officials Announce 62% Turnout." Dec. 2. http://www.bbc.com/news/world-africa-16007705.

———. 2012. "Egyptian Voters Back New Constitution in Referendum." Dec. 25. http://www.bbc.com/news/world-middle-east-20842487.

Electoral Institute for Sustainable Democracy in Africa. 2013. "Egypt: 2011/2012 People's Assembly Elections Results." Jan. https://www.eisa.org.za/wep/egy2012results1.htm.

Mohamed, Feisal G. 2012. "Slouching toward Jerusalem, Riyadh, and Washington to Be Born: A Conversation with Khaled Abou El Fadl on the Trials of Egyptian Democracy." *Dissent*, July 11. https://www.dissentmagazine.org/online_articles/slouching-toward-jerusalem-riyadh-and-washington-to-be-born-a-conversation-with-khaled-abou-el-fadl-on-the-trials-of-egyptian-democracy.

New York Times. 2014. "Timeline of Turmoil in Egypt Mubarak and Morsi to Sisi." June 23. http://www.nytimes.com/interactive/2013/07/02/world/middleeast/03egypt-timeline-morsi.html?smid=pl-share#/#time259_8831.

Sabry, Bassem, trans. 2012. "Manal El-Tibi's Resignation Letter to Egypt's Constituent Assembly." *Ahram Online*, Sept. 26. http://english.ahram.org.eg/NewsContent/1/64/53896/Egypt/Politics-/Manal-ElTibis-resignation-letter-to-Egypts-Constit.aspx.

Spencer, Richard. 2012. "Egypt Election Result: Muslim Brotherhood's Mohammed Morsi Wins." *Telegraph*, June 24. http://www.telegraph.co.uk/news/worldnews/africaandindianocean/egypt/9352396/Egypt-election-result-Muslim-Brotherhoods-Mohammed-Morsi-wins.html.

4

Old and New Battles for Turkish National Identity

JOSHUA D. HENDRICK

On May 28, 2013, approximately fifty people protested the razing of Gezi Park in Taksim, Istanbul, Turkey's town center. Locked arm in arm in an effort to halt Taksim's redevelopment and to save one of the city's few remaining green spaces, these environmentalists stood their ground in a context that became brutally repressive. Scattered with tear gas and water cannons, the initial green-minded protesters quickly became national heroes. The following day, their numbers increased tenfold, only to be met with even more forceful suppression. On the night of May 29, a group set up camp in the park to reclaim it as public space. In the early-morning hours of May 30, the police shot more tear gas into the park, and once the protesters vacated, the police set fire to their tents. Later in the day, however, protesters returned en masse, and over the course of the following two weeks, millions of citizens in cities throughout the country took to the streets in an occupy movement that since became known as the "Gezi uprising." The Gezi uprising lasted six weeks and was a major political crisis for what its protagonists claimed to be a far too powerful single-party "Islamist-roots" Adalet ve Kalkınma Partisi (Justice and Development Party) government. More specifically, the movement was a crisis for then prime minister Recep Tayyip Erdoğan, the AKP's leader and arguably the most divisive figure in contemporary Turkish politics. Throwing fuel onto the Gezi fire was Erdoğan's initial response to the protesters. On June 1, he mocked them by challenging that if they were able to mobilize one hundred thousand people for their cause, he could respond by amassing one million in support of his (*Hürriyet Daily News* 2013). Shortly thereafter, Erdoğan passed off the protesters as "glue sniffers" and as çalpulcular (looters, vandals—pronounced *cha-pul-ju-lar*; singular, çalpulcu).

Who were Turkey's çalpulcular? According to a poll conducted during the height of the protests, the archetype çalpulcu came into focus as young (approximately 80 percent were younger than thirty), university educated (54 percent), and almost equally male and female (MetroPOLL 2013). According to another poll, 57 percent claimed never before to have attended a protest or political rally, and 70 percent felt no affiliation to any one political party—approximately 81 percent labeled themselves "libertarian" (Bilgiç and Kafkaslı 2013). My own firsthand account of the protests, which I attended as a participant-observer both at the park and in three other cities in Turkey between June 2 and July 6, 2013, attests to these data. I would add, however, that especially in Istanbul at the center of the protest movement was a large constituency of artists and musicians, a significant number of Turkey's LBGTQ community, and self-designated feminists. Moreover, as the protests continued, various labor groups joined in solidarity, as did a wide variety of socialist and anarchist groups and even a small group whose participants called themselves "anticapitalist Muslims." On the one hand, therefore, it was a diverse crowd of primarily nonviolent antagonists; on the other hand, it was a distinctly left-of-center mobilization that collectively viewed "their Turkey" as under siege by a socially conservative, economically liberal government and by the global forces of privatization and austerity.

Nonetheless, contradictions at the park were clear. Under large banners that read "anticapitalist," "antineoliberal," and "antifascist" slogans, protesters proudly adorned Guy Fawkes masks, cheap gas masks, and hard helmets that were all made in China. They wore T-shirts, sneakers, and backpacks that displayed a certain taste for US-style bourgeois consumerism—North Face, Low Alpine, Nike, and other markers of contemporary casual fashions were all ubiquitous in the park. Moreover, nearly universal was a constant reliance upon for-profit global information and communication technologies, which were cited by protesters, journalists, and analysts alike as instrumental to galvanizing the crowd inside the park—smartphones and other tech devices, together with Facebook, Twitter, and other social media, were central to the protest's mobilization. Either oblivious or indifferent to the irony, the architects of Gezi Park's anticapitalist rhetoric were fashionable young men and women who were all covered in global brands and who were regularly updating their statuses, "tweeting," and "FaceTiming" about their experiences at Gezi. When observing these contradictions, I in no way meant to trivialize the desires of Turkey's çalpulcular—quite the contrary; it was not difficult to empathize with their concerns.

Correlating with the coming to power of the AKP to single-party rule in 2002, and continuing after two successive reelections (2007, 2011), two majority victories in local and municipal elections (2004, 2009), and two popular constitutional referendums (2007, 2010), was more than a decade of dramatic economic and social change in Turkey. In that time and driven by hot capital investment, Istanbul (and much of the country) had become awash with ubiquitous construction, consumer advertising, and unmanageable urban sprawl. Many historical sites had undergone demolition to make way for office parks, skyscrapers, shopping malls, and hotels, and a rapidly growing new consumer class of social conservatives who supported the governing party had moved into areas of the city that had long been, culturally speaking, restricted to Turkey's old elite. Such physical changes were exacerbated by a party and prime minister that had become consumed by the possibilities of repeated electoral success, which in addition to pervasive construction produced an era, especially since the party's third electoral victory in 2011, of consolidation. What sparked the protest was the razing of a park and the AKP's plan to redevelop the area into a hypermodern shopping complex in the image of an Ottoman military barracks, a Las Vegas–style commoditized re-creation of a precommoditized time and place. Although this plan was the spark that led to mass protest, however, tensions at Gezi Park dug much deeper into the country's political soul.

At Gezi a boiling point was reached. The plights and yearnings of the grandchildren of Turkey's so-called old guard, that is, those whom Turkey's liberal critics designated the country's "white Turks" and whom the international media often chose to simplistically term Turkey's "secularists," perceived of their city (and their country) as under siege by the unfettered processes of economic globalization and by the demographic changes that accompanied them. Having facilitated these changes, protesters framed their grievances as a critique of Recep Tayyip Erdoğan and the AKP's consolidation of power, coupled with the perceived inability of opposition parties to effectively represent the criticisms and demands of AKP foes. A telling episode for me as a researcher occurred one evening in the early days at Gezi after I accepted an invitation to join a group of protesters for dinner—a mishmash of vegetable sandwiches on white bread and over-the-counter snack food, sustenance that had become readily available at "grab some food, leave some food" stands scattered throughout the park. This group of ten to twelve people consisted of both men and women in their midtwenties. When I told them more about my interest in their cause, they were all eager to explain to me why they were there. One protester indicated, "Our Turkey has been stolen," and another followed yelling loudly, "Bring back Istanbul . . . return Turkey to the people" (field notes, June 4, 2013). When I asked what she meant by "stolen," the young woman brought up a number of recent reforms enacted by the governing party to curb public displays of intimacy and to limit the consumption of alcohol in public and the sale of alcohol after 10:00 p.m. outside of restaurants, bars, and clubs. The last reform went into effect less than two weeks before the events at Gezi Park, and when she explained this point to me, the group spontaneously held up their bottles of Efes Pilsen (Turkey's national beer) and shouted in unison, "Her yer Taksim, her yer direni!" (Everywhere is Taksim, everywhere is resistance!).

Throughout the protest period (the height of which lasted from May 30 to June 13, 2013), many protesters were keen to visibly display their affection for one another by kissing in front of cameras and by dancing, playing music, and expressing jubilation. When they did so, it was alongside exaggerated displays of national pride, which was expressed by waving Turkish flags, singing nationalist tunes, and crying out regularly in masse, "Mustafa Kemal'in askerleriyiz!" (We are soldiers of Mustafa Kemal!). This particular brand of Turkish national pride was also on display every night of the protest and for weeks thereafter at 9:00 p.m. sharp when neighborhoods throughout Istanbul (and throughout the country) came alive with the music of pots and pans banging from apartments to illustrate solidarity with Turkey's çalpulcular.[1]

One of the regular refrains at Gezi Park, "Hukumet Istifa! Tayyip istifa!" (Government, resign! Tayyip, resign!), led many in the international media and in policy circles in Europe and Washington, DC, to falsely designate this event as "Turkey's Spring," that is, as an event comparable to the 2010–11 Arab uprisings in Tunisia, Egypt, and elsewhere in the region (Giraldi 2013; Henri-Levy 2013; Rubin 2013; Seymour 2013). It is important to understand that although similar in an abstract way to the Arab Spring (that is, social dissent), and although similar mobilization strategies were used (for example, social media), Turkey's Gezi Park uprising was not an effort on the part of the masses to overthrow an entrenched dictator, military regime, or monarchy. Gezi Park was certainly symptomatic of deep-seated unrest, but the social composition of the protesters in particular, and the political and economic context of Turkey in general, was not analogous to the Egyptian, Tunisian, Libyan, or Syrian cases. Despite the use of "authoritarianism," "dictatorship," and "democracy" as categories to describe grievances and aims, the fact remains that the AKP's Turkey was leading a general, albeit piecemeal and

1. A group of musicians called Kardeş Türküler (Turkish Brothers/Sisters) put "the sounds of pots and pans" to a beat, wrote lyrics expressing their meaning, and in so doing wrote Gezi Park's unofficial anthem. A performance can be viewed (with English subtitles) at https://www.youtube.com/watch?v=o-kbuS-anD4.

flawed, democratization effort for more than a decade before this event, and well before the AKP's rise, Turkish state-society relations, however imperfect, were far more democratic than the conditions of its Arab counterparts. So what happened at Gezi Park?

Sharing much in common with the US-spawned Occupy movement, the Gezi uprising evinced a contradictory reality in contemporary Turkey. Although among the beneficiaries of the country's integration in terms of access to consumer tastes and information technologies, Turkey's çalpulcular were also party to the contradictions of the neoliberal era. That is, similar to political environments elsewhere, Turkey's three-decade shift to the center Right since the 1980s produced a milieu wherein mainstream, left-of-center political parties had become absorbed by the very system they originally mobilized to contest. Blindsided by the events at Gezi Park only slightly less than the AKP itself, Turkey's left-of-center leadership lacked the capacity to represent the desires of these technologically sophisticated, hyperindividualized, consumer-driven, socially liberal, and politically libertarian çalpulcular. The result was social discontent that could not be expressed through traditional means. The aim of this chapter, therefore, is to briefly explain how Turkey's çalpulcular got to this point of political activism and, in so doing, to briefly explain the diversification of modern Turkish nationalism more broadly. In order to understand the events at Gezi Park, I argue that it is first necessary to understand the ways in which Turkish national identity was universally internalized in a deeply divided twentieth-century political public. In this context, it is important to underscore that for much of Turkey's republican history, state-society relations were administered in accordance with a restrictive development model that catered to an urban-based, insular-oriented elite. Following a penetrating military coup in 1980, however, Turkey began to integrate with the emerging post–Cold War world economy, which impacted the country's political divisions in significant ways. Those who benefited most from these changes were previously marginalized constituencies of rural-to-urban Anatolian migrants, who, over the course of the late twentieth century, moved into Turkey's major cities to compete for public and private resources. This situation was compounded by a shift in the country's development model to favor export-oriented small to medium-size businesses whose leaders established themselves in newly industrialized towns in central Anatolia. Formerly holding a monopoly on cultural legitimacy and social prestige, Turkey's elite was forced to make room for an increasingly more prosperous, more diversified, and more conservative public sphere.

The Making of Turkish National Identity

The Turkish Republic emerged in the context of a coup d'état within the middle ranks of the Ottoman military following World War I. As a result, the military became entrenched as part of the new state bureaucracy. Although more often than not in the political background, the Turkish Republic was long administered by a secular state elite under the "tutelage" of military oversight. Linking leaders in a small industrial sector with labor, agriculture, and mass media, social power in the new republic was hoarded by an emergent managerial network whose actors sought to engineer society in their own interests. In so doing, both culture (that is, Islam and ethnically defined "Turkishness") and economics (that is, capital) fell under state authority. Operating as the self-appointed guardian of the Republic, the Turkish Armed Forces (*Türk Silahlı Kuvvetleri* [TSK]) either forcefully or passively overthrew elected governments on four occasions between 1923 and 1997. With the exception of a two-and-a-half-year junta (1980–83), however, Turkey's generals never sought to directly administer the state apparatus; rather, they preferred to act as its supervisors. The generals were able to achieve this position because "ideological allies, particularly in the judiciary, political parties, and the media[,] in addition to some segments of society[,] provided . . . necessary political power and encouragement . . . [because] they regarded the military's oversight in politics as the most effective way of avoiding [Islamic, Kurdish, and communist] threats" (Kuru 2012, 38). It was not until the 1980s that Turkish state-society relations began to change, and it was not until the 2002 emergence of the AKP that the country's era of military tutelage met the beginning of its end.

Defined in terms of chauvinist militarism and based on "blood, purity, boundaries and honor," Turkish national identity was created by a domestic elite of beneficiaries known as "Kemalists" (White 2012, 3). *Kemalism* refers to the political, economic, and social doctrine associated with Turkey's first president and national patriarch, Mustafa Kemal (d. 1938). Developed in stages over the course of many years, what were eventually termed "the six arrows of Kemalism" laid a foundation upon which military tutelage was institutionalized. Two of Kemalism's six arrows were *revolutionism/reformism* and *republicanism*. Mustafa Kemal rose to prominence as an Ottoman commander who exhibited tremendous prowess on the battlefield. After becoming the "hero of Çanakkale" (the western Anatolian coastal town known to Europeans and Americans as Gallipoli), Kemal emerged as a leader during Allied occupation of Istanbul in 1920. Commanding what was later termed Turkey's "War of Independence" (1920–23), Kemal set up a provisional government in the provincial city of Ankara before forcing the Allies to capitulate on Istanbul. The resulting Treaty of Lausanne (1923) marked the recognition of a new Turkish Republic in place of a defunct Ottoman Empire. The Ankara-based regime was recognized as the country's official government and Mustafa Kemal as its leader. Having already developed a constitutional government in 1921, the new Grand National Assembly continued what was to become a long process of revolution/reform of Turkey's legal system, civil code, and public sphere.[2] The regime abolished the Ottoman sultanate and the religious minority-defined millet system in 1922 as well as the thirteen-century-old Sunni caliphate in 1924. It replaced Islamic law with the Swiss Civil Code in 1926 and standardized a Latin-script Turkish alphabet in 1928. In addition to numerous other reforms,

2. For diverse and detailed accounts of Turkey's reform period under Kemal, see Mango 2002; Parla and Davidson 2004; and Zürcher 2004.

Kemal oversaw the creation of a constitutional republic that institutionalized a new political order based on "a common state-produced national, culturally ethnic, territorial, linguistic, and Muslim identity" (White 2012, 28).

Contrasting with the cosmopolitan configuration of the empire, the new republic was imagined from the outset to be a nation of Turks. Arguably the most penetrating (and successful) of Kemalism's arrows was thus the top-down manufacturing of Turkish nationalism. Building on foundations laid by the late-Ottoman "Young Turk" movement (1908–9), Turkish nationalism began with efforts to standardize language and then shifted to focus on racial purity through a lens of "ethnic Islam." Often confusing for observers of the Turkish case, in the early republic "Turkish" connoted "Muslim." Enamored with European notions of modernization, Kemalists viewed Islam as an alien import that caused Turkish ethnic identity to stagnate. Nonetheless, because if one was not Muslim he was understood to be Jewish, Greek, or Armenian, to be Turkish meant, secondarily, that one was Muslim. Understood and promoted simultaneously as an existential necessity and as a glorious blessing of communal exception, "religion retained its capacity to transcend cleavages institutionalized by non-ideological power (e.g., social class) and perpetuated its grip on interpersonal ethics and familial relations" (Jacoby 2004, 83). Thus, building upon nationalism were the remaining three Kemalist arrows: *populism*, *secularism*, and *statism*.

Unlike the Ottomans, who organized a cosmopolitan society of corporately autonomous groups based on confession (the *millet* system), Kemal's regime sought to engender a society by and for *Turkish* people. Rather than acknowledging difference, the young regime invested heavily in creating a collective consciousness of sameness. "Modern Turkey" was imagined as a society devoid of ethnicities, class antagonisms, and linguistic variation. The state thus continued Ottoman reforms and investments in national education, industry, and infrastructure, but it did so in the name of the nation. Overseeing this effort was Kemal himself who, as president, took on the honorific "Atatürk" (Father Turk) to signify the paternal state's alleged equidistance to all citizens. The reality of class, ethnic, and linguistic divisions, let alone patriarchal male privilege, was muted in official state discourse, which, although positively affecting the creation of a proud national community, was also characterized by "more exclusive, supremacy-oriented ethno-racialist elements as well" (Parla and Davidson 2004, 80). Anchoring Turkey's ethno-racialist supremacy was the Kemalist institution of secularism or, more specifically, *laïcism* (*laiklik*). Rather than an effort to separate matters of faith from matters of state, however, Turkish *laïcism* constituted an effort to bring matters of faith under the control of the state. Early in the republic's history was the creation of the Presidency of Religious Affairs (Diyanet, established in 1924), a massive bureaucracy charged with the task of consolidating faith in a way that would serve the interests of the regime. But because Turkishness was linked to Muslimness, Islam (in itself) was not the regime's primary fear; rather, the influence of religious communities, brotherhoods, and orders was viewed as potentially destabilizing. As such, brotherhoods were closed, Sufi orders and the veneration of shrines were outlawed, and various rituals and practices associated with Islam were "Turkified." According to Kemalists, "The elimination of the orthodox and Sufi religious establishments and traditional religious education and their replacement with the original sources available to all in the vernacular language would help pave the road to producing a new vision of Islam open to progress, modern life, and society ruled by science and Turkish national ideology" (Hanioğlu 2012, 43).

The last of Kemal's arrows was *statism* (étatisme), which referred to the regime's efforts to create a classless, corporatist society, wherein the state was envisaged to be the primary director and manager of economic growth and development. Both the last to come into fruition and the first to wither away, statism in Turkey was a midcentury effort to apply economic management principles to mitigate a middle way between Soviet-style planning and US-style markets. In addition to controlling heavy industry, large-scale banking, and certain key commodities (for example, sugar, alcohol, tobacco), statism was also employed to subsidize the emergence of a nationally

Turkish capitalist class by seizing property from non-Turkish minorities. Via this system, the regime sought to create an industrial society for Turks that "emphasized capital accumulation and work for national economic development . . . [that] . . . both protected local capital and encouraged the formation of a class of national merchants" (Parla and Davidson 2004, 129–30). Although successful in the creation of a cadre of economic elites whose affiliates managed to industrialize several western cities (for example, Istanbul, Izmir, and Edirne), domestic and international pressure brought on by, among other factors, rapid rural-to-urban migration between the 1950s and 1970s ushered in a decade of economic and political unraveling. The 1970s in Turkey were marked by numerous social contradictions that reached their apex.

Champions of early to midcentury Kemalism simply could not handle the pressure brought on by a ballooning population, increasing inequality, and high unemployment, which together created political spaces for ideological Left–Right political mobilization, conservative Islamic revivalism, and eventually Kurdish ethnic awakening. The result was political and economic turmoil that ended with a military-led coup in September 1980. Following a junta-led government from 1980 to 1983, a period of restructuring began that continued through the 1990s, which was followed by a global era of social transformation in the 2000s. In other words, if there was ever a "Turkish Spring," it occurred slowly over the course of two decades, and it did so atop a wave of economic liberalization, export-based expansionism, pious conservative revivalism, and ethnic Kurdish uprising. That is, it did so upon the crumbling foundation of Turkish Kemalism.

Turkey's New Elite

The 1970s in Turkey (as in much of the world) were tumultuous. Economic development slowed, investment came to a near halt, and debt increased dramatically. Left–Right politics escalated to low-level urban war, seven coalition governments came and went in collapse, and in the early autumn of 1980 the military decided that its role as guardian of the republic was needed. On September 12, tanks rolled and generals seized power. After appointing a parliament to draft a military-approved constitution in 1982, a technocrat named Turgut Özal who was retained by the military to oversee economic restructuring positioned himself for victory when the military returned power to civilian politics in 1983. In addition to banning all parties operating before the coup, the new constitution limited partisan participation by mandating a 10 percent electoral threshold for parties to pass in order to win parliamentary seats. The Özal-led Anavatan Partisi (Motherland Party [ANAP]) won with 45.2 percent of the vote, which allowed it to enjoy single-party rule for much of the decade.

Although contradictory in its approach to political liberalization, the 1982 Turkish Constitution did create a foundation for social transformation. Key to the postcoup era was an effort on the part of the junta to create the conditions for a post–Cold War Turkey by reviving Islam as a nationalizing beacon in the face of Left-Right politics. Known as the "Turkish-Islamic synthesis," this effort sought to allow religious communities a chance to compete for hearts and minds in the public sphere so as to provide an antidote to leftist ideology and to Iran-inspired Islamic revolutionism. Devised by the generals and administered by the Özal-led ANAP government, this policy consciously promoted Turkish Islam as bedrock to secular Turkish nationalism, thus opening the gates of Turkey's political public to pious populism. Coupled with extensive efforts to liberalize the Turkish economy, to expand export-oriented growth, and to develop new industrial centers in the Anatolian countryside, Turkey witnessed the economic rise of its famous "Anatolian Tiger" cities and the partisan rise of political Islam.

Exemplified by rapidly industrializing provincial capitals such as Kayseri, Gaziantep, and Denizli, "Turkey's Tigers" became engines for the country's late-century development. Indeed, throughout the 1980s and 1990s, Turkey experienced uneven patterns of growth marked by increased debt, expanded International Monetary

Fund–administered adjustment, and fluctuating periods of financial crisis (for example, 1989, 1991, 1994, 1999, 2001). Nonetheless, Turkey's Tiger cities continued to grow in a relatively uninterrupted fashion and created a new economic base of social power. Led by entrepreneurs in construction, textiles, and light manufacturing, what some analysts designate as Turkey's "Islamic capital" came into its own. A new elite emerged whose actors, however prideful as Turks, were most certainly not Kemalists. According to Gülalp, "Not all these petty entrepreneurs, whether the small-scale industrialists in provincial towns or the intermediaries in poor neighborhoods of Istanbul, [were] necessarily Islamists, but the Islamist segment of the business class comes primarily from among this sector" (2001, 438). Socially conservative, pious Muslims were among the primary beneficiaries of Turkey's economic liberalization in the 1980s and 1990s. Linked to one or another revived religious community and having a newfound interest in matters of policy and development, leaders in Turkey's Tiger cities found political representation in Turkey's National Outlook (Milli Görüş) Islamist movement. By the mid-1990s, the political power of Turkey's Islamists was formidable, which allowed its party at the time, the Welfare Party (Refah Parti), to come to power in a coalition government in 1996.

Offering a more outward-oriented and religiously motivated understanding of wealth accumulation and national identity, the RP based its model of development on a neoliberal understanding of a shrinking state apparatus as expressed through an Islamic idiom. Despite owing its growing success to its affiliates' abilities to increase their share of Turkish capital accumulation, "what ultimately differentiated Welfare from other parties . . . was its emergence as the visible tip of a populist iceberg, a movement that [used Islam and markets to] . . . appeal to different orders of people, across class and ethnic lines" (White 2002, 124). Notwithstanding its rising popularity (or, more precisely, because of it), the TSK took it upon itself to control the flood that swelled since the implementation of the "Turkish-Islamic synthesis" and again to assume its self-appointed role as guardian of the republic. Viewing the RP's Islam-identified face, coupled with the country's increasingly more conservative public sphere, as trending too far toward "Islamicization," the military held a Security Council meeting on February 28, 1997. Known infamously as Turkey's "postmodern coup," this event was enough to force a collapse of the RP government. In the year following, the RP was closed, its senior leadership was banned from politics, and a series of reforms was enacted to allay the military's fears of encroaching religion. Rather than putting an end to Turkey's conservative social transformation, however, the February 28, 1997, soft coup actually marked the last time the TSK was able to effectively influence the path of Turkish democracy because, by the late 1990s, all of Turkey was experiencing the winds of change of the global era. New wealth (and new wealth inequality) was on display in cities and neighborhoods throughout the country, satellite and Internet telecommunications were connecting Turks of all stripes to the outside world, and aspirations for accession to the European Union were widespread. In short, the forces of globalization had taken root.

Atop the RP's ashes, a split within Turkey's Islamist movement led younger generations to reframe their Islamic social views in terms of neoliberal conservatism. After a few years of political navigation following February 28, 1997, the former RP mayor of Istanbul, Recep Tayyip Erdoğan, collaborated with a small group of younger-generation former RP deputies to form the AKP. And although Erdoğan was officially banned from politics when the AKP ran in its first election in 2002, the party won approximately 34 percent of the national electorate, which allowed its acting leader, Abdullah Gül, to form a single-party government. Shortly thereafter, Erdoğan was reinstated to national politics and assumed the role of Turkey's prime minister, a position he held from 2003 to August 2014, when he was elected president in Turkey's first national presidential election.

Upon coming to power, the AKP managed to mobilize a coalition in terms of what its leaders designated "conservative democracy." Included in its ranks and throughout its constituency was a collection of "new elites" that included, among other groups, so-called ex-radicals in Turkish Islamism. These individuals, though not previously interested in legitimizing Turkey's political processes, were attracted to the AKP's inclusion of faith and piety as part of its platform and were already in a process of becoming "absorbed" by Turkey's post-1983 integration into the world economy. As Tuğal explains, "The liberalization of the radicals was overdetermined. . . . Adapting to Istanbul, increasing involvement with business, and reading liberal Islamic and well as radical sources . . . already had an influence. . . . What changed was the emergence of political leadership that could channel this flux in a definite direction" (Tuğal 2009, 149). In other words, when opportunity spaces emerged to increase "the Muslim share" of Turkey's political economy, radicalism moderated and conservative democracy took root (Hendrick 2013, 24–26, 52–55, 164–70, 233–42; Tuğal 2009). Nonetheless, in addition to upwardly mobile former Islamists, the AKP also managed to secure support from a majority of Turkey's voting Kurds, from liberal-minded "anti-Kemalist" democrats, and from a number of small to medium business owners who saw in the AKP's brand of populism a form of political leadership that could crack Turkey's historically restricted pathway to social mobility. Succeeding where the RP failed, the AKP reoriented Turkey's domestic and foreign policies to position the country for regional leadership, made significant progress in its first two terms toward European Union integration, and was successful in effectively removing the TSK from political oversight. Uniting with both like-minded social conservatives and globally minded democrats, this final AKP achievement was nothing short of revolutionary.

The Corruption of Power

In late January 2007, approximately seven months before the AKP's first reelection, a military-issued weapons cache was discovered in an apartment in Istanbul. This discovery led to an investigation into the source of the weapons, which resulted in more caches being found throughout the city, as well as to the uncovering of documents that allegedly implicated a number of active and retired military personnel in planning a coup to overthrow the AKP. For the next five years, the Istanbul prosecutor's office led a wide-reaching investigation into Turkey's infamously conspiratorial "deep state" (*derin devlet*), an alleged shadow network of military men, journalists, party leaders, and academics that Turkish society has long feared exists behind the scenes of social power. Believed to call itself "Ergenekon," this incarnation of Turkey's deep state was conspiratorially believed to have perpetrated a wide array of assassinations, smear campaigns, and acts of public disturbance so as to create the image of public unrest, which, if the network perceived necessary, could create the social conditions necessary to effect the AKP's political collapse. According to the AKP, together with a coalition of supportive "new media," in Ergenekon Turkey's deep state was caught red-handed.

Although initially hailed with widespread legitimacy, shortly after the first indictment in 2008 the Ergenekon trials turned infamous. By 2011 hundreds of well-known members of Turkey's social elite, including approximately two hundred active and retired military men, were held in Turkish prisons on charges of being a member of a terrorist organization or for being part of a broad conspiracy to topple the AKP or both (Jenkins 2011). Critical analysts argued, however, that the AKP missed an opportunity to democratize Turkish state-society relations by allowing other interests to take control of the investigation. Highlighting an alleged counterconspiracy, critics pointed to what they termed an "infiltration" of the prosecutor's office by the increasingly influential Gülen movement, a faith-based advocacy community whose actors accumulated tremendous influence in education, media, trade, and finance since 1983 and who operated as a partner with the AKP since 2002 in a mutually interested effort to destroy the remnants of Turkish Kemalism.[3] Allied

3. Turkey's "Gülen movement" began in the early 1970s in accordance with the teachings of Fethullah Gülen, a charismatic Muslim writer and preacher who encouraged his followers to become educated in modern sciences, education, business, and trade. Widely believed to be the most powerful nonelected, nonmilitary social force in contemporary Turkey, the GM established its influence by managing hundreds of math- and science-oriented schools throughout Turkey and, after

by mutual interests, the AKP and the GM shared enemies and operated in tandem for much of the early 2000s. The AKP supported GM initiatives in education, trade, and international outreach, and, in turn, GM-affiliated media offered nearly unconditional support for AKP domestic policies, provided the AKP with a needed presence in foreign countries where Turkey had no official relations, and played a significant role in grassroots outreach in the United States and throughout Europe promoting the AKP's agenda. This alliance proved to be widely beneficial for both groups, but by 2011 some contended that, through this partnership, the AKP had allowed the GM to become too powerful as an unelected force:

> To date [July 2011], no evidence has emerged to tie Fethullah Gülen . . . personally to the [Ergenekon] investigations. Nevertheless, there is no question that elements from within the [GM] community are heavily involved. Gülen sympathizers now dominate large swathes of the judiciary and the police force, particularly the intelligence branches, which have been providing most of the evidence for the investigations. Since the outset [of the Ergenekon trial], the [GM] media outlets have sought to shape domestic and international public opinion about the cases by running vigorous disinformation campaigns, including inaccuracies, distortions and outright untruths. (Jenkins 2011)

Despite credible claims of falsified evidence, shortly after the cessation of the Gezi Park protests, in August 2013 the Ergenekon trial came to a close. Twenty-one of 275 defendants were acquitted.

1990, throughout the world. Linked with the schools are networks of small to medium-size business ventures that use the schools as means to generate client portfolios, to establish inroads to domestic and foreign markets, and to generate human resources for the network's reproduction (Hendrick 2009, 2011, 2013). On the eve of a failed coup attempt on July 15, 2016, it was widely believed across Turkey's political spectrum that GM actors had made their way into strategic institutions of appointed state power, specifically prosecutors' offices, police forces, the high judiciary, the Ministry of Education, and the Turkish Armed Forces.

Among those individuals convicted were six retired generals, two retired colonels, a veteran journalist, the head of Turkey's Workers' Party, and a lawyer, who all received one or more life sentences. Two senior members of the People's Republican Party, Mustafa Kemal's original party, were sentenced to more than ten years in prison, along with dozens of former state bureaucrats, military personnel, lawyers, and minority-party operatives who joined their ranks. In September 2012, a linked case called "Sledgehammer" (*Balyoz*) came to an initial close when a Turkish court sentenced another 236 current and retired military personnel, party elites, and media figures to various prison terms, ranging from six months to twenty years. Regardless of the controversial context, by the late summer of 2013, the AKP seemed to have accomplished a feat unlike any other in the history of the republic: it rendered the Turkish military powerless in domestic political affairs. Left in its way, however, was its ally who allegedly orchestrated both the Ergenekon and the Sledgehammer investigations: the Gülen movement.

In the months that followed the events at Gezi Park and the final verdict associated with the Ergenekon trials, a curious set of events transpired—the AKP and its allies associated with the GM had a falling-out. With the military removed from its oversight capacity, and with a country that the international community understood to be illustrating signs of social and political unraveling after the events at Gezi Park, the AKP and the GM stoked tensions that were brewing for some time. By the summer of 2016, tensions reached an existential tipping point. On July 15, forces within the Turkish TSK attempted to overthrow the AKP government. In what proved in hindsight to be a poorly executed failure, the coup attempt resulted in more than 260 people killed, thousands wounded, and the country in turmoil. Former prime minister turned president Erdoğan and the AKP leadership very quickly assigned blame to Fethullah Gülen and the GM and subsequently oversaw a three-month state of emergency, which allowed the government to suspend Turkey's obligations to uphold the European Convention on Human Rights. The AKP-led government renewed the state of emergency numerous times, finally lifting it on July 19, 2018. The state of emergency allowed the government to purge more than 100,000 people from the bureaucracy, hold tens of thousands of people under arrest without due process, and lead a number of world human rights organizations and foreign governments to criticize the AKP (and Erdoğan specifically) for serious and rampant abuses of power (Human Rights Watch 2016; Reynolds 2016).

Although a former ally whose actors helped the AKP consolidate authority in Turkey, President Erdoğan began his pursuit of what he called "the parallel state" (referring to the GM) only a few months after the 2013 events at Gezi Park. Rattled by the threat to his legitimacy posed by the çalpulcular, Erdoğan was at his most vulnerable in late 2013. On December 17, 2013, Turkish persecutors widely believed to be associated with the GM opened criminal investigations that implicated several deputies in the AKP government as well as President Erdoğan's son. GM-affiliated media outlets broke the story of alleged graft, bribery, and illegal smuggling, citing leaked audio evidence that was posted on the Internet. Shortly thereafter, several GM-affiliated journalists were arrested for alleged links to illegal networks within the Turkish police force and the state prosecutor's office. In the months that followed, hundreds of policemen were fired or reassigned, and dozens of prosecutors were removed from their posts. Not only determined to liquidate "Gulenists" from the institutions of law and order, the AKP also encouraged divestment from the GM's Bank Asya (and sought its nationalization), blocked state contracts with GM-affiliated firms, and canceled the state's support for GM-sponsored events. And despite having once declared himself the head prosecutor of the Ergenkon trials, in a bewildering move in March 2015, President Erdoğan publicly apologized to the Turkish military for "being deceived" along with the rest of the nation into believing the allegations levied against the institution regarding alleged coup plans (*Hürriyet Daily News* 2015). On March 31, 2015, all 236 suspects convicted in the Sledgehammer coup case were acquitted after a retrial proved evidence against them was fabricated. Dozens of Ergenekon suspects remain in prison or await their own retrials. In this context, the events of July 15, 2016, were framed by the AKP, and widely believed by the Turkish public across the political spectrum, to constitute a last-ditch effort by the GM to oust its former ally from power. The result thus far, however, is exactly the opposite. In today's Turkey, any person or organization now fears being labeled "Gülenci" (Gülen-ist), as the repercussions of such suspicions are certain only to begin with arrest and detention. Meanwhile, in the shadows of this state of Islamist fratricide remain the çalpulcular, Turkey's underground, but in no way forgotten, repoliticized youth.

Conclusion: Out with the Old, in with the . . .

Taking advantage of both domestic and transnational opportunities in the post-1983 era, a diverse composition of new social elites emerged in Turkey to influence the transformation and diversification of the country's political, economic, and social landscape. The country's old beneficiaries were forced to make room for an upwardly mobile constituency of new actors who found economic success through liberalization and who found both domestic and international support for having long suffered under the brutal oversight of military tutelage and Kemalist subjugation. However pious they were as Muslims, and however comfortable their leaders became with neoliberal reform, the new elite proved to be no less Turkish than their counterparts. That is, their brand of conservatism was just as nationalist as their predecessors' and their thirst for power just as fierce. Following a final run-in with military tutelage in the late 1990s, they rebranded their identity as "conservative democracy," joined forces against mutual foes, and attempted to forge a renewed Turkish national identity that embraced both markets and ballots, both the glorious Turk and the esteemed Ottoman. In so doing, they managed to successfully frame their efforts as being in the interests of Turkish democratization (vis-à-vis military tutelage) and cosmopolitan prosperity. The events at Gezi Park in the summer of 2013, however, called the AKP out on its charade. The unraveling of conservative democracy followed as hubris and ambition ripped the AKP-GM coalition apart.

According to çalpulcular, Erdoğan's, the AKP's, and the GM's interest in participatory democracy has always been instrumental and opportunistic, and all have an outright contempt for social dissent. For the youth mobilized at Gezi Park, the forces of "conservative democracy" in Turkey had far more in common with "the old Turkey" they claimed to have replaced than with something called "the new Turkey" they so often claimed themselves to represent. Nonetheless, following Gezi Park, the AKP continued to consolidate its political authority by overseeing another set of local election victories in March 2014, and in August 2014 Erdoğan became Turkey's first-ever president to be elected by popular vote, with just under 52 percent voting in his favor. Since then, the emblazed leader has been criticized both domestically and abroad for cracking down on all forms of dissent, for curbing press and academic freedoms, and for expanding government corruption. Arguably the most powerful Turkish individual since Atatürk himself, Erdoğan has continued to exploit his victory at the ballot box as rationale for undermining his rivals and for removing obstacles in his way. Moreover, he stated with increasingly regularity that his ultimate aim was to transform Turkey from a parliamentary to a presidential state system, a feat he very narrowly achieved in April 2017 through a popular referendum that amended the constitution to this end.

As far as President Erdoğan is concerned today, the only force standing in his way is his old ally Fethullah Gülen. But now that he enjoys power and influence unparalleled since Atatürk himself, the question remains: Is the new Turkey, in fact, new? That is, beyond creating more space for new actors to participate in distributing the share of social power in Turkey, is the country's new elite facilitating diversification, inclusion, participation, and, for lack of a better word, democracy? All indicators suggest the contrary.

Those protesting at Gezi Park shone a light on one side of a broad divide that sees Turkey's experience in the global era (1983 to the present) as inherently unstable. Its protagonists were primarily young, educated, and well connected (virtually). Moreover, they did not hail from Turkey's working classes, from the country's ethnic minority populations, or (despite a few exceptions) from conservative social groups. Exemplifying the ways in which social schisms in Turkey were reorganized and rebranded by a new conservative elite, the grandchildren of Turkey's old beneficiaries became defined by the events at Gezi Park. By adopting a discourse of empowered victimhood, they perceived of their country as having been taken from them. Moreover, the very violent and very disruptive split between the AKP's and the GM's "new Turkey coalition" all but proved to Turkey's çalpulcular that their country had, in fact, been "stolen." But although they articulated their cause with traditional nationalist symbols (for example, the Turkish flag, images of Atatürk, and so on), they did so in such way that repudiated Kemalism and that celebrated ethnic and religious diversity. They comprised Alevis and Kurds, feminists and greenies, industrial workers and the children of old capitalists, "anticapitalist" Muslims and queer activists. In many ways, they were "post-Kemalists"—they were çalpulcular. They negated chauvinist patriotism in favor of individual freedom and libertine consumerism. At the same time, they criticized an ambiguous enemy called capitalism for having been adopted with too much fervor and in such a way that has transformed cities and stripped Turkish society of safety and security.

Today's Turkey, however, is defined not only by the events of Gezi Park of 2013 but also by the failed coup attempt of 2016. Both events have become symbols, albeit symbols in opposition, for a new Turkish national identity. As a former ally and partner in Turkey's conservative democratic transformation, the GM has even latched on to Gezi Park in solidarity with what they only very recently express to be their own repression at the hands of Erdoğan's regime. Emphatically denying all allegations levied against them, leaders associated with the GM now routinely cite their struggles as evidence of an attack on the forces of democratization and liberty more broadly. Unsatisfied with the opposition's ability to compete with the AKP, and not at all convinced of the GM's sincerity, Turkey's çalpulcular challenge Turkey's worldviews past and present while simultaneously reviving imagery from the country's national past to stake a claim for a more secure future. They are individually identified and profoundly skeptical (if not outright fearful) of all forms of organizational power. They thus reject the GM's efforts to link the latter's infighting with the AKP as somehow connected to their struggle. Indeed, in the months that followed the breakout of the AKP-GM war of position, opinion polls routinely indicated that Turks by and large viewed both the AKP as guilty of corruption *and* the GM as having infiltrated the Turkish state bureaucracy in an effort to perpetuate ulterior communitarian goals (approximately 60 percent in both categories [MetroPOLL 2014]). This distrust of both the AKP and the GM is precisely the point; perceived as under siege, Turkey's çalpulcular continue, albeit underground, to rage against ever-increasing market competition and ever-decreasing political choice. They vent against majoritarianism while simultaneously demanding promise and purpose. In so doing, they have become a signifying political trope for a new generation of postpolitical (that is, postpartisan) activism in Turkey and thus point to cleavages that will no doubt continue to redefine Turkey's political public for years to come.

Sources Cited

Bilgiç, Ezra Ercan, and Zehra Kafkaslı. 2013. "Gencim, Özgürlükçüyüm, Ne İstiyorum? (I Am Young, I Am Libertarian, What Do I Want?): Gezi Park Report." Istanbul: Bilgi Univ. Press. http://www.bilgiyay.com/Content/files/DIRENGEZI.pdf.

Giraldi, Phillip. 2013. "Turkish Spring." *American Conservative* (July–Aug.).

Gülalp, Haldun. 2001. "Globalization and Political Islam: The Social Bases of Turkey's Welfare Party." *International Journal of Middle East Studies* 33 (3): 433–48.

Hanioğlu, M. Şükrü. 2012. "The Historical Roots of Kemalism." In *Democracy, Islam and Secularism in Turkey*, edited by Ahmet Kuru and Alfred Stephan, 32–60. New York: Columbia Univ. Press.

Hendrick, Joshua D. 2009. "Globalization, Islamic Activism, and Passive Revolution in Turkey: The Case of Fethullah Gülen." *Journal of Power* 2 (3): 343–68.

———. 2011. "Media Wars, Public Relations, and 'the Gülen Factor' in the New Turkey." *Middle East Report* 260: 40–46.

———. 2013. *Gülen: The Ambiguous Politics of Market Islam in Turkey and the World*. New York: New York Univ. Press.

Henri-Levy, Bernard. 2013. "Towards a Turkish Spring." *World Post*, June 4.

Human Rights Watch. 2016. "A Blank Check: Turkey's Post-Coup Suspension of Safeguards against Torture." Oct. 25. https://www.hrw.org/report/2016/10/25/blank-check/turkeys-post-coup-suspension-safeguards-against-torture.

Hürriyet Daily News. 2013. "PM Erdoğan Calls on Demonstrators to End Gezi Park Protest, No Step Back from Project." June 1.

———. 2015. "We Were All Deceived, Erdoğan Says, Accusing 'Parallel Structure of Misinformation.'" Mar. 20.

Jacoby, Tim. 2004. *Social Power and the Turkish State*. New York: Routledge.

Jenkins, Gareth. 2011. "Ergenekon, Sledgehammer, and the Politics of Turkish Justice: Conspiracies and Coincidences." *MERIA* 15 (2). http://www.rubincenter.org/2011/08/ergenekon-sledgehammer-and-the-politics-of-turkish-justice-conspiracies-and-coincidences/.

Kuru, Ahmet. 2012. "The Rise and Fall of Military Tutelage in Turkey: Fears of Islamism, Kurdism, and Communism." *Insight Turkey* 14 (2): 37–57.

Mango, Andrew. 2002. *Atatürk: The Biography of the Founder of Modern Turkey*. Woodstock, NY: Overlook Press.

MetroPOLL Stratejik ve Sosyal Araştırmalar. 2013. "Gezi Parkı Protestoları" (Gezi Park Protesters). June.

———. 2014. "Yolsuzluk ve Cemaat-Hükumet Tartışmaları" (Corruption and Government: Religious Community Conflict). Jan.

Parla, Taha, and Andrew Davidson. 2004. *Corporatist Ideology in Kemalist Turkey*. Syracuse, NY: Syracuse Univ. Press.

Reynolds, Michael A. 2016. "Damaging Democracy: The U.S., Fethullah Gülen, and Turkey's Upheaval." *Foreign Policy Research Institute* (Sept. 26).

Rubin, Michael. 2013. "The Roots of the Turkish Uprising." *Wall Street Journal*, June 4.

Seymour, Richard. 2013. "Istanbul Park Protests Sow the Seeds of a Turkish Spring." *Guardian*, May 31.

Today's Zaman. 2013. "Long Sentences for Ergenekon Suspects, Life for Ex-Army Chief." Aug. 5.

Tuğal, Cihan. 2009. *Passive Revolution*. Stanford, CA: Stanford Univ. Press.

White, Jenny. 2002. *Islamist Mobilization in Turkey: A Study in Vernacular Politics*. Seattle: Univ. of Washington Press.

———. 2012. *Muslim Nationalism and the New Turks*. Princeton, NJ: Princeton Univ. Press.

Zürcher, Erik. 2004. *Turkey: A Modern History*. New York. I. B. Tauris.

5

Security Challenges in Tunisia, Libya, Morocco, and Algeria in the Wake of the Arab Uprisings

RAMAZAN ERDAĞ

The revolts and protests that began in late 2010 in North Africa greatly impacted international politics and security. It was assumed that economic discontent caused the revolts, but political dissatisfaction and demands for freedom, justice, and democracy turned revolts to revolution. The impact of the Arab uprisings in these states differed from one another: Tunisia, Libya, Morocco, and Algeria experienced mass popular protests that brought regime change in Tunisia and Libya, whereas their effect in Morocco and Algeria was slight. While Tunisia experienced a gradual and relatively smooth regime change and transition process, political instability in Libya after the toppling of the Qaddafi regime devolved into civil war, threatening regional and international security.

This chapter focuses on paradigm change in the security sector of four North African states—Tunisia, Libya, Morocco, and Algeria—during and after the Arab uprisings. It analyzes the security situation of each state before the uprisings and the changes in politics brought about by the uprisings. Security threats within individual countries and a lack of central authority, such as we see in Libya, cause human rights violations and directly affect neighboring states. Additionally, increasing tensions in the region and insecure borders raise the possibility of renewed external military intervention.

Revolution and Beyond: Breakdowns and Security Challenges

The Arab uprisings were caused by popular discontent against existing regimes and reaction to the aggressive tactics of security forces. The primary mission of security forces in North African and the Middle Eastern states—both military and police—is to protect regimes against their own citizens. One of the aims of the Arab Spring was to pressure regimes into reform in the security sector in order to provide well-structured security forces that are accountable to the people and maintain policies consistent with human rights; the demands for freedom, justice, and transparent and accountable governance were aimed in particular at the security sector (Perito 2015). With the Arab Spring, long-lasting autocratic regimes came to an end. The postrevolutionary era constituted a "historic rupture in authoritarian stability and a strategic surprise for both local actors and outside observers" (Ammour 2012, 1). Failures in transitioning from "authoritarian stability" to "democratic peace and stability" during the Arab Spring posed new security challenges at the local, regional, and international levels. New security challenges in the Middle East and North Africa (MENA) include divided security structures, uncontrolled armed groups, human rights violations, political chaos, and large swaths of territory under the control of terrorist organizations such as the Islamic State of Iraq and Syria (ISIS).

The prospect of a new influx of refugees from North Africa, fleeing the struggling economies of their home states and the onset of civil war in Algeria, alarmed Europeans back in 1993 (Lesser 1993, 9–11); the Arab Spring uprisings produced exactly such a wave of migrants from North Africa to Europe.

The uprisings in North Africa produced different social, cultural, economic, and political changes in each state: the regimes of Tunisia and Libya were overthrown, but the regimes of Morocco and Algeria remained in place. Morocco and Algeria had already undergone a partial democratization process after the end of the Cold War.

Tunisia

Unquestionably, the Tunisian street vendor Mohammed Bouazizi is the symbol and launcher of the Arab Spring. Bouazizi's self-immolation on December 17, 2010, opened a new era in Tunisia and the MENA region. His suicide prompted a series of street protests in Tunisia that culminated in the collapse of the Ben Ali regime and inspired uprisings elsewhere in the Arab world. The army played a crucial role in the success of the Tunisian revolution. The army was initially deployed to impose security, but the military's ultimate refusal to fire on protesters allowed the revolution to succeed (Joffé 2011, 519). Had the army reacted differently, the Tunisian rebels would probably have faced brutal repression, and the country might have suffered the chaos and civil war we currently see in Syria, Yemen, and Libya. In this way, the army was one of the leading actors in the Tunisian revolution, whereas the police were hostile and aggressive toward the rebels. Police forces in Tunisia both before and after the Arab Spring were seen as proregime and were viewed negatively by the public (Aleya-Sghaier 2014, 46–47).

Although military coups are a main characteristic of Middle Eastern states, Tunisia gained its independence without a coup d'état. Moreover, the power of the Tunisian army was restricted by Habib Bourguiba and Zine El Abidine Ben Ali in order to protect their regimes. The army was positioned to defend the country against external threats and cooperate with police forces on domestic security issues (Taylor 2014, 73–75). Political restrictions and the limited capacity of the army led them to favor the protesters during the Arab Spring in Tunisia.

Before the Arab Spring, Tunisia's policy with regard to its neighbors (Algeria and Libya, in particular) was cautious, lest the instability in those countries affect Tunisia's own security (Sorenson 2014, 385). After the revolution, Tunisia was able to hold two elections, have a successful democratic transition, and maintain relative political stability. In the 2011 elections, the moderate Islamist party Ennahda won a majority in parliament, but in the 2014 elections voters preferred the secular Nidaa Tounès (Call of Tunis) party, which won 85 of the 217 seats in parliament. Both elections indicate that Tunisia was able to attain democratic consolidation after its Arab Spring uprising, a model that remains unique in the Middle East.

Despite its successful democratic elections and political transition after the revolution, Salafi jihadism poses a serious security concern in Tunisia. Jihadist-Salafi groups such as Ansar al-Shari'a and al-Qaeda took advantage of the new freedoms during the democratic transition to regroup. The release of many prisoners and the return of former jihadist leaders from exile enabled these groups to gain new recruits. Young men join these groups not only because of poverty or lack of education, but also because these groups symbolize "power and identity" (Khatib 2014). From another point of view, the lack of successful political transition and ongoing civil war in Libya after the fall of Qaddafi jeopardize the security of the border between the two countries. Uncontrolled border crossings allowed easy passage of weapons and fighters from Libya into Tunisia. The Syrian civil war and the expansion of the area under ISIS's control also attracted young Tunisians to join jihadist groups (Malka 2015, 99–100). Jihadists have been blamed for the assassination of two secular politicians in Tunisia in 2013, as well as the attack on the Bardo National Museum in Tunis on March 18, 2015, that killed twenty-two people and injured fifty. The Bardo museum attack was symbolically significant because of the museum's location next to the Parliament building. The attack aimed to undermine the economy by targeting a popular tourist destination. Another such attack was staged on June 26, 2015, when a gunman opened fire on tourists at a beach and in the lobby of the Hotel Riu Imperial Marhaba near the city of Sousse, Tunisia, killing thirty-nine people. Tunisian president Beji Caid Essebsi placed the country on high alert and declared, "Tunisia is in a war against terrorism" (BBC 2015). ISIS claimed responsibility for both terrorist attacks, highlighting the linkage between threats to Tunisia's security and ISIS's activities in the region, the ongoing civil war and insecurity in Libya, and increased extremist activity near the Algerian border. Security challenges are a top priority for the Tunisian government, especially since the Tunisian economy is highly dependent on tourism and foreign investments (Pierini 2015). Rached Ghannouchi, cofounder of Ennahda, recognized the linkage of Tunisian security to the situation in Libya when he observed, "If the situation in Libya isn't resolved, Tunisia will remain under attack" (Doucet 2015).

Therefore, despite Tunisia's successful democratic transition, regional instability directly impacts its economy and security and threatens to jeopardize the sole success story of the Arab Spring.

Libya

Mu'ammar al-Qaddafi seized control of Libya through a coup d'état that toppled King Idris I on September 1, 1969. He was strongly influenced by the Arab nationalism and socialism of Egyptian president Gamal Abdel Nasser, adopting his slogan ("Freedom, socialism, unity") and imitating his speeches. In 1977 he announced that the country would thenceforth be known as the Libyan Arab Jamahiriyya. *Jamahiriyya* is a neologism meaning "government of the masses"; the apparatus of the state was to be dismantled, and the people were to rule themselves through popular committees. Qaddafi's three-volume *Green Book*, published in 1975, 1977 and 1979, was to be the main source of norms and rules regulating administration. In reality, the government remained autocratic. Libyan relations with regional and global actors were problematic; Qaddafi supported terrorist and liberation organizations in diverse countries and was linked to a number of specific terrorist acts (Danahar 2013, 348–49). Libya attracted the attention of Western countries because of its support for terrorism rather than because of any strategic importance in the region (Chivvis 2013, 21–23). Although Qaddafi tried to normalize and rebuild relations with Western countries in the 2000s, the Libyan people remained discontented with his government.

After forty-two years of Qaddafi's repressive rule, Libyans were inspired by the Tunisian and Egyptian revolutions that brought about the fall of autocratic regimes in those countries. The Libyan uprising was touched off by the arrest of a well-known attorney, Fathi Terbil, in February 2011; Terbil represented the relatives of some 1,270 prisoners gunned down by security forces at Abu Salim prison on June 29, 1996. Relatives of some of these prisoners held a protest in Benghazi on February 15, 2011; using the language of the Egyptian uprising, they called for a "day of rage" to protest Terbil's arrest. The government's violent response to peaceful protests rapidly led regime opponents to take up arms. By the end of February, the regime had lost control of Benghazi, on the eastern shore of the Gulf of Sidra, and Misrata, on the Gulf's western shore. In March 2011, Qaddafi's forces pushed back the rebels with brutal force, alarming people around the world about the potential of a massive slaughter of regime opponents. Citing the "Responsibility to Protect" principle adopted in 2005, the UN Security Council passed Resolution 1973 on March 17, 2011, which authorized an international campaign of air strikes against the Libyan regime, with the stated goal of protecting civilians. Ultimately, NATO forces went beyond the mandate to protect and forced the downfall of the regime. On August 23, 2011, rebels captured Qaddafi's compound in Tripoli. After a bloody battle in Qaddafi's hometown of Sirte beginning on September 15, Qaddafi was captured and violently killed at the hands of vengeful rebels on October 20, 2011.

Libya was a source of insecurity and instability in North Africa before the Arab Spring (Zoubir and Dris-Aït-Hamadouche 2013, 79), and it remained so in its wake. The National Transitional Council, formed in March 2011, took over state administration immediately after Qaddafi's death and remained in power until general elections held in July 2012 allowed the General National Congress (GNC) to take power on August 8, 2012. However, because of the rise of competing armed groups, a lack of political consensus, and the capture of cities by terrorist groups, Libya continued to face great security risks in the postrevolutionary era.

The most important security risk and challenge for Libya was the collapse of all existing institutions immediately after the revolution. In the absence of legally authorized security forces, the gap was filled by local armed groups. The new government's attempts to unite these groups to form an official, legal security structure failed, heralding a new crisis and further threats to public security; armed groups were able to reinforce their power and exercise control throughout the country (Mangan and Murtaugh 2014, 12–13). The rising power of nonstate actors and militias deepened political polarization and regional discrimination. Diplomatic missions became a major target of attack: al-Qaeda attacked the US consulate in Benghazi on September 11, 2012, killing US ambassador Christopher Stevens and three other Americans; the embassies in Tripoli of France, Pakistan, the United Arab Emirates, and Russia were all attacked in 2013; the embassies of Egypt and the United Arab Emirates were attacked on November 13, 2014; and the embassies of Algeria, Iran, South Korea, Morocco, Spain, and Tunisia were all attacked in the first half of 2015. Humanitarian groups, airports, and hotels also came under attack. The large number of terrorist attacks provides solemn testimony to the weakness of the state and the gravity of the security crisis in Libya. The duality in the security sector and the government's failure to control the militias produced a security dilemma and political fracture.

Libya faced a new civil war in 2014 with the launch of Operation Dignity by General Khalifa Haftar, a Libyan general, against Islamist militias in Benghazi. In response to Haftar's operation, militias in Misrata, with the support of other militias in the West, joined to form Libya Dawn (*Fajr Libya*), which battled government forces and seized control of Tripoli's international airport (Office of the Commissioner General for Refugees and Stateless Persons 2014, 20–21).

The Libyan general elections of 2014, intended to form a house of representatives to replace the GNC, brought a new political impasse. The GNC did not dissolve; on the contrary, the house of representatives took its seat but was forced to flee Tripoli after the elections and take refuge in the eastern town of Tobruk. Libya was divided both politically and in terms of the security forces, deepening the divide among local tribal actors and militias.

Once again, the failure of state building in Libya drew the attention of the international community. The United Nations Support Mission in Libya, led by the special representative of the secretary-general, Bernardino León, has been urging all parties to come together for a peaceful solution to the government crisis. The UNSMIL's role in unity dialogues has failed to inspire confidence; no progress has been achieved in the continuing negations. Furthermore, the ongoing civil war in Syria and chaotic conditions in Iraq have created new insecurity and threats, as ISIS has grown in power and captured large territories in the region, encouraging extremism and recruiting youth from all over the globe. ISIS in Libya first captured international attention when militants linked to ISIS beheaded twenty-one Egyptian Christians in Sirte on February 15, 2015. ISIS's activities in Libya have constituted a major security threat to Libya and its neighbors and a signal to the entire Mediterranean and southeastern Europe that its violence can extend beyond the Arab world.

In the postrevolutionary era, the security situation in Libya is alarming and threatens the region as a whole. The failure to control numerous militias and the ongoing government crisis demonstrate that Libya has finally become the "stateless state" that Qaddafi had claimed in 1977, though undoubtedly not as the erstwhile leader had envisioned. Terrorist groups in Libya take advantage of the chaotic situation to cross borders, smuggle arms, and recruit in other countries. Libya's ongoing crises and chaos have the potential to prompt a second international military intervention.

Morocco

Unlike Tunisia, Libya and Egypt, the Arab Spring did not bring about regime change in Morocco or Algeria. The protests that began in Morocco on February 20, 2011, did not demand the removal of King Mohamed VI from the throne; rather, they demanded constitutional and political reform. Although Moroccan security forces forcibly broke up some of the protests, they did not open fire on them, and there were no fatalities. Instead, in a televised speech on March 9, King Mohamed VI promised comprehensive reforms, laying the groundwork for a relatively smooth political transition. This approach was facilitated by reform moves the king had launched before the protests began. He initiated a social, cultural, economic, and political reform package aimed at establishing a "'Moroccan-style' democracy" (Sater 2011). Morocco's democratization process was nonetheless limited by the status of the king as commander of the faithful (*amir al-mu'minin*) and the main political actor in the kingdom (Darif 2014, 121). The 20 February movement's demands did not threaten the particularities of the king's status.

The strategy of the monarchy in response to protesters' demands was to pledge constitutional changes that would guarantee human rights and grant more powers to the parliament. After a new constitution was passed through a national referendum on July 1, 2011, the "modernist Islamist" Justice and Development Party (Parti de la Justice et du Développement), inspired by the Turkish party of the same name (the Justice and Development Party), won the parliamentary elections held in November 2011. Since then the PJD has been head of the ruling coalition. The adoption of a new constitution and gradual power sharing allowed Morocco a smooth transition process, although the monarch continues to dominate the political system. The uncertain outcomes of the uprisings in other Arab countries led Moroccans to be wary of seeking a dramatic regime change that would adversely affect political stability. Morocco's Arab Spring experience has been characterized as a "gentle revolution" (Lewis 2011).

Although the dominant Islamist group in Morocco is the moderate PJD, Morocco has had its share of extremists who have launched terrorist attacks in the country, such as a massive coordinated attack by a dozen suicide bombers in four different locations in Casablanca on May 16, 2003, killing thirty-three civilians, and the bombing of a café in Marrakesh on April 28, 2011, that killed seventeen people. At least fifteen hundred Moroccans have joined ISIS to fight in Iraq and Syria, and hundreds have gone to train with them in Libya (Winsor

2016). In March 2016, the Moroccan government announced the discovery of ISIS cells in the country that were planning terrorist attacks. Morocco's geographical proximity to Europe makes it an attractive launching point for terrorist attacks against Europe. Indeed, Moroccans have been involved in terrorist attacks in Europe; Morocco's northern Rif mountains are said to have become "a breeding ground for Europe's jihadi terrorists" (Jacinto 2016). Morocco has been trying to strengthen its cooperation with the United States against terrorism (Arieff 2013, 6–7). Hence, despite its relative political stability, Morocco's security is adversely affected by the ongoing civil wars in Libya and Syria and increased activities by ISIS and other extremist groups in Tunisia and Algeria.

Algeria

Despite the fact that 23 percent of the Algerian population lived below the poverty line and 10 percent were unemployed (but 21 percent or higher of the youth), and with a high cost of living, the Arab Spring largely bypassed Algeria (Dennison 2014, 3). Nonetheless, protests began on December 28, 2010, and continued episodically over the next two months. While corruption and restrictions on the freedom of speech were among the protesters' complaints, their main grievances were economic: unemployment, a lack of affordable housing, a sharp spike in food prices, and generally poor living conditions. The government responded with food subsidies, increasing the supply of wheat; increased public spending by 25 percent, including funds for public housing and salaries, creating "soft loan facilities for the youth"; and lifting the state of emergency that had been in place for nineteen years (ibid.). What Morocco achieved through constitutional change, Algeria did through measures that were largely economic. It was able to do so thanks to the oil and gas revenue that has enabled President Abdelaziz Bouteflika to remain in power since 1999. Whether these welfare measures will be enough to guarantee long-term stability remains unknown. On the one hand, promised political reforms have not materialized, and corruption remains rampant. On the other hand, Algerians have reason to fear the consequences of shaking the boat too vigorously.

Algerians' reticence to wage a large campaign demanding reform can be explained by the vivid memory of the civil war following the military coup on January 13, 1992, that preempted the expected victory of the Islamic Salvation Front in national elections. As many as two hundred thousand people died in that brutal catastrophe, which traumatized the country and left its people wary of provoking new violence. This wariness has been reinforced by instability and turmoil in other countries where governments were brought down by the Arab Spring uprisings.

Algeria plays a key role in the international energy market, especially in the supply of energy to Europe. It ranks tenth in world gas reserves and third in supplying natural gas to Europe (Le Sueur 2014, 12). Hence, Algeria's political stability and domestic security are important to both regional and global politics. In the aftermath of the Arab Spring uprisings, Algeria faced security threats from migrants fleeing conflict in neighboring countries and illegal trafficking from Libya and Mali. The Algerian government felt threatened by the potential of demands for democratic reform, but even more by the rising power of Islamists in the region—both Islamist parties coming to power in Tunisia, Morocco, and Egypt through the electoral process and radical Islamist groups seizing territory and conducting terrorist operations in countries with which Algeria shares a border: Libya, Mali, and Niger.

The Qaddafi regime was supported in part by expatriate forces from African countries, including Tuaregs from Mali and Niger. After his regime collapsed, a Tuareg separatist group, the National Movement for the Liberation of Azawad in northern Mali, revolted against Mali's central government, using weapons brought from Libya. The revolt was rapidly taken over, however, by two radical Islamist groups, Ansar Dine and al-Qaeda in the Maghreb. Despite pressures from the European Union to take an active role in promoting security in the region, the Algerian government chose not to involve itself in the conflict on its border in Mali, fearing possible

Islamist retaliation in their own country, where security remains fragile. But in January 2013 it allowed France to fly through Algerian airspace to stop the extremists in Mali. The Islamist response was swift and brutal: on January 16, 2013, 32 terrorists from an al-Qaeda-affiliated group calling itself "Those Who Sign in Blood" attacked the In Amenas gas plant in eastern Algeria, near the Libyan border. The plant, which supplies 10 percent of Algeria's natural gas production, was operated by the Algerian state oil company, Sonatrach, jointly with British Petroleum and Statoil, a Norwegian firm. Three of the attackers were Algerian; the others were from eight different countries, including 11 from Tunisia and 2 from Canada. Some 686 Algerians worked at the plant, along with 146 foreigners. Determined not to negotiate with terrorists, the Algerian government brought in helicopter gunships. By the time it was all over, four days later, 37 foreign hostages, 29 terrorists, and an Algerian security guard had been killed. The attack was a shock in part because the plant was considered to be quite secure, with approximately 150 gendarmes on site (ibid., 9). It was a bitter reminder of Algeria's vulnerability to attacks across its borders, especially from Libya and Mali. Algerian prime minister Abdelmalek Sellal commented, "We would need two NATOs to monitor our borders" (Nossiter and Cowell 2013).

The economic incentives the Algerian government gave to protesters in 2011 are threatened by the falling prices of oil on the global market. The collapse of oil prices in 1986 is seen as a direct contributor to the unrest preceding Algeria's brief democratic opening that collapsed into civil war in the 1990s. The government has reassured its people that Algeria can withstand the current slump in the oil market, but it has nonetheless frozen hiring in the public sector and postponed large public projects in an attempt to economize. High youth unemployment and housing shortages drive hundreds of young people to seek refuge in Europe (Buzzetti 2015). Algeria's economy is also threatened by corruption. As one author noted, "Part of the 'rentier state bargain' is a tacit understanding on the part of Algeria's population that while they accept a wide range of controls on their personal and political freedoms, the government will at least manage the country's natural resources wisely" (Dennison 2014, 5). Unrest is likely to increase if the Algerian government proves unable to provide adequately for its people.

Conclusion

This chapter analyzed the security challenges that Tunisia, Libya, Morocco, and Algeria faced after the Arab Spring. The Arab uprisings brought an end to business as usual for the autocratic regimes of North Africa. Each of these countries experienced the Arab Spring differently: Tunisia had a relatively successful revolution and democratic transition; the governments of Morocco and Algeria calmed protests in those countries by making political and economic concessions, respectively; and Libya, which responded to protests with the greatest severity, was overthrown with the aid of international military intervention. Despite these differences, all four countries face increased security challenges in the postrevolutionary era. The euphoria that followed the collapse of regimes in Tunisia, Egypt, and Libya has given way to careful politicking in Tunisia, the return of military rule in Egypt, and utter chaos in Libya, and all countries of the region have become more susceptible to terrorist attacks. As one commentator wrote, "The Arab Spring has morphed into the War on Terror" (Helman 2013). The failure to build coherent state institutions after the toppling of the Qaddafi regime and the move of jihadist groups linked to al-Qaeda and ISIS into the power vacuum have deepened existing insecurity in the entire region and have made border security a top priority for its neighbors. The humanitarian crises precipitated by the Arab Spring have also driven thousands to seek refuge in Europe. The more Libya's security situation worsens, the more regional security will be threatened. In the postrevolutionary era, the struggle to find peaceful resolutions and bring political stability to the Libyan crisis will determine the future of security in the entire Mediterranean.

Sources Cited

Aleya-Sghaier, Amira. 2014. "The Tunisian Revolution: The Revolution of Dignity." In *Revolution, Revolt, and Reform in North Africa: The Arab Spring and Beyond*, edited by Ricardo René Larémont, 30–52. London and New York: Routledge.

Ammour, Laurence Aïda. 2012. "New Security Challenges in North Africa after the 'Arab Spring.'" Geneva: Geneva Centre for Security Policy. https://www.files.ethz.ch/isn/143681/GCSP_PP_1204.pdf.

Arieff, Alexis. 2013. "Morocco: Current Issues." Congressional Research Service, Oct. 18. https://www.fas.org/sgp/crs/row/RS21579.pdf.

BBC. 2015. "Tunisia Attack on Sousse Beach 'Kills 39.'" June 27. http://www.bbc.com/news/world-africa-33287978.

Buzzetti, Pilar. 2015. "Algeria, Serious Risks to the Economic and Political Stability." *Mediterranean Affairs*, June 8. http://mediterraneanaffairs.com/algeria-serious-risks-to-the-economic-and-political-stability/.

Chivvis, Christopher S. 2013. *Toppling Qaddafi: Libya and the Limits of Liberal Intervention*. Cambridge: Cambridge Univ. Press.

Coupe, Jeffrey A., and Hamadi Redissi. 2014. "Tunisia." In *The Middle East*, edited by Ellen Lust, 789–829. 13th ed. Los Angeles: Sage.

Danahar, Paul. 2013. *The New Middle East: The World after the Arab Spring*. New York: Bloomsbury Press.

Darif, Mohammed. 2014. "Morocco: A Reformist Monarchy?" In *Revolution, Revolt, and Reform in North Africa: The Arab Spring and Beyond*, edited by Ricardo René Larémont, 105–24. London and New York: Routledge.

Dennison, Susi. 2014. "Algeria after the Arab Spring: Vindicated Model or Regime on the Rocks?" In *Algeria Three Years after the Arab Spring*, by Daniela Huber, Susi Dennison, and James D. Le Sueur, 3–8. Washington, DC: German Marshall Fund of the United States.

Doucet, Lyse. 2015. "Tunisia Museum Attack Tests Transition." BBC News, Mar. 22. http://www.bbc.com/news/world-africa-32011143.

Helman, Christopher. 2013. "Algeria Attack Shows the Arab Spring Morphing into the War on Terror." *Forbes*, Jan. 18. http://www.forbes.com/sites/christopherhelman/2013/01/18/algeria-attack-shows-the-arab-spring-morphing-into-the-war-on-terror/.

Jacinto, Leela. 2016. "Morocco's Outlaw Country Is the Heartland of Global Terrorism." *Foreign Policy* (Apr. 7). http://foreignpolicy.com/2016/04/07/the-rif-connection-belgium-brussels-morocco-abdeslam/.

Joffé, George. 2011. "The Arab Spring in North Africa: Origins and Prospects." *Journal of North African Studies* 16 (4): 507–32. doi:10.1080/13629387.2011.630881.

Khan, Mohsin, and Karim Mezran. 2014. "No Arab Spring for Algeria." Atlantic Council, May. http://www.atlanticcouncil.org/publications/issue-briefs/no-arab-spring-for-algeria.

Khatib, Lina. 2014. "Tunisia's Security Challenge." Carnegie Endowment for International Peace, Nov. 26. http://carnegieendowment.org/2014/11/26/tunisia-s-security-challenge-pub-57289.

Layachi, Azzedine. 2014. "Algeria: Untenable Exceptionalism during the Spring of Upheavals." In *Revolution, Revolt, and Reform in North Africa: The Arab Spring and Beyond*, edited by Ricardo René Larémont, 125–47. London and New York: Routledge.

Lesser, Ian O. 1993. *Security in North Africa: Internal and External Challenges*. Santa Monica, CA: RAND Project Air Force. http://www.rand.org/pubs/monograph_reports/MR203.html.

Le Sueur, James D. 2014. "Algeria, the Arab Spring, and the Specter of Jihad." In *Algeria Three Years after the Arab Spring*, by Daniela Huber, Susi Dennison, and James D. Le Sueur, 9–15. Washington, DC: German Marshall Fund of the United States.

Lewis, Aidan. 2011. "Why Has Morocco's King Survived the Arab Spring?" BBC News, Nov. 24. http://www.bbc.com/news/world-middle-east-15856989.

———. 2015. "Tunisia Museum Attack: 'Arab Spring' Pioneer under Threat." BBC News, Mar. 20. http://www.bbc.com/news/world-africa-31978874.

Malka, Haim. 2015. "Tunisia: Confronting Extremism." In *Religious Radicalism after the Arab Uprisings*, edited by Jon B. Alterman, 92–121. Lanham, MD: Rowman and Littlefield.

Mangan, Fiona, and Christina Murtaugh. 2014. "Security and Justice in Post-revolution Libya: Where to Turn?" United States Institute of Peace, Sept 17. http://www.usip.org/publications/security-and-justice-in-post-revolution-libya.

McQuinn, Brian. 2013. "Assessing (In)security after the Arab Spring: The Case of Libya." *PS: Political Science & Politics* 46 (4): 716–20. doi:10.1017/S1049096513001170

Nossiter, Adam, and Alan Cowell. 2013. "Algeria Says at Least 37 Foreigners Dead in Siege." *New York Times*, Jan. 21. http://www.nytimes.com/2013/01/22/world/africa/algeria-hostage-siege.html?hp&_r=0.

Office of the Commissioner General for Refugees and Stateless Persons, Netherlands Ministry of Foreign Affairs, Netherlands Ministry of Security and Justice, Landinfo, and Lifos. 2014. "Libya: Militias, Tribes and Islamists." Dec. 19. http://www.landinfo.no/asset/3025/1/3025_1.pdf.

Perito, Robert M. 2015. "Security Sector Reform in North Africa: Why It's Not Happening." Security Sector Reform Resource Center, Jan. 7. http://www.ssrresourcecentre.org/2015/01/07/security-sector-reform-in-north-africa-why-its-not-happening/.

Pierini, Marc. 2015. "Tunisia's Difficult Road to Security and Diversity." Carnegie Europe, Apr. 2. http://carnegieeurope.eu/publications/?fa=59616.

Sater, James N. 2011. "Morocco's 'Arab' Spring." Middle East Institute, Oct. 1. http://www.mei.edu/content/morocco%E2%80%99s-%E2%80%9Carab%E2%80%9D-spring.

Sorenson, David S. 2014. *An Introduction to the Modern Middle East.* 2nd ed. Boulder, CO: Westview Press.

Taylor, William C. 2014. *Military Responses to the Arab Uprisings and the Future of Civil-Military Relations in the Middle East: Analysis from Egypt, Tunisia, Libya, and Syria.* New York: Palgrave Macmillan.

Winsor, Morgan. 2016. "As ISIS Expands in North Africa, Morocco Faces Rising Threat of Islamic State Group Terrorism." *International Business Times*, Jan. 14. http://www.ibtimes.com/isis-expands-north-africa-morocco-faces-rising-threat-islamic-state-group-terrorism-2263641.

Zoubir, Yahia H., and Louisa Dris-Aït-Hamadouche. 2013. *Global Security Watch: The Maghreb: Algeria, Libya, Morocco, and Tunisia.* Santa Barbara, CA: Praeger.

Part Two

Human Rights in the Middle East

6

Islam, Non-Muslim Minorities, and Human Rights in the Middle East

VALERIE J. HOFFMAN

The Middle East has been convulsed in the past decade with public protests and revolutions demanding freedom, democracy, and dignity, key components of human rights. This part of the book explores this important theme. The current chapter discusses the ways that human rights have been defined in international conventions, debates about the universality of human rights and about the compatibility of human rights with Islamic teachings, the problems of pervasive authoritarianism and the abuse of power in the Middle East, and the legal disabilities of non-Muslim minorities in some Middle Eastern states. Tadros's chapter discusses sectarianism and the abuse of the rights of Coptic Christians in post-Mubarak Egypt. Rubenberg's chapter lays out the systematic abuse of Palestinian human rights in Israel and the Occupied Territories, an issue that lies at the heart of nearly seventy years of conflict.

Defining Human Rights

A human right is a universal moral right that belongs to human beings simply by virtue of being human. The United Nations' Universal

Portions of this chapter were previously published in Valerie J. Hoffman, "Muslim Perspectives," in *A Force Profonde: The Power, Politics, and Promise of Human Rights*, edited by Edward A. Kolodziej, 45–68 (Philadelphia: University of Pennsylvania Press, 2003).

Declaration of Human Rights (UDHR), endorsed by the General Assembly on December 10, 1948, is the foundation of international human rights law. The document recognizes "the inherent dignity and . . . the equal and inalienable rights of all members of the human family" as "the foundation of freedom, justice, and peace in the world." It declares that "the advent of a world in which human beings shall enjoy freedom of speech and belief and freedom from fear and want has been proclaimed as the highest aspiration of the common people." The document states that human rights are a common entitlement of all people, "without distinction of any kind, such as race, color, sex, language, religion, political or other opinion, national or social origin, property, birth, or other status," regardless of the nation or territory to which a person belongs. The rights proclaimed by this document include:

1. the right to life, liberty, and security of person
2. the right not to be enslaved
3. the right not to be subjected to torture or to cruel, inhuman, or degrading treatment or punishment
4. the right to recognition everywhere as a person before the law
5. the right to equal protection of the law, without discrimination
6. the right to take legal complaints to court
7. the right not to be subjected to arbitrary arrest, detention, or exile
8. the right, in the case of any criminal charge, to a fair and public hearing by an independent and impartial tribunal
9. the right to be presumed innocent until proved guilty
10. the right not to be subjected to arbitrary interference with one's privacy, family, home, or correspondence or to attacks upon one's honor and reputation
11. the right to freedom of movement and residence within the borders of each state
12. the right to leave any country, including one's own, and to return to one's country

13. the right to seek and to enjoy in other countries asylum from persecution
14. the right to a nationality and the right not to be arbitrarily deprived of one's nationality or denied the right to change one's nationality
15. the right to marry and to found a family
16. equal rights to men and women in marriage and divorce
17. marriage must be entered into only with the spouses' free and full consent
18. the right to own property alone as well as in association with others
19. the right not to be arbitrarily deprived of one's property
20. the right to freedom of thought, conscience, and religion, including the freedom to change one's religion or belief, and the freedom, either alone or in community with others, and in public or private, to manifest one's religion or belief in teaching, practice, worship, and observance
21. the right to freedom of opinion and expression; this right includes freedom to hold opinions without interference and to seek, receive, and impart information and ideas through any media and regardless of frontiers
22. the right to freedom of peaceful assembly and association and not to be compelled to join an association
23. the right to take part in the government of one's country, directly or through freely chosen representatives
24. the will of the people shall be the basis of the authority of government; this will shall be expressed in periodic and genuine elections that shall be by universal and equal suffrage and shall be held by secret vote or by equivalent free voting procedures
25. the right to social security
26. the right to work, to free choice of employment, to just and favorable conditions of work, and to protection against unemployment
27. the right to equal pay for equal work

28. the right to just and favorable remuneration ensuring for oneself and one's family an existence worthy of human dignity, and supplemented, if necessary, by other means of social protection
29. the right to form and to join trade unions for the protection of one's interests
30. the right to rest and leisure, including reasonable limitation of working hours and periodic holidays with pay
31. the right to a standard of living adequate for the health and well-being of oneself and of one's family, including food, clothing, housing, and medical care and necessary social services, and the right to security in the event of unemployment, sickness, disability, widowhood, old age, or other lack of livelihood in circumstances beyond one's control
32. the right to education

Are Human Rights Universal?

Are these human rights natural and self-evident, as the writers of the UDHR claim? Although representatives of non-Western countries took part in the drafting of the UDHR, the document reflects the values of the European Enlightenment and of Western society more generally. The UDHR is part of a larger package known as the International Bill of Rights, a name with a decidedly American flavor. Not surprisingly, some non-Western countries have seen the document as just one more offense in the West's long history of cultural imperialism—the imposition of Western values on non-Western countries. Riffat Hassan, for example, has written, "What needs to be pointed out to those who uphold the Universal Declaration of Human Rights to be the highest, or sole, model, of a charter of equality and liberty for all human beings, is that given the Western origin and orientation of this Declaration, the 'universality' of the assumptions on which it is based is—at the very least—problematic and subject to questioning. Furthermore, the alleged incompatibility between the concept of human rights and religion in general, or particular religions such as Islam, needs to be examined in an unbiased way" (Hassan n.d.).

A number of Muslim countries have claimed that some of the rights contained in the UDHR are incompatible with Islam, although the fact that Muslims disagree on these issues and do not object to the same rights or have the same basis for their objections undermines the notion of a universal "Islamic" objection to these rights (Mayer 2013, 22–26). Furthermore, the principles expressed in the UDHR reflect an ever more global aspiration of people around the world. Even Islamists have increasingly identified Islam with democracy and human rights (Hoffman 2010). The conflicting sentiments regarding the applicability of human rights in the non-Western world can be illustrated by audience reactions to a panel on female circumcision held at the University of Illinois at Urbana–Champaign in the 1990s: a man from China charged that human rights are a form of Western cultural imperialism, to which a man from Malawi retorted that he wants those rights for himself. Non-Westerners who claim that certain human rights are inapplicable to their own cultures are generally in a position of power and have a vested interest in not granting rights to those who are not. Although we must respect the perspectives of people who resist Western norms, any Westerner who declares that human rights belong only to Westerners may be said to engage in the worst sort of ethnocentrism.

Human Rights Problems in the Middle East

Human rights violations are a global problem from which no region of the world is exempt. Nonetheless, the Middle East has had more than its share of governments that have engaged in persistent abuses of human rights. Human rights problems in the Middle East include the persistence of authoritarianism and the abuse of power in much of the Middle East; lack of freedom of opinion, expression, and assembly in many countries; widespread use of arbitrary arrest and torture against dissidents; lack of political and social equality granted to religious and ethnic minorities; and the persistence of gender inequality and forced marriages. Another issue that has only recently come to widespread acceptance in the West is the rights of sexual minorities. This point has not yet emerged as a major issue in the Middle East, where there is little acceptance of nontraditional sexualities, although Iran has become a major venue of sex-change operations (Najmabadi 2013). The region has had to cope with far more urgent humanitarian crises.

Military conflict in many countries of the Middle East, especially Syria, Libya, Yemen, and Iraq, puts all human rights inherently at risk; today, a sizable population lacks the basic rights of life, liberty and security of their persons, let alone the other rights listed in the UDHR. But discussion of human rights has mainly to do with governments' abuse of authority, which is the focus of this chapter.

The Middle East has been home to some of the most notorious dictators in the world, including Saddam Hussein, Mu'ammar al-Qaddafi, Hafez al-Assad, and Bashar al-Assad, men who have imprisoned, tortured, and killed with impunity. The mass graves discovered after the fall of Saddam Hussein, the massacre of 1,270 prisoners at Abu Salim prison in Libya in June 1996, Hafiz al-Assad's brutal assault on the city of Hama in 1982—which killed anywhere from ten thousand to thirty thousand people—and the systematic killing of about 11,000 detainees in the custody of Bashar al-Assad's security forces between March 2011 and August 2013 (Black 2015) all speak to the horrific abuse of human rights in the region. The first three of these rulers are deceased, but the fourth maintains his grip on power, while ceding control of much of his country to rebel forces and the "Islamic State." The Islamic State, also known as ISIS or ISIL, lacks legitimacy in the international community and is unequaled in its brutality, as is clear from the stories told by recently rescued captives (Gordon 2015a), by a recent UN report that some 8,493 Iraqi civilians were killed and 15,782 Iraqis were injured by ISIS in the summer of 2014 alone, and by the discovery of mass graves in areas seized from them (Gordon 2015b).

Is There an "Islamic" Perspective on Human Rights?

There is no single Muslim perspective on the topic of human rights. Although virtually all Muslims believe that Islam guarantees human rights, there is a great deal of disagreement on specifics. Many Muslims believe that there is no incompatibility between Western notions of human rights and Islam; some would even argue for an Islamic derivation of Western human rights concepts. Islam has also often provided the idiom through which Muslims have expressed their demands for human rights in the face of the government oppression. On the other hand, Islamization programs instituted by governments have often involved human rights violations that have been justified in the name of Islam. There is broad divergence among Muslims on the definition of Islam itself and on the extent to which Islam contains within itself a comprehensive and unchangeable blueprint for society. It is virtually impossible to locate an authoritative definition of Islamic human rights.

The Nature of Islamic Law

Muslims sometimes claim that Islam is distinct from Christianity in that it is not only a religion but a complete way of life. This claim is based on the fact that the massive volumes of Islamic jurisprudence (*fiqh*) have something to say on all aspects of life, even the most mundane. Although the initial chapters deal with religious obligations, there are others that deal with social, economic, and political relationships. Islamic jurisprudence is concerned not only with commands and prohibitions but also with an ethical analysis of all acts, which are classified according to one of five categories: obligatory, recommended, permitted/neutral, reprehensible/disliked, or prohibited. Of these categories, only the first and last would concern government, as only these two would entail punishment for omission or commission. Although Muslim scholars were eager to classify the relative ethical value of acts, they rarely prescribed punishments unless they were already mentioned in the Qur'an for a similar or analogous situation. Even in cases for which scholars did prescribe penalties—for example, for neglect of obligatory prayer—these punishments have rarely been enforced by governments. Hence, despite the theoretical inclusion of all aspects of life in a publicly mandated system, from the beginning of Islam large segments of life were relegated de facto to the private sphere.

Despite slogans issued by Islamist groups like the Muslim Brotherhood or the Saudi regime proclaiming, "The Qur'an is our constitution," the legal content of the Qur'an is minimal, and it nowhere approaches the comprehensiveness of Islamic law. Islamic law is based not only on the Qur'an, which Muslims believe to be God's word, but also on Hadith, the huge and highly flawed body of literature that organizes under topical headings the various and often conflicting accounts of what the Prophet said and did. Concerning new issues that were not discussed in these two sources, qualified scholars exercised their individual judgment (*ijtihad*) through analogical reasoning based on a common motive or element existing between the new issue and precedents contained in the Qur'an and Hadith. Finally, the law is based on the consensus of scholars, such as it might exist.

Furthermore, Muslim scholars have allowed for differences of opinion on matters of law, differences that are often based on divergent hadith. Divergence of purportedly authentic textual sources and differences in legal interpretations are accepted in Islam. There is even a hadith to reassure Muslims concerning this: the Prophet allegedly said, "Disagreement among the legal scholars (*mujtahidin*) of my community is a blessing." As one European scholar of Islam observed, Islamic law is not a code of law but a discussion on the duties of Muslims (Gibb 1953, 68). The first attempt to codify Islamic law occurred in the eighteenth-century Ottoman Empire. Such attempts have always been problematic, because they inevitably eliminate the traditional allowance of different interpretations of the law.

We have established, then, that Islamic law is not monolithic and that there have been divergences in its interpretation. We also see, however, the high priority given to the model of the prophet

Muhammad as the basis for articulation of the law. What this primacy means is that the norms of a rudimentary seventh-century society, as reported and interpreted by Muslim scholars of the ninth century, became the basis of Islamic law. This issue has been problematic for Muslims trying to articulate a modern Islamic identity.

Conservatives, Modernists, and Fundamentalists

In order to give some structure to our discussion of Muslim perspectives on the application of Islamic law today, we will employ broad categories and terms that necessarily camouflage the very real diversity that exists within those categories: we may distinguish conservative Muslims, who claim that the model for the present is essentially that of the past, from modernist or liberal Muslims, who distinguish the essential, unchanging teachings of Islam from the social laws of the Qur'an, Hadith, and *fiqh*, which are tied to specific sociohistorical contexts and are inappropriate or even offensive for application in modern contexts. Modernists believe that the interpretation of Islamic law requires looking at the "spirit," purpose, or "moral thrust" of Qur'anic teachings, rather than following the letter of the law as traditionally understood (Rahman 1982; Cooper, Nettler, and Mahmoud 1998). Modernist Muslims believe that the liberal potential of Islam has been limited or stifled by concessions to human stubbornness, cruelty, and traditional culture. They believe that Islam embodies within itself the spirit of freedom, justice, and equality among people and that all laws purporting to derive from Islam that inhibit human rights are the result of the limitations and selfishness of the men who composed the books of Islamic law. Rather than examining the laws derived from Hadith and other ninth-century texts, modernists believe it is the responsibility of modern Muslims to examine the moral teachings of the Qur'an in a fresh light, to discern their high ethical values, and then devise laws embodying those values that are suitable for contemporary society and its aspirations. For modernists, what cannot change and evolve is stagnant and lifeless, and Islamic law as traditionally conceived is precisely such a lifeless and stifling body of tradition that has choked initiative and the spirit of freedom from Muslims for many centuries.

Some modernists, such as the Iranian Jamal al-Din al-Afghani (1838–97) and the Egyptian Muhammad ʻAbduh (1849–1905), saw the earliest Muslim community as embodying a flexibility, intellectual vitality, and liberality of spirit that must be recovered by modern Muslims in order for them to survive and prosper in the modern world. Other modernists, however, such as Lebanese scholar Nazira Zein-ed-Din (1908–76), Sudanese reformer Mahmoud Mohamed Taha (1909–85), and Tunisian historian Mohamed Talbi (born 1921), fault the early Muslim community for its inability to receive the true message of the Qur'an in its earliest egalitarian form, necessitating the imposition of regulations in the Medinese period of Muhammad's rule (622–632) that—according to them—were intended to die away in time.

Fundamentalists challenge both conservatives and modernists: they reject many aspects of Islamic tradition and claim to derive law and doctrine directly from the Qur'an and Hadith. Islamists belong to movements that aim to apply Islamic law as the foundation of political and social life. There have been a large number of such movements and their ideological approaches vary, but they tend to be fundamentalist in theology and conservative in jurisprudence. There are exceptions; Rached Ghannouchi, leader of Tunisia's Ennahda party, has often spoken as if he were a modernist. Hasan al-Turabi (1932–2016), an influential figure in modern Sudanese politics, cunningly employed Western vocabulary to give the impression that he was a democrat, but when he was the power behind the Bashir regime in Sudan he demonstrated authoritarian and fundamentalist tendencies.

Is Islam Compatible with Democracy?

Historical manifestations of states claiming validity on the basis of Islam have been highly variable, even in the premodern period. Advocates of democracy, socialism, and totalitarianism have all been able to find justifications in Islamic principles and precedents. Even if we admit that the basic feature of an Islamic state is that it applies

Islamic law, we find that "Islamic" states have been variable and highly selective in their application of that law. The questions of who has the authority to define an Islamic state, which precedents constitute genuine models for Islamic states, which interpretations and what parts of Islamic law should be applied in an Islamic state, and whether the Prophet ever even intended to establish a theocratic state are all hotly contested and debated among Muslims today.

We will attempt to answer the question of whether an "Islamic state" is compatible with democracy by comparing political theories based on Islamic law with the elements inherent in international standards of democracy.

Popular Sovereignty

Although many Islamists, such as the Egyptian Sayyid Qutb (1906–66) and the Indian/Pakistani Abul A'la Mawdudi (1903–79), have argued that sovereignty belongs to God and not to people, the combined thrust of the Qur'anic concept of human vicegerency (2:30) and the Qur'anic injunction "Rule among you shall be by consultation" (42:38) have often been interpreted as meaning nothing less than popular sovereignty. In practice, however, power in the Muslim world has often been concentrated in the hands of a single man and his cohorts. Before the creation of modern nation-states, there was no tradition of popular elections. The oath of allegiance (*bay'a*) given to the early caliphs has sometimes been seen as providing the foundation for an electoral process, but even when an actual selection by a group of people took place in premodern times, the group was always limited to a few leading Muslim men. The *bay'a* has also been theorized by some modern Muslims as a type of contract, but there are no procedures in Sunni law (that is, the interpretations followed by 87 percent of the world's Muslims) to remove rulers who fail to uphold their side of the contractual relationship; there is a good deal of discussion of this matter in the Ibadi school, which is neither Sunni nor Shi'ite and is followed by fewer than 1 percent of the world's Muslims. In the modern Middle East, elections that have taken place have often been flawed or fraudulent.

The Rule of Law

Even the direst Western critics of Islam have had to admit that Islamic tradition certainly contains a deep respect for the rule of law, which ought to bind the ruler as well as his subjects. Nonetheless, despite the existence of judicial courts that could rule independently of the opinion of the caliph, we have no instances in Sunni history of these courts actually functioning in such a way as to limit the authority of the ruler or remove him from office.

The Creation of Legislative Bodies

There is no tradition of legislative bodies in Islam before the creation of modern nation-states. Such bodies as do exist have often been rubber-stamp legislatures, lacking real power to create laws or to limit the power of the head of state. Until recently, Islamists often argued that the sharia is so complete that human legislation is both unnecessary and illegitimate. It is on this basis that Saudi Arabia resisted the formation of any representative body for decades. Nonetheless, many Islamists recognize the need to create laws that reflect both the ideals of Islam and the needs of modern societies. In its early years, Pakistan articulated the principle that laws should not be repugnant to the sharia. But when General Zia-ul-Haq overthrew Prime Minister Zulfikar Ali Bhutto in 1977, he inaugurated an Islamization program that was designed to implement sharia laws directly. The question of whether sharia laws as traditionally understood can foster economic prosperity and social harmony today is a matter of tremendous controversy among Muslims.

Freedom of Thought, Conscience, Religion, and the Press

Many Muslims cite the Qur'anic verse "There shall be no compulsion in religion" (2:256) to indicate that Islam favors freedom of thought, conscience, religion, and the press. Nonetheless, some Muslims believe that the legal weight of this passage was overridden by later-revealed verses that order Muslims to fight unbelievers "until idolatry is no more and God's religion reigns supreme" (2:193) and to slay unbelievers wherever they may be found (2:191). The policy of the early Muslim community was to deal harshly with polytheists but to allow Jews, Christians, and others who could be construed as monotheists, such as Zoroastrians or even Hindus, the freedom to practice their religion, provided they did not oppose Muslim rule, paid a special tax (*jizya*), and did not propagate their religion or repair existing houses of worship. The Qur'an says that God will harshly punish Muslims who renounce the faith (2:217), but Islamic law as written by Muslim scholars mandates capital punishment for apostates, an undeniable limitation on freedom of religion. Many modern Muslims, however, have embraced the notion of freedom of religion and believe that this concept is endorsed by Islam itself. They hold that the recourse to violence in the time of the Prophet was limited in scope and must be understood within that particular social context, when the renunciation of Islam was tantamount to a treasonous opposition to the state. When the Saudi representative to the United Nations protested the UDHR on the grounds that Islam does not condone freedom of religion, Pakistani representatives took great exception to this opinion (Mayer 2013, 22).

Although the press did not exist in the time of Muhammad or in the period when Islamic law was being formulated, poets often served as political satirists, and Muhammad was often the butt of poetic satire in the period before the Muslim conquest of Mecca. It is possibly significant that, when Mecca was conquered, a general amnesty was declared for all Meccans who had resisted Islam, except for the poets, who were executed. One would have to conclude that the model offered by the early Muslim community and traditional Islamic law is one that places severe constraints on these freedoms, although there are a number of contemporary Muslims who offer much more liberal interpretations. While nearly all Muslim countries constitutionally guarantee freedom of speech, this freedom is often curtailed by provisions excepting blasphemy. Governments are able to construe the statements of their opponents as either blasphemy or treason, thereby de facto prohibiting free speech.

A number of modern Muslim writers have advocated absolute freedom of religion. For Mohamed Talbi of Tunisia, faith has no meaning if there is no freedom of choice. He sees the human race as naturally and rightly fragmented and diverse in outlook and says that the refusal to deny equal validity to points of view other than one's own is against innate human nature (*fitra*) (Cooper, Nettler, and Mahmoud 1998, 133–35). *Fitra* is a concept broadly discussed in Islamic tradition, as Islam is described by the Qur'an as the religion that accords with the original pattern (*fitra*) upon which God created humanity. Mahmoud Taha of Sudan, who was executed in 1985 for his unusual interpretations of Islam, also proposed "absolute individual freedom" as a right enjoyed by all human beings, regardless of religion or race (Mahmoud 1998, 110). Talbi addresses the thorny issue of apostasy from Islam: "The cases of 'apostates' killed during the Prophet's life or shortly after his death are without exception those persons who, as a consequence of their 'apostasy,' turned their weapons against the Muslims, whose community was at that time small and vulnerable. The penalty of death appears in these circumstances as an act of self-defense." Talbi (1988) considers the issue of real apostasy largely theoretical, for Muslim conversion to other religions is rare in most of the world.

Rached Ghannouchi, leader of the Ennahda party in Tunisia, considers the application of the death penalty in the time of the Prophet and in the so-called War of Apostasy during the caliphate of Abu Bakr (632–34) to emanate from the point of view that apostasy is a political crime. He adds that there are "examples during and after the Prophet's life in which the apostate was not executed, but was forgiven." He points out that the Hanafi school of law does not allow the execution of a female apostate, since women are not expected to carry arms, "which supports the view that apostasy is a political crime left for the leader to judge the most appropriate method for its treatment." Ghannouchi favors freedom of belief and prohibition of compulsion, as it is in keeping with Qur'anic injunctions not to try to compel people to believe (10:99, 50:45). He explains that his refusal to sign a declaration condemning Ayatollah Khomeini's fatwa (legal opinion) issued in 1988 against Salman Rushdie was not because he agreed with the fatwa, but because he wanted the declaration to be more general, "defending the freedom of writers of any tendency and condemning the repression they are subjected to" (Ghannouchi 1998).

Nonetheless, calls for the application of the death penalty for apostasy have been made not only against individuals who have publicly disavowed Islam but also against individuals whose views have been deemed insufficiently Islamic. While the Salman Rushdie case is the most famous one in the West, the court conviction of Egyptian professor Nasr Hamid Abu Zayd of apostasy (with the intention of forcing the dissolution of his marriage), the execution of Mahmoud Taha in Sudan, and the assassination of secular journalist Farag Foda in Egypt and countless individuals from all walks of life in Algeria illustrate the possible ramifications of rigidity and intolerance, threatening even professing Muslims with charges of apostasy.

Freedom of Peaceful Assembly and Association

This issue is not a topic with which Islamic law deals, but there is an incident mentioned in the Qur'an that provides a fairly disturbing precedent in this regard. A group of Muslims in Medina had built a mosque in which they could meet and pray separately from the Prophet's mosque (the courtyard of which was right outside his wives' apartments, so it was virtually an extension of the Prophet's house, although a public space). The Qur'an describes this mosque as a rival and a source of discord and ordered it destroyed (9:107–10). This incident could give paranoid rulers a precedent legitimating the denial of the right of peaceful assembly and association.

Existence of Political Parties

The Qur'an looks unfavorably on any divisions among Muslims, and the Arabic word for political party, *hizb*, is mentioned with great disfavor in the Qur'an. The unity and brotherhood of all believers is emphasized in numerous verses, and the Qur'an speaks disparagingly of people who separate themselves from "the party of God" (*hizb Allah*, from which Hezbollah derives its name) to form separate factions (5:56, 30:31–32). Many modern heads of state have also decried the "factionalism" of political parties, thereby justifying the hegemony of a single ruling party.

Freedom from Arbitrary Arrest, Detention, Exile, Torture, and Cruel or Unusual Punishment

Although these issues are not discussed as such in Islamic law, there are innumerable Qur'anic verses and prophetic sayings enjoining justice and kindness, and it may be assumed that none of the impingements on human rights mentioned above would meet official approval among Muslim legal experts, despite the fact that they are common in the Middle East. Modernist and conservative Muslims agree that Islam accords full dignity to the individual. Islam is widely seen as a religion that promotes social justice among individuals, guaranteeing them the right to life, a minimal standard of living, and freedom from torture, seizure of their property, arbitrary imprisonment, or execution without just cause. Muslims generally agree that the weak elements of society, such as women and ethnic or religious minorities, should be protected by the state.

Nonetheless, many people, both Muslim and non-Muslim, fear the imposition of Islamic criminal law, which mandates penalties deemed harsh by contemporary standards. International Muslim reactions to the execution of sharia penalties may be illustrated by an exchange that came over a Muslim email network in east-central Illinois in the 1990s. One man wrote, "Praise be to God! Shari'a has come to Nigeria!" He proceeded to illustrate this joyous news with the description of the amputation of the hand of a cattle thief before a crowd of thousands of cheering onlookers. This message prompted the following response from another local Muslim: "We're talking about ripping somebody's hand off! Is this the kind of Islam we want to see? Wouldn't it be something if Muslims came up with a Shari'a-based law that gave greater honors and privileges to non-Muslims, so they would see that Islam is a religion of peace?"

Free Choice in Marriage

Islamic law grants fathers, grandfathers, and other guardians of minors and women the right to choose spouses and contract marriages for those in their care. Minors may dissolve the marriage bond by mutual agreement once they come of age. In the case of a woman marrying for the first time, her silence is often construed as consent, whereas a divorcée or widow must give explicit consent for marriage. The social reality of marriage is often even more coercive than these sharia regulations indicate, however, as women are frequently forced into marriages against their will, even when they express their aversion to the match. Although there have been significant social shifts in parts of the Middle East on this issue, with young people in urban areas in particular postponing marriage in order to pursue careers and education and insisting on having a say in the selection of their spouse, this issue remains an area of contention. The cultural constraints on marriage choices extend, however, even to guardians, because most schools of Islamic law require that a woman not marry beneath her social station. Furthermore, although Muslim men may marry Jewish or Christian women, according to Islamic law, Muslim women may only marry Muslim men. A traditional interpretation of Islamic marriage law would obviously not accord with modern notions of free choice in marriage. Nonetheless, Tunisia's Personal Status Law of 1956 allows men and women complete freedom in marriage, and its drafters saw this right as consonant with the spirit of Islam.

Equality of All Citizens before the Law

This most fundamental of all topics has been left for last, not because it is less important but precisely because it is the most problematic and requires detailed examination. The word *equality* (*musawat*) does not exist in the Qur'an, although the verses that proclaim the brotherhood of all Muslims are often taken today in the sense of equality. The Qur'an says that the only distinction among Muslims is in their piety (49:13). But the notion of human equality is clearly a Western import into the Muslim world, introduced in the wake of the French Revolution and Napoleon's conquest of Egypt. Nonetheless, of the three principles of the French Revolution—freedom, fraternity, and equality—it was the first two that appealed most to Westernizing Muslims. The concept of human equality is clearly problematic for a society accustomed to making divisions between Muslim and non-Muslim, male and female, and free versus slave, of which, in each category of paired opposites, those persons who fall into the first group are accorded significantly superior legal rights. Slavery was gradually abolished under British pressure, finally ending at the end of the nineteenth century. Constitutions drawn up in the newly modernizing nation-states until the last quarter of the twentieth century often granted Muslims and non-Muslims equal rights, but nations like Pakistan and Saudi Arabia, whose very raison d'être is Islam, found it far more difficult to allow such equality. Moreover, in most countries gender equality was never realized, even on paper, although a number of governments worked to improve women's legal status. The concept of human equality did make some headway in the early twentieth century, when the ideas of European socialism and Marxist communism became fashionable among some sections of the Westernized intelligentsia. "On the whole, however," wrote British scholar C. E. Bosworth, "Middle Eastern peoples have viewed the idea of human equality as a chimera, to which lip service is paid by political leaders in political manifestos, but which is rarely taken into account in practice" (1999).

Conservative Muslim Human Rights Documents

Ann Elizabeth Mayer, in her examination of conservative Muslim human rights documents, such as the Universal Islamic Declaration of Human Rights (UIDHR) and the Iranian constitution, finds that conservative Muslims assert that Islam endorses the principle of equality and requires equal treatment of individuals under the law, regardless of race, ethnicity, or language. Conspicuously absent is inclusion of gender and religion in the list of categories among which discrimination is not allowed. Just as eighteenth- and nineteenth-century Americans did not imagine that the egalitarianism articulated in the Declaration of Independence should apply to women or nonwhites, Muslims have generally been socialized to believe that the innate differences between the sexes go well beyond their reproductive roles and that men are inherently superior.

> Reading the English version [of the UIDHR], one could get the impression that many of the UIDHR provisions are subject to qualifications imposed by secular laws because the wording of the qualifications is consistently "according to the Law." Although the authors have obviously tried to mislead the readers of the English version by disguising the centrality of Islamic qualifications, in reality there is no similarity between the qualifications placed on rights in the UIDHR and those found in international law. After scrutiny, it turns out that in the UIDHR the *shari'a* is the law that qualifies rights when the term "according to the Law" is used. (Mayer 2013, 77)

Mayer discerns "a pattern of borrowing substantive rights from international human rights documents while reducing the protections that they actually afford. This is accomplished by restricting them so that the rights can only be enjoyed within the limits of the *shari'a*, which are unspecified. These emendations leave virtually unlimited discretion to states in deciding what the scope of the affected rights should be" (1991, 76).

The fact that the drafters of the UIDHR tried to pattern their document after the UDHR and camouflage divergence from it indicates their sensitivity to international opinion and their desire to be recognized in the international community as preserving human rights in their domains, even as they arrogate to their governments vast areas of authority to curtail human rights in the name of Islam.

Mayer sees in the writings of many conservative Muslim theorists on human rights a tendency to make individual rights subordinate to their obligations to the community, "a confusion of the traditional pattern of communal solidarity in premodern society and normative Islamic prescriptions, which are not viewed in relation to their original historical context. One sees the rejection of the idea that in the modern state there will naturally be conflicts between the competing interests of individual citizens and the government" (ibid., 64–65).

While Islamists (ideologues agitating for Islamic government) actively oppose governments they see as un-Islamic, they assume that it is the role of governments to take responsibility for the ethical character of the public arena (Ayubi 1991, 35). Their writings often reflect a vision of an idealized, altruistic society, in which government and society will naturally cooperate to bring about God's will on earth and advance the welfare of society, despite the fact that they readily acknowledge the absence of such a government and society since the time of the Prophet and his immediate four successors. Such a perspective is in radical opposition to the notion of constitutionalism, which places limitations on the power of the government over individual freedoms and guarantees the autonomy of different branches of government. The system of checks and balances assumes that self-interest is the main operative principle at the level of both individuals and government.

The UIDHR says that people have equal rights *under the sharia*, a code of law that retains discriminatory categories, making distinctions between free and slave, male and female, and Muslim and non-Muslim. Although slavery has no legal existence in the Muslim world anymore and most Muslims agree that it is a retrograde institution, application of the same assessment to sharia distinctions on the basis of sex and religion is much more problematic. The equality of which the UIDHR speaks is an equality of all Muslim men with each other and of all Muslim women with each other, not an equality of Muslim men and Muslim women or of Muslims and non-Muslims. As Mayer observes, "People are not being guaranteed the equal protection of a neutral law, but 'equal protection' under a law that in its premodern formulations is inherently discriminatory and thereby in violation of international standards" (2013, 91).

Regardless of the lack of real democracy and the reality of political oppression in much of the Muslim world, most Muslim theorists endorse the notions of democracy and free political expression. The problem is not, therefore, so much one of theoretical objections to democracy as that the regimes in power simply do not allow democracy to exist. Likewise, Muslim theorists would all agree on the equality of Muslim men, regardless of ethnicity, so the actual instances of persecution of ethnic minorities, such as the Kurds in Iran and Turkey, have no religious justification. However, the rights of women and religious minorities remain the most universally problematic theoretical human rights issues in the Muslim world, because they come into direct conflict with Islamic law and precedent.

Non-Muslims under Muslim Rule: Historical and Theological Perspectives

In addition to restrictions placed on religious minorities propagating their religions and repairing their houses of worship, the policy toward minorities attributed to the second caliph, ʻUmar ibn al-Khattab (ruled 634–44), was that Jews and Christians, in accordance with their "protected" (*dhimmi*) status, were denied the right to carry arms and were required to show their subservience to Muslims by not riding horses, by showing humiliating deference to any Muslim they passed on the road, and by wearing distinctive colors and belts that would immediately let people know of their inferior status. They were not to hold political office. Actual application of these rules has varied, and it is fair to say that Christians and Jews were treated relatively well under Muslim rule, compared to the treatment of Jews in medieval Christian Europe. Nonetheless, it is obvious that the second-class status accorded to "People of the Book" and the official intolerance of those persons not belonging to a recognized "heavenly" religion do not accord with modern international notions of human rights.

The social disadvantages of Jewish and Christian minorities were later reversed under European colonialism, as they were disproportionately represented in the new systems of modern education and in government bureaucracies. Muslims have often viewed non-Muslims with suspicion, as allies or potential allies of Islam's enemies, and such suspicions have naturally been exacerbated by events such as the Crusades and the establishment of a Jewish state in Palestine. The attacks on and intimidation of Jews in Arab countries in the 1950s are now finding an echo in attacks on and intimidation of Christians, leading to an exodus of many Arab Christians from their homelands. These attacks are often linked to radical Islamist groups, who see the presence of religious minorities as an impediment to the implementation of Islamic law in their countries. The imposition of sharia law in some northern Nigerian states prompted intense Muslim-Christian violence, and this issue also figured in the long civil war in Sudan (1955–72, 1983–2005). The treatment of minorities is clearly an area on which Islamists who favor the application of traditional Islamic law differ with liberals, who advocate complete equality of all citizens before the law.

Conservative Muslim Perspectives on the Rights of Non-Muslims

Conservative Muslims have sought to justify and preserve traditional discriminatory practices against non-Muslims, such as disallowing marriage between Muslim women and non-Muslim men and prohibiting the election of non-Muslims to high offices. The Iranian constitution explicitly limits recognized protected religious minorities to Iranian Zoroastrians, Jews, and Christians; Baha'is are excluded because only those monotheistic religions that existed prior to Islam are recognized, since Muslims see Islam as the completion and perfection of earlier forms of monotheism. Baha'ism, a faith that emerged in nineteenth-century Iran with Baha'ullah's claim of prophethood, challenges the finality of Islam and seeks converts among Muslims. Baha'is have, therefore, met with considerable persecution in Iran, both before and since the Iranian Revolution. In Pakistan members of another sect that emerged in the nineteenth century, the Ahmadis, see themselves as Muslims but are perceived as heretics by other Muslims; in 1974, bowing to pressure from Islamists, the Pakistani government declared Ahmadis to be non-Muslims. The consequences of failing to follow one of the "heavenly" religions are clear in the writings of the Iranian Sultanhussein Tabandeh in the 1960s: the non-Muslim who is neither a Jew nor a Christian is so base that he cannot be considered human. Those individuals who have not accepted the one God are "outside the pale of humanity" (Mayer 2013, 139). Baha'is and Ahmadis are further tainted by being of formerly Muslim ancestry. As is clear from the previous discussion on apostasy, most Muslims have not been able to tolerate the notion that a Muslim may change his religion.

In most Muslim countries, the application of Islamic law is limited to matters of personal status, and recognized religious minorities are allowed to follow the personal-status regulations of their own faith. In Egypt, for example, Coptic Christians cannot obtain a divorce, but Muslims can; therefore, the only option for Christians caught in an unhappy marriage is to convert to Islam. In matters of litigation involving Muslims and non-Muslims, judgment in an Islamic state (that is, a state in which all aspects of government are based on Islam) would be in an Islamic court, where non-Muslims may reasonably expect bias.

Modernist Muslim Perspectives on the Rights of Non-Muslims

Liberal Muslims often emphasize the essential unity of humanity as the foundation for religious equality and freedom, in addition to quoting the Qur'anic verse "There is no compulsion in religion" (2:256). Mohamed Talbi says, "To be a true Muslim is to live in courteous dialogue with peoples of other faiths and ideologies, and ultimately to submit to God. We must show concern to our neighbors. We have duties to them, and we are not islands of loneliness. The attitude of respectful courtesy recommended by the Qur'an must be expanded to embrace all mankind, believers and unbelievers, except for those who 'do wrong'—the unjust and violent, who resort deliberately to fist or argument" (Talbi 1998).

Humayun Kabir (1906–69), an Indian Muslim who remained in India after the partition of 1947, was concerned with Muslim coexistence not only with Jews and Christians but also with Hindus, who are the majority of the Indian population. He held that ethnic and religious diversity, with a balanced distribution of power among a number of different centers, is a source of strength for a nation and is the very essence of democracy. He recalled that the Qur'an itself says that all religions were initially the same (2:213) and that prophets have been sent to every country in every age, each bringing the message of God in the language of his people (14:4). If so many prophets were sent to Palestine within a few hundred years, he reasoned, surely many prophets must have been sent to such a vast and ancient country as India. He finds that the Vedas' description as *shruti* accords with the Qur'anic concept of revelation and that the Hindu concept of *avatar* is merely an Indian version of a prophet. He urges Muslims to recognize the truths embedded in Hinduism and Buddhism and to recognize Hindus and Buddhists as People of the Book, like Jews and Christians (Kabir 1998).

Religious Minorities in the Muslim Middle East Today

Attitudes and Policies toward Christians

The linkage between religion and nationalism has varied, as has the impact of that linkage on actual treatment of religious minorities. Nationalism, a solidarity based on shared ethnicity, language, history, or territory, entered the Middle East with colonialism and the movements of independence from Ottoman rule in Greece (1821–32) and the Balkan states in the nineteenth and early twentieth centuries. Nationalism need not be linked to religion. In Egypt and other Arab countries, nationalists in the nineteenth and early twentieth centuries debated the role of Islam in their national identity; some claimed a necessary linkage between Islam and Arab nationalism, while others insisted that, for example, Egypt must be for all Egyptians, including Egyptian Copts and Jews (Bezirgan 1981; Cleveland 1981; Jankowski 1981). Jamal al-Din al-Afghani believed that language is a more durable basis for national unity than religion and saw Europe's secular nationalism as the source of its strength (Afghani 1968, 56, 87).

The Ottoman Empire derived much of its legitimacy from Islam, but it made no attempt to force conversion to Islam and allowed the different religious communities in its domains to be largely self-governing, provided they paid taxes to the central government. The growth of nationalism led some non-Muslim minorities to demand equal status with Muslims. When the Ottomans violently suppressed Christian uprisings in the Balkans in 1875, the Great Powers of Europe (Britain, Russia, Prussia, Austria, and France) claimed the right to protect the empire's Christian minorities. The Armenian patriarch of Constantinople complained to the Powers of the extreme persecution of Armenians in Ottoman domains; entire Armenian communities were massacred during the Russo-Turkish War of 1877–78. In 1890 Sultan Abdul Hamid II created a paramilitary organization that was given free rein to deal with the Armenian population. Ottoman persecution of the Armenians culminated in the genocide of 1915–17, in which up to 1.5 million people were killed (Akcam 2004). Other Christian groups in Ottoman domains were similarly targeted for extermination (Levene 1998; Jones 2006). After the Ottomans were defeated in World War I, the Anatolian peninsula was to be divided among the Allied victors. But when Greece invaded Anatolia in 1919 to claim its part in the spoils, the Turks met the invasion with a popular nationalist resistance. The conflict was marked by atrocities on both sides. The solution to the conflict, proposed by the Greek prime minister to the League of Nations in October 1922, was a compulsory exchange of Greek and Turkish populations. As one scholar put it, "The League of Nations came to consider ethnic cleansing the best option for dealing with the refugee crisis" (Shields 2013).

Ironically, the establishment of the only avowedly secular republic in the Middle East was accomplished by creating an ethnicized religious identity, according to which 1.5 million Christians in Anatolia were labeled "Greek" and 500,000 Muslims in Greece were labeled "Turk." The population exchange resulted in near-religious uniformity in formerly diverse areas. As Shields (2015) wrote, "The leaderships inaccurately insisted that identity determined political goals, that religion could predict earthly loyalty, and that security could only come with the creation of a purified populace. Despite centuries of alternative realities, the new ideologies of the nation-state required a new form of 'sectarianism' whose manifestation was, simply, evil."

Not all nationalisms in the Middle East were similarly constituted, although Israel was also formed through the expulsion of non-Jews from parts of its territories. Christian Arabs were among the most ardent supporters of Pan-Arab nationalism, an ideology in which Islam would be accepted as a component of Arab national identity, but non-Muslim Arabs would enjoy equal status (Cragg 1991, 141–66). In the period of Pan-Arabism, from the late 1940s through the 1960s, Arab nations with a Muslim majority tended to de-emphasize the importance of religious difference; religion was subordinated to nationalism and socialism. Egypt's National Charter of 1962 stated that, "in their essence, all divine messages [that is, the Bible and the Qur'an] constituted human revolutions which aimed at the re-instatement of human dignity and happiness. It is the prime duty of religious thinkers, then, to preserve for each religion the essence of its divine message" (Haddad 1982, 28).

Nonetheless, Copts have not enjoyed total equality with Muslims in Egypt. They have encountered bias in obtaining jobs, especially in higher administration, and in obtaining grants to study abroad. The curriculum in public schools is explicitly Islamic. Radio and television are also full of Islamically oriented programming, whereas Christian programming is lacking. Christians are not allowed to build or repair churches without special permission (Hasan 2003). When the former Egyptian foreign minister Boutros Boutros-Ghali, was appointed UN secretary-general in 1992, Africans celebrated this first-time appointment of one of their own to the position, but many Egyptian Muslims were annoyed that the person so honored was a Copt.

Islamists in Egypt and other Arab countries with Christian minorities (Syria, Iraq, Palestine) have seen the presence of non-Muslims as an obstacle to the implementation of the sharia; the rising prominence of Islamism in the 1970s was accompanied by a rise in violent attacks on Christians (Kepel 1984, 195–201; Weiner 2005), which dramatically increased in the chaotic wake of the Arab Spring, as Tadros's contribution to this volume attests. Radical Islamists such as Sayyid Qutb and Osama bin Laden have cited Qur'anic verses that call Christians and Jews the enemies of the Muslims—for example, "Believers, take neither the Jews nor the Christians for your friends. They are friends of one another. Whoever among you seeks their friendship becomes one of them" (5:51). Less radical Muslims argue that these verses need to be understood within the context of the war between the Muslims of Medina and the pagans of Mecca, in which the Jews of Medina were accused of supporting the pagans. They point out that there are other verses of the Qur'an that take a very different attitude toward Christians and Jews. The Muslim Brotherhood has, over time, come to accept democracy as a legitimate system (Gerecht 2011) and has gradually moved toward affirming equal rights for non-Muslims, with the exception that only a Muslim could become the head of state. Shadi Hamid (2014), however, has argued that Islamists embraced democracy only under the pressure of participating in opposition political parties under authoritarian regimes and that once they come to power they embrace very different policies and values.

Attitudes toward Jews

The rise of Zionism, the surge in Jewish migration to Palestine in the early twentieth century, and the establishment of the state of Israel in 1948 led many Arab Muslims to regard Jews as enemies. The establishment of the state of Israel was followed by attacks on

Jewish populations in Arab countries, forcing most Jews in the Arab countries to flee (Aharoni 2003). Arab media and textbooks have frequently portrayed the Jews as innately immoral (Lewis 1986). A chapter on the prophet Muhammad's interactions with Jews in an Egyptian secondary school textbook emphasizes his benevolence and the Jews' treachery but omits any mention of the harsh sentence the Prophet pronounced against the Jews of Banu Qurayza for allegedly conspiring with the pagan Meccans against the Muslims in Medina—the execution of all their men and the enslavement of their women and children—except for an oblique statement that "the tables were turned on them" after the Meccans failed to take Medina. Not only does the textbook depict the Jews of Muhammad's day as ungrateful, petty, jealous, and treacherous, but it also says, "The Jews of yesterday are the same as the Jews of today and tomorrow, all cut from the same cloth [literally, made from a single lump of clay]. So it is necessary to study them and their ambitions and to arm oneself with every weapon against them. The Ramadan War [or the Yom Kippur War of October 1973], what preceded it, and its aftermath are a clear embodiment of the Jews' arrogance, deception, and disdain for all moral values" (Hashim et al. 2006–7, 74–77). Hence, thirty years after Egypt became the first Arab state to make a separate peace with Israel, Egyptian schoolchildren continued to be taught that Jews are innately crooked, devious, and devoid of morality.

While Jewish communities in Syria, Iraq, Yemen, Egypt, Morocco, and Algeria have all but vanished, a small Jewish community remains in Iran; estimates of its size vary from nine thousand to twenty-five thousand. The Jewish population is less than half as large as it was before the 1979 revolution. Jews have tried to compensate for their diminishing numbers by adopting new religious fervor: whereas before the revolution only a few old men went to the synagogue, now the synagogues are full. Tehran has eleven functioning synagogues, many of them with Hebrew schools, and it has two kosher restaurants, a Jewish hospital, an old-age home, and a cemetery. There is a Jewish representative in the Iranian parliament. A Jewish library holds twenty thousand titles, with a reading room adorned with a photograph of Ayatollah Khomeini. Before the revolution, Jews were well represented among Iran's business elite, holding key posts in the oil industry, banking, and law, as well as in the traditional bazaar. The wave of anti-Israeli sentiment that swept Iran during the revolution, along with large-scale confiscations of private wealth, sent thousands of affluent Jews fleeing to the United States or Israel. Khomeini met with the Jewish community upon his return from exile and issued a fatwa that the Jews were to be protected, as would Iran's tiny Christian minority. The societal shift toward religiosity affected Jews in Iran as well; some who had been secular in the 1970s began to keep kosher and observe rules against driving on the Sabbath. As many restaurants, cafés, and cinemas were closed in the wake of the revolution, the synagogue became a focal point for their social life (Hakakian 2014; Cohler-Esses 2015; Inskeep 2015; Sanasarian 2000).

A report by the International Federation of Human Rights (IFHR) on discrimination against religious minorities in Iran states, "The peculiarity of the Islamic Republic of Iran is not the mere fact that Islam is the religion of the State (other States share the same feature) but rather the fact that the State itself is conceived as an institution and instrument of the divine will. In this system, which can best be described as a clerical oligarchy, there is an identification between divine truth and clerical authority" (2003, 5). The report points out the many ways that the constitution of the Islamic Republic officially discriminates against religious minorities. Although Article 13 grants official recognition to Zoroastrians, Jews, and Christians and stipulates their religious freedom, the IFHR report demonstrates that these non-Muslim minorities nonetheless face discrimination in employment and upward mobility and points out that religion must be reported when applying for the general examination to enter any university in Iran.

Article 14 of the constitution guarantees that non-Muslims must be treated "in conformity with ethical norms and the principles of Islamic justice and equity [but not equality], and to respect their human rights." This principle applies only to those persons "who refrain from engaging in conspiracy or activity against Islam and the Islamic Republic of Iran" (ibid., 7).

Baha'is in Iran

Unlike Jews, Christians, and Zoroastrians, Baha'is are not a recognized minority in Iran and enjoy no legal protection to practice their religion. Baha'ism was established in Iran in 1863 by Mirza Husayn 'Ali Nuri, known as Baha'ullah (1817–92), as an outgrowth of an earlier movement, Babism. The overwhelming majority of Iranians belong to Twelver Shi'ism, which holds as a core doctrine the expected return of the twelfth imam as the Mahdi, who will "fill the world with justice, as it is now filled with iniquity." In 1844 Sayyid 'Ali Muhammad Shirazi (1819–50) claimed to be the "Bab" (Gate), meaning the Mahdi. As the Mahdi, the Bab signaled a break with Islam and the start of a new religious system, abrogating the provisions of Islamic law. The mullahs denounced Babis as apostates from Islam and enemies of God. Mobs attacked them, and many were tortured and publicly executed; the Bab himself was executed in 1850. In August 1852, two Babis attempted to assassinate the shah in revenge for the Bab's execution. In response, the government engaged in an extensive pogrom in which more than twenty thousand Babis lost their lives. The Bab allegedly foretold the coming of a person who would be a living manifestation of God. Baha'ullah claimed to be this person. He taught that humanity had reached a point of maturity that enabled every person to seek God and truth independently, thus calling into question the need for the clerics. Unlike the Bab, Baha'ullah forbade the use of violence. He tried to engage various governments in dialogue, but his claim to prophethood makes Baha'is apostates in the eyes of many Muslims.

At approximately three hundred thousand members, Baha'is are the largest religious minority in Iran. They are seen not only as apostates but also as supporters of the West and Israel; indeed, the global headquarters of Baha'ism is in Haifa. Between 1979 and 1989, more than two hundred Baha'is were killed or executed, hundreds more were tortured or imprisoned, and tens of thousands were expelled from schools and workplaces and denied various benefits, including registration of their marriages. Baha'i cemeteries, holy places, historical sites, administrative centers, and other assets were seized shortly after the 1979 revolution. Baha'is are allowed to bury their dead only in specifically designated wastelands, in which they are forbidden to mark individual graves or construct mortuary facilities. They are barred from attending legally recognized public and private institutions of higher education. In response, the Baha'i community established its own educational program, but the government has tried to suppress this initiative: faculty members have been arrested, and textbooks and other materials have been seized.

In early 1993, a secret government document was issued, "giving precise instructions for the slow strangulation of the Baha'i community" (ibid., 11). Measures include expulsion from universities and denial of employment. The document states, "A plan must be devised to confront and destroy their cultural roots outside the country" (19).

Authorities regularly disrupt Baha'i religious meetings, and the community has been ordered to dissolve all its administrative institutions (11). In 2001 a judge of the Supreme Office of Control and Review ruled that "seizure and confiscation of the properties belonging to the misguided sect of Baha'ism is legally and religiously justifiable" (12). Baha'is dismissed from their jobs because of their religious beliefs are deprived of their pensions, and some have been required to pay back pensions previously granted. The government also denies Baha'is the right to inherit (14).

After Mahmud Ahmadinejad became president in 2005, persecution of Baha'is intensified; hundreds were arrested. Since 2007 the Baha'i International Community (2015) has documented more than 780 incidents of economic persecution against Baha'is in Iran, including shop closings, dismissals, and the revocation of business licenses. In 2008 seven Baha'i leaders were arrested; in 2010 they were sentenced to twenty years' imprisonment. The Islamic Republic often states that arrested Baha'is are detained for security reasons. However, they have been offered their freedom if they recant

Baha'ism and convert to Islam, which indicates that their arrest has little to do with security.

On February 4, 2009, a group of Iranian artists and intellectuals wrote an open letter to the Baha'i International Community, apologizing and expressing shame for the "century and a half of silence towards oppression against Baha'is" (Iran Watch Canada 2009). On January 3, 2013, the US House of Representatives called on Iran to release Baha'is imprisoned solely for their religious beliefs. Perhaps the most touching expression of sympathy offered to the Baha'i community is a gift presented to it in 2014 by a distinguished Iranian Shi'ite cleric, Ayatollah Abdol-Hamid Masoumi-Tehrani: a paragraph from the writings of Baha'ullah written in illuminated calligraphy. Ayatollah Tehrani wrote on his website that he prepared the calligraphy as a "symbolic action to serve as a reminder of the importance of valuing human beings, of peaceful coexistence, of cooperation and mutual support, and avoidance of hatred, enmity and blind religious prejudice" (Baha'i World News Service 2014).

Hindus

Hindus live in the Gulf countries as migrant laborers in the United Arab Emirates (490,000), Saudi Arabia (390,000), Qatar (240,000), Kuwait (230,000), Oman (150,000), Yemen (150,000), and Bahrain (120,000). They have been granted the freedom to practice their faith only in Oman and the United Arab Emirates; Sultan Qaboos, the ruler of Oman, donated several tracts of land for the building of Hindu temples.

Oman's Religious Policy

The Sultanate of Oman stands out among the Muslim states of the Middle East for its cordial and even warm interfaith relations and for the freedom of religion it grants to residents of all faiths. The only country where the majority of Muslims belong to Ibadism rather than Sunnism or Shi'ism, Oman's Bu Sa'idi dynasty has long embraced religious tolerance, which deeply impressed British officials when Omanis ruled the Swahili coast (Ingrams 1931, 191). Sa'id ibn Sultan (ruled 1805–56), who moved the capital of the Omani empire to Zanzibar in 1832, instructed his governors to respect the religious customs of the people they ruled and prohibited the slaughter of cows in Hindu quarters, out of deference to Hindu religious sensibilities (Al Barwani 1997, 33). Barghash ibn Sa'id (ruled Zanzibar 1870–88) approved the building of a huge Anglican cathedral in the center of Zanzibar town, and British and French missionaries were allowed to function freely in nonproselytizing capacities among Muslims. The current sultan of Oman, Qaboos bin Sa'id, who came to power in 1970, has taken pains to promote religious harmony in Oman and in the region. Even Muslim groups are not allowed to proselytize in Oman.

In 1997 Oman's Ministry of Justice and Islamic Affairs was renamed the Ministry of Endowments and Religious Affairs, to signal its concern with promoting harmony among all religious groups. In 2003 the ministry inaugurated a journal titled *al-Tasamoh* (Tolerance), renamed in 2011 as *al-Tafahum* (Mutual Understanding). The journal describes itself as an Islamic journal, but it explicitly promotes interfaith understanding. The ministry also, in cooperation with the Reformed Church of America, sponsors the Al Amana Centre, an academic institute that promotes Muslim-Christian cooperation and understanding and introduces delegations of students and officials to Oman's religious and cultural landscape.

Seven lectures delivered by Oman's minister of religious affairs, Abdullah bin Mohammed Al Salmi, have been published in Arabic, English, German, Hebrew, and Chinese in a book titled *Religious Tolerance: A Vision for a New World*. These speeches took place in diverse venues: Aachen Cathedral in Germany, a meeting of the American Society of Missiology in Illinois, a meeting in Cairo of the Conference on the Islamic Forum, Cambridge University's Inter-Faith Programme, the Centre of Islamic Studies at Oxford University, and the National Defense College of Muscat. In these lectures, Al Salmi argues that all religions are based on a common foundation of values such as freedom, equality, and tolerance. It is not religion that causes conflicts, he says, but conflicts of interest, power contestations, and power imbalances. He endorses Hans Küng's statement at the Conference on Religions in Chicago in 1991 that there can be no peace between nations without peace between religions, and there can be no peace between religions without dialogue, which must go beyond the Abrahamic religions. Dialogue, says Al Salmi, will overcome fear and allow for the cooperation necessary for the survival of the planet in today's globalized world (2016, 184, 187). In his lecture at Muscat's National Defense College, he spoke strongly against the politicization of religion or making it the basis of the legitimacy of a political party or state. "The state's body has a highly abrasive digestive system, which would cause the religion to disintegrate and break down" (244). No one should interfere with the beliefs of others, but neither should one react violently to proselytizing efforts. "There should be a reforming effort to instill openness, a balanced and human vision of the religious other," he says. Belief "should always be an incentive for doing good works" and be based on a system of values that includes human equality, freedom, dignity, and compassion (188–89, 224).

In a region that is increasingly torn by brutal sectarian violence, Oman presents a unique balance between religious devotion and social cosmopolitanism; its people are religiously devout but lack religiopolitical fanaticism, exemplifying the spiritual courtesy (*adab*) that many Muslims believe to be the hallmark and heart of Islam. Sultan Qaboos's foreign policy dovetails with his religious policy; Oman has played an important mediating role in regional disputes and in the negotiations between the United States and Iran that led to the nuclear agreement of 2015.

Sufism and Interfaith Relations

Perhaps the main counter to Islamist extremism in the Muslim world is in Sufism. Often called "Islamic mysticism," Sufism is a spiritual movement found in both Sunni and Shi'ite Islam. Until the advent of

Wahhabism in the eighteenth century, Sufism was barely challenged as the foundation of popular Islam throughout the Muslim world. It continues to be an important aspect of Islamic religious life for people of different social classes. Sufi intellectuals in Egypt have made important attempts to grapple with the incompatibilities between the sharia and human rights and to articulate a spiritually and intellectually informed advocacy of human rights and theological pluralism. Perhaps the most distinctive Muslim perspective on interfaith relations in Egypt is that of the Egyptian Society for Spiritual and Cultural Research (ESSCR). This group is based on the teachings of Rafi' Muhammad Rafi' (Rafea Mohammed Rafea [1903–70]), a Shadhili Sufi master and a descendant of the well-known reformer Rifa'a al-Tahtawi (1801–73). After the death of the group's founder, leadership was assumed by his three children, Dr. Ahmad 'Abd al-Wahid Rafi' (known as Ali Rafea), a professor of engineering at the American University in Cairo; Dr. Aliaa Rafea, a professor of anthropology at 'Ain Shams University; and Aisha Rafea, a journalist. The ESSCR emphasizes religious pluralism and interfaith cooperation. Its primary teaching is that all religions, even polytheistic religions, have as their source and focus the same absolute reality and that the purpose of all revelations is to experience and act in harmony with the element of divinity that is within each person. All religions grow out of the one primordial religion (*din al-fitra*) but have deviated from the truth because of legalism, dogmatism, and ethnocentrism—not wrong theology. The ESSCR publishes books and journals, holds conferences, offers a "spiritual training system," and has centers in many major Egyptian cities, including Cairo, Helwan, Alexandria, and Aswan. Its explicitly pluralistic approach to theology enables its members to go well beyond the standard recognition of the Abrahamic religions and to have excellent relations with groups like the Baha'is (Hoffman 2010).

Is it possible that Sufis may lead the way to a new approach toward both Islam and people of other faiths? Such a possibility was envisaged by a symposium held in Cairo on January 18–21, 2008, entitled "Sufi Perspective on World Peace and Responsibility." The event was attended by officials from the US Embassy in Cairo and a number of other foreign diplomats, as well as some three thousand representatives of various Sufi orders. Criticized by the media as an American attempt to promote Sufi thought in order to counter fundamentalist tendencies in Egypt, the conference recommended the dissemination of Sufi principles through participation in various social and cultural activities. Mahmud 'Ashur, a scholar at the Islamic Research Center, told a journalist, "With their large gatherings and loyalty to their teachers, the Sufis are a true paragon of the genuine, peaceful religious spirit, but I don't think they are capable of countering religious fundamentalism," because they lack the qualified scholars necessary for such a mission (Maged 2008). Such a statement, however, belies the fact that many Sufi leaders do have the necessary qualifications. Ahmed Maged wrote in *Daily News Egypt*, "Many Sufis believe the future of the Muslim world hinges on the spread of Sufi ideals which have offered serenity and psychological relief through the ages, as well as peaceful participation in political life at a time when fundamentalists have wreaked havoc and instigated violence likely to endanger Egypt's stability" (ibid.). This point is undoubtedly true, but the teachings of many Sufi leaders offer more than serenity and psychological relief; they offer an intelligent critique of Islamist discourse and suggest that Sufis have a great deal to contribute to current debates on Islam, human rights, and interfaith relations.

Sufism has been promoted as a solution to global conflicts at conferences in other countries as well, including the World Sufi Forum in New Delhi in March 2016, which defined its goals as strengthening global peace, repudiating violence and extremism, calling for unity in multiplicity, spreading the spiritual and universal messages of Islam, and unconditional love, tolerance, and acceptance; the Third International Sufi Conference in Karachi, held in May 2017; and the Third Fez International Conference on Sufism and Global Peace, also held in May 2017.

The contemporary relevance of classical Sufi ideals may perhaps be indicated by the global popularity of Rumi and by the selection of a poem by Sa'di, a Persian poet of the thirteenth century, for an inscription over the entrance to the United Nations' Hall of Nations:

> All humans are members of one body; every person is a glint,
> shining from a single gem
> When the world causes pain for one member, how could the other
> members ever rest in peace?
> If you lack grief for another one's sorrow, why call yourself a
> human being?
>
> (Fideler and Fideler 2010, 167)

Conclusion

There is much that is omitted from this discussion of some of the challenges facing interfaith relations and the human rights of non-Muslims in the Middle East. I have not, for example, discussed ISIS's abuse of religious minorities or their horrific attacks on the Yazidi population, which are unprecedented. However, regardless of the status claimed by ISIS, it is not a state recognized by the international community and could be labeled a criminal enterprise. I have focused instead on issues pertaining to human rights in general and to the treatment of non-Muslim religious minorities in the Arab world and Iran. The problems are considerable, but they cannot be viewed in isolation from global political events or seen as a simple consequence of Islamic teachings. This fact is evident from the public statements and gestures of many Muslims, indicating that they find in Islam the spiritual and intellectual foundation to promote human rights and equality.

Sources Cited

Afghani, Jamal al-Din. 1968. *An Islamic Response to Imperialism: Political and Religious Writings of Sayyid Jamal al-Din al-Afghani*. Translated and edited by Nikki R. Keddie. Berkeley: Univ. of California Press.

Aharoni, Ada. 2003. "The Forced Migration of Jews from Arab Countries." *Peace Review* 15 (1): 53–60.

Akcam, Taner. 2004. *From Empire to Republic: Turkish Nationalism and the Armenian Genocide*. New York: Zed Books.

Al Barwani, Ali Muhsin. 1997. *Conflicts and Harmony in Zanzibar (Memoirs)*. Dubai: n.p.

Al Salmi, Abdullah bin Mohammed. 2016. *Religious Tolerance: A Vision for a New World*. Hildesheim, Zurich, and New York: Georg Olms Verlag.

Ayubi, Nazih N. 1991. *Political Islam: Religion and Politics in the Arab World*. London and New York: Routledge.

Baha'i International Community. 2015. "Situation of Baha'is in Iran." Oct. 2. https://www.bic.org/focus-areas/situation-iranian-bahais/current-situation#UMRVCS4s4uy58CTQ.97.

Baha'i World News Service. 2014. "In an Unprecedented Symbolic Act, Senior Cleric Calls for Religious Coexistence in Iran." Apr. 7. http://news.bahai.org/story/987.

Bezirgan, Najm A. 1981. "Islam and Arab Nationalism." In *Religion and Politics in the Middle East*, edited by Michael Curtis, 43–53. Boulder, CO: Westview Press.

Black, Ian. 2015. "Syrian Army Photographer Describes Torture and Killing in Assad's Prisons." *Guardian*, Oct. 1. https://www.theguardian.com/world/2015/oct/01/syrian-army-photographer-describes-torture-prisons.

Bosworth, C. E. 1999. "Musawat." In *Encyclopaedia of Islam*. 2nd ed. Leiden: Brill.

Cleveland, William L. 1981. "Sources of Arab Nationalism: An Overview." In *Religion and Politics in the Middle East*, edited by Michael Curtis, 55–67. Boulder, CO: Westview Press.

Cohler-Esses, Larry. 2015. "How Iran's Jews Survive in Mullahs' World." *Forward*, Aug. 18. http://forward.com/news/319269/irans-jews-win-secure-place-in-mullahs-world-with-strings-attached/#ixzz3rrqXQOjh.

Cooper, John, Ronald L. Nettler, and Muhammad Mahmoud, eds. 1998. *Islam and Modernity: Muslim Intellectuals Respond*. London: I. B. Tauris.

Cragg, Kenneth. 1991. *The Arab Christian: A History in the Middle East*. Louisville, KY: Westminster / John Knox Press.

Fideler, David, and Sabrineh Fideler. 2010. *Love's Alchemy: Poems from the Sufi Tradition*. Novato, CA: New World Library.

Gerecht, Reul Marc. 2011. "How Democracy Became Halal." *New York Times*, Feb. 6.

Ghannouchi, Rached. 1998. "IntraView: With Tunisian Sheikh Rached Ghannouchi." *Muslim Students Association News*, Feb. 10.

Gibb, H. A. R. 1953. *Mohammedanism: An Historical Survey*. 2nd ed. Oxford: Oxford Univ. Press.

Gordon, Michael R. 2015a. "ISIS Captives Say They Faced Blade as Rescue Came." *New York Times*, Oct. 27.

———. 2015b. "Kurds Investigate Report of Mass Grave of Yazidis in Sinjar." *New York Times*, Nov. 14.

Haddad, Yvonne Yazbeck. 1982. *Contemporary Islam and the Challenge of History*. Albany: State Univ. of New York Press.

Hakakian, Roya. 2014. "How Iran Kept Its Jews." *Tablet*, Dec. 30. https://www.tabletmag.com/jewish-news-and-politics/187519/how-iran-kept-its-jews.

Hamid, Shadi. 2014. *Temptations of Power: Islamists and Illiberal Democracy in the New Middle East*. New York: Oxford Univ. Press.

Hasan, S. S. 2003. *Christians versus Muslims in Modern Egypt: The Century-Long Struggle for Coptic Equality*. New York: Oxford Univ. Press.

Hashim, Ahmad 'Umar, et al. 2006–7. *Al-Tarbiyya l-Islāmiyya li-l-mar?ala l-thāniya min al-thanawiyya l-'āmma*. Cairo: Wizārat al-Tarbiyya wa-l-Ta'līm.

Hassan, Riffat. N.d. "Are Human Rights Compatible with Islam? The Issue of the Rights of Women in Muslim Communities." http://www.religiousconsultation.org/hassan2.htm.

Hoffman, Valerie J. 2003. "Muslim Perspectives." In *A Force Profonde: The Power, Politics, and Promise of Human Rights*, edited by Edward A. Kolodziej, 45–68. Philadelphia: Univ. of Pennsylvania Press.

———. 2010. "Islam, Human Rights and Interfaith Relations: Some Contemporary Egyptian Perspectives." *Journal of Political Theology* 11 (5): 690–716.

Ingrams, William Harold. 1931. *Zanzibar: Its History and Its People*. London: H. F. G. Witherby.

Inskeep, Steve. 2015. "Iran's Jews: It's Our Home and We Plan to Stay." NPR, Feb. 19. http://www.npr.org/sections/parallels/2015/02/19/387265766/irans-jews-its-our-home-and-we-plan-to-stay.

International Federation of Human Rights. 2003. "Discrimination against Religious Minorities in Iran." Aug. https://www.fidh.org/IMG/pdf/ir0108a.pdf.

Iran Watch Canada. 2009. "Century and a Half of Silence towards Oppression against Bahais Is Enough." Iran Watch Canada, Mar. 12. http://moriab.blogspot.com/2009/03/century-and-half-of-silence-towards.html.

Jankowski, James P. 1981. "Nationalism in Twentieth Century Egypt." In *Religion and Politics in the Middle East*, edited by Michael Curtis, 91–107. Boulder, CO: Westview Press.

Jones, Adam. 2006. *Genocide: A Comprehensive Introduction*. London: Routledge.

Kabir, Humayun. 1998. "Minorities in a Democracy." In *Liberal Islam: A Sourcebook*, edited by Charles Kurzman, 145–54. New York: Oxford Univ. Press.

Kepel, Gilles. 1984. *Le Prophète et Pharaon: Les mouvements islamistes dans l'Egypte contemporaine*. Paris: Editions La Découverte.

Levene, Mark. 1998. "Creating a Modern 'Zone of Genocide': The Impact of Nation- and State-Formation on Eastern Anatolia, 1878–1923." *Holocaust and Genocide Studies* 12 (3): 393–433.

Lewis, Bernard. 1986. *Semites and Anti-Semites: An Inquiry into Conflict and Prejudice*. New York: W. W. Norton.

Maged, Ahmed. 2008. "Debating Political Sufism." *Daily News Egypt*, Sept. 10.

Mahmoud, Mohamed. 1998. "Mahmud Muhammad Taha's Second Message of Islam and His Modernist Project." In *Islam and Modernity: Muslim Intellectuals Respond*, edited by John Cooper, Ronald L. Nettler, and Muhammad Mahmoud, 105–28. London: I. B. Tauris.

Mayer, Ann Elizabeth. 1991. *Islam and Human Rights: Tradition and Politics*. 1st ed. Boulder, CO: Westview Press.

———. 2013. *Islam and Human Rights*. 5th ed. Boulder, CO: Westview Press.

Najmabadi, Afsaneh. 2013. *Professing Selves: Transsexuality and Same-Sex Desire in Contemporary Iran*. Durham, NC: Duke Univ. Press.

Rahman, Fazlur. 1982. *Islam and Modernity: Transformation of an Intellectual Tradition.* Chicago: Univ. of Chicago Press, 1982.

Sanasarian, Eliz. 2000. *Religious Minorities in Iran.* Cambridge: Cambridge Univ. Press.

Shields, Sarah. 2013. "The Greek-Turkish Population Exchange." *Middle East Report* 267. http://www.merip.org/mer/mer267/greek-turkish-population-exchange?ip_login_no_cache=bc5ed48d01d2a78eb3f73ad92cc60ec2.

Tadros, Mariz. 2013. *Copts at the Crossroads: The Challenges of Building Inclusive Democracy in Egypt.* Cairo: American Univ. in Cairo Press.

Talbi, Mohamed. 1998. "Religious Liberty." In *Liberal Islam: A Sourcebook*, edited by Charles Kurzman, 161–68. New York: Oxford Univ. Press

Weiner, Justus Reid. 2005. *Human Rights of Christians in Palestinian Society.* Jerusalem: Jerusalem Center for Public Affairs. http://www.jcpa.org/christian-persecution.htm.

7

Regime Ruptures and Sectarian Eruptions in Post-Mubarak Egypt

MARIZ TADROS

This chapter examines the changing status and role of Egypt's largest religious minority, the Copts, in the period between Egypt's two regime ruptures: between February 11, 2011, when Mubarak's thirty-year rule came to an end following the January 25 revolution, up to the second regime rupture in 2013, when the multitude rose again, this time against Morsi's one-year tenure in office. The chapter critically addresses a number of postulates regarding revolutions, regime change, and majority-minority relations in the Arab world, with specific reference to the Egyptian case study. The first postulate that the chapter will engage with is that religious minorities prefer authoritarian regimes, with which they can consolidate pacts to secure their communal interests, over democratic systems. The second is that the Arab revolts have been inimical to the rights of religious minorities. The third is that Copts' diminished citizenship status can be largely explained by their lack of political agency as citizens and their preference for using the church as their political mouthpiece.

In engaging with these key issues, the approach has been to try to capture the wide array of voices and perspectives among Coptic Egyptians, with a view to contributing to grounded theory. The findings presented here are a synthesis of several studies that the author has conducted that relied on focus groups, in-depth case studies, and participant observation. This approach is premised on the belief that some scholarship on religious minorities in Egypt has suffered from pitfalls that led to the negation of the narratives and experiences of the subjects of their study. These pitfalls are to focus on interviews with elites within the community, on the assumption that they serve as proxies for the views and agency of a widely diverse community; to interpret the views of the church leadership and clergy as representing the political views and choices of all Coptic lay members; the objectification of Copts, with minimal attention to their voices, perspectives, and agency; and insufficient attention given to how the researchers' standing as outsiders affects how their subjects perceive and engage with them.

The first part of this chapter discusses the popular uprisings of 2011 in terms of the shifting power configurations before and after the fall of Mubarak. It discusses changes in the pattern of sectarianism, its manifestations, and implications for state-society relations. The second part examines church-state relations under a new president (Morsi) and a new pope (Tawadros II) and their interface with microlevel politics. The third part furthers the discussion of political mobilization from below against the regime and its outcome in the events after the second popular uprising of June 30, 2013. The chapter concludes with some reflections on what the rapid political change means for state-society-citizen relations.

Defiance of Several Red Lines

Mubarak's thirty-year authoritarian rule came to an end on February 11, 2011, after eighteen days of sustained protests by millions of citizens in several public squares across the country. The army allowed the regime to fall. In examining the political actors and arrangements that propped up the Mubarak regime, some have pointed to the political support of the country's religious minority, the Copts.[1] The patriarch of the Coptic Orthodox Church, Pope She-

1. Egypt has the largest religious minority in the Arab world, the Coptic Christians. Christianity has deep roots in Egypt, believed to date back to 48 CE. Since

nouda III, whose papacy lasted forty years (November 14, 1971–March 17, 2012) had entered into an entente with Mubarak's regime that involved the church rendering political support in return for its protection as an institution, though such a pact, by the end of Mubarak's tenure, had come under extreme pressure, as the church could no longer assume the role of mediator of the Copts' demands vis-à-vis the state (Tadros 2009). When the revolts against the regime intensified in the January 25 revolution, Pope Shenouda urged Christians not to join, just as Muhammad al-Tantawi, the grand sheikh of al-Azhar, urged the Muslims not to join. However, there is a growing body of scholarship indicating that Copts defied these instructions and took part in the uprisings, together with Muslims. People from different political ideologies (leftist, right of center, Islamist) cooperated and coordinated their efforts to a large degree, and Muslims and Christians stood side by side, holding the Egyptian flag. Images of men holding the Qur'an and the cross were widely disseminated in the media and were intended to promote the notion that there was religious unity in the face of a common oppressor. However, narratives that focus on the position of Pope Shenouda seem to suggest that the Copts followed his instructions and that incidents (rather than groups at large) of protest began to emerge only after the revolution. Avi Asher-Schapiro wrote in an article for the Carnegie Endowment for International Peace's Middle East Analysis website, *Sada*, "The crisis of political authority ushered in by the fall of Mubarak (which genuinely surprised church leaders) opened new space for Coptic activists to operate outside of traditional hierarchies" (2012). While he acknowledges earlier in the article that Copts had been mobilizing

---

the spread of Christianity in Egypt, followers who did not convert to Islam have gone through phases of ebb and flow in their position and relations vis-à-vis the social and political order. Today it is estimated that Christians constitute around 10 percent of the wider population—although some estimates put it at 20 percent (see Tadros 2013a for further details), and some put it down to 6 percent. Of the roughly 10 percent, it is estimated that about 9 percent follow the Coptic Orthodox faith, with the remaining 1 percent following the Protestant and Catholic faiths.

in expressions of public dissent against the government's practices as early as 2009, the large-scale participation of ordinary Coptic citizens in the 2011 revolution is never acknowledged in the article. Asher-Schapiro's suggestion that Coptic activists began to operate outside the traditional hierarchy of the Coptic Orthodox Church only after space opened up in 2011 is part of a larger argument that is based on the notion that Copts, via the church leadership, are supportive of authoritarianism.

This argument is highly problematic on two fronts: it ignores the active participation of Copts against Mubarak's authoritarian regime in the January 25 revolution and the significance of the level and scope of dissent against the security apparatus in defiance of the church shortly before the January 25 revolution. Several analysts have argued that the Copts' demonstrations against the security forces and the Mubarak regime, days after the bombing of a church in Alexandria on December 31, 2010, were a precursor to the revolution. Sherif Azer, a human rights activist, was at the scene of the violent confrontations that ensued in Shubra, Cairo, when security forces clashed with citizens who had congregated to remember those individuals who died in the Alexandria bombing. He wrote, "I saw with my own eyes, for the very first time, protesters clashing with such violence with security forces and burning police cars. It was a scene that was to be repeated frequently after January. But on that night in Shubra, I witnessed a foreshadowing of the future, one that was very close to arriving. I knew then how angry people were at the regime and what that anger might bring about" (2015).

What connects the Coptic dissent of early January and the dissent of the January 25 revolution is that Copts overcame the fear barrier through collective action that openly defied the regime. It is this collective defiance of the red lines of a security state that has convinced many analysts that this issue is important for understanding why people reached a tipping point in January 2011. Notwithstanding that some church leaders did forge ententes with the autocrats, as did their Islamic counterparts, the evidence cited above suggests that Coptic defiance of oppressive orders is no less than the dissent of

Muslims. In many ways, Coptic dissent against the state has at some points been more indicative of the general mood among the Muslim citizenry than the political will of the Coptic Church leadership.

The spirit of Tahrir Square did not have a ripple effect, spatially or temporally, on Muslim-Christian relations after the common mission of ousting Mubarak had been accomplished. The Supreme Council of Armed Forces (SCAF), which took over, forged an informal alliance with the Muslim Brotherhood that came to represent the political settlement of organizing power in the post-Mubarak phase (Tadros 2012). The new configurations of power after the overthrow of Mubarak did not bode well for the Coptic citizenry; perhaps the early signals of encroachments by SCAF were a precursor of more violence to come. In other words, the revolt against Mubarak did not impinge upon recognition of religious authorities or constitute a break with the status quo; on the contrary, those individuals who participated reported a feeling of immense patriotic pride and a sense of an empowered, emancipated citizenship. Rather, the threat came from the new power configurations that assumed authority.

Incidents of sectarian violence against Christian minorities, Baha'is, and Sufis increased in 2011. An important question is whether increased sectarianism was a consequence of the policies pursued by the new authorities or whether the removal of the regime's heavy-handed measures exposed underlying sectarian tensions. I would argue it is a combination of both, in addition to another important factor: the informal political ascendancy of the Islamists.

SCAF's governance of Egypt from February 2011 to June 2012 was characterized by the absence of a political will to uphold the rule of law in dealing with incidents of sectarian violence, a trend that was amplified after President Morsi took over. The army was responsible for the "Maspero massacre," the single worst incident of sectarian violence against Christians in contemporary Egyptian history, which involved army vehicles running over peaceful protesters. SCAF took no measures to hold the perpetrators accountable, signaling a high level of tolerance for religiously based discrimination and injustice. Social cohesion had been eroding in Egypt between

Muslims and Christians in many communities for several decades, and there were incidents involving collective violence against religious minorities living in the community (including the Baha'is). The security vacuum generated by the withdrawal of the police force from maintaining law and order was seized upon by religiously motivated as well as nonreligiously motivated criminal elements. No doubt, the revolution did not create sectarianism; it only brought to the surface tensions that had been simmering for years. The new political configuration in Egypt, which bestowed substantial formal and informal power on the Muslim Brotherhood and the Salafis to influence governance at all levels, had a direct impact on sectarianism relations. Their power was not reflected in the formal sphere in the form of new laws, decrees, or regulations, per se. It was in the informal arena that the encroachments were most apparent.

In 2008 there were 33 incidents of sectarianism reported in the press. In 2009 there were 32. There were 45 in 2010. The number increased to 70 sectarian incidents after the revolution in 2011 and increased again in 2012 to 112. The number of incidents for the two years after the revolution (2011 and 2012) comes to 182, representing a striking increase over the number of total incidents for 2008, 2009, and 2010 combined. The number of incidents nearly doubled from 2010 to 2011 and increased by a third from 2011 and 2012. Not only did the number of sectarian incidents increase in 2011 in quantitative terms, but, qualitatively, the level of intensity of assaults also increased. In analyzing the key "triggers" that led to the escalation of sectarian conflict for the period between 2008 and 2012, it is possible to note a number of important patterns.

The most frequent trigger of sectarian violence in the period from 2008 to 2010 was the escalation of nonreligious, small-scale disputes into full-fledged sectarian incidents. Since there is a power differential in many communities as a consequence of the Copts' minority status (though this situation is also mediated by geographic location, status, class, and gender), once an ordinary dispute assumes a sectarian character, Muslim mobilization is usually directed not only against the person involved in the dispute but also against the Copts in that community (be it an urban neighborhood, village, or hamlet). An examination of incidents that fall under this category provides us with important insights into the most significant source of sectarian strife.

While in some cases the disputes are criminal, in most cases they are simply heated discussions on everyday matters that can occur anywhere between any two citizens. This point is highly significant in that it shows that there is a great deal of sectarian antagonism beneath the surface that can be sparked easily, even when the original dispute had nothing to do with religious affiliation. It shows that social cohesion is under strain. In every case in which mobs rose against a minority, there have been Muslims who have sought to protect them, to stand up for them, and to disassociate themselves from the acts of the majority. However, they have been a minority and have often paid a heavy social price for their stance.

What is particularly alarming about the fact that ordinary citizen disagreements are being transformed into full-scale communal clashes is the spontaneity and unpredictability of such incidents. Whereas, for example, in the case of the construction or upgrading of a church, policy makers can assume the worst and take precautions to protect the premises and raise awareness; on the other hand, one cannot predict that haggling over prices between a vegetable seller and a shopper will escalate into sectarian strife. It makes the possibilities of developing an early warning system against the occurrence of such incidents far more difficult. This difficulty indicates that it requires years—possibly a generation—to change social mores, values, and ideas about the religious other. It also means that it is impossible to predict when disputes will escalate into sectarian violence (though, arguably, predicting their occurrence is also difficult in other instances). Unlike, for example, churches, which have a known geographical location, a heated debate, an incidence of fraud, a disagreement can happen anywhere, any time.

What is striking is the increase in the number of small-scale disputes turning into incidents of violence against Christians following the revolution. The total number of such incidents for the period from 2008 to 2011 was twenty-six; in 2011 there were eleven in a single year; in 2012 they rose to twenty-four. This escalation is cause for serious concern, for the reasons highlighted above. When undertaking ethnographic research in rural communities in December 2012, I was told in a village that had experienced such incidents that the increasing power of Salafis on the ground, and the perception in the community that Islamists are now in power and have the upper hand, has created an environment in which the spread of any rumors of Copts' wrongdoing against Muslims aggravates sectarian tensions that are very difficult to contain. The perception that Islamists are no longer accountable to a higher authority because they are in power has meant that those individuals who perpetrate violence against Christians feel they have little to fear.

The second most frequently cited trigger for sectarianism in the Egyptian context has been the construction, expansion, or renovation/upgrading of a Christian place of worship (there were nineteen incidents between 2008 and 2010). Egypt does not have a unified law regulating matters pertaining to construction and maintenance of places of worship. There are no legal restrictions on the construction of mosques, but Christian places of worship are governed by a discriminatory legal decree that makes it very difficult to construct new churches (Tadros 2013a, 51–55). Since population increases created a situation in which existing churches were no longer able to accommodate the growing number of worshipers, a de facto situation emerged in which churches were built having the status of illegality despite enjoying government approval. The process was succinctly articulated by Judge Noha el Zeiny, who highlighted that the standard practice was for people to apply for a permit to construct a church, which would be officially denied by the state security investigations (SSI), who nonetheless allowed them to convert a place into a house of worship that would be used informally as a church. There are many churches that were denied an official permit but were allowed by the SSI to function for decades as if they were "legal" entities (el Ibrashy 2011). The SSI was usually more lenient in granting official permits to renovate churches or build an annex to be used for church-related activities (such as Sunday school). However, the acquisition of such official permits sometimes took months, even years, to obtain. During the Mubarak years, the realization that a building was being used as a church or that an annex was being constructed or a fence or wall was being renovated provoked unknown persons believed to belong to various Islamist groups to mobilize residents to express their opposition to the construction or renovation. In other words, not only "illegal" churches were assaulted, but so were renovation or extension works that had official permits. The outcome was often the attempted or actual destruction of the church. Usually, the security forces intervened, though perpetrators were rarely brought to justice.

Following the revolution, a new phenomenon emerged that makes it difficult to classify incidents as prompted by church expansion or construction related. These acts neither involved the construction or renovation of churches nor were induced by any visible triggers. They included the Salafi occupation and attempted annexation of church-owned buildings, the mobilization of citizenry to force the closure of a church on the premise that it was unlicensed, or the sudden destruction of church fences and annexation of parts of the premises; all of these events occurred in the governorates of Minya, Cairo, Beni Suef, and Sohag, among others. This experience shows a rather serious new development of incidents of "untriggered" assault on Coptic Christians. It suggests that the level of intolerance has risen to the point that the very existence of churches in an area is cause for sectarian assault.

The third main trigger of sectarian assault during the period 2008–10 had to do with matters connected with Muslim-Christian gender relations (there were nineteen such incidents in total). Political critic Ibrahim Eissa noted that "most of the incidents of sectarian strife in Egypt are caused by a Christian boy falling in love with a Muslim girl or a Muslim boy wanting to marry a Christian girl or something to do with relations between the opposite sexes" (2012). In a society such as Egypt, where religious divisions are mirrored in deep social cleavages, interreligious marriages are anathema. Legally, a Muslim man can marry a Christian woman, but a Muslim woman cannot marry a Christian man. There are no social prohibitions against Muslim men marrying Christian women, especially since the latter convert to Islam upon marriage. However, these women's families normally reject such marriages and believe they bring dishonor upon them and upon the wider Christian community. What causes sectarian strife is often when Christian women disappear and their families discover that they converted to Islam and married Muslim men, and the families have no way of finding out whether they did so voluntarily or under pressure. Matters become particularly aggravated when the missing daughters are minors (under sixteen years of age), in which case, legally, they are under the guardianship of their families and the state is obliged to help them find their daughters, which it is reluctant to do.

However, after the revolution, a new phenomenon emerged that is difficult to classify under "gender relations": the disappearance of young girls and women (there were at least eight incidents in 2012) when there is no evidence of a previous relationship with a Muslim man. These were incidents in which women were out on errands or returning from a social engagement and never returned. In one instance, a Salafi leader admitted that such a young woman was in his company, stating that she intended to convert and that the family should not try to get in touch with her. These incidents led to the organization of protests and marches by Coptic citizens, sometimes directly confronting the powers that be.

The most dramatic change in sectarian violence that occurred after the Islamists informally rose to power in 2011 and formally assumed office in 2012 was the rise of "untriggered" incidents of assault against Christians. There were three such incidents in 2010, sixteen in 2011, and thirty-one in 2012. In each incident, there was no dispute or other spark of the acts of violence. For example, there were several incidents in which Coptic Christian women were assaulted for not wearing the veil. Although unveiled Muslim women were also exposed to such acts, assaults on Coptic women would be accompanied by verbal abuse against the "infidels." The overwhelming majority of violent sectarian incidents occur at the community level, rather than being confrontations between religious leaders or state figures, but this situation changed with the new power configuration in Egypt after the ascendancy of the Muslim Brotherhood candidate, Mohamed Morsi, to the presidency.

New Pope, New President: New Hope?

The ascendancy of Dr. Mohamed Morsi to the presidency was supposed to represent a new phase in Egypt's history, as the country would be led by its first democratically elected leader. It also coincided with the inauguration of a new Coptic pope four months later, in November 2012, Tawadros II. In principle, new leadership in the presidency and papacy could have signaled the possibility of turning a new leaf and forging a new rapport between the Coptic Church and the Muslim Brotherhood and Islamist leadership in power. It was also a perfect opportunity to demonstrate that Coptic anxieties about an Islamist-led government were unfounded and that a new inclusionary order was in the making. However, Coptic rejection en masse of the Muslim Brotherhood's presidential nominee had left a bad taste in the mouth of the new leadership that was not going to go away quickly.

Throughout his presidential campaign in the summer of 2012, Mohamed Morsi was keen to emphasize that he would be a president for all Egyptians, not just supporters of the Society of Muslim Brothers, and that he believed in equal citizenship for all, irrespective of religious affiliation. The majority of Egypt's Coptic Christians were nonetheless suspicious of the Muslim Brotherhood candidate, and in the first round many voted for one of the other main contenders, Ahmed Shafik, Amr Moussa, or Hamdeen Sabbahi. When Ahmed Shafik won 49 percent of the vote in the presidential election, it was attributed to the Copts, but it is statistically impossible, as the governorates with the highest concentration of Christians (Cairo, Alexandria, Minya, and Asyut) offered a negligible percentage of votes for Shafik (see Tadros 2013a for detailed description and analysis of the presidential elections).

Nonetheless, there can be no doubt that the Coptic vote had consistently gone to Morsi's non-Islamist opponent. Political commentators suggest that there were a number of missed opportunities for the new president to warm relations with the new pope: he could have attended the pope's inauguration ceremony and attended the Christmas Mass to convey holiday wishes to the pope and Christians. Whether on a macropolicy level or in terms of micropolitics, the Coptic vote against Morsi created serious misgivings and bitterness among not only Islamists but the broader support base that had voted him into office. In focus groups undertaken in 2012, Coptic women and men consistently reported that they were approached and reproached in their daily interactions: "Why don't you like Morsi? Why did you vote against him?" It is interesting that the same rebuke was leveled against the church leadership in the aftermath of the events of April 7, 2012, which marked a phase of open hostility between church and state.

On April 7, 2012, for the first time ever, the cathedral was attacked by men throwing stones in the presence of riot police, who were captured on live television firing tear-gas canisters into the building, effectively besieging it. Pope Tawadros II was not inside, but hundreds of mourners were. They had gathered for the collective funeral of those persons killed in sectarian violence in the village of al Khusous in Giza Province days earlier. A protest against President Morsi was planned for after the funeral, and a group of demonstrators was indeed about to exit the cathedral doors, shouting slogans against the Muslim Brotherhood. While the identity of the stone throwers is not certain, it is believed that they were thugs, perhaps hired for the occasion by parties unknown. The mourners retreated inside the cathedral, and the ensuing televised melee left two dead and nearly a hundred injured, including a number of police. Four hours later, masked men with high-powered rifles were observed on top of a small building at the entrance to the cathedral, shooting back at the security men and other besiegers. Were they also thugs, or were they Copts who decided that something had to be done to defend the cathedral and the people choking on tear gas inside? To this day, there is no answer to this question. As for the precipitating incident, the narrative preferred by the Islamists is that the police were attacked by Copts who had gone to the funeral armed for battle. As Freedom and Justice Party member of parliament ʻAbd al-Rahman Mitwalli put it, "He [a Coptic youth] is praying with a machine gun" (*Egypt Independent* 2013b). Yet this story line was challenged by footage that showed mourners, many of them women in black, grieving their loved ones. Mitwalli's statement was highly reminiscent of the statement made by the Supreme Council of the Armed Forces on October 9, 2011, when the army crushed protesters under the treads of armored personnel carriers at a rally outside the Maspero state broadcasting facility. That rally had concerned impunity for church burnings. In both instances, the reference to armed Copts was intended to provoke public sentiment that Muslims are under threat from the religious other.

Following the events, President Morsi said, "I consider any attack on the cathedral an attack on myself," but then he did not go to the cathedral to offer condolences to the pope, sending a delegation of advisers in his stead. Analysts contrasted this behavior with his speedy personal visit to young men who had suffered food poisoning at al-Azhar University the same week. There were no deaths in the food-poisoning case.

Emad Gad, who was then the deputy head of both the Egyptian Social Democratic Party and the al-Ahram Center for Strategic and Political Studies, recounted that the presidential delegation visiting the papal residence following the assault on the cathedral asked, "No offense, but why do you hate President Morsi?" (Gad 2013). Copts interviewed in focus groups said that when they themselves were asked this question, what they read between the lines was that they were reaping what they sowed. They had rejected Morsi, so they should expect revenge and to be treated like opponents of the regime.

Relations between church leadership and the state deteriorated rapidly in April 2012. In the very same hour that the presidential delegation was at the cathedral, presidential adviser ʻIsam al-Haddad disseminated a statement in English explaining the cathedral events in a different way: "On Sunday, April 7, events further escalated during the funeral procession of the Christian Egyptians killed, when angry mourners vandalized cars lined up on Ramses Street. This led to stone throwing and [the setting off] of firecrackers by people in the neighborhood of the cathedral. The situation further escalated, with [live ammunition] and pellets being fired, according to the neighborhood's security official." The statement added: "Camera lenses also captured individuals carrying live weapons, Molotov cocktails and rocks to the roof of the cathedral, as well as inside and outside of it, which prompted police to intervene and disperse the clashes with tear gas. The individuals seen to be firing firearms have been vehemently disavowed by the mourners. Investigations are still being conducted to reveal the identity of those involved in this incident" (*Egypt Independent* 2013a). It is evident from this statement that the government holds Copts responsible for instigating the April 7 violence by vandalizing cars. The statement does not identify the men on the roof as Copts, but suggests that they were, further making it seem as if there was an exchange of fire between actors inside and outside the cathedral walls, with a neutral security force trying to tamp it down. As the statement came from the presidential palace, some wondered if there was any point to the general prosecutor's investigation—the finger of blame had already been pointed from the highest office of the state.

The dual discourse espoused by the Muslim Brothers, one for the papal seat and one for international media consumption, seems to have been a tipping point for Pope Tawadros II, who abandoned his measured pleas for an inquiry into the assault and launched an open accusation of state negligence. In a telephone call to ON TV, the pontiff said that Morsi had "promised to do everything to protect the cathedral, but in reality we don't see this." When asked why, Tawadros said he believed "it comes under the category of negligence and poor assessment of events." He added, "This flagrant assault on a national symbol—the Egyptian church has never been subjected to this in 2,000 years" (Kaldaya.Net 2013). It was not the first time that the pope had criticized the powers that be, but these words were certainly the most scathing up to then.

When Squeezed, Exit, Duck, or Demonstrate

In reaction to the perceived or experienced sense of encroachment and pending threats to Coptic citizens under the growing powers of the Islamists, the reaction of different segments of the Coptic citizenry was diverse. Some Christians, after witnessing the growing political strength of the Islamists and the growing number of cases of kidnappings, imposition of levies, and so on, chose to leave.[2] One estimate suggests that some 350,000 Copts left Egypt in 2011 (Nkrumah 2012). Dennis Ross of the Washington Institute for Near East Policy estimates that no fewer than 100,000 Coptic Christians have emigrated since the Brotherhood came to power in 2012. If these figures are correct, it suggests that almost a half-million Coptic citizens left the country within the space of two years. Prior to the 2011–13 surge of emigration, it was estimated that there are about 2 million Copts living in the diaspora who had migrated in waves since the 1950s.

However, the majority of Coptic Egyptians engaged in more local-level forms of adaptation to the surge of Islamist and economically driven activity against them. Some Copts chose to maintain a low profile, to avert confrontations and aim for survival. In focus groups, they mentioned daily acts of minimizing mobility and public engagement, keeping to themselves. It is important, however, to understand this situation in the broader Egyptian context in which all Egyptian citizens, across religion, class, geographic location, and gender, were suffering from the absence of personal and public safety

2. Over the past sixty years, Christians have witnessed several periods of emigration, first in the 1960s, then in the 1970s, and more recently, since the Egyptian Revolution of 2011. Coptic emigration has been driven by aspirations for a better life economically, as well as subjection to discrimination and, in some instances, persecution.

as a consequence of the security vacuum created by the police force's abandonment of the task of maintaining a modicum of law and order.

One of the key characteristics of Egypt in the period from 2011 to 2013 was the sustained wave of citizens' engagement in contentious forms of expression of voice, through sit-ins, protests, marches, and occupation of buildings.

While it may be expected that Copts would "cocoonize," that is, retreat from public engagement in order to circumvent confrontation with the authorities, it was not the case. Increased encroachment on their rights led to increased activism. In other words, there was a positive relationship between increased levels of repression and increased levels of political dissent. Copts participated in street politics on both national issues and communal grievances. Copts participated in revolutionary youth movements and political parties that were involved in challenging Morsi's government's policies. When hundreds of thousands of protesters flocked to Ittihadiyya Palace in November 2012 to protest Morsi's presidential decree that granted him sweeping powers, Mohamed el-Beltagy, head of the Freedom and Justice Party, the Muslim Brotherhood's political arm, claimed that 60 percent of the protesters were Christian (*al-Yawm al-Sabi'* 2012). The inferences from such a statement are significant in a deeply polarized political environment of pro-Morsi versus anti-Morsi citizens and political forces. By claiming that the majority of the protesters in front of the palace were Christians, Beltagy was attempting to reframe the lines of contestation as being aligned on religious rather than political grounds. In other words, the Christian minority was dissenting against Muslims (and, by default, Islam). This allegation was intended to delegitimize the protests as well as heighten and deepen the desire for revenge by pro-Morsi supporters, a majority of whom were Islamists, against the Christian population. Even so, the Coptic citizenry who participated in broad-based antigovernment campaigns continued to seek to avoid making any claims on religious grounds and were not easily visible, in view of the absence of any ethnic differentiation between Christian and Muslim protesters.

On the other hand, there were a number of identity-specific forms of protests that Coptic citizens instigated, albeit with smaller numbers. In 2012 there were fifteen reported protests pertaining to the cases of individual Copts or matters of religious discrimination—following seventeen such reported events the previous year—though their demands were rarely met. It is critically important to note that these incidents were reported in the Egyptian press, so there is a possibility that there were other protests that took place but were not covered in the press. The identity-specific forms of contestation were organized by Coptic social movements, as well as ordinary Christian citizens; Christians were sometimes joined by Muslim friends, neighbors, and colleagues in solidarity. Crucially, the protests happened at public sites rather than inside church walls, as was most often the case prior to the 2011 revolution. Five of the 2012 protests were organized to press the security forces to be more proactive in investigating the disappearances of Coptic girls who were allegedly kidnapped for religious reasons, namely, their conversion to Islam and marriage to Muslim men. Three protests were organized to protest the enforcement of the *jizya* levy and the resort to kidnapping to extort it. Others were for failure to administer justice whether in particular lawsuit cases (in Minya) or in demanding retribution for those individuals killed in the Maspero massacre by the army.

While the table documents incidents of protest up to the end of 2012, Copts continued to participate in protest activity well into 2013, both against Coptic-specific grievances and as part of broader social and political movements that pressed for reform in the government's political and economic governance policies. Following the issuance of the Presidential Decree in November 2012, a countercoalition, or at least a loose informal bloc, had begun to form against the Morsi regime, comprising different non-Islamist political parties, a number of revolutionary youth movements, some influential broadcasting channels and the press, and various leading intellectuals. In addition to the political mobilization "from above," there was grassroots mobilization "from below." Tamarrod (Rebel), a newly formed

Table 8
2012 protests about Coptic-related issues

Cause	*Location*	*Date*	*Participants*
Incarceration of blogger Michael Munir, sentenced by a military tribunal for insulting SCAF	March from Tahrir Square to High Court (Cairo)	Jan. 18	Civil rights activists (Copts and others)
Killing of two Copts who refused to pay *jizya* to gangster Ahmad Sabir	Nag' Hammadi police station	Jan. 26	Over 500 Copts and Muslims
Kidnapping for ransom and assault of two Copts	Roadblock near al-Tahna al-Gabal (Minya)	Feb. 1	Villagers
Decision of committee led by Salafi sheikh to evict eight families in village of Sharbat	Parliamentary building (Cairo)	Feb. 12	Copts
Disappearances of Coptic girls	Cairo	Feb. 28	Coalition of the Victims of Kidnapping and Disappearance
Return of Mary Qudays, disappeared and later found married to a Muslim and wearing a face veil; prosecutor told the family they could not see her	Prosecutor's office at Ballina (Suhag)	Mar. 4	Local Copts and Copts of Egypt coalition
Life sentences for twelve Copts in Abu Qurqas clashes of 2011	High Court (Cairo)	May 22	Coptic activists and Maspero youth movement
Life sentences for twelve Copts in Abu Qurqas clashes of 2011	High Court (Cairo)	May 26	Copts of Egypt coalition
Disappearance of Hind Faruq Fu'ad, fourteen; parents accuse a young Muslim man	Police station in al-Qusayr (Red Sea district)	July 4	Copts from Luxor

Table 8 (*Cont.*)
2012 protests about Coptic-related issues

Cause	*Location*	*Date*	*Participants*
Repeated assaults on unveiled women, predominantly Copts, on public transportation and threats of forced veiling	Presidential palace (Cairo)	July 7	Copts
Looting and burning of Copts' property after a Coptic ironer of clothes was accused of burning a Muslim's shirt	Security headquarters (Giza); presidential palace (Cairo); march from Tahrir to High Court	Aug. 2	Copts of Egypt coalition and evicted families from Dahshour, joined by priests and ordinary citizens from Giza
Protection from gang attacking Copts' houses and demanding *jizya*	Security headquarters	Aug. 14	Around a hundred Copts from Gawaly (Asyut)
Justice for twenty-eight dead in the October 9, 2011, Maspero massacre	March from Shubra to Maspero (Cairo)	Oct. 9	Non-Islamist parties, April 6 and other youth revolutionary movements, Maspero youth movement, and ordinary citizens
Disappearance of fourteen-year-old girl	Mallawi police station (Minya)	Oct. 24	Family, relatives, and friends
Disappearance of 'Agabi 'Isam, a thirteen-year-old girl; parents accuse a woman wearing a face veil who works at her school	Alexandria library	Dec. 30	Family and friends

youth-led movement, issued a petition calling for early presidential elections and called to people to take to the streets on the first anniversary of Morsi's rule, to press for change. It announced by the third week of June 2013 that it had raised thirteen million signatures (Assran 2013). The pro-Morsi political bloc created a counterpetition, named Tagarrod (Stripped of Shackles/Hindrances) and announced it had collected fifteen million signatures and said it could easily reach twenty million.

But the litmus test was in people's participation in street protests. Starting on June 28, 2013, people took to the streets again. There were protests comprising thousands of pro-Morsi supporters, but the protesters against the regime were in the millions (Fayed and Saleh 2013).

The Muslim Brotherhood may have underestimated the large numbers that responded to Tamarrod's plea to take to the streets on June 30 to call for early presidential elections, but they did bet correctly on the Coptic contingent. A few days before the protests and throughout the week of demonstrations, media sympathetic to the Brotherhood launched a campaign that represented the protests as a Christian conspiracy against Islam. The campaign was staged with an intensity that was sufficient to catalyze bloody sectarian clashes. On the Muslim Brotherhood–affiliated television channel, Misr 25, Noureddin, a program presenter, made a fictitious announcement that Christians were attacking mosques. On an Islamist-affiliated channel, program guest Sheikh Mahmoud Shaaban, a Salafi, concocted a story that Christians had congregated in Tahrir Square and that their main chant was "Jesus is the solution," as if Christians were countering the Muslim Brotherhood slogan, "Islam is the solution." The campaign was also accompanied by threats that warned Copts not to participate in the protests (Egyptian Initiative for Personal Rights 2013). However, such threats did not deter Copts from taking to the streets, and they deliberately framed their participation in patriotic rather than sectarian terms.

The Brotherhood and sympathetic Islamist movements have consistently represented the opposition as remnants of Mubarak's old regime and Copts. However, if the above narrative shows a deliberate attempt to vilify the opponents as infidels, it also indicates an awareness on the part of the Muslim Brotherhood that the Copts do represent a political constituency that they should fear. Why else would the Brotherhood incite such sectarian hatred against the Copts right before the June 30 protests?

What drove Copts to go out in large numbers? Some factors are the same as the ones that drove all Egyptians to revolt: the absence of safety and security, increasing impoverishment, and the political monopolization of power in the hands of the Brothers. However, there are religiously mediated forms of encroachment that were specific to Copts. Social cohesion suffered a deep blow under Morsi's rule (see Tadros 2014 for specific case studies). Politically, the Muslim Brotherhood used the Copts as a scapegoat for its failure to build legitimacy within the wider polity. On a macro and micro level during Morsi's reign, the Copts were at the receiving end of intense hostility for their opposition to the president. Socially, the discourses and practices intended to vilify Christians as infidels or blasphemers against Islam permeated villages, towns, and cities alike. Economically, the imposition of ransoms and levies on Copts became quite prevalent in many parts of Upper Egypt, affecting whole villages in Asyut and Minya.

But it was not just the day-to-day living conditions that drove Copts to abhor the Muslim Brotherhood. Well before the Brotherhood came to power, Copts had an ideological resistance to notions of religiously mediated citizenship. For many Copts, the ousting of Morsi brought a sense of hope in the possibility of a different system of governance not mediated by religious affiliation.

On the night that Defense Minister Abdul Fattah el-Sisi announced the ousting of Mubarak, pro-Morsi factions roamed some of the main streets in Minya, firing shots in the air and chanting, "Oh how pathetic, oh how shameful, the Copts have become revolutionaries!"[3] For pro-Morsi supporters, the Copts' participation in the uprisings represented an affront on many levels: it indicated that non-Muslims do not know their place, that is, subservience to the Muslim ruler; that Muslims allied themselves with non-Muslims, the infidels, against them; and that a war of infidels against Islam is under way.

3. Interviews with Coptic citizens living in Minya's city center, July 2013.

There were several attacks on Christian places of worship, property, and individuals throughout July and into August (see, for example, Wahib 2013 and Hanna 2013). Human Rights Watch announced that several attacks on Christians had taken place in governorates across Egypt, including Luxor, Marsa Matrouh, Minya, North Sinai, Port Said, and Qena, during a period of less than three weeks after Morsi's ouster (Human Rights Watch 2013). In many of the incidents, witnesses told Human Rights Watch that security forces failed to take necessary action to prevent or stop the violence.

The greater the intensity of the security crackdown on the Muslim Brotherhood, the more ferocious the latter's backlash against the Copts. On August 14, the pro-Morsi protests at Rabi'a al-'Adawiyya and al-Nahda Squares in Cairo were cleared using excessive force by the security forces, leading to the deaths of many protesters as well as several police officers. In the space of the twelve hours that followed, pro-Morsi factions attacked sixty-four places of worship belonging to Christians (Rahuma 2013). Furthermore, there were large-scale attacks involving looting and torching of Copt-owned private and commercial property and several murders. Undoubtedly, the scale of the assault on places of worship was testament to the failure of the government to provide the most minimal of security provisions and the adoption of an almost laissez-faire attitude toward the systematic targeting of places of worship nationwide.

Surprisingly, unlike other incidents in which Copts were very vocal in condemning security negligence for the failure to protect churches against attacks, the narratives of many Copts captured in focus groups hardly mentioned security laxity and spoke about the intensity of the vengeance of the pro-Morsi faction against them, using both religious and patriotic language. The language used to describe the torching of their places of worship was full of references to "sacrificial giving," to "the cross that we must carry," and to the "history of a persecuted church not shying away from giving." In patriotic terms, people spoke of the price they were willing to pay to "save Egypt from the Brothers" and to "restore Egypt to the Egyptians." The language bordered almost on a patriotic struggle against foreign occupation. While the narratives were underpinned by ideas about a better future, this point is relative. What does "better" look like? There was no consensus. Some hoped for full-fledged citizenship in which there would no longer be any discrimination on the basis of religion. Others hoped for the minimal survival that they more or less enjoyed under Mubarak (though this notion featured more in the narratives of the older generation, not the younger). What cut across gender, location, and age in these focus groups was a sense that *anything* would be better than what they had experienced under Morsi, which they used in their narratives as a proxy for Islamist rule. Such perspectives were shared in October 2013 and January 2015. The question is in what ways the narratives of their experience of 2011–13 will be affected by how they experience the new status quo in a few years' time.

Concluding Reflections: What Went Wrong?

In this section we revisit the earlier postulates described in the introduction and the links between them. While they were formulated as questions specific to majority-minority relations between Muslim and Coptic citizens, in reality the lines of demarcation are sometimes more heavily drawn along other identifiers. They include political stance, with or against the regime in power (Copts were united with Muslims against both the Mubarak and the SCAF regimes) or pro- or anti-Morsi (political and ideological lines against the rule of the Islamists). The variations also manifest themselves politically along generational lines: some Coptic youth, for example, showed voter preferences similar to other youth rather than their parents and the older generation, more generally, in the first round of presidential elections of 2012. This point is critical because, in many instances, the political agency of Copts is more reflective of the political pulse of a large segment of the Egyptian population at large than, for example, the will of the pope. Having disentangled the singular political agency of all the Copts as being encapsulated in that of the pope, the claim that the Coptic minority prefer dictatorial regimes can be dismissed. Pope Shenouda showed a preference for ententes with authoritarian regimes, whether with Mubarak or later SCAF, which supports the idea that the church leadership, as with the Islamic leadership represented by al-Azhar University, did support authoritarian rulers. However, this orientation was incongruent with the political will and behavior of the thousands of Copts who protested against both regimes. While the Morsi regime came to power through elections, the governance policies pursued were not regarded as democratic by large segments of the Egyptian population, whether Copt or otherwise (even though Morsi had a large constituency and support base). Hence, Coptic participation in the uprisings of June 30 cannot be interpreted simply as a rejection of democracy in favor of a return to military rule, because the choice was not between democratic and authoritarian systems of governance but between two different kinds of authoritarian rule (Islamist or military).

This point brings us to the second contention that has been discussed in this chapter, namely, that Arab revolts are bad for the rights of religious minorities. Without generalizing for the entire region, the Egyptian experience shows that it is not so much the regime rupture that is inimical to minority rights as the ideology of the political order that is most important. The January 25 revolution has been celebrated as an instance of unity between Christians and Muslims, often compared with the show of unity demonstrated in the 1919 uprising against British occupation. In my earlier writings (2012, 2013a), I suggested that it is majoritarian democracy that is inimical to minority rights. In the case of Egypt, the Islamist ideological bent of the masses who were mobilized in 2011 and 2012 is what undermined the prospects of an inclusive political order. This Islamist orientation was not so much manifest in the policies and laws that were issued in this period as it was felt on a number of other levels and in a number of other spaces.

The Islamists' victories at the ballot box provided a golden opportunity to abate external and internal fears that an Islamist democracy is antithetical to minority rights. Such assurance could have been demonstrated in the use of an inclusive public discourse not only at a macro level but also in mosques, public establishments, transportation, and day-to-day interactions in which supporters of the Islamist political forces interacted with people on a daily basis. The narratives of the Copts who were interviewed and in focus groups in different parts of the country suggest otherwise. They indicate that discourse, speech, and day-to-day interactions became increasingly conceived in terms of their status and role being mediated by their belonging to a Christian minority.

The argument that religious minorities such as the Copts experienced increased discrimination not because of the Islamist ascendancy to power but because of the structural sources of oppression laid by the previous authoritarian regime also needs to be examined carefully. There is strong evidence that Mubarak's security apparatus manipulated sectarian violence to achieve its own ends, sometimes playing a key role in its creation and exacerbation (Tadros 2013a). However, what the second part of this chapter sought to show is that sectarianism increased in scope, frequency, and intensity after Mubarak's resignation. New patterns of discrimination emerged that had not existed during Mubarak's era (though they had certainly existed in Egypt's long history). These new forms include the imposition of *jizya*, ransoms, and kidnappings. Transitions from authoritarian rule often bring a sense of social chaos as well, with women and minorities particularly vulnerable to attack amid the breakdown of law and order. Undoubtedly, Christian and Muslim Egyptians alike are suffering the effects of lax security, but, as shown throughout, the targeting of Copts because of their religious identity was deeply unsettling, confirming Copts' suspicions that Islamists as political actors who aspire to enact a kind of governance premised on their political conceptions of the sharia will produce an order that is ideologically and politically exclusionary toward them as a minority. In short, the 2011–13 experience only increased their preexisting Ikhwanophobia further (see Tadros 2012 for the history of relations between the Muslim Brothers and the Copts).

Finally, closely related to the first and second contentions on regimes and political agency, this chapter has challenged the conception that Copts were simply "flocks" of the church or "cocoonized" instead of claiming their rights in the public space. What has been argued is that no generalization can be made for an entire religious group; many Coptic citizens have long been politically active, both in national struggles as well as in making demands for the recognition of their own rights. As such, they represent a political constituency whose power emanates from numbers. What is critically important to note, however, is that they are the constituency neither of a political party nor of the church. Instead, they have been a political constituency against the Brotherhood regime and are likely to act as such against any regime that marginalizes them. While the Copts are not a monolithic entity, as they exhibit diversity in their political, class, and geographic affiliations, they have nonetheless been experiencing a growing collective self-awareness owing to the increasing attacks against them based on religious grounds. In other words, increased encroachment led to increased incidence of collective mobilization rather than cocoonization. While such awareness has not produced a unified political group, there is nonetheless a constituency that is capable of rising en bloc. In the Egyptian context, in which opposition parties have struggled to forge a constituency with limited success, no doubt the Coptic political constituency has and will affect local politics.

Any new regime will have to contend with the fact that, while the Copts' political activism will not lead to a complete reconfiguration of power, there is still power in numbers. It may not be enough to determine the political outcome, but it is sufficient to stabilize or destabilize the status quo.

Fears abound among many of the Copts interviewed that, just as the participation of Copts in the January 25 revolution did not translate into their empowerment in the new status quo, so too this time their activism will be followed by nonrecognition under Sisi's new regime. Whatever the outcome, these years between the ruptures will most certainly influence future perceptions of their position in state and society in two fundamental ways: first, the power of collective action, both with the rest of Egyptians and together on Coptic issues; second, that anything is better than being governed by a system that, formally or informally, brings the Islamists to power. The question then becomes not under what regime Copts enjoy *more* citizenship rights that are not mediated by religion, but under what regime they enjoy *less* violation of their rights on account of their religious affiliation.

Sources Cited

Asher-Schapiro, A. 2012. "Is the Government-Church Alliance a Coptic Marriage?" *Sada Bulletin* (Carnegie Endowment for International Peace). http://carnegieendowment.org/sada/?fa=47343.

Assran, Mahitab. 2013. "Further Competition between Tamarod and Tagarod." *Daily News Egypt*, June 22. http://www.dailynewsegypt.com/2013/06/22/further-competition-between-tamarod-and-tagarod/.

Azer, Sherif. 2015. "The Prior Coptic Revolution." *Madamisr*, Jan. 7. http://www.madamasr.com/opinion/prior-coptic-revolution.

Egyptian Initiative for Personal Rights. 2013. "Letters to Christians in Minya" [in Arabic]. http://eipr.org/sites/default/files/pressreleases/pdf/letters_to_christians_in_minya_30_june.pdf.

Egypt Independent. 2013a. "Presidency Statement Blames Copts for Clashes." Apr. 9. http://www.egyptindependent.com//news/presidency-statement-blames-copts-clashes.

———. 2013b. "Shura Council Bitterly Divided over Cathedral Violence." Apr. 11. http://www.egyptindependent.com/news/shura-council-bitterly-divided-over-cathedral-violence.

Eissa, Ibrahim. 2012. "Jokes That Lighten the Tragedy" [in Arabic]. *Al-Dustur*, Feb. 15.

El Ibrashy, Wael. 2011. Interview with Noha el Zeiny Wael. Dream TV, Dec. 16. https://www.youtube.com/watch?v=vF_B1gwjS6o.

Fayed, Shaimaa, and Yasmine Saleh. 2013. "Millions Flood Egypt's Streets to Demand Mursi Quit." Reuters, June 30. http://www.reuters.com/article/us-egypt-protests-idUSBRE95Q0NO20130630.

Gad, Emad. 2013. "Hal Takrahun Mursi?" *Takfik Ni'mati*, Apr. 12. https://takfiknamati.tv/.

Hanna, Tariz. 2013. "Supporters of the Uprooted [President] Attack the Church in Digla" [in Arabic]. *Watani*, July 28. http://www.wataninet.com/watani_Article_Details.aspx?A=43278.

Human Rights Watch. 2013. "Egypt: Sectarian Attacks amid Political Crisis." July 23. https://www.hrw.org/news/2013/07/23/egypt-sectarian-attacks-amid-political-crisis.

Kaldaya.Net. 2013. "Angry Egypt Pope Accuses Morsi of Negligence." Apr. 10. http://www.kaldaya.net/2013/News/04/Apr10_E1_MeNews.html.

Nkrumah, Gamal. 2012. "Hail the Holy Synod." *Al-Ahram Weekly*, March 22–28.

Rahuma, Mustafa. 2013. "*Al-Watan* Records 64 Cases of Assaults on Churches and Copts in 12 Hours" [in Arabic]. *Al-Watan*, Aug. 15. http://www.elwatannews.com/news/details/260930.

Tadros, Mariz. 2009. "Vicissitudes in the Coptic Church-State Entente in Egypt." *International Journal of Middle East Studies* 41 (2): 269–87.

———. 2012. *The Muslim Brotherhood in Contemporary Egypt: Democracy Redefined or Confined?* London: Routledge.

———. 2013a. *Copts at the Crossroads: The Challenges of Building an Inclusive Democracy in Contemporary Egypt.* Cairo: American Univ. in Cairo Press; New York: Oxford Univ. Press of America.

———. 2013b. "Copts under Mursi: Defiance in the Face of Denial." *Middle East Report* 267. http://www.merip.org/mer/mer267/copts-under-mursi.

———. 2014. "Devolving the Power to Divide: Sectarian Relations in Egypt (2011–2012)." *IDS Bulletin* (Institute of Development Studies) 45 (5): 69–80.

Wahib, Jirjis. 2013. "Supporters of the Uprooted [President] Surround Diocese in Beni Suef and Raise al-Qaeda Flag on Marqus Church" [in Arabic]. *Watani*, Aug. 8. http://www.wataninet.com/watani_Article_Details.aspx?A=43675.

al-Yawm al-Sabi'. 2012. "Beltagy Claims in Words Spoken a Short Time Ago That Investigations Discovered That Sixty Percent of the Demonstrators in Front of Ittihadiyya Palace Were Copts" [in Arabic]. Dec. 13. http://www.copts-united.com/node13/Article.php?I=1380&A=79046.

8

The Palestinians

Justice Denied

CHERYL A. RUBENBERG

Palestinian Arabs refer to the expulsion of Palestinians from their lands at the time of the establishment of the state of Israel in 1948 as the Nakba, "catastrophe." Of the estimated 950,000 Arabs who lived in the territory before the establishment of Israel in 1948, more than 80 percent fled or were expelled, while some 156,000 remained (Pappe 2006a; Masalha 1992; Morris 1987). At the same time, Israel razed more than four hundred Palestinian villages (Khalidi 1992). An additional 250,000–300,000 Palestinians, some of them refugees from 1948, were displaced and became refugees in the 1967 War (Raz 2012). Approximately 45.6 percent of the global Palestinian population of 11.6–11.8 million is in historic Palestine (Israel, East Jerusalem, the West Bank, and the Gaza Strip), and 54.4 percent live in exile. In 2013 there were 2,719,112 Palestinians in the West Bank, 1,701,437 in the Gaza Strip, and 1,650,000 Palestinian citizens of Israel. Of the 400,000 Palestinians in the Jerusalem governorate, 62.1 percent live in areas annexed by Israel in 1967 (Palestinian Central Bureau of Statistics 2013; Al Sahli 2013).

Palestinian Citizens of Israel

Seventy-eight percent of historic Palestine, through UN Resolution 181 and land seized in the course of conflict, became the state of

Israel in 1948. At present, Palestinians, living mainly in the Galilee, constitute approximately 20 percent of the Israeli population. Israeli Palestinians have the right to vote and serve in the Knesset unless they are "present absentees," Palestinians who fled or were expelled from their homes by Jewish or Israeli forces before and during the 1948 war but remained within the area that became the state of Israel, or if they live in "unrecognized" villages. One in four Palestinians living in Israel is a "present absentee"; estimates of the total number of internally displaced people in Israel are between 250,000 and 420,000 (Pappe 2011; Rempel and Boqai 2005; Human Rights Watch 2008). Myriad laws and institutional arrangements discriminate against Israeli Palestinians. The "Law of Return," passed on July 5, 1950, allows all Jews from anywhere in the world the right to live in Israel and automatically gain citizenship. In 1970, to accommodate the influx of Russians, many of whom had very weak or no "Jewish" credentials (that is, direct matrilineal descent), this right was extended to people of Jewish ancestry and their spouses. On the other hand, all of the exiled Palestinians are prohibited from returning to their homeland (Lustick 1999; Boling 2001).

Palestinians remaining in Israel were subject to martial law until 1966; travel permits, curfews, administrative detentions, and expulsions were part of life. Israeli legislation "legalized" the transfer of land abandoned by Palestinians in 1947–48. This legislation, along with the use of emergency regulations to declare land belonging to Palestinian citizens "closed military zones," enabled the confiscation of Palestinian citizens' land. These laws are regularly used in Israel, East Jerusalem, and the West Bank to confiscate Palestinian land. Especially in East Jerusalem, Palestinian families are daily dispossessed from their homes as Jews "reclaim" property they abandoned in 1948 when the city came under Jordanian occupation.

The Bedouin, who have lived in the Negev Desert in southern Israel since the seventh century, are the most vulnerable community in Israel. For more than sixty years they have faced a state policy of displacement, home demolitions, and dispossession of their ancestral land. Today, 70,000 Bedouin citizens live in thirty-five villages that either predate the establishment of the state in 1948 or were created by Israeli military order in the early 1950s. The state considers the villages "unrecognized" and the inhabitants "trespassers on State land," so it denies them access to state services, such as water, electricity, sewage, education, health care, and roads, in order to "encourage" them to give up their land. The Prawer–Begin Bill, approved by the Israeli Knesset in June 2013, entrenches the state's historic injustice against its Bedouin citizens (Adalah 2013). The bill was met with almost universal condemnation: the UN Committee on the Elimination of Racial Discrimination called on Israel to withdraw the proposed legislation on the grounds that it was discriminatory; in January 2012 thousands of Palestinians and Israelis protested the Prawer Plan; in July of that same year the European Parliament passed a resolution calling on Israel to halt the Prawer Plan and its policies of displacement, eviction, and dispossession; and in September 2013 both Human Rights Watch and the United Nations Office of the High Commissioner for Human Rights issued statements condemning Israel's ongoing destruction of Palestinian homes and other structures, particularly in the occupied West Bank and the Negev Desert. The outcry was such that, on December 12, 2013, the government announced it would "shelve" the plan, but its reactivation could occur at any time.

On January 4, 2014, *Ha'aretz* reported that Foreign Minister Avigdor Lieberman said he would not support any peace agreement that did not include an exchange of Israeli Arab land and population. People living in the predominantly Arab regions in central and northern Israel would not be expelled, but the border between Israel and Palestine (if Palestine were recognized as a state) would move so the Arabs would be included in the Palestinian state. He categorically rejected the idea of allowing "the return of even one Palestinian refugee to Israel" (Ravid 2014). Lieberman maintained that it makes no sense to create a Palestinian state with no Jews while Israel is turned into a dual-population state with more than 20 percent Arabs. The Israeli Left and nearly all Palestinian citizens of Israel oppose this plan, which was first proposed in May 2004, and consider it racist.

The Lieberman plan proposes a territorial exchange whereby Israel would annex almost all Israeli settlements in the West Bank while withdrawing from a few deep inside the Palestinian territories and transferring Arab–Israeli areas in Israel to the Palestinian state. All Arab residents of these areas would lose their Israeli citizenship. The Druze community, whose leaders are mainly pro-Israel, would remain part of Israel. The city council of one Israeli Arab town denounced the proposal as a "second Nakba" (Khoury 2014; *Ha'aretz* staff 2014b).

The disadvantages of Arab citizens of Israel include the following:

1. Arab municipalities control only 2.5 percent of the overall land within Israel. While the government has created more than seven hundred new Jewish communities since the formation of the state, no new Arab communities have been authorized, despite natural population growth, leading to large housing shortages.
2. Arab citizens contribute only 8 percent of Israel's gross domestic product (GDP), despite constituting 20 percent of the population.
3. Arabs and Jews have unequal access to health care; the life expectancy of Arab men is 4.0 years lower than it is for Jewish men, and life expectancy of Arab women is 3.2 years lower than it is for Jewish women.
4. Approximately 12 percent of undergraduate students and 4 to 8 percent of graduate students in Israeli universities are Arab, but only 2 percent of the academic staff is Arab. The education gaps result from unequal allocation of budgets, higher dropout rates, insufficient school facilities, lower matriculation rates, and a lack of funds for special education. Because of the inadequate provision of education to the Arab population, more than 50 percent of Arabs in Israel live below the poverty line and more are at risk of falling into poverty. No university in Israel uses Arabic as a language of instruction, ensuring the disproportionate benefit to Jewish

students of educational funding from the United States and the European Union (Mossawa Center 2013).

5. Of the 120 members of the Knesset, only 12 are Arab.
6. The fact that Arabs do not serve in the military means they are excluded from the many benefits provided to former service personnel, including preference in hiring, housing mortgages, salaries, student housing, higher education, and allocation of land for housing. The Contributors to the State Bill, approved by the Ministerial Committee for Legislation on June 16, 2013, states that such preferential treatment shall not be considered discrimination. On January 1, 2015, a new law was put into effect exempting discharged Israeli soldiers from paying national insurance fees.
7. Inequitable distribution of public funds between Jews and Arabs has led to growing socioeconomic gaps (UK Task Force on Issues Relating to Arab Citizens of Israel 2013).

The Occupied Territories

The Occupied Territories are the areas that Israel conquered in the 1967 War; they constitute the 22 percent of historic Palestine that remained outside Israeli borders after the war of 1948. They include East Jerusalem, the West Bank, and the Gaza Strip. All peace negotiations since the 1993 Oslo Accords concern these occupied areas. By 2014 Israel, in contravention of international law, had established more than 150 settlements, in addition to hundreds of illegal (by Israeli law, but with the assistance of government agencies) "outposts," with a combined population exceeding 600,000 Israeli citizens, and Israel was "negotiating" the retention of the settlements and their integration under Israeli sovereignty.

The fenced or patrolled areas of the settlements cover only 3 percent of the West Bank, but 43 percent of the West Bank is off-limits to Palestinian use because of its allocation to the settlements' local and regional councils. Virtually all the land viewed by Israel as public or "state land" (27 percent of the West Bank) has been allocated to settlements rather than for the benefit of the local population. About one-third of the land within the settlements' outer limits is privately owned by Palestinians (OCHA 2012a). By 2013 Israel controlled more than 60 percent of the West Bank through settlements and their jurisdictional areas, settlement blocs, outposts, military bases, closed firing zones, nature reserves, the Separation Barrier, and the matrix of settler-only bypass roads, leaving Palestinians clustered in isolated, disconnected cantons.

These conditions leave the West Bank a deeply carved-up area of disconnected Bantustans without access to water resources, little access to their former agricultural lands, and no prospects for Palestinian self-determination in an independent Palestinian state alongside Israel—to which the Palestine Liberation Organization (PLO) had agreed as far back as 1988, recognizing Israel's "right" to exist on the 78 percent of Palestine they had taken in 1948. This commitment was the basis of the Oslo Accords and all subsequent peace initiatives, but Israel has unilaterally created "facts on the ground" that have altered the physical reality to such an extent that a "two-state" solution looks increasingly impossible. At the same time, Israel wishes to see as many Palestinians as possible leave the territories and, to that end, has implemented policies that make life for the Palestinians so restrictive, humiliating, and economically debilitating that they are under constant pressure to move elsewhere.

In April 2014 an Israeli commentator noted that, for forty-six years, Passover in Israel has begun with an announcement that a total closure had been imposed on the Occupied Territories. He decried the logic that "our freedom = their oppression" and the discrimination that allows Arabs to be arrested without trial, imprisoned for years, kept behind walls, and beaten and tortured with impunity. Israel, he wrote, had become "a nation of prison wardens" (Laor 2014).

In late April 2014 *Ha'aretz* reported that Israel had imprisoned more than 800,000 Palestinians since conquering the West Bank and Gaza in the 1967 War. The editorial commented, "The numbers reflect one of the worst experiences of imprisonment in contemporary history, designed to break the will of an entire nation seeking freedom." At that time, 5,224 Palestinians were held in Israeli jails (*Ha'aretz* staff 2014c).

East Jerusalem

Israel endeavors to force Palestinians out of the city as one of various measures to make it impossible for East Jerusalem ever to become the capital of a Palestinian state. In the immediate aftermath of the 1967 War, Israel destroyed three villages southwest of Jerusalem, expelled the residents, and depopulated four other villages as well as half the city of Qalqilya (MIFTAH 2011). In occupied East Jerusalem, Israel disbanded the local municipal council, illegally extended Israeli law and jurisdiction, and, on June 28, 1967, passed the Reunification Law, a de facto annexation of East Jerusalem. Israel expelled all non-Jews from the Jewish Quarter in the Old City of Jerusalem (Benvenisti 1966, 64–67) and depopulated and demolished the Mughrabi quarter adjacent to the Western Wall, including one of the remaining mosques from the time of Saladin (Hasson 2012), to make room for a public square for Jewish worshipers, and built the Western Wall Plaza over the area. Israel also began immediately constructing settlements in its newly expanded borders. In 1980 Israel formally annexed East Jerusalem and declared it their "united and eternal capital," though this designation is not recognized by the world's governments, including the United States until December 6, 2017, when President Trump announced that the United States would recognize Jerusalem as Israel's capital. All other governments consider Jerusalem to be Occupied Palestinian Territory.

Following the 1969 Rogers Plan, housing construction in Jerusalem took on new intensity and went beyond demographic considerations to "a military conquest by architectural means," designed to preempt any possibility of Israeli withdrawal (Dumper 1997, 114; Raz 2012; Ir Amin 2010; Territorial Jerusalem 2013). Since that time, Israel has built nine Jewish settlements in East Jerusalem. The international community considers these settlements illegal because they are on occupied land. Aside from two small projects, no public planning or building was conducted for Palestinians throughout this period. Palestinian communities in East Jerusalem encountered bureaucratic and planning barriers designed, both overtly and covertly, to prevent their potential growth. Israel has used "urban planning" as a state tool to limit the development of Palestinian neighborhoods, while simultaneously expropriating Palestinian-owned land, constructing illegal Jewish-only settlements, and populating those areas with Jewish settlers (Lein 2002a, 85–90). After Likud's rise to power in 1977, the 1950 Absentee Property Law was used sporadically to take over East Jerusalem properties and houses, particularly in the Muslim Quarter of the Old City and in the Holy Basin (Rothman 2012). Most of these properties were turned over to extremist religious settler organizations. Creating Jewish enclaves and settling Jews in Palestinian villages and towns has inevitably meant the displacement of Palestinians. Under the 1993 Oslo Accords, East Jerusalem was supposed to become part of the independent Palestinian state, but, after the Accords were signed, a vast settlement project has been relentlessly colonizing and Judaizing Jerusalem. The current government of Prime Minister Benjamin Netanyahu has pursued this endeavor especially intensely, making clear publicly and behind closed doors that there are no restrictions on settlement expansion in municipal East Jerusalem (Territorial Jerusalem 2011).

Israel conferred "permanent residency" to Palestinians living in what became Municipal Jerusalem; in other words, the 66,000 Palestinians living in Jerusalem in 1967 were classified as resident aliens. Yehudit Oppenheimer describes as an "urban legend" the commonly told story that in 1967 Israel offered the city's Palestinian residents Israeli citizenship and they rejected it. Rather, Israel wanted the territory of East Jerusalem, but not its residents, and so "created a status that is without parallel in the world, a situation in which a native community of 300,000 people lives without citizenship in the place where they were born and have lived forever" (Oppenheimer 2012). Subsequently, Israel instituted a policy of "revocation of residency rights" in conjunction with house demolitions in an attempt to depopulate East Jerusalem of its Palestinians.

In East Jerusalem Palestinian housing, most of it already inadequate and severely overcrowded, is confined to 7.5 percent of the land dedicated to housing (Seidemann 1997). Palestinians who apply for permits to expand existing houses or to build new ones are virtually always refused on various "zoning or bureaucratic grounds." A Palestinian with an expanding family faces a hard choice: continued serious overcrowding for his family, building without a permit and ensuring demolition, or leaving for somewhere else, in which case he will lose his residency status. In East Jerusalem, an estimated twenty thousand homes, housing one-third of the population, have demolition orders.

Although East Jerusalem residents pay taxes, the Jerusalem Municipality has continuously failed to invest in infrastructure and services such as roads, sidewalks, and water and sewage systems in Jerusalem's Palestinian villages. It has built almost no new schools, public buildings, or medical clinics for Palestinians; the lion's share of investment has been dedicated to Jewish areas. An Inter-Ministerial Committee on Jerusalem decided that the Palestinian population there should remain at a steady ratio of no more than 20 to 28 percent of the total population of the city. Family reunification became the only mechanism by which West Bank residents could obtain permission to live in East Jerusalem. From 1967 to 1994, Palestinian women residents were not allowed to submit family reunification applications for their nonresident husbands. From 1982 until the mid-1990s, Israel's Ministry of the Interior did not allow Palestinian mothers residing in Jerusalem to register their children, thereby denying them access to public health services and education in Israeli public schools. Jerusalem-born Palestinian children registered according to their father's status in the West Bank lost the right to legal status in the city. According to official Israeli sources, Jerusalem residency status was revoked from at least 5,000 Palestinians in the period of 1968–95 because they had failed to retain a valid reentry visa while studying abroad (Gassner-Jaradat 2010).

The period of Israeli-Palestinian peace talks was characterized by a deterioration of Palestinian residency rights in the city. As Israel hoped to assert its claim for sovereignty over the entire city, unilateral Israeli activity intensified and policies were reshaped to strengthen this claim. A new Israel-entry permit system was installed in 1991–93, which restricted access of West Bank Palestinians to East Jerusalem. Under the pretext that Jerusalem was slated for discussion in future "final status negotiations," Israel's 1993 policy on family reunification was not applied to Palestinian Jerusalemites. East Jerusalem was excluded from the interim agreements reached between Israel and the PLO. Unlike Palestinian residents of the rest of the Occupied Territories, whose right to reside in the area was protected under the interim agreements, revocation of Palestinian residency rights in Jerusalem increased dramatically. The new policy conditioned Palestinian residency rights on proof of "center of life in Jerusalem" and required papers documenting employment and study. Permanent domicile had to be submitted by Palestinian holders of Jerusalem identity cards in any interaction with the Interior Ministry. Failure to prove "center of life" resulted in the revocation of residency rights not only from persons staying abroad but also from those individuals who had moved to live in the surrounding West Bank. Between 1995 and 1998, the Jerusalem residency status of some two thousand Palestinians and their dependents was thus declared "expired," and affected families were left in legal limbo (ibid.).

More recent official and unofficial proposals for dividing sovereignty over the city do not consider the basic right of Palestinians in Jerusalem to family unity. Ideas presented at the Camp David summit between Israel and the PLO, and by President Bill Clinton in 2000, as well as the so-called Geneva Initiative of 2003, treat Palestinians in Jerusalem as a population that can be separated and diminished by political compromise. With no such compromise in sight, Israel's Separation Barrier, currently under construction in eastern Jerusalem, is about to achieve a similar objective: when it is completed, between 70,000 and 100,000 Palestinians, lawful residents of the city, will be cut off from Jerusalem's center and stripped of their right of access to family, work, and public services. Their legal status as residents of Jerusalem is likely to be revoked in the future (ibid.).

Palestinians currently constitute 38 percent of Jerusalem's total population. Since 1967 the residency status of 14,084 Palestinians has been revoked. Seventy-eight percent of Palestinians in Jerusalem and at least 84 percent of the children live below the poverty line; the poverty rate rose 10 percent between 2009 and 2013 and is estimated at 86 percent (Oppenheimer 2013). Palestinians are permitted to build on only 7.5 percent of the area of East Jerusalem, most of which has already been exhausted by previous construction. Between 2005 and 2009, only 13 percent of the Jerusalem housing units that were granted building permits were in Palestinian neighborhoods (Association for Civil Rights in Israel n.d.b). There is a shortage of some thirty-one miles of sewage pipes, and residents instead use septic tanks. Repeated flooding of these systems causes serious health hazards (Association for Civil Rights in Israel n.d.a). There is a chronic shortage of some one thousand classrooms in East Jerusalem's educational system, despite Israeli commitments to the courts to provide them. The dropout rate for twelfth grade students in East Jerusalem is 40 percent.

East Jerusalem is home to 6,150 at-risk children; the rate of family violence is rising. Children are also at risk of arrest and detention; from 2000 to 2011, more than 8,000 Palestinian children between the ages of twelve and fifteen were arrested and detained in the West Bank and East Jerusalem. Nearly all were handcuffed and blindfolded during their arrest, which was most often carried out on suspicion of stone throwing, and they were almost always interrogated and held without access to a lawyer or their parents. Nearly all (98 percent) were subjected to physical or psychological violence during their arrest and detention (Save the Children and the East Jerusalem YMCA Rehabilitation Program 2012). A report released by Human Rights Watch highlights the abusive treatment of children in detention, including choke holds, beatings, and coercive interrogations (Human Rights Watch 2015).

The building of eighty-eight miles of the Separation Barrier, the closing of passage points, and the implementation of an "entry-permit regime" have effectively cut off East Jerusalem from the West Bank, exacerbating the poor economic and social conditions of its residents. The Separation Barrier and restrictions on entry from the West Bank imposed on both patients and medical staff led to a severe financial crisis in East Jerusalem's hospitals, which provide the bulk of medical services for the entire West Bank (World Health Organization 2011; Reuters 2012a; Shuttleworth 2015).

The most explosive issue in the Old City is the Israeli effort to change the status quo on the Haram al-Sharif, or Temple Mount, site of the third most important Muslim holy site. The only remaining wall of the Second Temple, known as the Western Wall, is holy to Jews. By allowing Jews to pray on the Haram, accompanied by Israeli soldiers, while imposing restrictions on Muslim worshipers, and, as a consequence of the growing movement to destroy the Dome of the Rock and the al-Aqsa Mosque and replace them with a Third Temple, Israel is responsible for greatly increased conflict over the site. There have been frequent clashes between Muslims who oppose the Jewish presence on al-Haram al-Sharif and the police who protect them and who frequently prevent Muslims from entering the Haram, in order to accommodate the Jews. After visiting the Haram in September 2000, accompanied by hundreds of soldiers and sparking the Second Intifada, Prime Minister Ariel Sharon in 2003 gave permission to non-Muslims to visit the Haram, despite Palestinian warnings that the move could destroy any hope for peace and would inflame violence (BBC 2000). Over the past two decades, both Jewish and fundamentalist Christian groups have advocated building a Third Temple on the site (Shragai 2005). In 1984 a Jewish terrorist group attempted to blow up the Dome of the Rock and other Muslim holy sites on the Haram but was foiled by Israeli authorities (Lis, Shragai, and Yoaz 2004).

From August to October 2013 conflict on the Haram al-Sharif intensified owing to the increasing frequency of visits by rabbis and Jewish worshipers to the site, the activities of various messianic Third Temple groups, and mounting prohibitions on Palestinians' access and prayer. The situation became so intense that Jordan sent a letter of complaint to UN Secretary-General Ban Ki-moon over Israeli occupation authorities' repeated violations against al-Aqsa Mosque and other holy sites in Jerusalem and escalating assaults by Jewish extremists on al-Aqsa Mosque, carried out under the protection of Israeli occupation forces (Abdullah 2013). A March 18, 2014, European Union internal report warned that the violations could "spark extreme reactions locally as well as across the Arab and Muslim world, and have the potential to derail the peace negotiations."

The report also says that almost 100,000 East Jerusalem residents are in danger of losing their homes owing to Israeli building restrictions. It details Israeli infringements on the rights of Palestinians in East Jerusalem, such as limitations on their freedom of movement and access to housing. The report says, "Israeli policies in Jerusalem are aimed at cementing its unilateral and illegal annexation of East Jerusalem" and points to "the unprecedented surge in settlements activity" since the negotiations resumed in July 2013, suggesting that this escalation appears to be part of Israel's strategy to use the settlement construction and infrastructures "to expand Jerusalem deeply into the West Bank" (Hass 2014a).

The West Bank

Israeli scholars Ariella Azoulay and Adi Ophir (2005) have characterized Israel's control over the West Bank as the interplay between "spectacular violence" that kills instantly and "suspended violence," meaning measures that are not immediately lethal, such as the permit system; the destruction of homes, roads, and wells; restrictions on movement; denial of access to water resources; the system of Jewish-only bypass roads; the Separation Barrier; and other means of dividing Palestinian territory into separate parcels. Both are apparent in analyzing the occupation. During the 1967 War, 280,000 to 325,000 Palestinians fled or were expelled from the Occupied Territories (Bowker 2003, 81). Between the 1967 War and the establishment of the Palestinian Authority (PA) in 1994, Israel stripped more than 250,000 residents of the West Bank of their residency rights (Eldar 2012). In 1967 the occupation forces pushed Palestinians to cross to the East Bank (Jordan) and prevented most of those persons who had fled or been expelled from returning to their homes. Israeli tactics included the demolition of villages; intelligence squads equipped with loudspeakers driving through towns and villages, telling the people to go to Jordan within two hours, because their houses would soon be bombarded; providing free bus rides for some 100,000 Palestinians to the Allenby bridge, from which they could cross into Jordan; forcing at gunpoint approximately 4,000 Palestinians daily to cross the river into Jordan; and destroying homes (Raz 2012, 103–35).

Palestinians in the West Bank are ruled by martial law implemented by an army bureaucracy called the Israel Civil Administration (ICA) under the control of the Israel Defense Forces (IDF). The June 1967 War had not yet ended when Israeli defense minister Moshe Dayan told Lieutenant General Yitzhak Rabin, the chief of the General Staff, that the aim of Israeli conquest in the West Bank was to empty it of its inhabitants (Raz 2012, 3). Since then, Israel has pursued direct depopulation policies in the region. Additionally, through indirect policies and processes, Israel hopes that Palestinians will despair of ever achieving a viable, sovereign state and will leave the territory and be willing to accept any settlement offered by Israel. The main components of indirect depopulation include military orders and incursions, mass arrests, arbitrary "administrative detention," military courts, home demolitions, the permit system, the Separation Barrier, and collective punishment, including curfews, closures, nighttime raids of villages, and attacks on civilian offices.

Home and Village Demolitions

Israel formally demolishes Palestinian homes for one of three "official" reasons: for lack of a permit, as a punitive measure (for example, if a family member is deemed to be a terrorist), or for alleged military reasons. In fact, the policy is grounded in strategic considerations, including restricting the areas where Palestinians can live. The Israeli Committee against House Demolitions estimates that between 1967

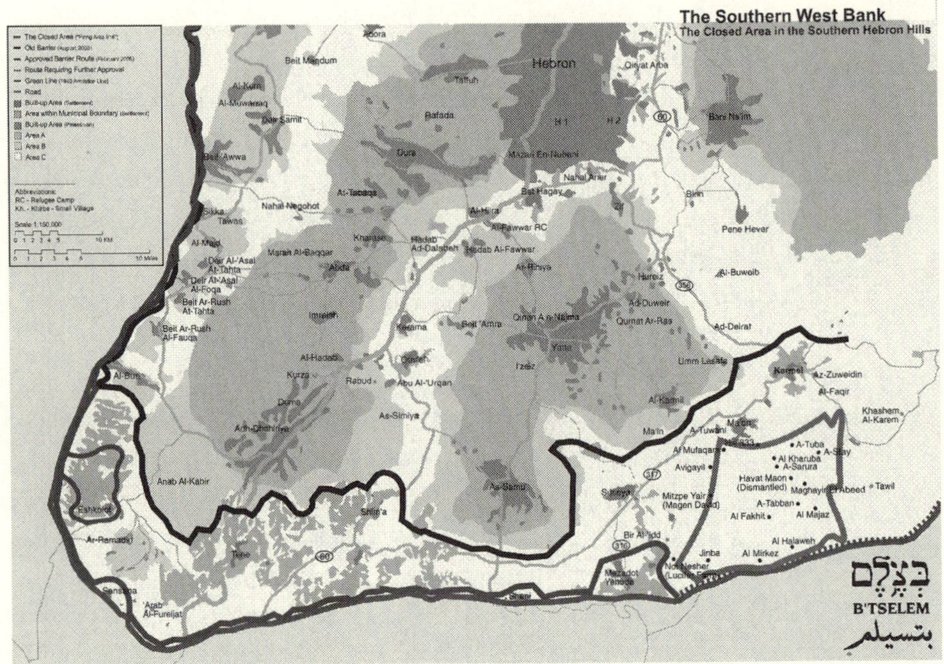

1. The closed area in the South Hebron Hills. A portion of the map found at http://www.btselem.org/sites/default/files2/map/southern_hebron_hills_map_eng.pdf. By permission of B'Tselem.org.

and 2011, Israel demolished twenty-five thousand homes in the West Bank, East Jerusalem, and Gaza, leaving hundreds of thousands of people homeless (Halper 2010). In 2012 alone, Israel demolished twenty-one hundred Palestinian homes and other structures, including tents, farm buildings, wells, and residential and industrial units (*Middle East Monitor* 2013). The human suffering entailed in the process of destroying a family's home is incalculable. A home is the center of people's lives; the site of their most intimate personal lives; a refuge; a physical representation; an expression of their identity, tastes, and social status; an extension of their very "selves." Traditionally, upon marriage sons in Palestine construct a home close to their parents, thus maintaining both physical proximity and continuity on ancestral land (Landau 2013).

Israel often demolishes entire villages. Eight villages in the South Hebron Hills were slated for destruction in July 2012 (figure 1, area outlined in red), allegedly "because the territory is needed for Israel Defense Forces training exercises." In reality, destruction of these villages is meant to empty the area of Palestinians. The IDF and the ICA regard all the residents of the targeted villages, particularly the ones in Firing Zone 218, as "squatters," even though the villages have existed since at least the 1830s. In areas of the West Bank that under the Oslo Accords are deemed Area C (areas under Israeli control), Israeli authorities do not allow residents to build more structures, including schools or clinics, to accommodate natural growth. These communities are not included in the master plans that were prepared for building settlements and are not connected to the road system, the water system, or the electrical grid (Hass 2012b; Jaradat 2012).

The Permit System

Of all the elements in Israel's suspended violence over the Palestinians, none is more all encompassing or more effective than the permit system. Permits regulate Palestinian employment, access to medical care, attainability of education, where they can worship, and their ability to travel—abroad, between Gaza and the West Bank, and within the West Bank, as well as to Jerusalem. The permit system negatively affects the Palestinian economy as well as Palestinians' ability to build or enlarge a home, develop their municipalities, tend their fields, dig or repair a well, or live in their village of origin, and it determines what roads they can travel on. It even determines the ability of families to live together as married couples with their children. The permit system allows Israel to control 2.3 million people in the West Bank (and, until 2005, the Gaza Strip), many of whom do not comprehend its integrated magnitude. Every vehicle—private automobiles, taxis, buses, ambulances, and trucks—must have multiple special permits just to move (in addition to licenses) to travel between and within various areas, to move commercial goods, and to travel within the "seam zone" (the area between the Separation

Barrier and the Green Line), among others (B'Tselem 2011a, 2015a). The principal question underlying this system is why any human being should need a permit to see a doctor, visit relatives in the next town, attend college, move from one place of residence to another, or pursue any other routine activity. Israeli authorities clearly view these movements as an exception or privilege, which they grant if they are convinced that the applicant is not a "security threat" and has a "justifiable reason" to go from one place to another inside the West Bank. For those Palestinians who are granted this privilege, the permit has become one of the most important documents for meeting daily needs and exercising rights, which cannot be achieved by means of other documents, such as an identity card or professional certificate.

Obstructions and Checkpoints

Israel has divided the West Bank into six major and several smaller cantons. The principal physical means Israeli security forces use to control and restrict Palestinian movement among the separated areas are obstructions and checkpoints—both permanent and temporary (known as "flying checkpoints"). Staffed checkpoints have existed in the Occupied Territories since the beginning of the occupation. During the years of the Oslo process (1993–2000), the number of checkpoints was vastly expanded to restrict freedom of movement from the Occupied Territories into East Jerusalem and Israel. With the eruption of the Second Intifada, a whole new system of checkpoints was imposed within the West Bank, to restrict movement from one area to another. Over the years, the checkpoints became the most conspicuous symbol of occupation. In early July 2007, there were eighty. Thirty-three of them were the last inspection point before entering Israel, but most were located a few kilometers from the Green Line, inside the West Bank (B'Tselem 2007b). In December 2012, there were ninety-seven fixed checkpoints in the West Bank; fifty-seven were internal checkpoints, which are all situated well within the West Bank. At some of the checkpoints, Israel prohibits private Palestinian vehicles to cross unless they have special permits and in principle allows crossing only for public transportation and commercial vehicles (B'Tselem 2007b). Seven checkpoints operate for the transfer of goods.

Some checkpoints are closed to motor vehicles; only pedestrians are allowed to cross. At these checkpoints, the residents are permitted to proceed to a few meters from the checkpoint, while at others the cars have to stop hundreds of meters away. Then the pedestrians cross the checkpoint, get into a vehicle (a bus or taxi) on the other side, and continue their journey (B'Tselem 2007a). Checkpoints are not only a matter of separation and control but frequently have extreme consequences. For example, between 2000 and 2007, sixty-nine pregnant Palestinian women were forced to endure labor or childbirth at a checkpoint, resulting in the deaths of at least thirty-five babies and five women during the period (Shoaini 2011). Human Rights Watch reported that in September 2000 three Palestinian laborers required hospitalization after being beaten by Israeli soldiers at a checkpoint. According to *Ha'aretz,* "In response to the event, the Israeli soldier commented, 'what we did was nothing special . . . everyone does it.'" The International Middle East Media Centre reported instances of strip searches being performed on women as well as young girls. B'Tselem reported that between 2000 and 2010, thirty-eight people died as a result of being stopped or delayed at checkpoints while they were on their way to the hospital (Weir n.d.; B'Tselem 2007b). Palestinians endure long waits at checkpoints, exposed to heat and cold, without food or drink. They are often humiliated or detained by soldiers wanting "to 'educate' them in response for what the soldiers consider arrogance, or an attempt to bypass the checkpoint, or even for trying to talk with a soldier at the checkpoint" (B'Tselem 2007b).

A few hours every day security forces set up dozens of "flying checkpoints" throughout the West Bank, stopping all passing vehicles carrying Palestinians, even if the travelers had already been checked at a permanent checkpoint. Since 2000 security forces have increasingly made use of flying checkpoints; 340 were set up in March 2012 (OCHA 2012b). For the most part, Palestinians are prohibited from using the modern “bypass” roads that crisscross the West Bank to facilitate settler travel among settlements and to Israel proper. Palestinians are mainly confined to old side roads and a few main roads. Movement along the side roads is blocked by physical obstructions (dirt mounts, concrete blocks, boulders, trenches, fences, and iron gates) to channel traffic to the main roads, where all Palestinian movement is subject to staffed “checkpoints” through which only those individuals with proper permits may pass. As of mid-July 2007, there were 455 physical obstructions throughout the West Bank (B’Tselem 2007b). Unlike staffed checkpoints, these obstructions do not allow the exercise of discretion in permitting movement along the road, so no accommodation is made for emergencies. The problem is exacerbated in winter, when the area is muddy and large puddles of water collect alongside the obstructions (B’Tselem 2011c; OCHA 2012b).

As a result of these restrictions on movement, hundreds of thousands of Palestinians daily spend many hours trying to get from one place to another. Given that they learn only at the last moment whether they will receive a permit, be allowed to cross the checkpoint, or how much time they will have to wait before crossing, the residents of the West Bank live in a constant state of uncertainty and are unable to make plans. Their lives often revolve around the attempt to reach their destination (B’Tselem 2007b). Therefore, many cut back as much as possible on the need to travel. The geographic division of the West Bank causes long-term harm to the economic, social, and political life of Palestinian society, making it very difficult for people to exercise their right to self-determination.

Siege

Siege is another means Israel uses to separate West Bank Palestinians; Israel blocks access roads to certain areas by placing physical obstructions, so that entry and exit are possible only via fixed checkpoints. A siege of this kind was imposed on the Nablus area from 2002 to 2008, causing terrible damage to the city’s infrastructure and creating hundreds of casualties. In order to take over the city, soldiers punched holes through walls, ceilings, and floors of homes, mosques, and commercial buildings, destroying soap factories and established landmarks (Leech 2012). Siege tactics were used in different areas through 2014, negatively impacting social institutions and impeding the development of business and health care.

The Separation Barrier

The Separation Barrier, on which construction began in 2000, has deeply and destructively distorted the geography, economy, and social life of Palestinians in the West Bank and East Jerusalem by confiscating more land; separating villages from their agricultural lands, further diminishing the agricultural sector; severing villages in half, separating villages from each other and from their "mother" cities; impeding access to education, health care, and employment; creating a new "closed military zone" referred to as the "seam zone"; and imposing an expanded "permit regime" whereby Palestinians must have permits to live in their own homes, work their own lands, or travel beyond their villages.

All official Israeli government decisions and documents on the Separation Barrier emphasize that the barrier does not signify a future political border and that the sole reason for its construction was "security." However, the main purpose was to expand Israeli settlements. The Separation Barrier was erected primarily *within* the occupied West Bank and has expanded Israel's area of control. The barrier's route, determined in part by the location of many of Israel's West Bank settlements, creates the infrastructure for de facto annexation of most of the settlements and settlers. Israel's settlement expansion is also taking place far to the east of the barrier, deep in the West Bank, in places such as Beit El, Ofra, Eli, Shiloh; throughout the Jordan Valley and the southern Hebron Hills; and through the process of "retroactively legalizing" outposts in remote areas. The barrier, like the settlements, leads to numerous infringements of the basic human rights of Palestinians over and above the direct damage inflicted by its construction, including violations of property rights, the right to free movement, the right to an adequate standard of living, and the collective right to self-determination (Lein and Cohen-Lifshitz 2005; Shalev 2012; Hareuveni 2010, 2012; Lein 2002a, 2002b, 2003; Dugard 2004). The Separation Barrier has also had severe environmental impacts, including land degradation, severe flooding, the destruction of water sources, and deteriorated waste management, which have compounded its adverse effect on the livelihoods of Palestinians in rural areas of the West Bank and on the already vulnerable Palestinian refugee population (UNRWA 2012; Rinat 2012).

The total length of the Separation Barrier, as approved in the last government decision on the matter in April 2006, and after changes to the route were carried out by order of the High Court of Justice, is 708 kilometers (440 miles). It is more than twice the length of the Green Line (the 1949 armistice line between Israel and the West Bank). The barrier's route is convoluted, with 85 percent running within the territory of the West Bank, mainly in areas where Israel has established settlements and industrial zones. In other areas, it runs mostly along the Green Line. To the west of the barrier, on its "Israeli" side, lies 9.4 percent of the territory of the West Bank, including East Jerusalem (UNRWA 2012).

The Separation Barrier includes a system of fences, an antivehicle component, patrol roads, a trace path on each side to disclose the footprints of infiltrators, and warning and surveillance systems. Its total width, including all these components, ranges between 35 and 100 meters (115 and 328 feet). According to the Israeli Ministry of Defense, along 4 percent of the route the barrier takes the form of an 8-meter-high (26-foot-high) concrete wall, primarily in urban areas such as East Jerusalem, Qalqilya, and Tulkarm (figure 3). In July 2013, approximately 62 percent of the barrier's approved route was complete, a further 10 percent was under construction, and 28 percent was planned but not yet constructed (OCHA 2013).

The Separation Barrier has reduced the access of Palestinians living in communities located behind the barrier to workplaces and

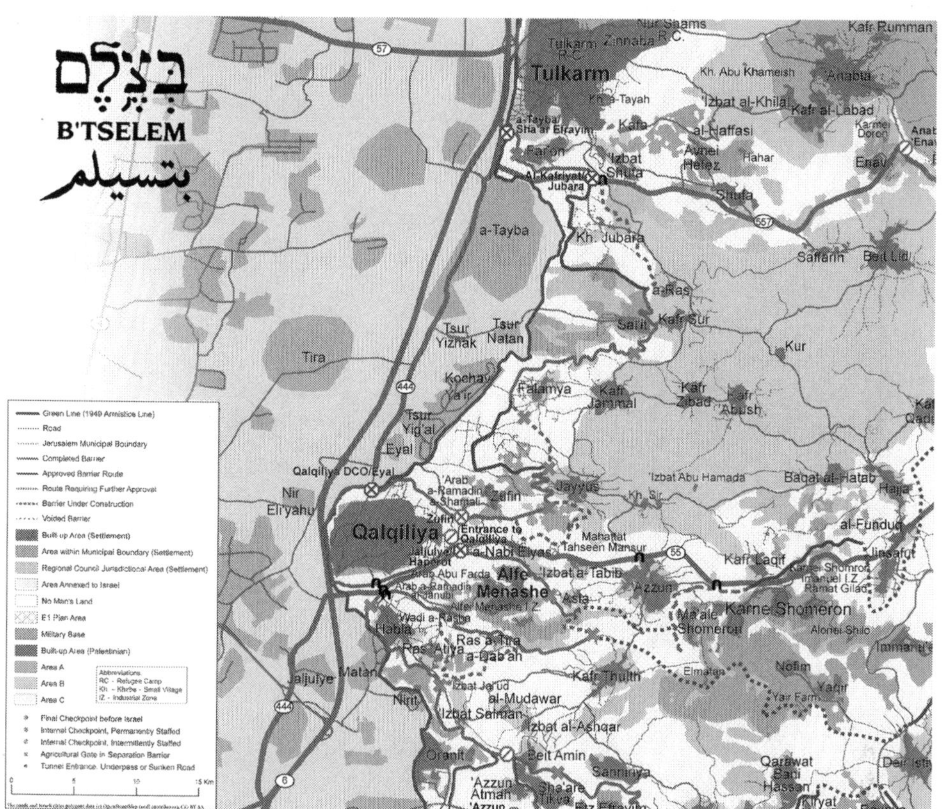

2. The Separation Barrier in the Tulkarm-Qalqiliya area. Map by Ofir Feuerstein. In Shlomi Suissa, *Not All It Seems: Preventing Palestinians Access to Their Lands West of the Separation Barrier in the Tulkarm-Qalqiliya Area* (Jerusalem: B'Tselem, 2004), 5. By permission of B'Tselem.org.

essential services. The agricultural livelihoods of thousands of families have been undermined by the permit and gate regime, which restricts access to farmland behind the barrier. Permit applications are regularly rejected on grounds that farmers failed to prove their "connection to the land" to the satisfaction of the Israeli authorities, as well as on security grounds. In 2011, "42 percent of applications submitted to the civil administration before the harvest to reach the olive groves beyond the barrier were rejected" (Greenberg 2012). The

3. The Separation Barrier between Abu Dis and East Jerusalem, June 7, 2004. Photo by Brendan McKay. Printed with permission.

limited opening of the agricultural gates has forced permit holders to stop cultivation or to shift from labor-intensive to rain-fed and low-value crops.

To enable construction of the Separation Barrier, Israel issued orders for expropriation of 30,261 dunams (7,477 acres) of land. Of that area, 88 percent is private land belonging to Palestinian residents, and 0.6 percent is owned by Israeli citizens. The remainder, amounting to 3,460 dunams (855 acres, 11.4 percent of the land), was confiscated by Israel from Palestinians and declared "state land" (Hareuveni 2012, 14). Between 2004 and 2007, more than 160 structures located near the barrier's route were destroyed (B'Tselem 2008a). The sections of the barrier that have not yet been built will encompass settlement blocs deep within the West Bank—"fingers" reaching far into the West Bank.

The Military Justice System

Since June 1967, the Israeli military authorities have issued some twenty-five hundred decrees with enormous impact on all aspects of Palestinian life. They are frequently revised, almost impossible to challenge, and can apply retroactively. These orders provide the "legal" basis for charging Palestinians with political and other offenses. They do not apply to Israeli settlers living in the West Bank, who are governed by Israeli civil law, a discrimination that contravenes international law. Palestinians are often unaware that new military orders have been issued because they have not been made public or translated into Arabic, and they only become apparent when they are implemented. Palestinians' most basic aspirations and normal activities, including education, marriage, work, health care, and movement, are regulated by military and emergency laws that impose criminal sanctions for breaches and violations. These decrees have allowed the military to control all West Bank water, expropriate Palestinian lands by simple declaration that it is "state land," conduct raids, arrest people, take over domestic rooftops under the pretext of observation, and harass the population (Hareuveni 2010; Shalev 2012; B'Tselem 2011e; Reuters 2012a).

Ha'aretz described a military raid in the West Bank village of Budrus in May 2013: Thirty Israeli soldiers arrived at a home at two in the morning, broke down the front door of a home, and tossed concussion grenades at its terrified residents. They dragged the mother by her hair, yelling insults and injuring her hand; they kicked the father and sprayed him with pepper spray; they beat one of the daughters; they threw a young man down the stairs, dropped a concussion grenade on him, and, without explanation, dragged him away nearly naked. When an adult daughter of the family arrived, the soldiers broke her arm. What happened, according to one of the authors, was "routine" (Levy and Levac 2013; Levy 2013a). In a representative week, from January 26 to February 1, 2012, the Israeli military conducted fifty-six such incursions into Palestinian communities in the

West Bank and a limited one into the Gaza Strip (Palestinian Center for Human Rights 2012). The intention is to engender a climate of fear and uncertainty.

Arrests

Arrests of Palestinians are a daily event and a well-established Israeli occupation practice. Most of these arrests and detentions have nothing to do with security but are intended to humiliate and create fear. Arrests of young men for throwing stones at soldiers are common and often result in imprisonment, sometimes followed by release after several months with a fine or without charge. More often, they are convicted of a "security offense"—anything Israel defines as such (for example, showing a prohibited flag, possessing a "banned" book or newspaper, and more)—and spend many long years in prison. Between 1967 and December 2012, an estimated 800,000 Palestinians were detained under Israeli military orders in the Occupied Territories—approximately 20 percent of the total Palestinian population under occupation and as much as 40 percent of the total male Palestinian population (Levy 2013b). As of August 2009, there were at least 7,834 Palestinians in Israeli prisons and detention centers, of whom 53 were women and 355 were children under the age of eighteen (Addameer 2009). From August 31, 2009 to November 30, 2012, 44,728 Palestinians were arrested. In 2012 alone, 4,500 Palestinians were arrested (B'Tselem 2016d). Prison conditions are bleak; interrogations are often conducted under torture, sometimes resulting in fatalities (Levy 2013b; Addameer 2016).

In March 2013, the United Nations Children Fund (UNICEF) revealed that 700 Palestinian children aged twelve to seventeen, most of them boys, are arrested, interrogated, and detained by the Israeli military, police, and security agents every year in the occupied West Bank. These children are often blindfolded, their hands tied, and they suffer physical and verbal abuse. They are often coerced into confession and do not have immediate access to a lawyer or family during questioning. All of this contravenes international standards for children's rights. Such practice, says the report, appears to be widespread, systematic, and institutionalized (Reuters 2013).

Administrative detention is a procedure by which governmental authorities detain individuals without charge and without judicial trial. Based on secret "evidence," an Israeli military commander may detain a suspect for up to six months, and the military court may extend detention indefinitely. Some administrative detainees spend as many as seven or more years in prison. The state is not required to disclose the evidence for the alleged threat posed by that individual, either to the detainee or to his or her attorney. If Israel had evidence of an individual's wrongdoing or lawbreaking, it would arrest, try, and convict that person; the vast number of convicted prisoners attests to this fact. Administrative detention, then, can be understood as political repression—punishing an individual for his or her speech, writings, or alleged associations. It has also been the primary method that Israel has used to eliminate emerging political leaders—whether nationalist or Islamist—in the Occupied Territories (B'Tselem and HaMoked 2009).

The Israeli military court system in the West Bank (and in Gaza prior to Israel's 2005 unilateral withdrawal), established in 1967, is distinct from the system used to court-martial Israeli soldiers and from the system that tries and punishes (or acquits) Israelis, including those persons who live in the settlements. The primary or only evidence in the vast majority of military court convictions is confessions (first or third-party, or both) extracted during interrogation. The IDF and police conduct some interrogations, but the main agency responsible for interrogation of Palestinians is the Israel Security Agency, Shin Bet. The age of "criminal responsibility" in the Occupied Territories is twelve (Hajjar 2006).

Many international observers were skeptical or reluctant to label Israel a torturing state; however, in 1977, the *Sunday Times* (London) published a detailed inquiry into "Arab allegations and official Israeli denials of the use of torture." The *Times* reported, "Torture of Arab prisoners is so widespread and systematic that it cannot be dismissed as 'rogue cops' exceeding orders. It appears to be sanctioned as deliberate policy." As a result, Prime Minister Menachem Begin ordered a curtailment of violent interrogation tactics, and for the next several years allegations of torture declined. To compensate, Shin Bet developed a new technique to gather information and extract confessions: the use of Palestinian collaborators (*'asafir*, literally "birds") in prisons. By the early 1980s, torture was resumed, including beatings, electric shock, death threats, position abuse, cold showers, sexual abuse, and denial of access to toilets (Hajjar 2010).

Control over the Economy

Israel has nearly absolute control over the economy of the West Bank, integrating it into the Israeli economy and creating a profound imbalance in the Palestinian economy. Israel has had this control since 1967; however, the 1995 Paris Protocol to the Interim or Oslo II Accord sanctioned and deepened Israel's strict control over the Palestinian economy, including all imports and exports. Israel collects all customs duties on behalf of the Palestinian Authority and has repeatedly withheld them as a form of blackmail and punishment. The Paris Protocol established a system whereby virtually every basic commodity from soap powder to cement to gasoline must be imported from Israel or through Israeli middlemen, who in some cases are former officers of the occupation army (Gordon 2008, 70–92).

Study after study, including studies by the World Bank, the International Monetary Fund, and other neoliberal Western institutions, show that Israel's grip on the Occupied Territories, its theft of land and water and control of movement, remains the principal obstacle to Palestinian economic activity (for example, World Bank 2011). On top of Israel's paralyzing domination of the economy of the West Bank, economic "development" has been channeled away from indigenous Palestinian business and into industrial zones where foreign and Israeli exporters can exploit unskilled Palestinian workers cheaply and without any accountability (World Bank 2012; Kanaan, Kock, and Sumlinski 2012; UNCTAD 2012). A 2012 World Bank report stated that virtually all the "growth" in the West Bank was the result of foreign aid, and, in the past few years, the PA "has become more donor dependent at an increasing rate," with "the majority of the recent donor aid" allocated "to pay PA salaries and arrears, which has pumped up consumption and imports of consumer goods." The same World Bank report found that investment had been close to nil, as the productive sectors of the Palestinian economy continued to shrink, with more people becoming dependent on PA salaries and aid handouts. Unemployment has continued to rise and remains at Great Depression levels of 26 percent (higher in Gaza), according to a new study by the United Nations Conference on Trade and Development (UNCTAD). Half of all infants under two years of age in the West Bank and Gaza Strip suffer from iron-deficiency anemia. Stunting and malnutrition levels have shown no signs of improvement, as millions of Palestinians in the West Bank and Gaza remain mired in poverty and food insecurity (World Health Organization 2005).

From 1993 to 2000 and beyond, Israel imposed a policy of "closure" in the West Bank and Gaza, with serious economic repercussions. The restrictions on movement of goods and people strangled the Palestinian economy; 80 percent of the 125,000 Palestinians who worked in Israel or joint industrial zones lost their jobs during the Oslo years, resulting in a huge drop in the Palestinian GDP. The Paris Protocol allowed Israel to check Palestinian goods for "security," to license business enterprises, to issue import and export licenses, and to stipulate the import or export partners to be used. The result was the closure or downsizing of the majority of Palestinian companies owing to high costs and ensuring that virtually all Palestinian imports and exports are with Israel (Kubursi and Naqib 2010).

Israel controls all water resources available to Palestinians and distributes them in an extremely unequal fashion (B'Tselem 2011b). Israel's citizens, including citizens living in West Bank settlements, as in developed countries worldwide, benefit from unlimited running water to meet their household needs and sustain their agricultural sector. On the other hand, hundreds of thousands of Palestinians suffer from a severe water shortage throughout the summer, and many also endure scarcities during the winter. The shortage of drinking water causes dehydration and the inability to maintain proper hygiene, leading to illness. Water shortages and land confiscation are the major causes of the severe decline of the agricultural sector, traditionally the largest sector of the Palestinian economy, since failure to water crops and animals leads to their degeneration. The regression of the agricultural sector has not been made up by a potentially flourishing industrial sector, because Israel has prevented the development of Palestinian industry.

According to military orders dating from 1967, there has been a drastic restriction on drilling new wells to meet Palestinian water needs. Drilling a well requires obtaining a permit, which entails a lengthy and complicated bureaucratic process, and the vast majority of applications submitted have been denied. The majority of permits sought were for wells that had ceased to be used owing to improper maintenance or because they had dried up. The few that were granted were solely for domestic use and were less than the number of wells that were in use before 1967 (B'Tselem 2011b). This Israeli power and its policies did not change after the Interim Accord. In October 2012, for example, Israeli forces destroyed five water wells and a water pump in a northern West Bank village near Jenin, claiming the structures were constructed without a permit. An Israeli bulldozer, accompanied by military vehicles, destroyed the wells in Kfar Dan village, without even giving the villagers any prior notification. Jenin governor Talal Dweikat commented, "By destroying water wells, Israeli authorities are targeting the Palestinian economy" (*Ma'an* news agency 2012).

The water shortage is especially hard on residents of Palestinian villages that are not connected to a water network. Some 191,238 Palestinians still live in 134 West Bank villages without a network of running water. An additional 190,000 Palestinians live in communities with very limited water systems. In the winter and fall, these residents collect rain in cisterns next to their homes and use it for all their needs. In spring and summer months, when the water in the pits runs out, the residents rely on water from nearby springs and water they purchase at extremely high cost from owners of private water tankers. Hundreds of thousands of other Palestinians live in communities with a central running water network that supplies water irregularly in limited amounts and does not reach everyone in the community. For this reason, some Palestinian authorities supply water in the summer months on a rotation basis: each neighborhood receives water once every few days, for one day and only for several hours at a time. To supplement this amount, residents buy water brought to them in privately owned tankers at very high prices (Lein 2001). To make matters worse, Israeli forces often destroy Palestinians' rainwater cisterns. In the first ten months of 2012, Israeli soldiers destroyed thirty-six rainwater cisterns in Israeli-controlled areas of the West Bank, affecting 1,600 people (Palestine News Network 2012). Most had been restored with European assistance. Most of the communities affected by these demolitions reside near Israeli settlements and unauthorized outposts that enjoy a regular water supply. In many of these cases, ancient cisterns were destroyed that had served the forefathers of the inhabitants of these communities long before the establishment of the state of Israel. Restoring an ancient cistern is considered an offense (*Ha'aretz* editor 2012a).

Israel provides the PA with 95 percent of its electricity in the West Bank and 75 percent of its electricity in Gaza. Israel can and does cut the power supply at will. The PA is powerless to determine the price of electricity, much less the supply. Because of its dependence on the Israeli electricity grid, Palestinian projects for solar energy in the West Bank received permission to supply electricity only to places that are not hooked up to the electricity grid. Moreover, Israel has demolished numerous "illegal" solar panels that are the only source of electricity for Palestinians in West Bank villages (Greenwood 2012).

Hoteliers, Israel Chemicals, and cosmetics firms that market products made of minerals from the Dead Sea claim that this body of water, one-third of which was conquered by Israel in 1967, is an economic asset solely belonging to Israel. In reality, however, 25 percent of it belongs to Palestinians. Nonetheless, Palestinians have been denied permission to build tourist hotels or industries using Dead Sea resources (Sadeh 2012).

Olive trees are a traditional mainstay of the Palestinian economy and remain the major commercial crop for Palestine, with many families dependent on olives for their livelihood. Numerous products are extracted from olive trees, including olives, olive oil, olive wood, and olive-based soap. Olive oil is the second export item in Palestine, and olive production contributes to 38.2 percent of all fruit trees' productive income. The olive industry in the Occupied Territories supports 80,000 families and accounts for 14 percent of the economy's agricultural income. The inability of farmers to cultivate or harvest their crops because of security-related pretexts or the physical destruction of trees undermines the fragile Palestinian economy and makes arable subsistence less feasible for communities. The destruction of olive trees by settlers is a constant phenomenon—soldiers do not protect Palestinian farmers—and the soldiers themselves implement government policy to destroy olive groves. With all the above-noted impediments, including water shortages, total agricultural output has been seriously damaged; the proportion of the GDP earned from agriculture has fallen from 28 percent to 5.6 percent in the past twenty years (Aviram 2012).

Israel controls all Palestinian borders, airspace, and much of its communications. Moreover, it has made clear that this situation will continue even if an independent Palestinian state is eventually negotiated. Palestinians were initially hopeful that the Oslo process was an opportunity to shake off the choking economic reliance on Israel; it was assumed that Palestinians would soon have control over their own border crossings. Palestinian officials fueled this optimism by speaking repeatedly about a Palestinian-controlled seaport, airport, and safe passage to link the West Bank and Gaza, all of which they claimed were promised under the provisions of Oslo and would be implemented at later stages. None of these hopes came to fruition.

Settler Violence

Residents of illegal Jewish settlements in the West Bank perpetrate acts of extreme violence against Palestinians, with the silent complicity of IDF forces (Hass 2012c; *Ha'aretz* editor 2012b; Levy and Levac 2014). Settler violence against Palestinians in the Occupied Territories began during the early 1970s and has continued unabated; indeed, it has increased exponentially. With increasing impunity, the scope and intensity of settler violence surged during the First Intifada (1987–93) and swelled dramatically during the Second or al-Aqsa Intifada (2000–2005). The judicial system fails to arrest, charge, or sentence settlers involved in violence against Palestinians. Settlers have killed hundreds of Palestinians and have carried out thousands of assaults on people and property. They abuse merchants and owners of market stalls, destroying their goods and ruining produce; they hurt Palestinian medical crews and attack journalists; they kill livestock, poison wells, destroy crops, uproot trees, shatter windowpanes and windshields, and torch automobiles, trucks, homes, and mosques. A common practice is to enter Palestinian residential areas, shoot and throw stones at houses, and damage property. In 2013 there were 399 settler attacks on Palestinians, resulting in 146 injuries, 306 attacks on private property, and 201 Palestinians harmed by the failure of Israeli security forces to protect Palestinians from settlers (Hass 2014b).

The objective of the attacks is to intimidate the Palestinians to such an extent that they will "leave voluntarily." Government acquiescence is further testimony to the state's objective of depopulating the West Bank. In October 2012, *Ha'aretz* reported that Israeli authorities have sought to limit Palestinian farmers' access to olive trees, the main source of their livelihood, to a few days a year and did not protect the olive trees from vandalism the rest of the year. "This system penalizes farmers by limiting their access, rather than enforcing the rule of law on violent settlers" (Greenberg 2012). In one case that went to court, settlers repeatedly assaulted two elderly brothers, beating them when they tried to access their fields, causing severe injuries, and burning their olive trees. They left messages such as "Death to the Arabs" (Hass 2013).

The Israeli government offers tacit support to settlers who engage in this behavior. Numerous organizations inside Israel and in the international community have written comprehensive reports documenting the violence and the collusion of the Israeli government (for example, United Nations Human Rights Council 2013; Amnesty International 2005; B'Tselem 2011e; Yesh Din 2014; Human Rights Watch 2005). In March 2013 an Israeli analyst described how soldiers protected settlers as they stole a Palestinian's horse, chain saw, and coat, which contained his identification. He commented, "Generations of officers have learned from experience that enforcing the law [on settlers] can be a major hindrance to their careers. . . . If they try to, they know that the military wing of the settlers—aka 'a small number of fanatics over whom we have no control'—will make them pay the price" (Gurvitz 2013).

While Palestinians in the West Bank are subject to military rule, Israeli settlers are subject to the Israeli judicial system and are afforded liberties and legal guarantees that Palestinians are denied. The government has created an extraterritorial personal status for Israeli civilians living in the Occupied Territories, regulations that the Knesset regularly extends. The Israeli government authorized settlers to carry weapons from the earliest days of the settlement project; the IDF issued Uzi and M-16 machine guns to early settlers. As the number of settlers grew, the IDF expanded the settlers' institutionalized security role. These "organic military units," composed of settler-residents, are granted authority to detain Palestinians but are mandated to operate only within settlement confines. The IDF provides them with weapons, training, and equipment.

Killings and Injuries Caused by the Israel Defense Forces

One former Israeli soldier describes the typical IDF attitude toward Palestinians:

> As soldiers, we preferred to relate to every Palestinian as a threat. In effect, there is no distinction between a Palestinian who fires at us and a Palestinian who throws a rock at us, a stone thrower and a demonstrator or a demonstrator and someone who simply does

> not obey our orders or gets insolent. All of them are attempting to undermine our control and at the end of the day, everyone is an enemy. And if every Palestinian is an enemy, then every Palestinian is also a target. And there is nothing he can do to stop being a target, in our view. (Gvaryahu 2013)

In 2013 IDF soldiers killed 27 Palestinians in the West Bank, the highest figure since 2008, and three times higher than in 2012, when 9 Palestinians were killed in the West Bank. Four of those persons killed in 2013 were minors. Six were armed, but Palestinian sources doubt that the IDF's intent was to arrest rather than kill them. IDF soldiers killed a worker trying to cross the Separation Barrier, as well as a minor who approached the barrier in another village and a woman walking along the fence in the al-'Arrub refugee camp. Israeli security forces injured 3,736 Palestinians in 2013, compared to 3,031 in 2012; 64 percent were wounded in popular protests against the occupation (up from 59 percent in 2012); 32 percent of the injured were minors (Hass 2014b).

During the First Intifada, which by all accounts was a movement of nonviolent resistance, Israel killed 1,100 Palestinians, and as many as 29,900 children required medical treatment for injuries caused by beatings from Israeli soldiers following Defense Minister Yitzhak Rabin's policy to use "force, might, and beatings" to suppress the uprising. More than 120,000 Palestinians were arrested (B'Tselem 2000; Abunima 2011; Institute for Middle East Understanding 2012). Between September 1993 (the beginning of the "Oslo Peace Process") until September 2000 (the beginning of the Second or al-Aqsa Intifada), Israel killed 276 Palestinians. The Second Intifada involved considerable violence: Palestinians killed 731 Israeli civilians (200 in the West Bank, including 35 minors and 45 women) and 332 military or security forces (146 in the West Bank); Israeli military or security forces killed 4,860 Palestinians, including 1,793 in the West Bank (of whom 317 were minors and 53 were women), and Israeli civilians or settlers killed 46 Palestinians, of whom 40 were in the West Bank. Of the 1,793 Palestinians in the West Bank who were killed by Israeli security forces, only 472 are known to have been taking part in hostilities (B'Tselem 2008c).

Israel also carries out targeted assassinations of persons it deems a security threat or terrorist, nearly always injuring innocent bystanders. On December 14, 2006, Israel's High Court ruled that targeted killing is a legitimate form of self-defense against terrorists (Wilson 2006), in violation of international law. International human rights law dictates that, even when persons are suspected of involvement in criminal activity, governments are obligated to exhaust all other available measures to charge them and bring them to trial. However, "willful killings" have long been part of Israeli policy in the Occupied Territories (Schiff 2006; al-Haq 2001). Between September 2000 and August 2011, Israel's targeted assassinations claimed 425 Palestinian lives, including 174 bystanders (B'Tselem 2008). The nature of proof required by the Israelis for the killings is classified, and the target of assassination is not given a chance to present evidence in his defense or to refute the allegations against him.

The Gaza Strip

At the end of 2013, 1,763,387 Palestinians lived under conditions of occupation in Gaza, even though in 2005 Israel withdrew its military bases and settlers from the Strip (Goldberg 2013). After Israel's 2005 unilateral "disengagement," Tel Aviv claimed that the Gaza Strip was no longer occupied. Nevertheless, international and Israeli nongovernmental organizations (NGOs) consider Israel a de facto occupying power in Gaza and thus responsible for the welfare of the population (B'Tselem 2016a). In fact, Israel assumes no responsibility for the humanitarian or any other needs of the Gazan population, while it continues to rule the Strip with an iron hand and continues to hold absolute control over important elements of Palestinian life there, including the crossing of people, the crossing of goods, airspace, territorial waters, population registry, and the tax system.

Israel's policies with regard to Gaza include its complete isolation and control over every aspect of the lives of the people living there—the latter reinforced by repeated military interventions ranging from targeted assassinations to massive military campaigns. In 2007 Israel imposed a total embargo on all people and products to and from Gaza that remains in effect at this writing. This blockade involves separating Gaza from the West Bank and East Jerusalem and from the remainder of the world, resulting in its almost total inaccessibility and causing countless hardships for Palestinians there. Gaza can thus be considered under "indirect occupation" that is as oppressive as the direct occupation of the West Bank, and in many ways more so. Israel's objective is to make life so arduous that people will "choose" to leave. Its policies in pursuit of this goal include restrictions on family unification; control over population registry; the permit system; control of the economy, water, and other resources; denial of safe passage between Gaza and the West Bank, including the failure to fulfill the Oslo Accord agreement on "Safe-Passage"; and control over Gaza's airspace, seaport, and coastal waters (HaMoked n.d.; Kadman 1999; Van Esveld 2012; B'Tselem 2016c).

Despite being physically separate, the territories of the West Bank and Gaza Strip constituted a single political unit prior to the peace process, owing to the national identity shared by the residents of the two areas, their common history prior to 1948, and the integration processes the two areas have undergone since the beginning of the occupation in all aspects of life: family ties, education, culture, and economy. Initially, Israel administered the occupation regime of the two areas in a similar and coordinated way. The Gaza Strip and the West Bank were acknowledged as a single integral territorial unit in international agreements between the Palestinians and the state of Israel signed under international patronage. However, the unilateral measures Israel has implemented to institutionalize and perpetuate a new factual and legal reality of separation between residents of the Gaza Strip and the West Bank, which severs the interdependent social, economic, and cultural ties between the two groups, have

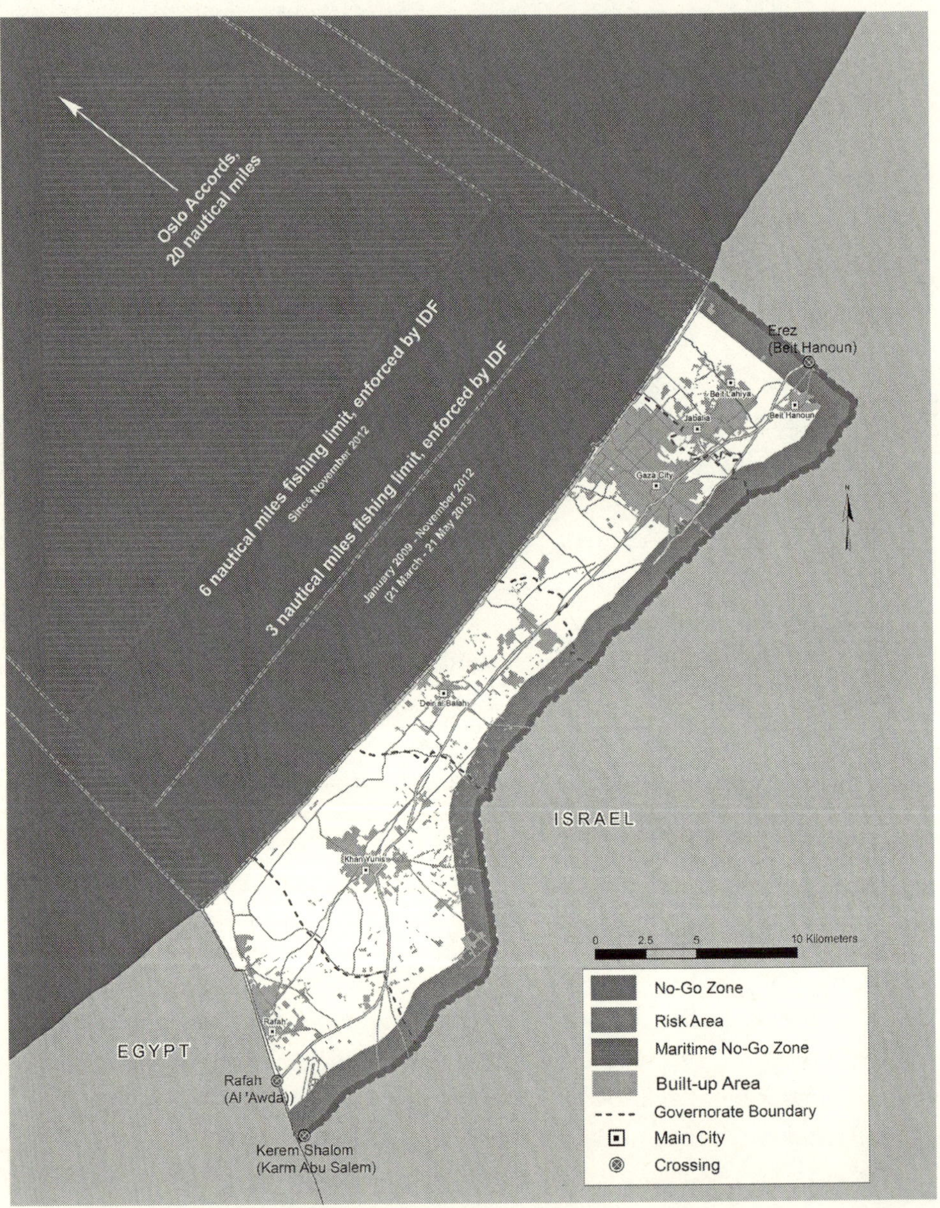

4. Gaza Strip: areas restricted to Palestinian access, 2013. Map provided courtesy of the UN Office for the Coordination of Humanitarian Affairs. The boundaries and names shown and the designations used on this map do not imply official endorsement or acceptance by the United Nations.

negated these documents and severely infringed on their rights, as well as impeding the possibility that the Palestinian people will realize their right to self-determination.

In 2009 Amira Hass wrote, "Friends and family [in Gaza and the West Bank] live just 70 kilometers [43.5 miles] apart but Israel does not allow them to meet. Today, a Palestinian born in Gaza who lives in the West Bank without Israeli permission is considered an 'illegal presence.' . . . Prior to Hamas' election victory in 2006, the PA's center of rule was in Gaza. That didn't hinder Israel from perfecting the conditions of separation and severance that turned the Strip into the detention camp it is today" (Hass 2009).

An IDF PowerPoint slide show, presented before the Turkel Committee for the investigation of the Israeli raid on the Gaza-bound flotilla in 2010 (Gross 2013; Harel 2013), revealed for the first time the official goals of Israeli policy regarding the Gaza Strip. The slide show, prepared by the Administration for the Coordination of Government Policy in the Territories—the IDF body in charge of carrying out Israeli government policies regarding the civilian population in the West Bank and Gaza—deals with the humanitarian conditions in the Strip regarding food, water, fuel, electrical supply, and the condition of medical facilities in Gaza. As one writer noted, "Despite the many obfuscations and dissimulations in the foregoing, the goal of Israel's policy regarding Gaza is clearly that of its separation from the West Bank and Jerusalem and, moreover, it is a violation of official and unofficial principles of previous agreements and negotiations between Israel and the Palestinians" (Sheizaf 2010).

According to IDF assumptions, there are 1.6 million people living in Gaza. The army does not occupy itself with the distribution of supplies, so there is no way of knowing if the population's needs are actually met, only that, according to the IDF, enough food and water is entering Gaza to prevent a total humanitarian catastrophe. Slide 50 details the goods found on the Gaza-bound flotilla: medical supplies, toys, school gear, construction materials, and powered wheelchairs—all of which were confiscated (ibid.).

Separation Fence

In 1994 Prime Minister Yitzhak Rabin ordered the construction of a separation fence along the Israeli-Gazan border on confiscated Palestinian land, running along the entire land border of the Gaza Strip. It was made up of wire fencing with posts, sensors, and buffer zones on lands bordering Israel and concrete and steel walls on lands bordering Egypt. In 2005, as part of its unilateral withdrawal, Israel further sealed off the Gaza Strip, appropriating more Palestinian land, with a three-layered security system that is one of the most impenetrable barriers in the world. The new barrier is far more sophisticated than the original, with high-tech surveillance and weapons systems. It includes electronic sensors, hundreds of video and night vision cameras, and watchtowers mounted with remote-control machine guns. The new Gaza barrier stretches for 60 kilometers (37 miles). Entry into the Gaza Strip by land is possible through five crossing points, all of which have remained completely closed since 2006.

Israel has created a "buffer zone" or an Access Restricted Area on land taken from Gazans along the fence and in the sea. In 2010 OCHA and the World Food Program reported, "The land areas along the fence affected by access restrictions have gradually expanded since the beginning of the Second Intifada in September 2000." The report concludes that approximately 35 percent of Gaza's cultivable land is located within the restricted area.

Since 2000 Israel has routinely denied permits to Gaza residents who want to study in the West Bank. In the twelve years since, it has given permits to only three Gazans to study at universities in the West Bank. On September 26, 2012, the High Court ruled against four female university students from the Gaza Strip who had been seeking to study at Birzeit University in the West Bank. The four petitioners, aged between thirty-seven and forty-nine, were registered for master's studies at Birzeit. The court also upheld the ban on a fifth woman, eighteen, who had been seeking to study law at the school (Hass 2012a). In December 2012, under Israeli pressure, the United

States quietly canceled a scholarship program for students in the Gaza Strip, as Israel refused to grant the students permits to travel to the West Bank. The program had offered about thirty scholarships to promising but impoverished Palestinian high school seniors from Gaza to study in West Bank universities. It was a rare opportunity for gifted students in Gaza, which has been under a hermitic closure since 2007 (Associated Press 2012).

Despite extensive family ties between Palestinian residents of the West Bank, Gaza, and Israel, in September 2000 Israel imposed an almost complete prohibition on Gazans from entering Israel for family visits and drastically restricted Israelis' ability to enter the PA-controlled areas of Gaza; permits to enter Gaza fell by 98 percent. Israel has thus made it almost impossible for couples, one of whom is Israeli and the other a resident of Gaza, to live together under one roof and consequently for their children to live with both parents. The same now applies to West Bank residents and Israel; moreover, Palestinians from Gaza can receive permits to enter the West Bank only for extreme medical emergencies. Marriages, deaths, education, and the like do not merit a permit. A common obstacle that Israel places on divided families is to suspend the permits of Israelis to enter Gaza. Israel suspends the permits in a wholesale manner with no notice of the decision or how long it will be in effect. The vast majority of those individuals holding such permits are women with Israeli citizenship or residency who are married to Gazans. Women who leave Gaza for a brief visit in Israel are frequently unable to return to their homes, husbands, and children. In January 2002, Israel decided to shorten the period of the entry permits for divided families, from three months to one month. Women who wish to obey the law must travel to the Erez checkpoint twelve times a year to renew their permits. Owing to harsh conditions, many women do not reach Erez to renew their permits on time. When they later try to get a new permit, their application is rejected on the grounds that they had "stayed illegally in the territory of the Palestinian National Authority" (Hass 2004).

Water Crisis

The water situation in the Gaza Strip is even more dire than in the West Bank. Gaza has suffered a steady increase in debilitating ecological and hydrological problems. After 1967 Israel invested even less in Gaza's water infrastructure than it did in the West Bank. These problems have crippled agricultural and economic production and damaged the health of Gaza's burgeoning population (Isaac 2010). In Gaza the coastal aquifer serves as its main water resource. Other Gaza water sources, such as runoff from the Hebron Hills, have been diverted for Israeli purposes (Kubursi and Naqib 2010). The aquifer has annually grown more polluted and salinized, a process that has worsened dramatically in the past decade with increased consumption of water. Overextraction has led to increasing salinization, while penetration of untreated sewage, pesticides, and fertilizers has caused pollution. Poor water quality and contamination negatively affect Palestinians' quality of life and expose them to serious health risks. By 2010 "almost 95 percent of the water pumped in the Gaza Strip was polluted and unfit for drinking" (B'Tselem 2010b). It is estimated that it will take at least twenty years to rehabilitate Gaza's underground water system, and any delay in dealing with the problem will lead to additional deterioration in the situation and thus might extend the rehabilitation process for hundreds of years. However, since it began its siege on the Gaza Strip in June 2007, Israel has forbidden the entry of equipment and materials needed to rehabilitate the water and wastewater-treatment systems there.

The daily per capita water consumption in Gaza was 91 liters (24 gallons), slightly higher than in the West Bank, yet lower than the minimum of 100 liters (26.4 gallons) recommended by the World Health Organization (WHO) (B'Tselem 2010b). Even this statistic is misleading because, as noted, the water is contaminated. Overpumping of the aquifer has been going on for several decades, causing penetration of saline water into the underground water system. Poor maintenance of wastewater-treatment facilities and damage caused by Operation Cast Lead (2008–9) led to further pollution of the underground water by wastewater and to greater salinity. Waste-disposal sites in Gaza are handled improperly; after Operation Cast Lead, they received more than six hundred thousand tons of waste, including asbestos, medical waste, oils, and fuels (Horowitz, Ratner, and Weiss 2011, 54–69).

Ninety-three of the 180 wells in Gaza have a chloride level four to eight times higher than the 250 mg/liter amount recommended by WHO, rendering it unfit for drinking. In addition, the concentration of nitrates in the wells is six times higher than the amount recommended by WHO and is a major cause of anemia among children and methemoglobinemia ("blue infants" syndrome) among babies, which frequently leads to choking and death; almost half the infants in a sample examined in 2007 suffered from troubling symptoms of the syndrome. The Palestinian Water Authority estimates that almost 40 percent of the incidence of all disease in Gaza is related to polluted drinking water. According to international aid organizations, 20 percent of Gazan families have at least one child under age five who suffers from diarrhea as a result of polluted water. A UN study published in 2009 estimates that diarrhea is the cause of 12 percent of children's deaths in the Strip. The lack of potable drinking water additionally causes malnutrition in children and affects their physical and cognitive development. Water pollution also harms the area's agricultural produce; the milk given by cows in Gaza is polluted, and farm crops that once characterized the area, such as oranges, have declined in quantity and quality (B'Tselem 2010b).

The siege on Gaza has prevented the entry of equipment and materials that can be used to improve water quality and taste and to develop and rehabilitate the water infrastructure and the wastewater-treatment facilities (B'Tselem 2010a, 2016b). Lack of construction materials and replacement parts has led to greater loss of water from the supply network in Gaza. Prior to the siege, the loss had been 30 percent of the amount of water supplied to consumers, generally resulting from leaks in the pipes. By 2009 the loss reached 47 percent, according to figures of the Coastal Municipalities Water Utility, and the loss has continued to grow annually (B'Tselem 2010b).

The Gaza Strip's power station has been working only at partial output since Israel bombed it in June 2006. There is also a shortage of industrial fuel needed to operate the station, which has led to frequent power outages. The outages prevent wastewater-treatment facilities from completing the fourteen-day treatment cycle and impair the frequency of water supply to houses. According to UN figures, water is supplied to houses in Gaza City for four to six hours once every five days and in the rest of the Gaza Strip for four to six hours once every three days. Owing to the low pressure, the water does not reach the top floors in tall buildings. In Operation Cast Lead, Israel severely damaged Gaza City's wastewater-treatment facility, leading to untreated wastewater flooding extensive farm areas. Thirty kilometers (18.6 miles) of water networks, eleven wells, and six thousand home water tanks were damaged during the operation (Horowitz, Ratner, and Weiss 2011). Most of Gaza's wastewater now flows to the Mediterranean Sea, polluting the shoreline and rendering it unfit for bathing. Proper wastewater treatment would have enabled use of the treated wastewater for agricultural purposes and reduced pumping of the underground water (B'Tselem 2010b).

Energy Crisis

As indicated earlier, Israel provides the PA with 75 percent of its electricity in Gaza. Power regularly goes out for six to eight hours daily. There have been many fatal house fires started by candles lit during power outages. Israel bombed the Gaza power station in 2006 and has long blockaded the territory from receiving supplies, including fuel needed to run the station (Akram 2013).

Restricted Sea Areas and Control over Territorial Water

Under the 1994 Gaza-Jericho Agreement between Israel and the PLO, areas within 20 nautical miles (37 kilometers/23 miles) off Gaza's coast should be open to Palestinian use for fishing, recreation, and economic activity. Israel's prohibitions on fishing from the Gaza exist even though there is no fence along Gaza's coastline, and residents do not have open access to the sea. Palestinians wanting to go to the sea need to request a permit from Israel, and any who obtain a permit are restricted in how far they can go. Israel does not issue permits to all fishermen who request them, and, during the course of Operation Cast Lead (December 2008–January 2009), Israel prohibited all fishing (B'Tselem 2012b). When fishing resumed after the operation, Tel Aviv reduced the distance to about 3 nautical miles (5.5 kilometers/3.5 miles).

Israel's prohibition on entering deep waters denies fishermen access to areas abundant with fish, limiting catches to small fish of poor quality. As a result, it is extremely hard to earn a living from fishing (traditionally second only to agriculture in the Occupied Territories' economy) or even to cover fishing expenses. Given the lack of other sources of income in the Gaza Strip, some fishermen were left no option but to violate the prohibition and endanger their lives (Schiano 2013; Palestine News Network 2013; Baker 2013). The restriction of fishing to shallow waters led to a sharp reduction of the fish population and harm to the habitat of young fish, endangering the future fish population; the entire fishing sector in Gaza suffered a sharp blow. The restrictions also raise the cost of fish, preventing many families from obtaining an important source of protein. Because of the short supply, the price of fish has risen (B'Tselem 2011d). In 2011 the livelihood of some 3,000 families in Gaza, constituting some 19,500 people, depended directly on the fishing industry, and another 2,000 families who made a living from affiliated industries, such as building and maintenance of boats and sale and maintenance of equipment, were severely harmed. Between 2000 and 2010, the number of fishermen in Gaza dropped from about 10,000 to fewer than 4,000 (OCHA and World Food Program 2010). The Fishermen's Association in Gaza Port said that, despite the significant decrease in the number of fishermen, the diminished fishing area could not accommodate all the fishermen, so they staggered their departures and sometimes even breached the prohibition on sailing toward Egypt, where they bought fish from Egyptian fishermen (B'Tselem 2011d).

Home Demolitions

During the Second Intifada, Israel employed a policy of demolishing houses, uprooting orchards, and destroying farmland, especially in the Gaza Strip. This policy was mostly applied before Israel implemented the disengagement plan in 2005, in areas surrounding the settlements and around army posts, usually along the Egyptian border. This policy was part of Israel's strategy in the Gaza Strip and the Israel-created "security strips" around places where Israeli civilians or armed forces were located. Palestinians were either totally prohibited from entry or allowed only with a special permit (B'Tselem 2012). The houses were usually demolished at night, without giving the residents any warning, and the possessions in the house were buried under the ruins. Israel called this policy "clearing," a name that concealed the destructive and long-term consequences for residents of the Gaza Strip. Thousands of people were made homeless. Israel caused this damage to people whom it did not accuse of being involved in aggression against Israeli civilians or security forces. During Operation Cast Lead, Israel again carried out wide-scale house demolitions. According to UN figures, Israel destroyed more than thirty-five hundred residential dwellings during the operation, leaving some 20,000 persons homeless.

Military Justice

In 1970–71, under the direction of General Ariel Sharon, the Israeli military undertook a violent "pacification" campaign in Gaza. The imposed quiescence provided the authorities with the latitude to institute more legalistic means of control, including expanding the military court system. Interrogation was increasingly aimed at producing confessions to be used for conviction. During this period Israeli and

Palestinian defense lawyers working in the military court system began reporting clients' complaints of ill treatment and torture during interrogations. Officials condemned these reports as anti-Israeli propaganda and anti-Semitic lies by Palestinians and other "enemies of the state" (Hajjar 2010).

Control after the 2005 "Disengagement"

In August 2005, Israel unilaterally withdrew its settlements and military installations from the Gaza Strip. Many assumed that this action meant that Gaza would no longer be under Israeli occupation. However, the occupation actually intensified in the years following. Israel imposed a complete blockade on the 1.7 million Palestinians living in the Gaza Strip; virtually no Gazans are permitted to leave. Exports are almost completely banned, and imports are restricted to a few basic humanitarian supplies. Fishing is limited to three nautical miles from the coast, compared to the twenty stipulated in the Oslo Accords. Many refer to Gaza as "one large outdoor prison," and Israel controls nearly every aspect of life in this tiny, isolated enclave. All of these restrictions together have severely damaged the economy, health, and well-being of Gaza's residents and their ability to attain education and contributed to a major rise in poverty and unemployment (B'Tselem 2007a). In 2014 Pierre Krähenbuhl, the United Nations Relief and Works Agency (UNRWA) commissioner-general, declared Israel's seven-year blockade of the Gaza Strip the "longest in history" and called it "a very extreme . . . and illegal collective punishment" (*Ha'aretz* staff 2014a).

Military Interventions after the Disengagement

After implementation of the disengagement plan, some Palestinian organizations in the Strip continued to fire rockets and mortars at Israeli communities close to the Green Line, killing 11 Israelis in the period from September 2005 to November 2009. Israel responded by permitting its forces to open fire on any Palestinians found in areas Israel had designated as "Access Restricted Areas," regardless of the threat posed by these individuals. Israel also increased targeted assassinations of Palestinians allegedly involved in attacks on Israel, killing many bystanders (B'Tselem 2008c). In addition, Israel has conducted major military assaults on Gaza:

1. "Summer Rains" (2006), in which the army bombed civilian infrastructure, particularly Gaza's only power station, and killed 522 Palestinians who were not taking part in the hostilities (B'Tselem 2008c).
2. "Operation Cast Lead" (2008–9), in which Israel bombed residences, industrial buildings, agriculture, and infrastructure for electricity, sanitation, water, and health care, killing more than 1,389 Palestinians, 759 of whom did not take part in the hostilities; wounding more than 5,400, 350 of them seriously; and destroying more than 3,500 residential dwellings, leaving 20,000 people homeless, in what one Israeli journalist called "pure, undiluted cruelty and hatred" (Levy 2013a; B'Tselem 2015b; Rudoren, Akram, and Kershiner 2012).
3. Operation "Pillar of Defense," which opened on November 13, 2012, with the targeted assassination of Ahmad Jaabari, Hamas's longtime military leader and chief negotiator with Israel. During eight days of hostilities, Israel launched air strikes against more than 1,500 sites throughout Gaza and, to a lesser extent, artillery fired from tanks and naval forces. Palestinian casualties from Israeli attacks were 165 dead, including 99 civilians, and 1,399 wounded, mostly civilians (OCHA 2012c). Human Rights Watch declared that Israel had "violated the laws of war" (Whitson 2013).
4. Operation "Protective Edge" (2014), the most ruthless assault yet, which killed 2,145 people in seven weeks, destroyed 60,000 homes, and made homeless more than 100,000. "Whole neighborhoods annihilated in an assault in which 20,000 tonnes of explosives were fired into one of

> the most densely-populated regions on earth" (Carr 2015). Breaking the Silence, a group of Israeli soldiers, published a 240-page report, *This Is How We Fought in Gaza, 2014*, refuting Israeli government claims that it took all necessary precautions to protect civilians. "A first serjeant serving in the Mechanized Infantry in Gaza explained, 'Anything inside [the Gaza Strip] is a threat. The area has to be "sterilised," empty of people.' . . . The IDF reduced whole neighborhoods to rubble for no clear operational reason, just to 'demonstrate presence in the area'" (Shaoul 2015).

Since the cease-fire that ended the assault on August 26, 2014, Israel has fired hundreds of times on farms and Palestinian fishing boats in Gaza (ibid.). Israeli historian Ilan Pappe has called Israeli policy toward the Gaza Strip "an incremental genocide" (Pappe 2006b) and condemned Operation Protective Shield as an "indiscriminate slaughter in the killing fields of Palestine" (Pappe 2014). A letter signed by 359 Jewish Holocaust survivors also condemned the slaughter and "Elie Wiesel's manipulation of the Nazi Genocide to attempt to justify the attacks on Gaza" and decried the "extreme, racist dehumanization of Palestinians in Israeli society, which has reached a fever-pitch. . . . 'Never again' must mean NEVER AGAIN FOR ANYONE!" (International Jewish Anti-Zionist Network 2015).

Conclusion

This chapter provides just some of the available documentation indicating Israel's persistent disregard for Palestinian human rights, including discrimination against Palestinian citizens of Israel, the creation of intolerable and inhumane conditions in which Palestinians are forced to live in the Occupied Territories, illegal confiscation of Palestinian lands and destruction of their homes, mass arrests and detainment without charges, the creation of arbitrary rules with disproportionately harsh penalties, and indiscriminate killings, especially in Gaza.

Sources Cited

Abdullah, Asrul. 2013. "Jordan Complains to UN over Israeli Violations in Jerusalem." Mi'raj Islamic news agency, Oct. 2. http://www.mirajnews.com/jordan-complains-to-un-over-israeli-violations-in-jerusalem/16305.

Abunima, Ali. 2011. "Force, Might and Beatings: Indelible Images of the First Intifada." Electronic Intifada, Dec. 9. https://electronicintifada.net/blogs/ali-abunimah/force-might-and-beatings-indelible-images-first-intifada.

Adalah. 2013. "The Prawer–Begin Bill and the Forced Displacement of the Bedouin." May. http://www.adalah.org/uploads/oldfiles/Public/files/English/Publications/Articles/2013/Prawer-Begin-Plan-Background-Adalah.pdf.

Addameer. 2009. "Isolation and Solitary Confinement of Palestinian Prisoners and Detainees in Israeli Facilities." Aug. 1. http://www.addameer.org/publications/isolation-and-solitary-confinement-palestinian-prisoners-and-detainees-israeli.

———. 2016. *Annual Violations Report: Violations of Palestinian Prisoners' Rights in Israeli Prisons, 2015*. Ramallah: Addameer Prisoner Support and Human Rights Association. www.addameer.org/sites/default/files/publications/website.pdf.

Akram, Fares. 2013. "Fire in Gaza Kills Family and Stirs Rage against the Power Company." *New York Times*, Jan. 31.

Al-Haq. 2001. "Wilful Killing: The Assassination of Palestinians in the Occupied Palestinian Territories by the Israeli Security Forces." Feb. http://www.alhaq.org/publications/publications-index/item/wilful-killing-the-assassination-of-palestinians-in-the-occupied-palestinian-territories-by-the-israeli-security-forces.

Al Sahli, Nabil. 2013. "Israel and Its Demographic Complex." *Middle East Monitor*, July 4.

Amnesty International. 2005. "Israel/Occupied Territories: Israeli Authorities Must Put an Immediate End to Settler Violence." London: Amnesty International, Apr. 24. MDE 15/027/2005.

Associated Press. 2012. "US Drops Gaza Scholarships after Israel Travel Ban." *Huffington Post*, Dec. 9.

Association for Civil Rights in Israel. N.d.a. "Health and Environment." http://www.acri.org.il/en/category/east-jerusalem/health-and-environment/.

———. N.d.b. "Planning and Building Rights." http://www.acri.org.il/en/category/east-jerusalem/planning-and-building-rights/.

Aviram, Alon. 2012. "The War on the Palestinian Oil Harvest." +972 *Magazine*, Oct. 30.

Azoulay, Ariella, and Adi Ophir. 2005. "The Monster's Tail." In *Against the Wall: Israel's Barrier to Peace*, edited by Michael Sorkin, 2–27. New York: New Press.

Baker, Ismail Jamal Faris Baker. 2013. "The Fisherman's Narrative: 'I Can Only Give False Assurances to My Children.'" *Palestine News Network*, May 1. http://reliefweb.int/report/occupied-palestinian-territory/jamal-ismail-faris-baker-fisherman%E2%80%99s-narrative-%E2%80%9Ci-can-only.

BBC. 2000. "'Provocative' Mosque Visit Sparks Riots." Sept. 28. http://news.bbc.co.uk/onthisday/hi/dates/stories/september/28/newsid_3687000/3687762.stm.

Benvenisti, Meron. 1996. *City of Stone: The Hidden History of Jerusalem*. Berkeley: Univ. of California Press.

Boling, Gail J. 2001. "Palestinian Refugees and the Right of Return: An International Law Analysis." BADIL Information and Discussion Brief, Jan. 1.

Bowker, Robert P. G. 2003. *Palestinian Refugees: Mythology, Identity, and the Search for Peace*. Boulder, CO: Lyne Rienner.

B'Tselem. 2000. "Statistics: Fatalities in the First Intifada." http://www.btselem.org/statistics/first_intifada_tables.

———. 2001. "End the Uprooting of Trees." Feb. 7. http://www.btselem.org/press_releases/20010207.

———. 2004. "Permit System to Cross Separation Barrier Is Racist." June 16. https://electronicintifada.net/content/btselem-permit-system-cross-separation-barrier-racist/1729.

———. 2007a. "The Gaza Strip: One Big Prison." May. https://www.google.com/search?q=The+Gaza+Strip%3A+One+Big+Prison&ie=utf-8&oe=utf-8.

———. 2007b. "Ground to a Halt: Denial of Palestinians' Freedom of Movement in the West Bank." Aug. http://www.btselem.org/publications/summaries/200708_ground_to_a_halt.

———. 2007c. "Israel Prevents All Boats and Fishing Off the Gaza Coast." Feb. 26. http://www.btselem.org/press_releases/20070226.

———. 2008a. "Demolition of Houses near the Separation Barrier, Far'un Village, Tulkarm District." Apr. 6. http://www.btselem.org/separation_barrier/20080406_farun_house_demolitions.

———. 2008b. "Palestinians Killed during the Course of a Targeted Killing in the Occupied Territories, 29.9.2000–26.12.2008." http://www.scottishpsc.org.uk/mass-killings/btselem-statistics-fatalities-2992000-26122008.

———. 2008c. "Statistics: Fatalities before Operation 'Cast Lead.'" http://www.btselem.org/statistics/fatalities/before-cast-lead/by-date-of-event.

———. 2010a. "The Siege on the Gaza Strip: 1.5 Million People Imprisoned." Sept. 27. http://www.btselem.org/gaza_strip/20100531_the_siege_on_gaza.

———. 2010b. "Water Supplied in Gaza Unfit for Drinking." Aug. http://www.btselem.org/gaza_strip/20100823_gaza_water_crisis.

———. 2011a. "Alternative Roads for Palestinians." Jan. 1. http://www.btselem.org/freedom_of_movement/alternative_roads_for_palestinians.

———. 2011b. "Background: Water Crisis." Jan. 1. http://www.btselem.org/water.

———. 2011c. "Checkpoints, Physical Obstructions, and Forbidden Roads." Jan. 16. http://www.btselem.org/freedom_of_movement/checkpoints_and_forbidden_roads.

———. 2011d. "Restrictions on Fishing." Jan. 1. http://www.btselem.org/gaza_strip/restrictions_on_fishing.

———. 2011e. "Settlements and Land: Yovel Outpost: Israel Retroactively Approves Theft of Private Land." July 14. http://www.btselem.org/topic-page/14-july-11-yovel-outpost-israel-retroactively-approves-theft-private-land.

———. 2012. "Demolition for Alleged Military Purposes." Jan. 1. http://www.btselem.org/topic/razing.

———. 2015a. "Checkpoints, Physical Obstructions, and Forbidden Roads." May 20. http://www.btselem.org/freedom_of_movement/checkpoints_and_forbidden_roads.

———. 2015b. "Statistics: Fatalities during Operation 'Cast Lead.'" Aug. 31. http://www.btselem.org/statistics/fatalities/during-cast-lead/by-date-of-event.

———. 2016a. "The Gaza Strip: Israel's Obligations under International Law." Jan. 1. http://www.btselem.org/gaza_strip/israels_obligations.

———. 2016b. "Gaza Strip: The Tightened Siege and Intensified Economic Sanctions." Jan. 1. http://www.btselem.org/gaza_strip/siege_tightening.

———. 2016c. "Residency and Family Separation: Implementation of the Family Unification Policy." Jan. 1. http://www.btselem.org/family_separation/implementation.

———. 2016d. "Statistics on Palestinians in the Custody of the Israeli Security Forces." May 30. http://www.btselem.org/statistics/detainees_and_prisoners.

B'Tselem and HaMoked. 2009. "Without Trial: Administrative Detention of Palestinians by Israel and the Internment of Unlawful Combatants Law." Oct. http://www.btselem.org/publications/summaries/200910_without_trial.

Carr, Matt. 2015. "Israel's Crazed Assault on Gaza Was 2014's Single Most Haunting and Revolting Event." Stop the War Coalition, Jan. 2. http://www.stopwar.org.uk/index.php/news-comment/36-matt-carr/1066-israel-s-crazed-assault-on-gaza-was-2014-s-single-most-haunting-and-revolting-event.

Dugard, John. 2004. "Question of the Violation of Human Rights in the Occupied Arab Territories, Including Palestine." Report of the Special Rapporteur of the Communion on Human Rights. United Nations Commission on Human Rights, 60th session; item 8 of the provisional agenda E/CN.4/2004/6/Add.1. Feb. 27, 2004.

Dumper, Michael. 1997. *The Politics of Jerusalem since 1967*. New York: Columbia Univ. Press.

Eldar, Akiva. 2012. "Israel Admits It Revoked Residency Rights of a Quarter Million Palestinians." *Ha'aretz*, June 12.

Gassner-Jaradat, Ingrid. 2010. "Family Reunification." In *Encyclopedia of the Israeli-Palestinian Conflict*, edited by Cheryl A. Rubenberg, 1:385–91. Boulder, CO: Lynne Rienner.

Goldberg, J. J. 2013. "Jews Now Minority in Israel and Territories." *Forward*, Sept. 19.

Gordon, Neve. 2008. *Israel's Occupation*. Berkeley: Univ. of California Press.

Greenberg, Joel. 2012. "Double Take: For Palestinian Olive Growers, a Bitter Harvest." *Ha'aretz*, Oct. 18.

Greenwood, Phoebe. 2012. "Palestinians Prepare to Lose the Solar Panels That Provide a Lifeline." *Guardian*, May 12.

Gross, Aeyal. 2013. "Turkel Panel Calls for IDF Commanders to Take Greater Responsibility." *Ha'aretz*, Feb. 7.

Gurvitz, Yossi. 2013. "Don't Blame Settlers for Violence against Palestinians." +972 *Magazine*, Mar. 13.

Gvaryahu, Avner. 2013. "The Real Rules of Engagement in the West Bank." *Ha'aretz*, Jan. 24.

Ha'aretz editor. 2012a. "Drying Out the Palestinians." *Ha'aretz*, Dec. 10.

———. 2012b. "Silent Deportation." *Ha'aretz*, Aug. 5.

Ha'aretz staff. 2014a. "Israel's Blockade of Gaza the 'Longest in History,' Says New UNRWA Head." *Ha'aretz*, Apr. 17.

———. 2014b. "Lieberman's Land, Population Swap Proposal Is Roundly Condemned." *Ha'aretz*, Jan. 9.

———. 2014c. "Over 800,000 Palestinians Imprisoned by Israel since 1967." *Ha'aretz*, Apr. 17.

Hajjar, Lisa. 2006. *Courting Conflict: The Israeli Military Court System in the West Bank and Gaza*. Berkeley: Univ. of California Press.

———. 2010. "Israeli Military Court System in the Occupied Territories." In *Encyclopedia of the Israeli-Palestinian Conflict*, edited by Cheryl A. Rubenberg, 2:663–77. Boulder, CO: Lynne Rienner.

Halper, Jeff. 2010. "House Demolitions." In *The Encyclopedia of the Israeli–Palestinian Conflict*, edited by Cheryl A. Rubenberg, 1:568–70. Boulder, CO: Lynne Rienner.

HaMoked. N.d. "Travel between the West Bank and the Gaza Strip." http://www.hamoked.org/Topic.aspx?tID=sub_30.

Harel, Amos. 2013. "The Turkel Report: A No-Confidence Vote in the IDF's Internal Investigations." *Ha'aretz*, Feb. 6.

Hareuveni, Eyal. 2010. "By Hook and by Crook: Israeli Settlement Policy in the West Bank." Jerusalem: B'Tselem. https://www.google.com/search?q=The+Gaza+Strip%3A+One+Big+Prison&ie=utf-8&oe=utf-8#q=By+Hook+and+by+Crook:+Israeli+Settlement+Policy+in+the+West+Bank.

———. 2012. "Arrested Development: The Long Term Impact of Israel's Separation Barrier in the West Bank." Jerusalem: B'Tselem. https://www.google.com/search?q=The+Gaza+Strip%3A+One+Big+Prison&ie=utf-8&oe=utf-8#q=Arrested+Development:+The+Long+Term+Impact+of+Israel%E2%80%99s+Separation+Barrier+in+the+West+Bank.

Hass, Amira. 2004. "Has the Transfer of Enclaves Begun?" *Ha'aretz*, Feb. 26.

———. 2009. "Gaza's Separation from the West Bank Is Israel's Greatest Triumph." bitterlemons.org, Apr. 26.

———. 2012a. "High Court Rejects Gaza Students' Petition to Study in West Bank." *Ha'aretz*, Sept. 27.

———. 2012b. "Israel Orders Demolition of 8 Palestinian Villages, Claims Need for IDF Training Land." *Ha'aretz*, July 23.

———. 2012c. "Lambs to the Settlers' Slaughter, Screaming and Unheard." *Ha'aretz*, Aug. 5.

———. 2013. "Israel to Urge Court: Drop Palestinian Farmers' Complaint against Settler Attacks." *Ha'aretz*, Jan. 28.

———. 2014a. "EU Diplomats Warn of Regional Conflagration over Temple Mount." *Ha'aretz*, Mar. 28.

———. 2014b. "Tensions in the West Bank Are Rising, Together with IDF, Settler Violence." *Ha'aretz*, Jan. 31.

Hasson, Nir. 2012. "Rare Photograph Reveals Ancient Jerusalem Mosque Destroyed in 1967." *Ha'aretz*, June 15.

Horowitz, Adam, Lizzy Ratner, and Philip Weiss, eds. 2011. *The Goldstone Report: The Legacy of the Landmark Investigation of the Gaza Conflict.* New York: Nation Books.

Human Rights Watch. 2005. "Promoting Impunity: The Israeli Military's Failure to Investigate Wrongdoing." June. https://www.hrw.org/report/2005/06/21/promoting-impunity/israeli-militarys-failure-investigate-wrongdoing.

———. 2008. "Off the Map: Land and Housing Rights Violations in Israel's Unrecognized Bedouin Villages." Mar. 30. https://www.hrw.org/report/2008/03/30/map/land-and-housing-rights-violations-israels-unrecognized-bedouin-villages.

———. 2015. "Israel: Security Forces Abuse Palestinian Children." July 19. https://www.hrw.org/news/2015/07/19/israel-security-forces-abuse-palestinian-children.

Institute for Middle East Understanding. 2012. "Fact Sheet: 25th Anniversary of the First Intifada." Dec. 16. http://imeu.org/article/25th-anniversary-of-the-first-intifada.

International Jewish Anti-Zionist Network. 2015. "More than 350 Survivors and Descendants of Survivors and Victims of the Nazi Genocide Condemn Israel's Assault on Gaza." http://www.ijan.org/projects-campaigns/nafa/survivors-and-descendants-letter/.

Ir Amin. 2010. "Absentees against Their Will: Property Expropriation in East Jerusalem under the Absentee Property Law." July. http://www.ir-amim.org.il/en/report/absentees-against-their-will-%E2%80%93-property-expropriation-east-jerusalem-under-absentee-property.

Isaac, Jad. 2010. "Water Resources and the Israeli-Palestinian Conflict." In *The Encyclopedia of the Israeli-Palestinian Conflict*, edited by Cheryl A. Rubenberg, 3:1592–1605. Boulder, CO: Lynne Rienner.

Jaradat, Ahmad. 2012. "50 Demolition Orders for South Hebron Hills." The Alternative Information Center, June 17. http://cjpp5.over-blog.com/article-fwd-the-alternative-information-center-org-palestine-israel-50-demolition-orders-for-south-hebron-hi-107141720.html.

Kadman, Noga. 1999. "Families Torn Apart: Separation of Palestinian Families in the Occupied Territories." Translated by Zvi Shulman. Jerusalem: HaMoked. http://www.hamoked.org/Document.aspx?dID=10700.

Kanaan, Oussama, Udo Kock, and Mariusz Sumlinski. 2012. "Recent Experience and Prospects of the Economy of the West Bank and Gaza: Staff Report Prepared for the Meeting of the Ad Hoc Liaison Committee." International Monetary Fund, Sept. 23.

Khalidi, Walid, ed. 1992. *All That Remains: The Palestinian Villages Occupied and Depopulated by Israel in 1948*. Washington, DC: Institute for Palestine Studies.

Khoury, Jack. 2014. "Israeli Arab Leaders: Lieberman's Land Swap Proposal Is Delusional." *Ha'aretz*, Jan. 7.

Kubursi, Atif, and Fadle Naqib. 2010. "Economy: The Economics of Occupation." In *Encyclopedia of the Israeli-Palestinian Conflict*, edited by Cheryl A. Rubenberg, 1:344–53. Boulder, CO: Lynne Rienner.

Landau, Idan. 2013. "House Demolitions: Zionism's Constant Background Noise." Translated by Ofer Neiman. +972 *Magazine*, June 17.

Laor, Yitzhak. 2014. "Pouring Out Our Wrath." *Ha'aretz*, Apr. 14.

Leech, Philip. 2012. "Why Jabal an-Nar? Researching Nablus." *Bulletin of the Council for British Research in the Levant* 7 (1): 30–35.

Lein, Yehezkel. 2001. "Not Even a Drop: The Water Crisis in Palestinian Villages without a Water Network." Translated by Zvi Shulman. Jerusalem: B'Tselem. http://www.btselem.org/press_releases/20010805.

———. 2002a. "Land Grab: Israel's Settlement Policy in the West Bank." Translated by Shaul Vardi and Zvi Shulman. Israel: B'Tselem. https://www.btselem.org/download/200205_land_grab_eng.pdf.

———. 2002b. "The Separation Barrier: Position Paper." Translated by Zvi Shulman. Jerusalem: B'Tselem.

———. 2003. "Behind the Barrier: Human Rights Violations as a Result of Israel's Separation Barrier." Translated by Zvi Shulman. Jerusalem: B'Tselem.

Lein, Yehezkel, and Alon Cohen-Lifshitz. 2005. "Under the Guise of Security: Routing the Security Barrier to Enable Israeli Settlement Expansion in the West Bank." Translated by Zvi Shulman. Jerusalem: B'Tselem. http://www.btselem.org/download/200512_under_the_guise_of_security_eng.pdf.

Levac, Alex, and Gideon Levy. 2013. "Death at a Cemetery." *Ha'aretz*, Feb. 1.

Levy, Gideon. 2013a. "The Cherry on Top of the IDF." *Ha'aretz*, June 2.

———. 2013b. "Eight Hundred Thousand." *Ha'aretz*, Feb. 28.

———. 2013c. "Israeli Cruelty Reached a Point of No Return in the 2008–09 Gaza War." *Ha'aretz*, Mar. 31.

Levy, Gideon, and Alex Levac. 2013. "A Battered House, a Shattered Palestinian Family." *Ha'aretz*, May 21.

———. 2014. "When Yitzhar Settlers Attack." *Ha'aretz*, Apr. 18.

Li, Darryl, and Yehezkel Lein. 2006. "Act of Vengeance: Israel's Bombing of the Gaza Power Plant and Its Effects, September 2006." Jerusalem: B'Tselem.

Lis, Jonathan, Nadav Shragai, and Yuval Yoaz. 2004. "Yatom: Jews Nearly Succeeded in 1984 Temple Mount Plot." *Ha'aretz*, July 24.

Lustick, Ian. 1999. "Israel as a Non-Arab State: The Political Implications of Mass Immigration of Non-Jews." *Middle East Journal* 53 (3): 101–17.

Ma'an news agency. 2012. "Local Official: Israel Destroys 5 Water Wells in Jenin." Oct. 24. http://www.maannews.com/Content.aspx?id=531724.

Masalha, Nur. 1992. *Expulsion of the Palestinians: The Concept of "Transfer" in Zionist Political Thought, 1882–1948*. Washington, DC: Institute of Palestine Studies.

———. 2013. "Separation between Gaza and West Bank." *Ha'aretz*, Feb. 26.

McGreal, Chris. 2002. "Israeli Retaliation Targets Oil Harvest and Waterholes." *Guardian*, Oct. 23.

Middle East Monitor. 2013. "PLO Report Gives Details of 266 Palestinians Killed by Israel in 2012." Jan. 22.

MIFTAH. 2011. "House Demolition Primer: Fact Sheet." Mar. 29. http://www.miftah.org/Display.cfm?DocId=14882&CategoryId=4.

Morris, Benny. 1987. *The Birth of the Palestinian Refugee Problem, 1947–1949*. Cambridge: Cambridge Univ. Press.

Mossawa Center. 2013. "The Mossawa Center's Briefing Paper for the U.S. State Department Human Rights Report on Israel: Discrimination against the Arab Minority in Israel." Mossawa Center (Haifa, Israel), Oct. 24. http://www.usacbi.org/wp-content/uploads/2013/11/US-State-Dept-2013-Report-Mossawa-Submission.pdf.

OCHA (United Nations Office for the Coordination of Humanitarian Affairs). 2012a. "The Humanitarian Impact of Israeli Settlement Policies." Jan. https://www.ochaopt.org/documents/ocha_opt_settlements_factsheet_january_2012_english.pdf.

———. 2012b. *The Monthly Humanitarian Monitor*. June. http://www.ochaopt.org/documents/ocha_opt_the_humanitarian_monitor_2012_07_27_english.pdf.

———. 2012c. *The Monthly Humanitarian Monitor*. Oct.–Nov. http://www.ocha_opt_the_humanitarian_monitor_2012_12_18_english.pdf.

———. 2013. "The Humanitarian Impact of the Barrier, July 2013: Key Facts." July 9. https://www.ochaopt.org/documents/ocha_opt_barrier_factsheet_july_2013_english.pdf.

OCHA and World Food Program. 2010. "Between the Fence and the Hard Place: The Humanitarian Impact of Israeli-Imposed Restrictions on Access to Land and Sea in the Gaza Strip." New York: United Nations Office for the Coordination of Humanitarian Affairs and the World Food Program. http://www.ocha_opt_special_focus_2010_08_19_english.pdf.

Oppenheimer, Yehudit. 2012. "Why Jerusalem Palestinians Are Applying for Israeli Citizenship." *Ha'aretz*, Oct. 26.

———. 2013. "Children with Swollen Bellies in East Jerusalem." *Ha'aretz*, Aug. 12.

Palestine News Network. 2012. "Aid Agencies Call for a Halt to Recurring Demolitions of Water Cisterns in Area C." Dec. 20.

———. 2013. "Israel Shoots at Fishermen, Seriously Injures in Gaza." May 1.

Palestinian Center for Human Rights. 2012. "Weekly Report on Israeli Human Rights Violations in the Occupied Territory (26 Jan.–01 Feb. 2012)."

Palestinian Central Bureau of Statistics. 2013. *Special Statistical Bulletin: On the 65th Anniversary of the Nakba.* Ramallah, May 14. http://www.pcbs.gov.ps/site/512/default.aspx?tabID=512&lang=en&ItemID=788&mid=3171&wversion=Staging.

Pappe, Ilan. 2006a. *The Ethnic Cleansing of Palestine.* Oxford: Oneworld.

———. 2006b. "Genocide in Gaza." Electronic Intifada, Sept. 2. https://electronicintifada.net/content/genocide-gaza/6397.

———. 2011. *The Forgotten Palestinians: A History of the Palestinians in Israel.* New Haven, CT: Yale Univ. Press.

———. 2014. "Israel's Incremental Genocide in the Gaza Ghetto." Electronic Intifada, July 13. https://electronicintifada.net/content/israels-incremental-genocide-gaza-ghetto/13562.

Ravid, Barak. 2014. "Lieberman: Several Israeli Arab Towns Must Be Made Part of Palestine under Peace Deal." *Ha'aretz*, Jan. 5.

Raz, Avi. 2012. *The Bride and the Dowry: Israel, Jordan, and the Palestinians in the Aftermath of the June 1967 War.* New Haven, CT: Yale Univ. Press.

Rempel, Terry, and Nihad Boqai, eds. 2005. *Survey of Palestinian Refugees and Internally Displaced Persons.* Bethlehem, Palestine: BADIL Resource Center for Palestinian Residency and Refugee Rights.

Reuters. 2012a. "East Jerusalem Hospitals Face Financial Crisis in Wake of Palestinian UN Bid." *Ha'aretz*, Nov. 6.

———. 2012b. "Israel Raids Palestinian NGO Offices amid Heightened Tension." *Ha'aretz*, Dec. 11.

———. 2013. "Israel Mistreats Palestinian Children in Custody, UNICEF Reports." *Ha'aretz*, Mar. 6.

Rinat, Zafir. 2012. "Separation Fence Threatens to Destroy Farming, Ecosystem around Jerusalem." *Ha'aretz*, Oct. 18.

Rothman, Moriel. 2012. "In East Jerusalem, Only Palestinian Property Seized as 'Absentee.'" *+972 Magazine*, Mar. 6.

Rudoren, Jodi, Fares Akram, and Isabel Kershiner. 2012. "Israeli Airstrike Kills Three Generations of a Palestinian Family." *New York Times*, Nov. 18.

Sadeh, Shuki. 2012. "West Bank Palestinians See an Israeli Roadblock to Economic Independence." *Ha'aretz*, Mar. 23, 2012.

Save the Children and the East Jerusalem YMCA Rehabilitation Program. 2012. "The Impact of Child Detention: Occupied Palestinian Territory."

Jerusalem: Save the Children Sweden and E-J YMCA Rehabilitation Program. http://resourcecentre.savethechildren.se/library/impact-child-detention-occupied-palestinian-territory.

Schiano, Rosa. 2013. "Two Fishermen Arrested by Israeli Navy and Their Boat Confiscated." *Mondoweiss*, June 17.

Schiff, Ze'ev. 2006. "On the Origins of Targeted Assassination." *Ha'aretz*, June 5.

Seidemann, Daniel. 1997. "The Struggle for Land in Jerusalem: An Interview." *Palestine–Israel Journal of Politics, Economics and Culture* 4 (2). http://www.pij.org/details.php?id=479.

Shalev, Nir. 2012. "Under the Guise of Legality: Israel's Declarations of State Land in the West Bank." Jerusalem: B'Tselem.

Shaoul, Jean. 2015. "Soldiers Reveal Israeli War Crimes in 2014 Gaza Assault." World Socialist Web Site, May 14. https://www.wsws.org/en/articles/2015/05/14/gaza-m14.html.

Sheizaf, Noam. 2010. "IDF Document: 'Policy Principle: Separating Gaza from West Bank.'" +972 *Magazine*, Sept. 5.

Shoaini, Halla. 2011. "Childbirth at Checkpoints in the Occupied Palestinian Territory." *Lancet*, July 5.

Shragai, Nadav. 2005. "Third Temple Culture." *Ha'aretz*, Jan. 26.

Shuttleworth, Kate. 2015. "Elderly Palestinian Woman Dies as Israel Blocks Access to Hospitals." National, Oct. 21. http://www.thenational.ae/world/middle-east/elderly-palestinian-woman-dies-as-israel-blocks-access-to-hospitals.

Territorial Jerusalem. 2011. "New Settlement Approval Issued for Gilo—Plan 13261." Sept. 9.

———. 2013. "Everything You Need to Know about Jerusalem and the Absentee Property Law." July 13.

UK Task Force on Issues Relating to Arab Citizens of Israel. 2013. "Israel's Arab Citizens: Key Facts and Current Realities." http://uktaskforce.org/docs/130625-israel-s-arab-citizens---key-facts-and-current-realities.pdf.

UNCTAD. 2012. "Report on UNCTAD Assistance to the Palestinian People: Developments in the Economy of the Occupied Palestinian Territory." Geneva: United Nations Conference on Trade and Development, 59th session of the Trade and Development Board, Sept. 17–28, TD/B/59/2.

United Nations Human Rights Council. 2013. "Report of the Independent International Fact-Finding Mission to Investigate the Implications of the Israeli Settlements on the Civil, Political, Economic, Social and Cultural Rights of the Palestinian People throughout the Occupied Palestinian Territory, Including East Jerusalem." Geneva: United Nations Human Rights Council. Twenty-second session. Agenda item 7. Feb.

UNRWA. 2012. "Jerusalem Study: West Bank Barrier Has a Devastating Impact on the Environment and Palestinian Communities along Its Route." Jerusalem: Barrier Monitoring Unit (BMU) of the UN Relief and Works Agency (UNRWA) for Palestine Refugees in the Near East, together with Applied Research Institute Jerusalem (ARIJ), June 7.

Van Esveld, Bill. 2012. "'Forget about Him, He's Not Here': Israel's Control of Palestinian Residency in the West Bank and Gaza." Human Rights Watch, Feb. 5. https://www.hrw.org/report/2012/02/05/forget-about-him-hes-not-here/israels-control-palestinian-residency-west-bank-and.

Weir, Alison. N.d. "Israeli Checkpoints and Their Impact on Daily Life." http://www.ifamericansknew.org/cur_sit/checkpoints.html.

Whitson, Sarah Leah. 2013. "Israel: Gaza Airstrikes Violated Laws of War; Israeli Attacks Killed Civilians, Destroyed Homes without Lawful Justification." Human Rights Watch, Feb. 12. https://www.hrw.org/news/2013/02/12/israel-gaza-airstrikes-violated-laws-war.

Wilson, Scott. 2006. "Israeli High Court Backs Military on Its Policy of 'Targeted Killings.'" *Washington Post*, Dec. 15.

World Bank. 2011. "Building the Palestinian State: Sustaining Growth, Institutions, and Service Delivery; Economic Monitoring Group Report to the Ad Hoc Liaison Committee." Apr. 13. http://siteresources.worldbank.org/INTWESTBANKGAZA/Resources/AHLCReportApril2011.pdf.

———. 2012. "West Bank and Gaza: Towards Economic Sustainability of a Future Palestinian State; Promoting Private Sector-Led Growth." http://documents.worldbank.org/curated/en/864951468140640370/West-Bank-and-Gaza-Towards-economic-sustainability-of-a-future-Palestinian-state-promoting-private-sector-led-growth.

World Health Organization. 2005. "The State of Nutrition: West Bank and Gaza Strip." http://www.who.int/hac/crises/international/wbgs/oPt_Review_of_nutrition_situation_June2005.pdf.

———. 2011. "East Jerusalem Hospital Network." http://www.emro.who.int/pse/programmes/east-jerusalem-hospital-network-project.html.

Yesh Din. 2014. "Law Enforcement upon IDF Soldiers in the Occupied Territories: Figures for 2013." Sept. https://www.google.com/search?q=Law+Enforcement+upon+IDF+Soldiers+in+the+Occupied+Territories%3A+Figures+for+2013&ie=utf-8&oe=utf-8.

Part Three

Gender Dynamics

What Has Changed?

9

Gender Norms in the Muslim Middle East

VALERIE J. HOFFMAN

In 2005 Freedom House issued a report finding that no issue presented a greater challenge to the attainment of democracy and justice in the Arab world than gender inequality. A twenty-month study surveying sixteen countries and the Palestinian territories found "a pervasive, gender-based gap in rights and freedoms. A substantial deficit in women's rights exists in every country reviewed in this study and is reflected in practically every institution of society: the law, the criminal justice system, the economy, education, health care, and the media" (Nazir and Tomppert 2005). A follow-up study published in 2010, which added Iran to the countries under review (Kelly and Breslin 2010), found that this deficit persisted, despite notable progress, especially in education, economic opportunities, and political participation. Although gender inequalities can be found in every region of the world, the gap between the rights of men and of women is widest in the Middle East and North Africa.

Westerners have long reflexively attributed women's suffering in the Middle East to Islam, a tendency that Western scholars began to seriously challenge in the 1990s (Kandiyoti 1992; Moghadam 2013, 1–10). Abu-Lughod (2013) points out that this reductionist logic is often genuinely shocking to Muslim women and reminds us that there is no uniform understanding of Islam or its implications for Muslim women. Moghissi, on the other hand, writes that the heroic effort to rescue "Islam" from culpability ends up serving the interests of Islamists who, regardless of their differences, all aim to curtail women's rights (Moghissi 1999). Mona Eltahawy writes even more vehemently:

> Name me an Arab country, and I'll recite a litany of abuses against women occurring in that country, abuses fueled by a toxic mix of culture and religion that few seem willing to disentangle lest they blaspheme or offend. When more than 90 percent of women who have ever been married in Egypt have had their genitals cut in the name of "purity," then surely we must all blaspheme. When Egyptian women are subjected to humiliating "virginity tests" merely for speaking out, it's no time for silence. When an article in the Egyptian criminal code says that if a woman has been beaten by her husband "with good intentions," no punitive damages can be obtained, then to hell with political correctness. . . . When it comes to the status of women in the Arab world, it's not better than you think. It's much, much worse. (2015, 5–6)

This chapter reviews gender in the Middle East from a number of perspectives: Western and Muslim discourses about Muslim women, women's rights in traditional interpretations of Islamic law, other cultural norms that impact women's status, conservative and revisionist interpretations of women's rights in Islamic law, legal reforms affecting women's rights in the last century, Islamic feminism, hypermasculinity in Middle Eastern culture, attitudes toward homosexuality and transgender in the Middle East, and new trends in gender relations making an appearance in the region.

Western and Muslim Discourses about Muslim Women

Women have been at the center of Christian discourses about Islam since at least the early eighth century, when John of Damascus noted with disgust that the Qur'an "clearly legislates that one may have four wives and one thousand concubines if he can, as many as he can maintain beside the four wives; and that one can divorce whomsoever he pleases, if he so wishes, and have another one" (Tieszen 2015, 19). Petrus Alfonsi, a Jewish scholar of Spain who converted to

Christianity in 1106, was just one of many Westerners to repeat the allegation that the prophet Muhammad was "burning so much with the fire of lust that he did not blush to befoul another man's bed in adultery just as if the Lord were commanding it" (ibid., 161). Western observers since the nineteenth century have targeted the veiling and oppression of Muslim women as an indication of the inferiority of Islam as a religion (Ahmed 1992, 144–68), forcing Muslims into defensive postures, either in the direction of defending traditional sexual segregation as morally superior to Western gender relations or in the direction of finding traditional sexual segregation and anti-feminist biases to be antithetical to the spirit of Islam, the result of Muslims' patriarchal rigidity and poor understanding of the exalted morality and human equality propagated by authentic Islam. As the following quotation from a book by American missionaries in 1902 indicates, Christian missionary activity in the Muslim world was suffused with concern to "liberate" Muslim women, and Westerners often saw the veiling and seclusion of women as the greatest cause of Muslim "backwardness": "In the twenty-fourth Surah of the Koran women are forbidden to appear unveiled before any member of the other sex, with the exception of near relatives. And so by one verse the bright, refining, elevating influence of women was forever withdrawn from Moslem society. The evils of the zenana, the seraglio, the harem, or by whatever name it is called, are writ large over all the social life of the Moslem world. Keene says it 'lies at the root of all the most important features that differentiate progress from stagnation'" (van Sommer and Zwemer 1902, 5–6; Keene 1879, 4). In another book, Zwemer acknowledged that the Qur'an abolished the practice of female infanticide, but he wrote, "Mohammed improved on the barbaric method and discovered a way by which not some but *all* females could be buried alive without being murdered—namely, the veil" (1900, 161).

Westerners were preoccupied with the veil and fascinated by the imagined sensuality of the harem (Porterfield 1998; DelPlato 2002). Edward Said went so far as to conflate Europe's penetration of the Middle East with the sexual conquests of individual Western adventurers in the Middle East: "The relation between the Middle East and the West is really defined as sexual: as I said earlier in discussing Flaubert, the association between the Orient and sex is remarkably persistent. The Middle East is resistant, as any virgin would be, but the male scholar wins the prize by bursting open, penetrating through the Gordian knot despite the 'taxing task.' 'Harmony' is the result of the conquest of maidenly coyness; it is not by any means the coexistence of equals" (1978, 309).

Said's critique of the West's pursuit of an unequal "harmony" with the Middle East could equally be leveled at Muslim gender discourses, which use marital harmony and the complementarity of the sexes as code phrases to promote starkly unequal gendered relationships. Muslim public intellectuals in the nineteenth and early twentieth centuries responded to Western criticism of Muslim gender norms in two distinct yet sometimes intertwined ways: by defending the reasonableness of Muslim customs while impugning the morality of the West and by proclaiming that Islam liberated Arab women from the shackles of misogyny and servitude in which they had lived before Islam. Some who took the latter rhetorical strategy acknowledged the disadvantages of women in Muslim societies but argued that these obstacles were contrary to Islam's original purpose and ethos; they sought to improve women's lives by reinterpreting Islamic law according to what they said were Islam's underlying ethical goals and principles, the most important of which is justice. These "modernist" interpreters of Islam claimed that the Qur'anic endorsement of polygamy in Sura 4:3 ("Marry other women as you like—two, three, four") was meant to be a short-term solution to the problems faced by women and girls who were suddenly widowed and orphaned after many men had died in war. They argue that the verse's closing admonition, "But if you fear that you cannot maintain equality among them, marry one only or [have relations with] any slave-girls you may own; this will make it easier for you to avoid injustice," constitutes a restrictive stipulation that actually implies a preference for monogamy, especially when considered in conjunction with verse 129 of the same Sura: "Try as you might, you will never be able to treat your wives impartially." The apparent contradiction between the two verses was customarily resolved by saying that the equality mandated in verse 3 is an equality of time and wealth, whereas the equality deemed impossible in verse 129 is equality in affection, which is beyond human capacity. This interpretation is rendered plausible by the example of the prophet Muhammad, who carefully distributed his time and property equally among his wives, although everyone knew he favored 'A'isha over the others. But some modernists took the contradiction as a virtual prohibition of polygamy, and on this basis Tunisia's Personal Status Code of 1956 did, in fact, prohibit it—the only country to do so based on a modernist interpretation of the Qur'an. Turkey, the only other Muslim country to prohibit polygamy soon after the establishment of its republic, abandoned all pretense of following Islamic precepts and patterned its family law on the Swiss Civil Code.

The modernists had limited success in persuading the masses to follow their agenda; leaders of Islamist movements such as the Muslim Brotherhood of Egypt and Jama'at-i Islami of India/Pakistan rejected modernist reinterpretations of Islamic law and insisted on traditional, unequal gender norms. Nonetheless, modernist discourse had a broad impact, and the worlds of Islamism and modernism overlapped and intersected in many instances. One of the ways that modernism and Islamism intersected in the second half of the twentieth century is in the widespread adoption of a rhetoric claiming that Islam gives women more rights than any other religion. Ann Elizabeth Mayer observed that conservative Muslims who had formerly been frank in their espousal of unequal rights for men and women had, by the 1990s, embraced a rhetoric that appeared to champion women's rights while, in fact, maintaining traditional misogyny (Mayer 1995).

Muslims, of course, have no monopoly on hypocritical rhetoric. Leila Ahmed has pointed out how Lord Cromer, the British consul-general of Egypt from 1883 to 1907, purportedly championed feminism in Egypt while maintaining the propriety of misogyny in British society (Ahmed 1992, 152–53). Likewise, American rhetoric justifying its invasion of Afghanistan in 2001 as having the goal of "liberating" Afghan women can easily be dismissed as camouflage for the real goals of defeating al-Qaeda and the Taliban, ensuring American security, and extending American influence.

Women's Rights in Traditional Interpretations of Islamic Law

As we have seen, both conservative and liberal Muslims often claim that Islam significantly improved the status of women in seventh-century Arabia. They claim that women were severely devalued in Arabia before Islam, that female infanticide and polygamy were rampant, that women had no right to own or inherit wealth, and that they were subjected to the whims of often brutal husbands who regarded them as little more than chattel. Islam banned female infanticide, limited polygamy, and gave women the right to own and manage property, rights that Western women came to enjoy only recently.

There is little historical evidence to substantiate most of the claims concerning the miserable condition of women in pre-Islamic Arabia (Abbott 1941; Ahmed 1992). Although the Qur'an does mention and prohibit female infanticide, there is little evidence that polygyny was common in either Mecca or Medina (Stern 1939, 62, 70). Although Muslims interpret the Qur'an as limiting the number of wives a man may take to four, the wording of the verse in question—"Marry other women as you like—two, three, four" (4:3)—could equally be seen not as limiting polygamy but as encouraging men to take more wives. It is not unlikely, not only because of the context (dealing with the problem of orphaned girls and widowed women after the death of many men in battle), but also because the form of the words connoting the numbers is not typical. Identical wording occurs in the Qur'an with respect to the number of pairs of wings angels have (35:1); in that instance, the phrase is sometimes translated "twos, threes, fours," suggesting imprecision because of the unusual form of the numbers, as well as the mystery inherent in such a topic. Likewise, the wording of the Qur'an in 4:3 suggests imprecision in the number of wives a man may take. Nonetheless, Muslim legal scholars have universally interpreted it as setting a limit on the number of wives a man may have at one time.

The claim that women did not own or inherit wealth in pre-Islamic Arabia is contradicted by the story of Muhammad's own life: he was a poor man until he married a wealthy widow who had employed him and later proposed marriage. The stories of Khadija, Hind, and other great female personalities of Muhammad's early life hardly suggest that women were chattel. But in an attempt to defend Islam against charges of misogyny, the advantages Islam gave to women have been exaggerated so consistently and repeatedly that even many Western scholars have come to accept them as true. The claim that Islam radically improved the rights of women has served the agendas of both conservatives, who wish to demonstrate the superiority of the sharia over Western norms, and modernists, who wish to demonstrate that Muslim scholars sabotaged the Prophet's originally feminist agenda.

Marriage

Islamic law provides that "marriage is in the hands of the guardian," meaning that male guardians have the right to contract marriages for women in their care. Men may marry more than one woman and may marry Jewish and Christian women, but no comparable rights are extended to Muslim women. The groom must pay a dower (*mahr*) to the bride in return for exclusive rights to her sexuality and reproductive capacity. Often, only a token part of the *mahr* is given at the time of marriage; the rest is payable if the man divorces her. Men are obligated to provide their wives with food, clothing, and shelter ("maintenance") in a manner befitting the women's social station before marriage, and in return husbands may demand their wives' obedience (Haeri 1993). Husbands are not allowed to take any of their wives' wealth without their permission. The Qur'an (4:34) allows men to take certain measures against disobedient wives, including striking them, although commentaries on the Qur'an and legal scholars mitigate this point somewhat by saying that beating should be a last resort and should not produce bruising, bleeding, or broken bones (Bauer 2006; Ammar 2007). Nonetheless, the subordinate position of women in marriage is clear.

Divorce

The Qur'an allows men to "replace one wife with another" (4:20) with ease, although it encourages men to treat their wives justly and fairly. Hadith records Muhammad as saying that of all permitted things divorce is the most hateful to God, but the Qur'an takes the matter in stride and Islamic law places no restrictions on a man's ability to divorce his wife by simple verbal pronouncement. If the divorce is initiated by the husband, he may not take back the dower, and any unpaid portion becomes due at that time. Divorce is effective only after a waiting period of three menstrual cycles, during which the husband may reconcile with his wife. He may divorce her and reconcile twice, but the third time the divorce is irrevocable, and he may not contract a new marriage with the same woman until she has married another man and been divorced by him. There is no alimony in Islamic law; the husband's obligation to maintain the wife ends with the end of the waiting period. The Qur'an urges women who are unhappy with their marriages to seek reconciliation (4:128). It allows women to ransom themselves from an unhappy marriage by returning the dower to their husbands (*khul'*) if the latter agree (2:229), but no recourse is mentioned in the Qur'an for women whose husbands do not agree to divorce. Most schools of Islamic law (though not the Hanafi school, which is favored in central Asia, South Asia, and many former Ottoman territories) grant women very limited grounds on which they may appeal to a judge for the dissolution of an unhappy marriage: failure of the husband to maintain the wife properly, the husband's sexual impotence, the husband's terminal illness, or abandonment. Only the Maliki and Hanbali schools include wife abuse among the grounds for court-ordered divorce.

Child Custody

After divorce, the child continues to belong to the father and his lineage. The mother may have temporary custody of the child up to a certain age, which varies among the different schools of Islamic law and sometimes also varies according to the gender of the child. The variations range from age two to age nine. The father is responsible to maintain the child, and if the mother is breast-feeding the child (normally expected until age two), he is responsible to maintain both of them until the child is weaned.

Inheritance

The Qur'an outlines specific shares that each relative will inherit of the wealth of the deceased (4:11–12). An earlier Qur'anic verse had encouraged people to make out wills specifying to whom they bequeath their inheritance (2:181), so legal schools generally allow one-third of the inheritance to be apportioned by a will, while the rest is distributed according to the Qur'anic shares. In general, children are favored over spouses in inheritance, and women receive about half the inheritance of men in a comparable kinship relation to the deceased. This discrepancy is justified by conservative Muslims on the basis of male financial provision for women.

Legal Testimony

According to the Qur'an, loan contracts require two male witnesses or, if two men cannot be found, one man and two women, "so if one of them forgets, the other will remind her" (2:282). The implication that women are more forgetful than men was not lost on medieval Muslim men, and in Islamic law a woman's testimony is always worth only half the statement of a man. Regarding crimes that have specified punishments in the Qur'an and Hadith, such as murder, adultery, slander, and theft, women's testimony is disallowed altogether. This prohibition creates problems in the case of women who are raped, because the testimony of four adult Muslim male eyewitnesses to the act of penetration is necessary to prove such an allegation. If such proof is not available, a woman who accuses a man of rape opens herself to a charge of slander, which is punishable by eighty lashes.

Freedom of Movement

The sharia grants men the authority to control the movements of their female guardians. Men thus have the right to keep women secluded in the home, although Hadith allows women to go the mosque—a right that was denied women for centuries but that they have reclaimed in recent decades. Some Middle Eastern countries do not allow a woman to travel abroad without permission from her male guardian. This legal mandate can result in such absurdities as the case of a female professor at the University of Damascus who needed the permission of her young brother to obtain an exit visa (Shaaban 1988, 35–36).

Right to Education

An oft-quoted hadith proclaims the obligation of all Muslim men and women to "seek knowledge," which was traditionally limited to the religious knowledge adequate to allow Muslims to perform all their religious obligations. Ghazali, an influential eleventh-century scholar, said that men should teach these duties to their wives in order to prevent them from having to leave the house to seek such knowledge. However, if a man does not teach the wife, Ghazali said she is obligated to seek religious knowledge from a qualified teacher outside the home (Farah 1984, 103).

Competence

Muslims find in the classical Islamic literature ample justification for the notion that men are innately superior to women. They interpret the "preference" God gives to men (Qur'an 4:34) and the "rank" men have over women (Qur'an 2:228) as referring to a vast array of natural, physical, social, and religious advantages, ranging from superior intelligence and physical strength to social authority and literacy, prophethood, and leadership in prayer—although, in the Qur'anic context, both the "preference" and the "rank" appear to refer to the advantages men have over women in marriage and divorce. Hadith has a number of misogynist sayings attributed to the Prophet indicating that women are morally and intellectually inferior to men, that women are dangerous to men, and that the majority of the inhabitants of hellfire are women. Although the Qur'an appears to make men and women equally responsible before the law, with equal punishments for adultery, for example, medieval Muslim scholars seemed to feel that women's moral and intellectual weakness necessitated male guardianship and responsibility even in the moral sphere. Given that presupposition, it is not surprising that conservative Islamic human rights documents grant women rights of dependence and maintenance by men, rather than rights of autonomy and self-determination.

Other Cultural Norms Affecting Women's Rights

Perhaps even more important than Islamically sanctioned limitations on women's rights are cultural norms that are common to patriarchal societies and are strong in many parts of the Middle East. Foremost among them is a high social priority placed on maintaining family honor and avoiding shame. This theme has been thoroughly explored in many studies (Antoun 1968; Shaaban 1988; Tillion 1983; Wikan 1984). A family's honor depends especially on the modesty and chastity of its women. It is critically important in traditional societies in the Middle East to avoid any hint of suspicion concerning the behavior of the women in one's family. This point is so important that any infringement of the honor code lays a burden on male family members to expunge the shame from their midst by murdering the offending women in so-called honor killings (Antoun 1968; El Saadawi 1980, 25–32; Husseini 2009; Tripathi and Yadav 2004; Welchman 2007). This cultural priority on family honor, rather than

Islamic law, is what lies behind the customs of veiling and secluding women. Originally, the custom of veiling was to denote women of high social status; only gradually did it come to be seen as an Islamically mandated practice for the maintenance of modesty and social morality across social classes (Stowasser 1997). Traditional perceptions of women's hypersexuality and limited intelligence and self-control legitimated these customs.

The decline in veiling and seclusion in urban areas in the twentieth century raised new anxieties and social tensions, which Fatima Mernissi documented in her classic work, *Beyond the Veil* (1975). The discrepancy between the new urban norms and traditional social values has led to an increase in the number of honor killings in many cases (Husseini 2009) and to the social legitimation of the rape of women who are deemed to be inadequately covered (Taha 2013; Kirollos 2016). In Pakistan rape is used as a political tool to shame and emasculate political opponents (Haeri 1995). Morocco, Algeria, the United Arab Emirates, and Egypt have all conducted "virginity tests" on women who dare to enter public spaces in contravention of local custom (Eltahawy 2015, 92–94; Kirkpatrick 2015), although Egypt banned virginity tests in December 2011 in response to a court case (Flock 2011). Such practices not only express the importance of female virginity before marriage, but are conducted on the assumption that unmarried women who engage in public activities are no better than prostitutes. The aggressive targeting of women who dare to enter public life is owing not only to the incompatibility of their public visibility with traditional gender norms, but also, according to Paul Amar, an attempt to compensate for weakness by establishing moral authority by degrading opponents and depicting them as immoral. During the 2011 protests in Egypt, revolutionaries were denounced as "fags, thugs, and prostitutes." "It was not enough to call them that," says Amar. "They literally started to make their bodies into that by creating evidence that they were thugs, fags and prostitutes, by creating data on prostitutes, by doing virginity tests" (2012). Under Mubarak, any woman arrested for protesting against the regime was registered as a prostitute in court records and press accounts, and then raped and sexually tortured in jail (Amar 2011, 309). Social injustices are articulated as gender disorder in political discourse.

Women's Human Rights: Conservative Muslim Perspectives

Ann Elizabeth Mayer has examined various conservative Muslim documents on human rights and analyzed their compatibility with international human rights standards as articulated in the Universal Declaration of Human Rights (UDHR) of 1948, the International Covenant on Economic, Social, and Cultural Rights of 1966, and the International Covenant on Civil and Political Rights (ICCPR), also of 1966. The documents she studied include the Universal Islamic Declaration of Human Rights of 1990, the Iranian constitution of 1979, the "Draft of the Islamic Constitution" of 1978 devised by al-Azhar University's Islamic Research Academy, and the writings of Iranian scholar Sultanhussein Tabandeh (1914–92) and of Pakistani writer Abul A'la Mawdudi (1903–79). While finding, not surprisingly, that these documents overwhelmingly uphold traditional interpretations of the sharia with regard to women's social roles, Mayer finds, perhaps more fundamentally,

> an absence of any willingness to recognize women as full, equal human beings who deserve the same rights and freedoms as men. Instead, discrimination against women is treated as something entirely natural—in much the same way that people in the West think it is natural that mentally defective persons and young children must be denied certain rights and freedoms. However, there is a general reluctance to spell out in ways likely to come to the attention of a Western audience the authors' beliefs in inherent female inferiority. In this regard, the invocations of *shari'a* law are very useful, since the *shari'a* qualifications that are placed on rights tend to look harmless to a casual observer but signal the authors' general intentions to an informed audience. (1991, 136)

All of these documents speak of women only in the context of marriage and assert the authority of men over women; the idea of an unmarried, autonomous woman is never contemplated. Among these sources, only Tabandeh was explicit in his opposition to the concept of gender equality and his belief that the political domain is innately alien to the domain of women. He said it is necessary for women to stay at home and avoid public gatherings attended by men unless absolutely necessary, in order to preserve public morality (ibid., 116–17). Mawdudi, on the other hand, "was a canny politician who seems to have appreciated the damage that it would do to the credibility of his human rights scheme if he admitted that it aimed at denying fundamental rights to one-half of the population," so he avoided discussion of women in his writing on human rights, although his views on the subject are amply expressed elsewhere, often in a highly polemical tone linking gender equality, female autonomy, and gender desegregation with moral disintegration, promiscuity, and perversion. Mawdudi listed as one of his "basic human rights" respect for the chastity of women, but, as Mayer points out, "the need to shield women's chastity has been exploited by Muslim conservatives like Mawdudi as a justification for denying women a broad spectrum of rights and for keeping them largely restricted to the home." Mawdudi was also not above making overtly false statements, such as that no law other than the sharia protects women from rape and that Muslim armies never engaged in prostitution or rape, as Western armies did (ibid., 117–19).

Islamic human rights statements like the Universal Islamic Declaration of Human Rights maintain an idealized vision of Muslim society in which all women are maintained by husbands or male relatives and have no need of financial autonomy, ignoring the hardships of indigent divorced women. Mayer also notes that one of Ayatollah Khomeini's first acts after the Iranian revolution was the abolition of the Family Protection Act, which had required that all divorces be pursued through a court, significantly broadened the grounds on which a woman could seek divorce, assigned custody based on the best interests of the child, and required a husband to get permission from the court before marrying a second wife. The Khomeini regime lowered the minimum marriage age from eighteen to thirteen and drastically curtailed women's activities outside the home, including educational and employment opportunities and the ability to participate in sports (ibid., 130–31). Mayer concludes that conservative Islamic human rights schemes violate the following provisions of the UDHR: Article 1 (guarantee of equality), Article 2 (guarantee against discriminatory treatment), Article 7 (guarantee of equal protection of the law), and Article 16 (guarantee of the freedom to marry the partner of one's choice), as well as the following provisions of the ICCPR: Article 2 (guarantee against discriminatory treatment), Article 3 (equal rights guarantee), Article 12 (guarantee of liberty of movement), and Article 26 (guarantees of equality, equal protection, and nondiscriminatory treatment). The persistence of discriminatory attitudes is evident in a public statement issued by the Muslim Brotherhood of Egypt in March 2013 affirming male guardianship over women, the need for women to receive permission from their guardians to work or travel or to use contraceptives, and the right of husbands to discipline their wives and condemning the notion of marital rape (Kirkpatrick and El Sheikh 2013). In November 2014, President Recep Tayyip Erdoğan of Turkey declared that gender equality is unnatural, that some jobs are inappropriate for women, and that feminists are at fault for "rejecting motherhood" (Arsu 2014).

Women's Human Rights: Modernist Muslim Perspectives

Modernists since Qasim Amin (1863–1908), an associate of Muhammad 'Abduh, have argued against the notion that men and women are fundamentally different or that biological differences regarding reproduction necessitate radically different social functions. Qasim Amin's book *Tahrir al-mar'a* (The Emancipation of Women), published in Egypt in 1899, articulated the essential early modernist position and catapulted the issue of women's rights into the forefront of Muslim consciousness, provoking a debate that has not abated to this day. Amin targeted women's veiling (meaning, at that time, the face veil) and seclusion, polygamy, divorce laws, and education as areas requiring reform. He did not advocate the adoption of Western dress for Muslim women, but felt, based on his experience as a judge in civil law court, that the face veil, which is not required by the sharia, resulted in many abuses of women in the legal system, as it allowed someone else to impersonate them. As a result, women were married and had their property sold without their knowledge. He argued that the face veil prevented women from participating in society in a healthy manner and that women should be educated (at least at the primary level) and learn marketable skills. As a judge, he was too close to real-life problems to disregard the problem of indigent, unskilled women with no male relatives to support them. Nor did Amin advocate radically new gender norms—like many early modernists and later Islamists, he advocated women's education mainly to enable women to be better companions for their husbands and better mothers to their children and in order to eliminate superstition among the people (which was seen as propagated mainly by women). But he argued that if women seem more infantile and lacking in intelligence than men, it is only because men have deprived them of education for so many generations; a girl, he said, has the same innate intelligence and curiosity as a boy (Hoffman-Ladd 1987, 25–27; Ahmed 1992, 142–45, 155–64).

Consistent with the tendency among modernists to regard the laws of the Qur'an as too contextually bound to be compatible with modern society, Mohamed Abed Jabri of Morocco (1935–2010) argued that the regulations of the Qur'an were the result of historical conditions that gave the fully Islamic principles of freedom of faith and equal rights for women a content that is below modern Muslim aspirations (Filali-Ansari 1998, 160).

Moroccan feminist scholar Fatima Mernissi (1940–2015) used the criteria of traditional Islamic scholarship to question the authenticity of some of the hadith that have been most frequently quoted to justify a gender ideology that views women as tainted through impure bodily functions (menstruation, postpartum bleeding) and mental and moral limitations, as well as the famous hadith that is typically used to justify denying women participation in the political process: "A nation that is ruled by a woman will never prosper."

Traditional Muslim scholarship examines the reliability of the individuals cited in the chain of authorities for each individual narrative (hadith) in order to assess its soundness. By this criterion and others, Mernissi undermined the credibility of these allegedly "sound" hadith and countered them with others that she believed had been deliberately suppressed by Muslim scholars. She wrote:

> All the monotheistic religions are shot through by the conflict between the divine and the feminine, but none more so than Islam, which has opted for the occultation of the feminine, at least symbolically, by trying to veil it, to hide it, to mask it. Islam as sexual practice unfolds with a very special theatricality since it is acted out in a scene where the *hijab* [veil, seclusion] occupies a central position. This almost phobic attitude toward women is all the more surprising since we have seen that the Prophet has encouraged his adherents to renounce it as representative of the *jahiliyya* [Arabian society before Islam] and its superstitions. This leads me to ask: Is it possible that Islam's message had only a limited and superficial effect on deeply superstitious seventh-century Arabs who failed to integrate its novel approaches to the world and to women? Is it possible that the *hijab*, the attempt to veil women, that is claimed today to be basic to Muslim identity, is nothing but the expression of the persistence of the pre-Islamic mentality, the *jahiliyya* mentality that Islam was supposed to annihilate? (1991, 81)

Feminism and Legal Reform in the Twentieth Century

Until the last quarter of the twentieth century, Islam played a minor role in the modernization discourse of most countries in the Middle East. Turkey, Iran, and the socialist regimes of the Arab world all included female education and women's participation in the public sphere as part of their modernization strategies. It became normal in many countries for Muslim women who attended university to wear Western dress. Nonetheless, women's expanding education and their participation in the public workforce and even in politics were not paralleled by equal expansion of their rights in the private sphere.

Although the Qur'an contains relatively few verses with a legal import in the social sphere, many of the verses that do issue specific regulations concern marriage, divorce, and inheritance. Thus, what has come to be called "personal status law" plays a central role in public conceptions of Islamic law. Most Muslim countries base their personal status laws on traditional interpretations of the sharia, sometimes with modest modernist revisions: raising the minimum age of marriage, mildly discouraging polygamy, requiring men to go to court to obtain a divorce, expanding somewhat the traditionally very restrictive grounds on which a woman can seek a divorce, and giving women a longer period of custody of their young children after divorce. In reality, these restrictions are often ignored. In Egypt, where the minimum marriage age is eighteen, there are no criminal sanctions against anyone who ignores the law, and some 17 percent of girls are married under that age (Girls Not Brides 2016).

Women and Islamism

The rise of Islamism's popularity in the 1970s was accompanied by a resurgence of extremely conservative gender norms (Hoffman-Ladd 1987). Hasan Hanafi wrote that Islamists are dominated by "a sexual perception of the world" (Ayubi 1991, 45). Nazih Ayubi noted that "sexually frustrated males do not normally externalise their feelings into a rebellion against *all* the manifestations of political, social and economic repression in society, but rather internalise the agony at the level of moral and religious defence" (ibid., 40–41). Around the world, Islamist movements are preoccupied with policing gender relations by placing restrictions on women. Saudi Arabia's increasing oil wealth allowed it to export its ideology, including its extremely restrictive gender norms, both through direct propaganda and through the recruitment of migrant labor from other Middle Eastern countries before the Gulf War of 1990–91 (Hoodfar 1996). Iran's Family Protection Act of 1975 modestly expanded women's rights in marriage and divorce, but the Islamic Republic founded in 1979 meant a shocking and abrupt reversal in women's rights, as Haideh Moghissi clarifies in her contribution to this volume.

But the Islamic Republic of Iran's withdrawal of rights granted to women by the shah was far from the worst development for women in the region: in the civil war that engulfed Algeria after the military takeover in 1992, radical Islamists conducted a broad campaign of assassination of unveiled women and girls (Bennoune 1995). This brutality was exceeded by the Taliban after they conquered Afghanistan in 1996: they not only forced women to wear a fully enveloping *burqa*, but also closed girls' schools, prohibited women from working or obtaining medical assistance, and savagely beat women who ventured out in public to buy food for their families (Rostami-Povey 2007). This extremist misogyny became normalized among radical Islamists, most notoriously in areas controlled by the so-called Islamic State of Syria and Iraq (ISIS) (Callimachi 2015). Women carry the burden of manifesting cultural authenticity and are an easy target for male assertions of power and control. Mernissi wrote, "It is no wonder that women, who have such tremendous power to maintain or destroy a man's position in society [by exposing them to the risk of shame], are going to be the focus of his frustration and aggression" (1985, 160–64).

Islamic Feminism

The Islamic revival was also accompanied by new efforts to redefine women's rights within Islam. There is no doubt that Islamic movements have been appealing to many women as well as to men (Hoffman 1995, 213–16; Mahmood 2005; Hafez 2011). Western feminist scholarship has sometimes celebrated women's participation in the new piety movements and pointed out that it may be Western bias that identifies feminism with women's autonomy, whereas Muslim women are carving out their own space within the framework of Islam, in what has often been labeled "Islamic feminism."

Western scholars have debated the appropriateness of labeling the Muslim Brotherhood's Zaynab al-Ghazali (1917–2005) an

"Islamic feminist" (Ahmed 1992, 207; Badran 1991; M. Cooke 1994, 1995, 2001, 83–106; Duval 1998; Sullivan and Abed Kotob 1999, 104–9). Ghazali is an intriguing character because she was the first woman to serve in an unofficial leadership capacity in the Muslim Brotherhood and because she was a strong woman who inserted clauses into the contracts of both her marriages that forced her husbands to accept her Islamic activism and gave her the right to divorce them if they interfered in her vocation—and indeed, she divorced her first husband for this reason (Hoffman 1985). In her writings in the Brotherhood magazine, *al-Da'wa*, she featured the lives of early Muslim women warriors, especially Kharijite women, but she also told women that they must fulfill their "first, holy, and most important mission" as wives and mothers before engaging in public activities (ibid., 236–37). She advised them not to work outside the home or enroll their children in day care centers, but to be fully devoted to motherhood.

The contradiction between her admonitions and her example became clear to me when I interviewed her a second time in 1988. She told me God had given her a blessing that most would not consider a blessing: she was unable to conceive. Furthermore, her (second) husband was very wealthy and employed servants to do housework, so she was entirely free to devote herself to the Islamic cause. Finally, she said, he had other wives, and whenever he was with them "it was like a vacation." When her second husband divorced her under government pressure during her imprisonment for her alleged involvement in a plot against Nasser's regime (1964–71), she felt she had fulfilled her duty of marriage and was thenceforth free to be a full-time activist (Hoffman 1995, 216). Needless to say, these circumstances are unusual; she cannot serve as an attainable model for most women. She called herself "the mother of the Muslim Brotherhood," legitimating her activism through the idiom of motherhood.

Ghazali declared that Islam "gave women everything—freedom, economic rights, political rights, social rights, public and private rights"—and that Muslim women must study Islam so they can know these rights (Hoffman 1985, 234–35), but she did not elaborate. It is unlikely that she meant that women ought to have the same rights as men, because at no time does she challenge traditional interpretations of the sharia. She stated clearly that secular feminism is "a mistake" (ibid., 234). She did not engage in critical examination of Muslim texts. She told me she was very upset when she first learned about the hadith that affirm women's intellectual and religious deficiency, but after several days during which she could not pray and challenged God's wisdom in allowing the Prophet to say these words, her distress drove her back to God. She decided she could do nothing but accept these words that contradicted her experience and her sense of justice. Shehadeh writes that Ghazali saw herself "as a 'woman-man' with a divine mission," perhaps "of a different nature or breed from other women" (2003, 135–37). Shehadeh sees Ghazali as ambitious and manipulative, promising women freedom and security in a future Islamic state in order to gain their support, "thus becoming their 'patron saint' while actually condemning them to a permanently inferior state" (ibid., 140).

Badran sees Hiba Ra'uf as a more promising candidate for the title "Islamic feminist" (2009, 214–41), although she rejected the appellation, because she strove for a new discourse of women's rights within the framework of Islam. Some scholars have embraced Islamic feminism as more appropriate for Muslim societies than Western-style feminism (El Guindi 1996), while others remain skeptical (Moghissi 1999). In Southeast Asia, Muslim women's organizations have had some success in advocating new interpretations of women's rights in Islam (van Doorn-Harder 2006; Anwar 2008). This activism has been more limited in the Middle East (Mughni 2010). A number of Muslim scholars in the West have taken a fresh look at the Qur'an and have suggested new hermeneutical strategies with liberatory possibilities (Wadud-Muhsin 1992; Afsaruddin 1999; Barlas 2002; Wadud 2006; Aslan, Hermansen, and Medeni 2013; Hidayatullah 2014; Mir-Hosseini, al-Sharmani, and Rumminger 2015), while others point out the limitations of these approaches (Mirza 2002; Moosa 2003, 124–25; Ali 2006; Silvers 2006; Tatari 2013; Bouachrine 2014).

Homosexuality and Transgender in the Middle East

President Mahmoud Ahmadinejad famously responded to a question at Columbia University in September 2007 regarding homosexuals in Iran by asserting, "In Iran, we don't have homosexuals, like in your country." Although homoeroticism, especially love for beardless youths, formed a major motif of medieval Persian poetry and was seen as unexceptional, it is not the same as identification as a homosexual. As William Beeman notes, "The notion that one must be either 'gay' or 'straight' does not accord with what we observe in pan-human sexual behavior, which is far more flexible and nuanced. The gay/straight categorization is an artifact of American culture, which glories in binary categories for classifying people" (2014, 151). Afsaneh Najmabadi claims that, in Iran, same-sex sexuality was not considered shameful until encountered by the West (2005, 3). Beeman notes that what is stigmatized in the Middle East is to take the passive role in a sexual relationship; in the case of male rape, stigma attaches only to the one who is penetrated, not to the one who penetrates: "Active partners in Iran do not consider themselves to be 'homosexual.' Indeed, it is a kind of macho boast in some circles that one has been an active partner with another male, as it signals a power differential between the two. In actuality, many men are 'versatile' in their sexual activity, but if they are known to have relations with other men, they will always claim in public to be the active partner" (2014, 154–55). In the Arab world, men may be raped by armed gangs (Longmann 2014) or by security forces (*Not Your Booty* 2013), in which case shame attaches only to the victim.

Homosexuality is prohibited in traditional understandings of Islamic law, although Scott Siraj al-Haqq Kugle (2010) controversially claims that there is no specific prohibition in the Qur'an against same-sex activity. Homosexuality is criminalized in Middle Eastern countries, where it is punishable by death in Sudan, Saudi Arabia, Yemen, Qatar, Kuwait, and Iran (Ungar 2002). Nonetheless, same-sex relations are informally recognized in many places (Beeman 2014, 156).

In recent years, there has been an emerging "gay" culture in Lebanon and demands for recognition of gay rights in several countries (Meehan 2007; Platt 2014), but such recognition appears to be a long way off.

The Iranian government insists that individuals must be clearly male or female and take on the characteristics of their gender. Its approach to ambiguous sexuality is interesting and unique: it encourages sex-change operations for those individuals whose gender is ambiguous or who feel their true gender identity is not the same as their biology. Consequently, Iran has emerged as a global center for sex-change operations (Najmabadi 2014).

Hypermasculinity

A gender system that dictates a strict male-female binary and assumes clear gender differences in personalities, aptitudes, and social roles may be expected not only to favor masculinity but also to exaggerate its attributes. Patriarchy has long been associated with "macho" cultural norms for men, which is certainly true of the Middle East. Around the world, anxieties caused by the weakening of classic patriarchy and anger prompted by political frustrations and military humiliations are often transmuted into attempts to control women or even violence against women, in an aggressive assertion of masculinity. Moghadam points out that hypermasculinity, "with its aspects of competition, rivalry, swagger, aggressiveness, and violence," is an underlying cause of many conflicts and wars and that men often experience invasion and occupation as a type of emasculation to which men reflexively respond with yet more hypermasculinity (Moghadam 2013, 163). Hypermasculinity is thus both a cause and a result of insecurity and conflict.

Hypermasculinity is often expressed through sexual harassment, which is routine and pervasive in many Arab countries (Eltahawy 2015, 76–84). Hypermasculinity is an integral feature of Islamist movements, which make control of women's dress and behavior a central focus of their ideology and activities. In the Algerian civil war of the 1990s, in Afghanistan under both the Mujahideen and the Taliban, and in Iraq and Syria under ISIS, violent assaults against women, including acid attacks, murder, and rape, have been pervasive tactics of war and social control.

Hypermasculinity and sexual violence are not limited to Islamists. Leaders and security forces of the current or former governments of Iraq, Syria, Libya, and Egypt are all on record as committing acts of brutal sexual violence against both women and men (ibid., 84–97; Amar 2011). Paul Amar describes the emergence of a "thug state" in Egypt during the presidency of Hosni Mubarak, when the regime paid working-class men generous amounts to terrorize people and brutalize regime opponents (2011, 308). He comments, "There is a rush of masculinity and a sense of authority and control. It's a kind of culture of thuggishness" (2012). This brutality was on full public display in the "Battle of the Camels" on February 2, 2011, when pro-Mubarak thugs on horses and camels attacked protesters in Tahrir Square, an event that many saw as pivotal in turning public opinion against the regime.

Sexual violence against women—and men—was a tactic used against antiregime protesters under multiple regimes in recent years: during Mubarak's presidency (1981–2011) (Eltahawy 2015, 94–97; Amar 2011), during the period when the Supreme Council of Armed Forces held the reins of state (2011–12) (Kirkpatrick 2015; Eltahawy 2015, 97–102, 104–8), and during the presidency of Mohamed Morsi (2012–13) (Langohr 2013). It was only after a gang rape in Tahrir Square during Sisi's inauguration as president in June 2014 that Sisi finally spoke out against this sexual violence, but even then he spoke of Egypt's honor, not of women's rights.

Changing Gender Dynamics

Shereen El Feki has written that, when it comes to sex and gender norms, there is a large discrepancy between appearance and reality in the Arab world and suggests that the sexual climate in the Arab world "looks a lot like the West on the brink of the sexual revolution" (2013, xvii). There is no doubt that the traditional pillars of patriarchy—male monopoly over economic resources and public life, the extended patrilocal family, and rigid social controls over the behavior of individuals—are unraveling. Today, women outnumber men in higher education in many Middle Eastern countries, more and more women work in the public labor market, and some even participate in government. These revolutionary steps exist side by side with the continuation of traditional attitudes toward sexual morality and appropriate behavior for women. The unevenness of social change has produced sometimes violent convulsions, not only in the Arab Spring uprisings, in which women often and even prominently participated alongside men, but also in violent reactions against the forces of liberalism. Socioeconomic crises in the Middle East are often perceived locally as caused by a decline in public morality, and the segregation of the sexes has traditionally been seen as the core of public morality. This perception explains, in part, why, wherever Islamist movements have gained power, they have immediately aimed to restrict the public visibility and mobility of women.

Women's rights groups are active throughout the region and have had important impacts on many fronts, from guaranteeing women's rights in the constitutions of Tunisia and Iraq to organizing creative responses to sexual harassment in Egypt (Moghadam 2013, 243–73; al-Ali and Pratt 2009, 121–61; Amar 2011, 310–13). Egyptian feminist Nawal El Saadawi challenged the virginity cult and its attendant customs back in 1972 in her pathbreaking work, *Al-Mar'a wa-l-jins* (Women and Sex), published in Beirut because no publisher in Cairo would dare to do so. Today young people read her books and discuss them openly (R. Cooke 2015). El Saadawi (2011) exulted in the ambience in the early days of the Egyptian uprising in January–February 2011: "Hundreds of young girls walk free, chanting—and not one has been sexually harassed or molested!" That exhilaration was not to last. Nonetheless, there are middle- and upper-class urban women who are willing to challenge traditional gender and sexual norms; a few are bold enough to speak about it publicly (Eltahawy 2015, 199–238). In the following chapter, Marshall analyzes feminist activities and accomplishments in Turkey. In chapter 11, Moghissi discusses the risks and opportunities presented to women by the current upheavals in the Arab world from the perspective of someone who was active in feminist groups in Iran before the revolution.

There is no doubt that Middle Eastern society is undergoing major transformations, but it is uncertain whether they will lead to major changes in gender norms any time soon.

Sources Cited

Abbott, Nabia. 1941. "Women and the State on the Eve of Islam." *American Journal of Semitic Languages and Literatures* 58 (3): 259–84.

Abu-Lughod, Lila. 2013. *Do Muslim Women Need Saving?* Cambridge, MA: Harvard Univ. Press.

Afsaruddin, Asma, ed. 1999. *Hermeneutics and Honor: Negotiating Female "Public" Space in Islamicate Societies*. Cambridge, MA: Harvard Univ. Press.

Aftab, Tahera, Shakila Rehman, and Zarin Saeed. 2008. "Living under the Axe: Story Narrated by *Karo Kari* Survivor." *Pakistan Journal of Women's Studies: Alam-e-Niswan* 15 (1): 85–96.

Ahmed, Leila. 1992. *Women and Gender in Islam: Historical Roots of a Modern Debate*. New Haven, CT: Yale Univ. Press.

Ali, Kecia. 2006. *Sexual Ethics and Islam: Feminist Reflections on Qur'an, Hadith, and Jurisprudence*. Oxford: Oneworld.

Al-Ali, Nadje, and Nicola Pratt. 2009. *What Kind of Liberation? Women and the Occupation of Iraq*. Berkeley: Univ. of California Press.

Al-Ali, Nadje Sadig. 2007. *Iraqi Women: Untold Stories from 1948 to the Present*. London: Zed Books.

Amar, Paul. 2011. "Turning the Gendered Politics of the Security State Inside Out? Charging the Police with Sexual Harassment in Egypt." *International Feminist Journal of Politics* 13 (3): 299–328.

———. 2012. Interview with Paul Amar by Valerie Hoffman at the Univ. of Illinois at Urbana–Champaign, Oct. 20.

Ammar, Nawal H. 2007. "Wife Battery in Islam: A Comprehensive Understanding of Interpretations." *Violence against Women* 13 (5): 516–26.

Antoun, Richard T. 1968. "On the Modesty of Women in Arab Muslim Villages: A Study in the Accommodation of Tradition." *American Anthropologist*, n.s., 70 (4): 671–97.

Anwar, Zainah. 2008. "Advocacy for Reform in Islamic Family Law: The Experience of Sisters in Islam." In *The Islamic Marriage Contract: Case Studies in Islamic Family Law*, edited by Asifa Quraishi and Frank E. Vogel, 275–84. Cambridge, MA: Harvard Law School.

Arsu, Sebnem. 2014. "Turkish President Says Women Shouldn't Be Considered Equals." *New York Times*, Nov. 24.

Aslan, Ednan, Marcia Hermansen, and Elif Medeni, eds. 2013. *Muslima Theology: The Voices of Muslim Women Theologians*. Frankfurt am Main: Peter Lang.

Ayubi, Nazih. 1991. *Political Islam: Religion and Politics in the Arab World*. London: Routledge.

Badran, Margot. 1991. "Competing Agenda: Feminists, Islam and the State in Nineteenth- and Twentieth-Century Egypt." In *Women, Islam and the State*, edited by Deniz Kandiyoti, 201–36. Philadelphia: Temple Univ. Press.

———. 2009. *Feminism in Islam: Secular and Religious Convergences*. Oxford: Oneworld.

Barlas, Asma. 2002. *"Believing Women" in Islam: Unreading Patriarchal Interpretations of the Qur'ān*. Austin: Univ. of Texas Press.

Bauer, Karen. 2006. "Traditional Exegeses of Q. 4.34." *Comparative Islamic Studies* 2 (2): 129–42.

Beeman, William O. 2014. "Few 'Gays' in the Middle East, but Significant Same-Sex Sexuality." In *Everyday Life in the Middle East*, edited by Donna Lee Bowen, Evelyn Early, and Becky Schulthies, 151–58. 3rd ed. Bloomington: Indiana Univ. Press.

Bennoune, Karima. 1995. "S.O.S. Algeria: Women's Human Rights under Siege." In *Faith and Freedom: Women's Human Rights in the Muslim World*, edited by Mahnaz Afkhami, 184–208. Syracuse, NY: Syracuse Univ. Press.

Bouachrine, Ibtissam. 2014. *Women and Islam: Myths, Apologies, and the Limits of Feminist Critique*. Lanham, MD: Lexington Books.

Callimachi, Rukmini. 2015. "ISIS Enshrines a Theology of Rape." *New York Times Magazine*, Aug. 13.

Cooke, Miriam. 1994. "Zaynab al-Ghazali: Saint or Subversive?" *Die Welt des Islams* 34 (1): 1–20.

———. 1995. "*Ayyam min hayati*: The Prison Memoirs of a Muslim Sister." *Journal of Arabic Literature* 26 (1–2): 147–64.

———. 2001. *Women Claim Islam: Creating Islamic Feminism through Literature*. New York and London: Routledge.

Cooke, Rachel. 2015. "Nawal El Saadawi: 'Do You Feel You Are Liberated? I Feel I Am Not.'" *Guardian*, Oct. 11. https://www.theguardian.com/books/2015/oct/11/nawal-el-saadawi-interview-do-you-feel-you-are-liberated-not.

DelPlato, Joan. 2002. *Multiple Wives, Multiple Pleasures: Representing the Harem, 1800–1875*. Madison, NJ: Fairleigh Dickinson Univ.

Duval, Soroya. 1998. "New Veils and New Voices: Islamist Women's Groups in Egypt." In *Women and Islamization: Contemporary Dimensions of Discourse on Gender Relations*, edited by Karin Ask and Marit Tjomsland, 45–72. Oxford: Berg.

El Feki, Shereen. 2013. *Sex and the Citadel: Intimate Life in a Changing Arab World*. New York: Anchor Books.

El Guindi, Fadwa. 1996. "Feminism Comes of Age in Islam." In *Arab Women: Between Defiance and Restraint*, edited by Suha Sabbagh, 159–61. New York: Olive Branch Press.

El Saadawi, Nawal. 1972. *Al-Mar'a wa-l-jins*. Beirut: al-Mu'assasa 'l-'Arabiyya li-l-Dirasat wa-l-Nashr.

———. 1980. *The Hidden Face of Eve: Women in the Arab World*. Translated by Sherif Hetata. London: Zed Press.

———. 2011. "Egyptian Feminist Nawal El Saadawi in Tahrir Square: The City in the Field." *Ms. Magazine*, Feb. 7. http://msmagazine.com/blog/2011/02/07/egyptian-feminist-nawal-el-saadawi-in-tahrir-square-i-saw-with-my-own-eyes-the-barbarism/.

Eltahawy, Mona. 2015. *Headscarves and Hymens: Why the Middle East Needs a Sexual Revolution*. New York: Farrar, Straus and Giroux.

Farah, Madelain. 1984. *Marriage and Sexuality in Islam: A Translation of al-Ghazali's Book on the Etiquette of Marriage from the "Ihyā'."* Salt Lake City: Univ. of Utah Press.

Filali-Ansari, Abdou. 1998. "Can Modern Rationality Shape a New Religiosity? Mohamed Abed Jabri and the Paradox of Islam and Modernity." In *Islam and Modernity: Muslim Intellectuals Respond*, edited by John Cooper, Ronald Nettler, and Mohamed Mahmoud, 156–71. London: I. B. Tauris.

Flock, Elizabeth. 2011. "Samira Ibrahim Is the Woman behind Egypt's Ban of Virginity Tests." *Washington Post*, Dec. 27. https://www.washingtonpost.com/blogs/blogpost/post/samira-ibrahim-is-the-woman-behind-egypts-ban-of-virginity-tests/2011/12/27/gIQACKNgKP_blog.html.

Girls Not Brides. 2016. "Child Marriage around the World: Egypt." http://www.girlsnotbrides.org/child-marriage/egypt/.

Haeri, Shahla. 1993. "Obedience versus Autonomy: Women and Fundamentalism in Iran and Pakistan." In *Fundamentalisms and Society: Reclaiming the Sciences, the Family, and Education*, edited by Martin E. Marty and R. Scott Appleby, 181–213. Chicago: Univ. of Chicago Press.

———. 1995. "The Politics of Dishonor: Rape and Power in Pakistan." In *Faith and Freedom: Women's Human Rights in the Muslim World*, edited by Mahnaz Afkhami, 161–74. Syracuse, NY: Syracuse Univ. Press.

Hafez, Sherine. 2011. *An Islam of Her Own: Reconsidering Religion and Secularism in Women's Islamic Movements*. New York: New York Univ. Press.

Hidayatullah, Aysha A. 2014. *Feminist Edges of the Qur'an*. New York: Oxford Univ. Press.

Hoffman, Valerie J. 1985. "An Islamic Activist: Zaynab al-Ghazali." In *Women and the Family in the Middle East: New Voices of Change*, edited by Elizabeth W. Fernea, 233–54. Austin: Univ. of Texas Press.

———. 1995. "Muslim Fundamentalists: Psychosocial Profiles." In *Fundamentalisms Comprehended*, edited by Martin E. Marty and R. Scott Appleby, 199–230. Chicago: Univ. of Chicago Press.

Hoffman-Ladd, Valerie J. 1987. "Polemics on the Modesty and Segregation of Women in Contemporary Egypt." *International Journal of Middle East Studies* 19 (1): 23–50.

Hoodfar, Homa. 1996. "Egyptian Male Migration and Urban Families Left Behind: 'Feminization of the Egyptian Family' or a Reaffirmation of Traditional Gender Roles?" In *Development, Change, and Gender in Cairo: A View from the Household*, edited by Diane Singerman and Homa Hoodfar, 51–79. Bloomington: Indiana Univ. Press.

Husseini, Rana. 2009. *Murder in the Name of Honor: The True Story of One Woman's Heroic Fight against an Unbelievable Crime*. Oxford: Oneworld.

Kandiyoti, Deniz. 1992. "Islam and Patriarchy: A Comparative Perspective." In *Women in Middle Eastern History: Shifting Boundaries in Sex and Gender*, edited by Nikki R. Keddie and Beth Baron, 23–42. New Haven, CT: Yale Univ. Press.

Keene, Henry George. 1879. *The Turks in India*. London: W. H. Allen and Co.

Kelly, Sanja, and Julia Breslin, eds. 2010. *Women's Rights in the Middle East and North Africa: Progress amid Resistance*. New York: Freedom House; Lanham, MD: Rowman and Littlefield.

Kirkpatrick, David D. 2015. "'Stripped, Beaten, Humiliated' and Barred from Her Own Trial in Egypt." *New York Times*, June 7.

Kirkpatrick, David D., and Mayy El Sheikh. 2013. "Muslim Brotherhood's Statement on Women Stirs Liberals' Fears." *New York Times*, Mar. 14.

Kirollos, Mariam. 2016. "Sexual Violence in Egypt: Myths and Realities." *Jadaliyya*, Jan. 16. http://www.jadaliyya.com/pages/index/13007/sexual-violence-in-egypt_myths-and-realities.

Kugle, Scott Siraj al-Haqq. 2010. *Homosexuality in Islam: Critical Reflection on Gay, Lesbian and Transgender Muslims*. Oxford: Oneworld.

Langohr, Vickie. 2013. "This Is Our Square." Middle East Research and Information Project, no. 268. http://www.merip.org/mer/mer268/our-square?ip_login_no_cache=fc68279b2070fb3f66ff5ccf27886014.

Longmann, James. 2014. "Gay Community Hit Hard by Middle East Turmoil." BBC, Oct. 29. http://www.bbc.com/news/world-middle-east-29628281.

Mahmood, Saba. 2005. *Politics of Piety: The Islamic Revival and the Feminist Subject*. Princeton, NJ: Princeton Univ. Press.

Mayer, Ann Elizabeth. 1991. *Islam and Human Rights*. 1st ed. Boulder, CO: Westview Press.

———. 1995. "Rhetorical Strategies and Official Policies on Women's Rights: The Merits and Drawbacks of the New World Hypocrisy." In *Faith and Freedom: Women's Human Rights in the Muslim World*, edited by Mahnaz Afkhami, 104–32. Syracuse, NY: Syracuse Univ. Press.

Meehan, Sumayyah. 2007. "Homosexuality in the Middle East." *Muslim Observer*, Nov. 8. http://muslimobserver.com/homosexuality-in-the-middle-east/.

Mernissi, Fatima. 1975. *Beyond the Veil: Male-Female Dynamics in Muslim Society*. Cambridge, MA: Schenkman.

———. 1985. *Beyond the Veil: Male-Female Dynamics in Muslim Society*. Rev. ed. London: Al Saqi Books.

———. 1991. *The Veil and the Male Elite: A Feminist Interpretation of Women's Rights in Islam*. Translated by Mary Jo Lakeland. Reading, MA, and New York: Addison-Wesley.

Mir-Hosseini, Ziba, Mulki al-Sharmani, and Jana Rumminger, eds. 2015. *Men in Charge? Rethinking Authority in Muslim Legal Tradition*. Oxford: Oneworld.

Mirza, Qudsia. 2002. "Islamic Feminism, Possibilities and Limitations." In *Law after Ground Zero*, edited by John Strason, 108–22. Sydney: Glasshouse Press.

Moghadam, Valentine M. 2013. *Modernizing Women: Gender and Social Change in the Middle East*. 3rd ed. Boulder, CO: Lynne Rienner.

Moghissi, Haideh. 1999. *Feminism and Islamic Fundamentalism: The Limits of Postmodern Analysis*. London: Zed Books.

Moosa, Ebrahim. 2003. "The Debts and Burdens of Critical Islam." In *Progressive Muslims on Justice, Gender, and Pluralism*, edited by Omid Safi, 111–27. Oxford: Oneworld.

Al-Mughni, Haya. 2010. "The Rise of Islamic Feminism in Kuwait." *Revue des mondes musulmans et de la Méditerranée* 128: 167–82.

Najmabadi, Afsaneh. 2005. *Women with Mustaches and Men without Beards: Gender and Sexual Anxieties of Iranian Modernity*. Berkeley: Univ. of California Press.

———. 2014. *Professing Selves: Transsexuality and Same-Sex Desire in Contemporary Iran*. Durham, NC: Duke Univ. Press.

Najumi, Mohadesa. 2013. "Your War Did Not Liberate Us." *Counterpunch*, Aug. 23. http://www.counterpunch.org/2013/08/23/your-war-did-not-liberate-us/.

Nazir, Sameena, and Leigh Tomppert. 2005. *Women's Rights in the Middle East and North Africa: Citizenship and Justice*. New York: Freedom House; Lanham, MD: Rowman and Littlefield.

Not Your Booty. 2013. Documentary on sexual violence in Egypt. https://www.youtube.com/watch?v=0DkdYPs_qfE.

Platt, Gareth. 2014. "Tortured in the Closet: Gay People in the Middle East Tell Their Story." *International Business Times*, Sept. 17. http://www.ibtimes.co.uk/tortured-closet-gay-people-middle-east-tell-their-story-1464735.

Porterfield, Todd. 1998. *The Allure of Empire: Art in the Service of French Imperialism, 1798–1836*. Princeton, NJ: Princeton Univ. Press.

Rostami-Povey, Elaheh. 2007. *Afghan Women: Identity and Invasion*. London: Zed Books.

Said, Edward W. 1978. *Orientalism*. New York: Vintage Books.

Shaaban, Bouthaina. 1988. *Both Right and Left Handed: Arab Women Talk about Their Lives*. Bloomington: Indiana Univ. Press.

Shehadeh, Lamia Rustum. 2003. *The Idea of Women in Fundamentalist Islam*. Gainesville: Univ. Press of Florida.

Silvers, Laury. 2006. "'In the Book We Have Left Out Nothing': The Ethical Problem of the Existence of Verse 4:34 in the Qur'an." *Comparative Islamic Studies* 2 (2): 171–80.

Stern, Gertrude H. 1939. *Marriage in Early Islam*. James G. Forlong Fund, vol. 18. London: Royal Asiatic Society.

Stowasser, Barbara Freyer. 1997. "The Hijab: How a Curtain Became an Institution and a Cultural Symbol." In *Humanism, Culture and Language in the Near East: Studies in Honor of Georg Krotkoff*, edited by Asma Afsaruddin and A. H. Mathias Zahniser, 87–104. Winona Lake, IN: Eisenbrauns.

Sullivan, Denis Joseph, and Sana Abed-Kotob. 1999. *Islam in Contemporary Egypt: Civil Society vs. the State*. Boulder, CO: Lynne Rienner.

Taha, Rana Muhammad. 2013. "Shura Council Members Blame Women for Harassment." *Daily News Egypt*, Feb. 11. http://www.dailynewsegypt.com/2013/02/11/shura-council-members-blame-women-for-harassment/.

Tatari, Muna. 2013. "Gender Justice and Gender Jihād—Possibilities and Limits of Qur'anic Interpretation for Women's Liberation." In *Muslima Theology: The Voices of Muslim Women Theologians*, edited by Ednan Aslan, Marcia Hermansen, and Elif Medeni, 155–66. Frankfurt am Main: Peter Lang.

Tieszen, Charles. 2015. *A Textual History of Christian–Muslim Relations: Seventh–Fifteenth Centuries*. Minneapolis: Fortress Press.

Tillion, Germaine. 1983. *The Republic of Cousins: Women's Oppression in Mediterranean Society*. Translated by Quintin Hoare. London: Saqi Books.

Tripathi, Anushree, and Supriya Yadav. 2004. "For the Sake of Honour: But Whose Honour? 'Honour Crimes' against Women." *Asia-Pacific Journal on Human Rights and the Law* 5 (2): 63–78.

Ungar, Mark. 2002. "State Violence and LGBT Rights." In *Violence and Politics: Globalization's Paradox*, edited by Kenton Worcester, Sally Avery Bermanzohn, and Mark Ungar, 48–66. New York: Routledge.

van Doorn-Harder, Pieternella. 2006. *Women Shaping Islam: Reading the Qur'an in Indonesia*. Urbana: Univ. of Illinois Press.

van Sommer, Annie, and Samuel M. Zwemer, eds. 1902. *Our Moslem Sisters: A Cry of Need from Lands of Darkness Interpreted by Those Who Heard It*. 2nd ed. New York: Fleming H. Revell.

Wadud, Amina. 2006. *Inside the Gender Jihad: Women's Reform in Islam*. Oxford: Oneworld.

Wadud-Muhsin, Amina. 1992. *Qur'an and Woman*. Kuala Lumpur: Penerbit Fajar Bakti Sdn. Bhd. Reprinted in 1999 by Oxford Univ. Press.

Welchman, Lynn. 2007. "Honour and Violence against Women in a Modern Shar'i Discourse." *Hawwa: Journal of Women of the Middle East and the Islamic World* 5 (2–3): 139–65.

Wikan, Unni. 1984. "Shame and Honour: A Contestable Pair." *Man*, n.s., 19 (4): 635–52.

Zwemer, Samuel M. 1900. *Arabia: The Cradle of Islam: Studies in the Geography, People and Politics of the Peninsula, with an Account of Islam and Mission-Work*. Edinburgh: Oliphant, Anderson, and Ferrier.

10

The Politics of Gender Equality in Turkey

GÜL ALDIKAÇTI MARSHALL

Since its establishment in 1923, the Turkish Republic has praised itself for being a Western-style democracy where women have citizenship rights equal to men's rights. Among them are the right to vote, run for office, work, divorce, have child custody, and inherit. Nonetheless, members of the second-wave feminist movement, which started in the early 1980s, have found these rights necessary but inadequate and consistently criticized the shortcomings of the legal framework. Turkey's bid for European Union membership, which became official in 1987, and the election of an Islamist party, Adalet ve Kalkınma Partisi—the Justice and Development Party—five times in a row to national government, in 2002, 2007, 2011, June 2015, and November 2015, have brought new actors with new perspectives on women's rights and gender equality to the political sphere in Turkey. In this chapter, I examine the convergence and divergence among the perspectives of feminists, the AKP government, and the EU. I also discuss the implications of these actors' viewpoints and actions. My aim is to provide insight into women's rights activists' struggle for justice within the dynamic political atmosphere of Turkey influenced by multiple local, national, and supranational actors.

Feminist Activism in Turkey

Turkey has a long history of feminist movements that aimed at improving women's rights and changing society toward establishing gender equality. At the end of the nineteenth century, feminist women living under Ottoman rule struggled to abolish polygyny, eliminate arranged marriages, ease restrictions on how to appear in public, and gain the right to vote. Sharia law under the Ottomans allowed men to be polygamous, ordered women to wear the *çarşaf* (long, loose garments) and *peçe* (a face cover) in public, and excluded women from participating in politics. Most of these feminist activists lived in the cosmopolitan cities of Istanbul, İzmir, and Selanik. They came from influential upper-class families and had a high level of education. Affected by feminist developments in Western countries, these activists made their views public, primarily in the journals they published (Demirdirek 1998).

Feminist activists were not alone in their endeavor. A group of elite men who wanted to reform the political system gave support to these women (Kandiyoti 1991). Most feminist scholars agree that in many societies, Turkey being no exception, change in women's status often represents change in the political, cultural, and even economic systems of those societies. Many reformist elite men of the late Ottoman Empire supported women activists principally because they equated change in these realms with change in women's rights.

This stand of the reformist elite became the mainstream approach to women's status and conduct in the Republic of Turkey, which was established in 1923 after a war of independence against European occupiers who wanted to take advantage of the decline of the Ottoman Empire. Secular-oriented members of the elite in the early republican era abolished the sharia and adopted a civil code that guaranteed women equal rights in marriage, divorce, child custody, and inheritance. The Law of the Unification of Instruction established secular, mixed-gender public education. Five years of primary education became compulsory by a constitutional mandate. This mandatory education was expanded to eight years in 1997. Without a legal provision, women were encouraged not to wear the *çarşaf* and *peçe* when they appeared in public, especially in government offices, state schools, hospitals, and courts. By 1934 women had attained the right to vote and be elected to office in local and national elections.

With its stand on the status of women, the Turkish state claimed progress and development in a Western fashion and, as Kandiyoti (1991) remarks, broke its ties with its Ottoman past, not only to create a nation-state but also to eradicate the power of the sharia in public administration. Nevertheless, the "new woman," who was encouraged by the state to be part of the public sphere, where she could obtain education and profession, was also expected to be modest in her appearance and conduct, in order to protect herself and her family's honor.

However supportive women were of the gender policies of the newly established secular republic, their daughters and granddaughters, some of whom were educated in Europe and the United States and witnessed the rise of the second-wave women's rights movements in these regions, began in the early 1980s to criticize the inconsistencies they saw in existing state policies and the discriminatory gender attitudes and behaviors women faced in their daily lives. This recognition was the beginning of the second-wave feminist movement in Turkey.

The feminist movement was initially composed of women in Istanbul, Ankara, and İzmir, three large cities in western Turkey. Just like the Ottoman feminists, the forerunners of the second-wave movement were highly educated and had middle- or upper-middle-class backgrounds. Unlike the Ottoman feminists, however, many had professions, thanks to the more women-friendly policies of the Turkish Republic, whose goal was to integrate women into the public sphere. Most forerunners of the movement had a radical or socialist feminist orientation. Consciousness-raising groups, which were an early form of organization, played significant roles in launching campaigns. Even if they were small, these early campaigns brought a lot of media attention to the street protests and petitions that the feminists instigated.

The focus of feminists in the 1980s was on the elimination of gender-discriminatory laws in the Civil and Penal Codes and the elimination of domestic violence against women. To this end, they launched their first campaign in 1986 to put pressure on the state to implement the Convention on the Elimination of All Forms of Discrimination against Women, which the Turkish state had signed in 1985 at the United Nations World Conference. The implementation of CEDAW required the Turkish state to amend its laws to remove articles that were gender discriminatory, specifically the two articles that led the Turkish state to enter reservations when signing CEDAW. These two articles endorsed the husband as head of the family and gave him the power to make decisions on family affairs, such as the place of residence and schooling for children (Berik 1990). The feminist campaign led to a petition signed by seven thousand women who called on the state to amend all discriminatory laws (Sirman 1989).

Further campaigns and protests in the 1980s were launched to draw public and state attention to violence against women. Feminist groups organized to protest domestic violence and street harassment and assaults against women. They campaigned to change the laws that did not regard domestic violence as a punishable crime. When necessary, to get media attention, activists used radical tactics, as in the example of a 1989 campaign during which participants distributed to women on the street seven-millimeter-long needles attached to purple ribbons, to be used against men who harassed or assaulted them on the streets and in other public spaces, such as public parks and transportation (Çaha 1996).

As the movement grew and attracted more women, not only in big cities but also in towns and regions other than the western and economically more developed parts of Turkey, these issues kept their significance for most feminist groups. The decline in street protests in the 1990s and accompanying institutionalization of feminist activism, with an increasing number of feminist organizations and a larger feminist presence in the universities, not only concentrated feminist activities in pressuring the state to amend laws that discriminated against women and to introduce laws that could prevent domestic violence, but also brought a new issue to the forefront of the feminist agenda. Increasing women's representation in political parties and in Parliament became a significant component of the feminist movement. The reason was the very low number of women in local and national elected bodies. Women constituted 4.5 percent in the first Parliament, on account of the unofficial quota used by the secular government of the early republic, but the number never reached this point again until the 2000s. Feminist efforts that started in the 1990s and continued into the 2000s to help women candidates for local and national elections and to pressure political parties to list more women candidates were pivotal in changing this low number. As a result, the number of women in Parliament went up to about 9 percent in 2007 and 14 percent in the 2011 elections. Still, women's groups were not the only actors causing this change. The considerable role that the EU played in this increase will be discussed further into this chapter.

Another issue was the employment of women. Because of the conscious efforts of the state elite in the early republican era, industrialization increased women's employment to 43 percent in 1955 (Zeytinoğlu 1998), only to decline to about 28 percent by 2000; it has remained low ever since. Women's low labor-market participation in manufacturing and services, gender inequalities in pay and promotion, and the fact that women worked mainly as unpaid labor in agriculture were discussed among feminists and publicized through publications by well-known feminist activists and scholars. Nonetheless, there were no significant campaigns or protests in relation to this issue. Women's employment and revisions to the Labor Law prompted feminist mobilization only after the mid-2000s, when the EU began to pressure Turkey to increase women's labor-force participation and amend its Labor Law.

The 1990s brought some progress toward meeting the demand of feminist groups to eliminate legal provisions. For instance, feminist groups criticized Articles 440 and 441 of the Penal Code, which mandated harsher punishment for a wife than for a husband in the case of adultery, a double standard that discriminated against women in legal judgments concerning what counts as adultery and its penalty. Feminists argued that it is not the state's business to criminalize adultery. These criticisms were influential in the Constitutional Court's decision to abolish statutes that made adultery a crime. The court cited CEDAW as the reason, emphasizing that Articles 440 and 441 violated CEDAW's principle of eliminating discrimination against women in marriage (Acar 2000). During this period, feminist campaigns were also influential in amending an article in the Penal Code that carried a reduced sentence for rape if it was committed against a prostitute and an article in the Civil Code that required married women to receive their husbands' permission to be employed. A major achievement of feminist groups was the passage of the "Family Protection Law" in 1998.[1] Their persistent public emphasis on the problem of domestic violence against women finally received the attention of the Turkish state, which introduced measures against offenders. Depending on the severity of the offense, these measures included actions such as the removal of the offender from the household and the termination of contact with the survivor. Turkey's international obligations toward the UN and the EU made the passage of the law timely. The law was passed before the 1999 Helsinki Summit, where the EU declared its decision regarding Turkey's official candidate status.

The main success of feminist groups during the 1980s and 1990s was in making so-called private issues public and drawing the public's attention to these issues. A lack of judicial leverage gave these women's groups limited opportunity to challenge the state's discriminatory policies, especially by bringing pressure from the supranational level. Even though CEDAW was binding, the UN did not have the means to put immediate pressure on Turkey to amend existing gender-discriminatory policies. It was after Turkey became an official candidate for EU membership that critical pressure began to build for policy changes.

1. The title of the law was criticized by a number of feminist groups, as it made the family the focus, rather than women. The law was originally proposed by women's groups as the "Violence against Women Law."

The Changing Political Terrain in the 2000s

The EU, along with the AKP government, became a significant influence in drawing the picture of gender politics in the 2000s. These two actors have altered the dynamics of participation in policy making and political alliances, as well as the forms of political activism for feminist women's groups.

It is not that the EU had no influence on Turkey in the area of gender politics before the 2000s. For example, the Turkish state signed CEDAW in 1985, not only because it had the confidence that it had progressive policies on women's rights, but also because it wanted to look good to the EU, which the country aimed eventually to join. Another example is the 1995 UN World Conference on Women in Beijing. During this conference, Turkey set 2000 as the date to withdraw its reservations to CEDAW, because again it hoped that doing so would positively influence the EU's perspective on Turkey's EU membership. Yet another example is the presentation of shadow reports by Turkish women's nongovernmental organizations at UN meetings. Beginning in 1997, Turkish feminists prepared shadow reports on women's rights in Turkey to present to the UN Committee on the Status of Women. These reports provided an alternative perspective to the information in the official reports presented to the Committee by the Turkish state. The goal of women activists was to influence not only the UN but also the EU, so they could put some pressure on the Turkish state from outside its national borders; however, there were no direct relations between Turkish feminist organizations and the EU.

The 1999 Helsinki Summit, where the EU finally declared Turkey an official candidate for membership, was the turning point. Increasing the influence of the EU on the Turkish state, this historic date prompted the coalition government headed by Bülent Ecevit, leader of the center-left Cumhuriyetçi Halk Partisi (CHP, the Republican People's Party), to embark on a policy-change process that included a number of packages passed by Parliament to transpose EU directives and align the laws of Turkey with the laws of the EU. The Civil

Code was amended in 2001 as part of this process. The Civil Code, which was adopted from the Swiss Civil Code in the early years of the republic, carried some of the same gender-discriminatory articles. With the change in the Civil Code, the Turkish state no longer had a reason to keep its reservations to CEDAW.

The changes to the Civil Code included replacement of the article that saw the husband as the head of the family. The revised Civil Code now recognizes the husband and the wife as equal partners in marriage, with equal decision-making power over family affairs. Unlike the old Civil Code, which treated only the husband as the representative of the family, the new Civil Code acknowledges both the husband and the wife as equal representatives of the family to a third party. The new Civil Code also accepts the equality of the husband and wife in contributing to the family union financially, according to their capacities. According to the new Civil Code, women can travel without the permission of their husbands; the previous Civil Code required the husband's permission for travel. Other significant changes include raising the marriage age for both men and women to eighteen, from fifteen for women and seventeen for men; the right of married women to keep their maiden names after marriage; and equal rights to property acquired during marriage. In the case of divorce, property is equally divided between the man and woman.

The campaign for the Civil Code amendments brought about the first large coalition of women's groups. Knowing that the Turkish government and Parliament were getting ready to alter the code, 126 women's organizations and groups from around Turkey, most of which were secular or feminist (or both) in orientation, created a forum to influence policy makers. Through press releases and contacting members of Parliament, these groups made their demands known and were able to influence the parliamentarians to make changes mostly in the direction they advocated. The success of these women's groups stemmed from having an agenda already developed before the new millennium with regard to what needed to be changed in the Civil Code, and how. By giving the green light to Turkey for membership candidacy, the EU provided an opportunity for these groups to insert their agenda into the process of gender-policy amendment. Many feminists recognize the significant role of the EU, as indicated by the following quote from an activist in Kadın Girişimcileri Destekleme Derneği (the Association for Supporting Women Entrepreneurs):

> I think Turkey's membership process is very important. We would not want it to come to an end quickly. We have been able to use the EU's leverage for change because Turkey is a candidate. Look at Greece. It is a member country. The EU does not have the same influence on member countries. For example, there are no legally binding documents on violence. There are recommendations; that is all. The EU's legal pressure on member states is mainly in the area of employment; but this is not the case with candidate countries. The EU uses the political criteria to pressure them. As a result, we have been able to utilize those criteria to push for change in women's rights. (Personal interview, May 17, 2007)

The EU treats women's rights and gender equality in candidate countries as political conditions for membership. It expects candidate countries to uphold democracy and respect human rights and links the fulfillment of these criteria to membership. These conditions give the EU power over candidate countries until membership is granted. The EU uses a methodical approach of regular screening to measure the level of transformation of directives into national structures and the alignment of laws and procedures (Usul 2011; Zielonka and Mair 2002). Under this approach, the EU began in 1998 to issue documents that addressed gender equality in Turkey. These releases included annual country progress reports and accession partnership documents. It also required national action plans from the Turkish state.

Even though gender equality and women's rights were not given much space in the initial documents, country reports and other documents issued by EU bodies put more emphasis on these matters after 2000. My research reveals that an important reason was the growing relationship between feminist organizations and the EU. As the EU representatives from influential EU bodies such as the European

Commission and European Parliament began to acquire more information from Turkish women's organizations by making personal visits, receiving feedback on EU documents on women's rights in Turkey, and using reports on women's status in Turkey prepared by Turkish feminist organizations, they reflected these organizations' views in their documents. A clear case can be observed in the EU's remarks on amendments to the Civil Code. The early country progress reports praised Turkey in a few sentences concerning its women's rights record, as can be seen in the following statement from the 1998 report: "The status of women in Turkey is increasingly in line with that prevailing in most EU countries" (European Commission 1998, 17). Starting in 2000, however, the European Commission emphasized the necessity of amending the Civil Code, especially the article that recognized the man as the head of the family. It also highlighted the persistence of violence against women, adding honor killings as a particular form of violence that needed to be eliminated, and pointed out that there is a gender gap in education, which is pronounced between the eastern and western parts of Turkey. After the amendment of the Civil Code, the European Commission congratulated Turkey in its 2002 country progress report for further aligning its laws with the laws of the EU: "The adoption of these reforms demonstrates the determination of the majority of Turkey's political leaders to move towards further alignment with the values and standards of the European Union" (European Commission 2002, 17). It encouraged Turkey to enforce the new code. At the same time, this and later reports echoed the feminist groups' position about what still needs to be changed in the Civil Code. These organizations, which have had a strong role in the amendments to the Civil Code, let the EU know, by increasing their lobbying efforts, that the equal property regime for which they pushed included only those marriages that took place after January 1, 2002, whereas it should have also included all marriages before this date. The EU became an ally of the feminist organizations in pressuring the state to take measures to eliminate violence against women and increase women's numbers in Parliament and the government. A further aim of the EU was to encourage women to become what Nancy Fraser (2000, 13) calls "citizen-workers," by participating in the formal labor market.

After the election of the AKP to government in 2002, gender-equality reforms continued with speed until 2005. During this period, under the AKP, the Penal Code, the Constitution, and the Labor Law were amended to align Turkish laws with EU directives (or hard laws).[2] Amendments to the Penal Code included the elimination of gender-discriminatory laws by eradicating the arbitrary decisions made by parents or school principals to force girls to undergo virginity tests, expanding the definition of rape to include rape in marriage, increasing punishment for rape, and raising punishment for sexual harassment in the workplace. The Constitution was amended to recognize the equality of men and women, and the Labor Code accepted the principles of equal pay for equal work or work of equal value and equal treatment. It required the equal treatment of part-time and full-time workers. It placed the burden of proof on the employer in claims of gender discrimination. Exceeding the EU legislation, which required a minimum of fourteen weeks of maternity leave, the new labor law raised paid maternity leave from twelve weeks to sixteen weeks—eight weeks before and eight weeks after birth.[3]

Despite these developments, the AKP government slowed its efforts to transpose the EU directives in many areas, including gender equality, after 2005. The declining pace of reforms received

2. Hard laws are binding legal measures that the EU uses to require member and candidate countries to introduce new laws in line with the EU or employ the required laws (Ferree 2008). Soft laws are nonbinding measures. They are in the form of guidelines, action plans, and recommendations. While some EU requirements on gender equality are hard laws, such as the equal-pay and parental-leave directives, others are soft laws, such as action plans on eliminating violence against women and positive action.

3. In February 2013, the minister of labor under the third-term AKP government announced the ministry's plans to increase maternity leave to twenty-four weeks and to take further measures to guarantee the worker's right to keep her job when her maternity leave ends.

strong criticism from the EU. In its 2005 report, the European Commission emphasized that "Turkey should urgently improve gender-equality and fight against discrimination" (2005, 97). This urgency resulted from the fact that "no progress" had been made "as regards the transposition of the EC Directives prohibiting discrimination on employment" and that Turkey had to further align its laws with the EU's in "parental leave, equal pay, access to employment, burden of proof, as well as statutory and occupational social security" (ibid., 96). Moreover, violence against women and honor killings were reported as continuing problems. The European Commission persisted in bringing the issues of women's low representation in politics, low participation in the labor market, high illiteracy rate, and early marriages to the attention of the Turkish state.

The 2006 Accession Partnership Document also emphasized the need to implement the new laws and grouped them with its short-term requirements, along with the need to enhance women's political and economic participation, to support women's organizations, and to tackle violence against women by opening shelters and training the appropriate parties, such as the police, health care workers, municipal workers, judges, and prosecutors. This focus on implementation was repeated in the country progress reports in the second half of the 2000s, putting further pressure on Turkey. As a result, a parliamentary commission was established to investigate the extent of honor killings and domestic violence against women. In response to the European Commission's criticisms about the lack of reliable data on domestic violence, the Kadının Statüsü ve Sorunları Genel Müdürlüğü (KSSGM, the Directorate General on the Status and Problems of Women), funded by the EU, conducted a nationwide survey on domestic violence in 2009.

In the domain of education, the Ministry of National Education, in collaboration with United Nations Children's Fund, launched an education campaign to decrease illiteracy among women, which has been a particular problem in the east and southeast. A similar campaign was launched in the private sector by the newspaper *Milliyet*, which belonged to the Doğan Media Group. As a result of these efforts, the rate of girls' enrollment in primary schools rose to about 98 percent in 2010 (European Commission 2010). The European Commission praised this development, but emphasized that the closing of the gender gap in primary education needed to be "sustained and improved" (2009, 23). In response to this notification, the Ministry of National Education set up an early warning system to track girls at risk of dropping out of school.

The EU continued to criticize the rate of women's labor-market participation in the second half of the 2000s, mainly because, despite the changes in the Labor Law and the existence of bylaws, women's employment rates had not risen. Women's labor has continued to be absorbed by the informal market, and many women have maintained the trend of leaving their jobs after they marry or become pregnant. The social security system, which covered only formal labor, left out many of those women who were within the informal economy. To combat this problem, Parliament passed the "employment package" in May 2008. According to this package, the social security premiums of newly hired women will be covered by the unemployment insurance fund for five years. The coverage is set at 100 percent in the first year and drops to 20 percent in the fifth year. The Turkish Unemployment Agency is responsible for helping the registered unemployed with vocational training, job matching, and counseling (European Commission 2008, 62).[4]

The unmet demands of the EU listed in the progress reports with regard to gender equality found their way into the 2008 revision of the Accession Partnership Document, which stipulated that Turkey must do the following:

> Pursue measures to implement current legislation relating to women's rights and against all forms of violence against women,

4. The efforts of the government brought down the informal market participation rate to 33.6 percent by 2014. However, women were still heavily represented in that vulnerable population (European Commission 2014).

> including crimes committed in the name of honour. Ensure specialised training for judges and prosecutors, law enforcement agencies, municipalities and other responsible institutions and strengthen efforts to establish shelters for women at risk of violence in all larger municipalities, in line with current legislation, further increase the awareness of the general public, and of men in particular, concerning gender issues, and promote the role of women in society, including through ensuring equal access to education and participation in the labour market and in political and social life; support the development of women's organisations to fulfil these goals. (European Council 2008, 7)

Turkey responded, in its 2008 National Programme, by promising that the maximum penalty in the Penal Code would be applied to those individuals guilty of honor killings and that measures would be taken to reduce violence against women. The state made further promises to increase collaboration with women's organizations to boost women's participation in "the education, labour force and political and social life" (National Programme for the Adoption of the Acquis 2008, 10). In addition to this document, Turkey mapped its objectives specifically in the Gender Equality Programme of 2008–13. Among these objectives was the establishment of a commission in Parliament on equal opportunity and of another body to focus on gender equality. Making gender awareness a part of budgeting and of cooperation among various institutions was part of the goal of mainstreaming gender issues. Women's education was one of the priority areas; specific goals included increasing women's enrollment rates in all levels of education, reducing the illiteracy rate of both girls and women, eliminating gender discrimination within textbooks, and increasing women's numbers in managerial positions within the education sector. The country pledged to increase women's participation in the labor force by increasing employment-guaranteed vocational training; improving care facilities for children, the sick, the disabled, and the elderly; enacting a comprehensive parental leave law; encouraging women's entrepreneurship; and expanding employment opportunities for women with a low level of education. Defining direct and indirect discrimination within a legislative framework and tracking and eliminating wage inequality between women and men were also employment-related specific pledges. Although a number of supportive strategies were listed to improve women's political participation, establishing a constitutional gender quota to increase the number of women in Parliament and amending election laws were not mentioned among the strategies in the political realm. The Gender Equality Programme also noted violence against women as a significant problem in Turkey and stated that there are ongoing campaigns to address it.

Most of what was revealed in the Gender Equality Programme was to satisfy Turkey's international obligations that stem from not only its negotiations with the EU but also being a signatory to CEDAW and the Beijing Declaration; thus, the document also had sections on media and women, health, poverty, and the environment. As noted above, some of the pledges were realized, such as literacy and education campaigns to reduce the gender gap between girls and boys and the passage of the employment package to encourage women's labor force participation. Even though an Equality Body is yet to be founded, in 2009 the Parliamentary Commission on Equal Opportunities for Women and Men was established.

Some might see the developments in the area of gender equality after 2002 as a sign of the influence of modernization on the governing Islamist party. It is true that the AKP has made great strides in its gender-policy platform to meet the demands of the EU and the feminist women's groups who took advantage of the EU membership process. However, the policies proposed or put in place by the AKP have also created questions with regard to its intentions and in some cases led to setbacks. The issues of adultery and gender quotas are examples. The AKP, under the influence of its conservative faction, tried to recriminalize adultery during the 2004 changes to the Penal Code. Prime Minister Recep Tayyip Erdoğan defended the AKP proposal by arguing that it is a measure that would benefit women whose husbands cheat on them. He also stated that his party's proposal treats men and women equally in the case of adultery. Eighty women's organizations, the majority of which were feminist and all of which had a secular orientation, came together to protest the proposal.[5] The proposal and the protests were widely covered by the media. The prime minister called the activists "a group of marginal women" who do not represent the majority of women in Turkey. The AKP's proposal was criticized by members of the center-left CHP in Parliament for deviating from European Union standards. Canan Arıtman, a member of the CHP, stated that adultery is treated not as a crime but as a reason for divorce in European countries, and thus the proposed law would not be accepted by the EU; such an action would put a stop to Turkey's EU membership process. She also emphasized that adultery should be treated as a private matter between a husband and wife. True to Arıtman's warnings, Günther Verhugen, the commissioner in charge of EU enlargement, cautioned the AKP government that recriminalizing adultery would prevent the opening of the accession negotiations between the EU and Turkey. In response, the AKP removed the proposal.

In another case, during the changes to the Constitution in 2004, the AKP voted overwhelmingly against the establishment of a constitutional quota system to increase women's political representation. As a result of the efforts of feminist women's groups, which launched a campaign in 2002 for a 30 percent quota system in the Constitution, two sympathetic female members of the CHP brought a proposal to the floor of Parliament that would open the way for the enactment of such a policy. The proposal stated, "Women and men are equal. The state has the responsibility to ensure the implementation of these rights. Temporary measures and regulations for this purpose should

5. Women with a liberal feminist and Kemalist orientation mobilized, along with radical and socialist feminists, to change discriminatory laws. Kemalist women strongly support secularism in Turkey and mobilize against Islamist movements. One Islamist women's organization was active and collaborated with secular-oriented women's groups during the changes to the Penal Code. Some Kemalist and Islamist women identify themselves as feminists.

not be regarded as preferential treatment and privilege." While CHP members supported the proposal, most AKP members, including most women parliamentarians from the AKP, were against it, arguing that there is no need for a positive-action measure because the revised Constitution already accepted the equality of men and women. An AKP member changed the proposal: "Women and men are equal. The state has the responsibility to ensure the implementation of these rights." The two parties compromised on this version and passed it as an amendment to Article 10 (Aldıkaçtı Marshall 2010). The following statement reveals the disappointment of feminist women's groups: "We were not able to persuade the state to establish a quota. What does this mean? It means 'you [as a woman] can't make decisions. Well, you can, but only in women-related areas. You can be a minister responsible for affairs related to women, but you cannot be a minister of energy, for example'" (personal interview with a member of Kadın Girişimcileri Destekleme Derneği, May 17, 2007). This quote sums up the position of female politicians in the AKP government. Since it came to power in 2002, the AKP has appointed few women to its cabinet, and they were assigned mainly to the Ministries of Education and Welfare. Nevertheless, feminist efforts to increase women's participation were supported by strong EU pressure, which prompted the AKP (and other parties) to list a higher number of women as candidates in each election, bringing the percentage of women in Parliament to a record high.

The above cases of discrepancies exemplify the conflict within the party over gender equality and women's rights. Among AKP members of Parliament there are some who have strong ties with Islamist as well as secular women's groups and organizations. They listen to women's demands. At the same time, a steadfast conservative group takes positions against demands for further improving women's rights. The AKP's conflicting stand on gender equality is creating further tensions with feminist women's organizations and the EU. Under its government, the relationship between KSSGM and secular-oriented feminist women's groups has deteriorated, to the point that the EU warned the AKP government in its 2009 and

2010 country progress reports about its dismissive attitude toward women's groups. The EU states that the relationship between the state and civil society is especially weak compared to member states and other candidate states.

Despite these warnings, the AKP has maintained its contradictory approach to women's rights. The government amended Article 10 of the Constitution one more time to categorize women as a group, like the elderly and children, that needs social protection. The party has been increasingly giving the message that women are mothers and that motherhood is their first and foremost duty (Güneş-Ayata and Tütüncü 2008). The party's leader, Recep Tayyip Erdoğan, has been encouraging married partners to have at least three children to maintain the country's young population, which is the main force behind the current economic boom in the country. In 2012 he attempted to ban abortion, which is legal up to the tenth week of pregnancy, and to eliminate all C-sections, arguing that they curb population growth. Strong opposition from grassroots women's groups and women-friendly parliamentarians, as well as heavy media coverage that put the issue under the spotlight, quashed Erdoğan's endeavor. Nevertheless, feminist women's groups remain wary.

Sources Cited

Acar, Feride. 2000. "Turkey: The First CEDAW Impact Study." Center for Feminist Research. Toronto: York Univ. and the International Women's Rights Project.

Aldıkaçtı Marshall, Gül. 2010. "Gender Quotas and the Press in Turkey: Public Debate in the Age of AKP Government." *South European Society and Politics* 15 (4): 573–91.

Berik, Günseli. 1990. "State Policy in the 1980s and the Future of Women's Rights in Turkey." *New Perspectives on Turkey* 4: 81–96.

Çaha, Ömer. 1996. *Sivil Kadın: Türkiye'de Sivil Toplum ve Kadın* (Civil Society and Woman in Turkey). Istanbul: Vadi Yayınları.

Demirdirek, Aynur. 1998. "In Pursuit of Ottoman Women's Movement." In *Deconstructing Images of "the Turkish Women,"* edited by Zehra F. Arat, 65–81. New York: St. Martin's Press.

European Commission. 1998. Regular Report from the Commission on Turkey's Progress towards Accession. Brussels.

———. 2002. Regular Report on Turkey's Progress towards Accession. Brussels, SEC (2002)/1412.

———. 2005. Regular Report on Turkey's Progress towards Accession. Brussels, SEC (2005)/1426.

———. 2008. Regular Report on Turkey's Progress towards Accession. Brussels, SEC (2008)/2699.

———. 2009. Regular Report on Turkey's Progress towards Accession. Brussels, SEC (2009)/1334.

———. 2010. Regular Report on Turkey's Progress towards Accession. Brussels, SEC (2010)/1327.

———. 2014. Regular Report on Turkey's Progress towards Accession. Brussels, SWC (2014)/307.

European Council. 2008. Council Decision of 18 February 2008 on the Principles, Priorities, Intermediate Objectives and Conditions Contained in the Accession Partnership with the Republic of Turkey (2008/157/EC).

Ferree, Myra Marx. 2008. "Framing Equality: The Politics of Race, Class, and Gender in the US, Germany, and the Expanding European Union." In *Gender Politics in the Expanding European Union: Mobilization, Inclusion, Exclusion*, edited by Silke Roth, 237–55. New York: Berghahn Books, 2008.

Fraser, Nancy. 2000. "After the Family Wage: A Postindustrial Thought Experiment." In *Gender and Citizenship in Transition*, edited by Barbara Hobson, 1–32. New York: Routledge.

Güneş-Ayata, Ayşe, and Fatma Tütüncü. 2008. "Party Politics of the AKP (2002–2007) and the Predicaments of Women at the Intersection of the Westernist, Islamist, and Feminist Discourses in Turkey." *British Journal of Middle Eastern Studies* 35 (3): 363–84.

Kandiyoti, Deniz. 1991. *Women, Islam and the State*. Philadelphia: Temple Univ. Press.

National Programme for the Adoption of the Acquis. 2008. Decision of the Council of Ministers Dated 10 November 2008, no. 2008/14481.

Sirman, Nükhet. 1989. "Feminism in Turkey: A Short History." *New Perspectives on Turkey* 3 (1): 1–34.

Usul, Ali Resul. 2011. *Democracy in Turkey: The Impact of EU Political Conditionality*. New York and London: Routledge.

Zeytinoğlu, Işık Urla. 1998. "Constructed Images as Employment Restrictions: Determinants of Female Labor in Turkey." In *Deconstructing Images of "the Turkish Women,"* edited by Zehra F. Arat, 183–97. New York: St. Martin's Press.

Zielonka, Jan, and Peter Mair. 2002. "Introduction: Diversity and Adaptation in the Enlarged European Union." In *The Enlarged European Union: Diversity and Adaptation*, edited by Peter Mair and Jan Zielonka, 1–8. London and Portland, OR: Frank Cass.

11

Between a Rock and a Hard Place

The "Arab Spring," Women, and Lessons from Iran

HAIDEH MOGHISSI

There is little doubt that the uprisings in Arab countries and the fall of several military regimes did not bring the long-awaited changes that bred the revolts. It is true that regime changes do not necessarily give birth to new orders that transform the aspects of society that bring people into the streets; regime changes brought about by a revolution are just the first stage of a lengthy process, the ultimate outcome of which is defined, in part, by the strategies adopted in the postrevolutionary period. Most notably, the outcome depends on whether efforts are made to control or expand the revolutionary demands and whether political participation by the citizenry is encouraged, motivated, or inhibited. The political elites who take up power in the aftermath of a revolution usually want to consolidate their position and restrain and overcome opposition. The democratic forces that revolt against deprivation, inequality, and tyranny want to see revolutionary demands met and promises delivered.

Sadly, the aftermath of the revolutionary activity in the Middle East and North Africa—growing political crisis, deepening divisions between change-seeking forces and the governing parties, senseless violence, the disintegration of Libya, and the establishment of yet another military junta in Egypt—run counter to the ideals and visions of the original change-seeking forces. For a variety of reasons, notably ongoing secular resistance in these countries, Islamist parties face serious challenges in establishing totalitarian theocracies à la Iran. But the very experience of Iran warns us that the democratic forces' challenges are no less serious in making the transition to democracy a reality. Perhaps the major challenge is how and with which forces to form a workable coalition in order to fend off authoritarianism in religious garb.

The social and political consequences of the 1979 revolution in Iran, a political milieu in which I took part, have no doubt influenced my wary outlook. On the one hand, it was hard not to be positively affected by the popular uprisings that swept the Middle East in recent years. On the other, however, past experience made me cautious in my reactions to revolutionary euphoria. A colleague of mine, a historian, recently told me that the problem with scholars outside the field of history is that they do not have long-term understanding about political events of this sort. That might be true. But just consider that, in the twentieth century alone, Iranians took part in several major nationalist and regional socialist movements, joined in two major transformative antidictatorial revolutions, and forced four kings into exile, yet still democracy and freedom seem an elusive dream. The most striking and devastating disappointment was, of course, after the 1979 revolution: the overthrow of the monarchy resulted in the establishment of an archaic, rights-negating, misogynist theocracy. This outcome bore enormous costs for women, who had supported the revolution by the millions and in different forms. For women, in particular, a revolution mobilized by demands for freedom, democracy, and social justice turned into a huge prison under the self-appointed guardians of the sharia. In fact, the repeated defeats of progressive social and political movements in Iran mean that activists' basic demand for women's right to "have the right to have rights," to use Hannah Arendt's profound concept, is the same demand that was first articulated in the early 1900s and has remained unfulfilled ever since.

The Iranian revolution and its consequences have been defining events for the region, and indeed for the world. The democratic forces throughout the region, wary of duplicating the Iranian experience in their own countries, seem determined to stop the advances of Islamists, as a young woman told me at Taksim Square in Istanbul in early June 2013. They had learned from the hard lessons of Iran that Islamist forces, once in power, resort to shutting down dialogue and silencing opposing voices. It is what Islamists did in Iran, during Morsi's one-year rule in Egypt, and by Recep Tayyip Erdoğan in Turkey.

Political circumstances don't change overnight, but through an extended process. For this reason, the experiences of the 1979 revolution's democratic forces in Iran, and in particular the experiences of women activists during and especially after the event, can still be enlightening, to enable women elsewhere in the region to avoid a similar fate. The sneaky movements evident in Arab countries to curb women's activism and to undermine their existing legal and civil rights are distressingly familiar to Iranian women. We worried from the start about the situations emerging in Arab countries. Self-identified Muslim human rights lawyer and 2003 Nobel laureate Shirin Ebadi expressed these concerns in March 2012, when she called upon Arab women to learn from the experiences of women in Iran and warned them against making the same mistakes (Ebadi 2012). So did Algerian scholars and women's rights activists, including Marieme Hélie-Lucas, Karima Bennoune, and others; from the events of the early 1990s in Algeria, they knew only too well the atrocities of which militant Islamists are capable in the name of Islamic justice, as well as the brutal response of the army.

The developments that have taken place in the region so far confirm our misgivings. For example, consider that after the devastating, bloody uprising in Libya, the first "revolutionary" statement of the interim government, as announced by Mustafa Abdel Jalil, was a promise to lift restrictions on polygamy and to follow the sharia in legal matters. Who knows how political elites would respond to the Salafis' campaign for gender segregation in education and other areas of public life? No amount of twisting and bending the facts can change the reality that when the sharia becomes the basis of legislation in a Muslim-majority country, any hope of fair and equal treatment for women in social and legal matters is rendered impossible.

In Egypt the new constitution hastily put together by an assembly heavily stacked with Salafis and members of the Muslim Brotherhood mentioned women's rights only in the context of the family and utilized the insinuating language of protection of their dignity and morality in a way remarkably similar to Iran's constitution.[1] Fear now loomed over the heads of women who thought that, by participating day and night alongside men in the Tahrir Square protests, they had gained respect and recognition as citizens with rights equal to men's. Now they feared rollbacks of the reforms to family law passed in 2000 and 2005 and the Islamists' push for abolishing the minimum age of marriage for girls (presently set at eighteen). Hope of equality had already been shattered by systematic and deliberate attacks on women, from virginity tests performed on arrested activists to sexual harassment of women protesters aimed at humiliating, frightening, and pushing women off the streets. In February 2013 the Shura Council's human rights committee blamed women protesters for the sexual harassment to which they had been subjected (*Egypt Independent* 2013).

Only in Tunisia did the secular forces' campaign succeed in keeping the parity between women's and men's rights and responsibilities, enshrined in the 1959 constitution, in the new 2014 constitution. The Tunisian government also committed itself to take concrete action to implement its National Plan of Action to end violence against women

1. The first assembly of the post-Mubarak national referendum in March 2011 put in place a set of constitutional amendments that was passed with an overwhelming 77 percent of the vote and heavily supported by Islamists. A year later, the Brotherhood, having won 47 percent of the seats in parliament, along with the Salafis, who won another 25 percent of the seats, tried to push through a constituent assembly heavily stacked with Islamists and their sympathizers. The assembly was suspended following a mass walkout by liberal parties, the Coptic Church, and even al-Azhar and a lawsuit challenging its constitutionality. For details, see Abdel Kouddous 2012.

(UN Women 2017). But there have also been worrisome developments: debates on legalizing polygamy, which was banned in 1957 in order to address social problems (Arfaoui 2009); repeated clashes between Salafis and liberal, left-leaning students at universities (Al Arabiya News 2012; Al-Monitor 2012); multiple violent attacks on secular journalists (Barrie 2012) and activists (*Al-Akhbar* 2012); and the assassination of leftist politicians Chokri Belaid and Mohamed Brahmi in 2013. The return of jihadists to Tunisia, against which Tunisians took to the streets in January 2017 (*Daily Star* 2017), is also a concern regarding future developments in the country.

For many of us who lived through and survived the establishment of the Islamic regime in Iran, these events, while not surprising, are nonetheless distressing. Iranian women from all walks of life also participated in the 1979 revolution. More important, secular women (believers and nonbelievers alike) waged the first mass protests against Ayatollah Khomeini's demand for the reveiling of women in public places, a directive that occurred just a few weeks after the collapse of the shah's regime—ironically, on the eve of International Women's Day. We rightly saw the ayatollah's statement as opening the floodgate to other regressive measures, which indeed did follow. The spontaneous insurrection of women, with no support from any of the leftist or liberal organizations and parties, led to massive protests, sit-ins, and work stoppages in ministries, hospitals, government agencies, and girls' high schools and lasted two weeks, despite continued attacks on the protesters by self-styled *hezbollahi* thugs. Women's associations and groups were formed in every university and in public and private institutions and agencies. The strength of the women's movement against reveiling forced the clerical state into a temporary retreat.

However, it was only a temporary and minor success. The *hijab* became mandatory several months later, after the bloody suppression of leftist antigovernment forces in the universities, the regime's invasion of Kurdistan and Turkmen Sahra, the closure of all universities, and the expulsion of leftist professors and students under the ploy of the Islamic "cultural revolution." All liberal daily newspapers were shut down on the ayatollah's direct order to the gangs to "break the pens of the journalists."

The alarming signs of the rising tide of authoritarianism in religious garb required the formation of a coalition and the mobilization of the middle classes, along with the working classes that had participated in the uprising in various ways, to form the broadest possible united front against the Islamists' ideological and organizational assaults. It did not happen. A few of us within the leadership of Etehad-e Meli-e Zanan (National Union of Women) persistently argued against the position of some of the women who acted as mediators between our organization and the Fedaii Organization, the largest leftist organization at the time, who thought the priority was anti-imperialist struggle, not women's rights.

In the end, the absence of the full support and assistance of the community of secular intellectuals, and the Left's theoretical confusion and silence or, at best, mild and flimsy criticism of the Islamic regime's attacks on democratic freedoms, and in particular on women's rights, facilitated the processes that made Ayatollah Khomeini the unchallengeable and uncompromising leader of the revolution. Women activists were accused by the state-run media of being royalists and supporters of the United States. A good part of the Left also began to articulate a discourse that the issues raised by women were peripheral to the goals of national and anti-imperialist struggles. Khomeini's support of the Muslim students' takeover of the American Embassy fooled many, particularly those on the Left, that the regime was "anti-imperialist." The Iran-Iraq War made the situation even worse and in the process silenced women's voices against the Islamists' gender agenda and assisted in rolling back the modest legal gains achieved by women under the shah's regime and introducing unimaginable new restrictions on women's social status and mobility.

The women's movement was not blameless in this process. At the outset, we failed to listen carefully to Khomeini's rhetorical pronouncements that "women and men are equal in the eyes of God."

The meaning of his statement that "the new government would provide women with all rights denied to them, within the confines of the sharia," was crystal clear, but the dominance of populist, anti-imperialist tendencies and unrealistic expectations about the revolution within the ranks of the most active, gender-conscious sections of the female population prevented us from seeing through the revolutionary promises and the Islamists' medieval agenda wrapped in nationalist garb.

Second, we had taken for granted our existing rights and personal liberties. We did not make any connection between our situation and women's experiences in anticolonial movements in Egypt, Algeria, Palestine, and other parts of the region. Nor did we try to learn from the experiences of the women's rights pioneers in our own country and their intense struggle to win minimal gains for women in personal status laws during the 1960s and 1970s. Worse, a good part of the opposition either chose silence or joined in the regime's hostile discourse against the social and legal reforms of the previous regime as a corrupting influence of the West.

This one-sided perception is now echoed in Egypt. As women's rights activist Hoda Elsadda pointed out in a conversation with Deniz Kandiyoti, one of the key obstacles faced by activists for women's rights in Egypt is "a prevalent public perception that associates women's rights activists and activities with the ex–First Lady, Suzanne Mubarak and her entourage, that is[,] with corrupt regime politics. This public perception is already being politically manipulated to rescind laws and legislative procedures that were passed in the last ten years to improve the legal position of women, particularly within Personal Status Laws" (Elsadda 2011).

In Iran the new regime's formidable and systematic suppression of the women's movement was also accompanied by discrediting the limited legal reforms of previous decades as dictated by the foreigners, un-Islamic, and benefiting only upper- and upper-middle-class women. The subsequent developments should not have surprised anyone. They included the abolition of the Family Protection Act, banning women from the bench, the introduction of sharia-based civil and criminal codes, and closing certain fields of education to women. Only then did women and minority groups appreciate how profoundly the shifts in political power would impact women's legal protections and access to resources.

None of what has been said is meant to suggest that the struggles of peoples in Arab countries to achieve social justice, democracy, and dignity are already lost because of the rising tide of Islamism. The phenomenon of present-day Islamism is not the cause but the result of a set of policies pushed on the region and obediently carried out by corrupt local tyrants. Decades of neoliberal economic policy, state retraction from welfare services, privatization, and the breakup and distribution of public assets among the regimes' cronies encouraged corruption and produced huge income gaps, poverty, unemployment, and the suppression of political freedoms. Consistent containment of democratic alternatives has been, with some variations, the familiar pattern everywhere. Universal resentment of Western powers for their pursuit of their own geopolitical and economic interests and their military adventures and double standards, particularly in relation to Israeli-Palestinian relations, added to the people's discontent. Decades of suppression of the Left had weakened liberal opposition and its mobilization possibilities and made mosques the only venue for mobilizing discontent, a circumstance that assisted in the growth of Islamist parties and in their ability to organize supporters. The post-uprising election results in Arab countries confirmed the obvious, that leftist and independent forces did not have the same opportunities to organize and could not effectively compete with the Islamist parties. Iran's Khomeinists, Egypt's Muslim Brotherhood, Algeria's Islamic Salvation Front, Morocco's Justice and Development Party, and Turkey's Justice and Development Party all grew and flourished as a result of this economic and political mess.

Granted, Islamists do not constitute an undifferentiated mass. No doubt, differences exist between, on the one hand, Egypt's Muslim Brotherhood, Tunisia's Ennahda, and Iran's Khomeinism, and, on the other hand, the al-Qaeda/Taliban criminals of Afghanistan, Lashkar-e Islam in Swat, northern Pakistan, jihadists in Mali

(Bennoune 2013), and the brutal so-called Islamic State in Iraq and Syria. However, when it comes to issues related to family, women, and sexuality, differences among these groups are matters of degree. Needless to say, the force of their political-ideological power is defined by the level of social and economic advances in the societies in which they operate and the strength of counterhegemonic forces. However, the Islamists' focus on the bodies and male-defined purity and honor of women signifies that, given the opportunity, they would try to control women within the confines of the sharia. Hence, everywhere, Islamists' political gains are accompanied by women's losses.

In fact, with the rising influence of Islamism since the mid-1970s, the gendered character of the practices associated with the state-society relationship has been transformed. Moreover, the region's patriarchal and neopatriarchal ideologies and institutions take as their most passionately articulated mission the restoration of conservative religious doctrine and teachings on the status of women. Indeed, contempt for women's intelligence and emotional and moral stability is the marker of religious prescriptions and the moral regime of various brands of fundamentalism (Moghissi 2001).

Hence, it would be misleading to argue, as some do, that Islamist parties in Egypt, Tunisia, and elsewhere are the same as Christian Democrats in Germany or Sweden or that these brands of Islamists are more flexible in their interpretation of the sharia. In such discourse, the measure of enviable moderation and democratic Islamism is usually whether an Islamist party or regime is hostile to the West. Donald Trump's visit to Saudi Arabia with much fanfare in May 2017 confirms this point.

It is stunning that the American and British governments are now full force in the business of promoting "moderate Islamism" for the region, in the hope of controlling the rising tide of resistance against their neocolonial and neoliberal economic policies. They continue the Cold War strategy of identifying the secular Left and nationalist forces in the region as enemies and the Saudi Arabia– and Qatari-backed Wahhabis as reliable partners in Afghanistan, Yemen, Bahrain, Egypt, and elsewhere.

Even more disturbing is the unjustified advocacy that radical Islamist groups receive from a portion of the Left and antiracist, antiwar scholars and activists of the West, who hail the political and moral challenge that Islamists pose to Western hegemony and its liberal values. Islamists' gendered practices, sometimes even their cruelty to women, do not seem to generate much concern, let alone open condemnation. The rationale sometimes is that populations suffering from poverty, unemployment, and neocolonial aggression should not be polarized by raising gender-related questions. Such a rationale fails to acknowledge that women represent the overwhelming majority of the armies of the poor, unemployed, and exploited in these societies, in addition to being daily targets of misogynist humiliation and violence. This type of reasoning made Egyptian journalist Mona Eltahawi the target of criticism for concerns she expressed about the Brotherhood's policies against women (Eltahawi 2012; Good 2012). Other times, the reality of anti-Muslim racism in the West is invoked to silence criticism of Islamic gendered practices. This was the case when a Palestinian hip-hop group, DAM, was denounced for a music video it produced about honor crimes. The critics argued that the group had presented Palestinians as uncivilized, blaming the community and devaluing the culture (Abu Lughod and Midashi 2012).

The point that is overlooked here is that social realities are multidimensional and integrated, and we do not have to choose between forces of oppression in an effort to determine whether one is more detrimental than another to a peaceful and dignified life for women.

Notwithstanding all of the foregoing, the societies that have gone through revolutionary upheavals in the past few years now face a new order of which the parameters, complexities, and contradictions are not yet sorted out. It is possible, and one should certainly remain hopeful, that the unfinished revolutions in the region will produce results more favorable to the democratic forces that started the uprisings. The opposition in both Tunisia and Egypt is very active and has some clout, especially in Tunisia.

What we see in Arab countries are continued political instability and clashes, with the propertied and business classes also engaged in the struggle for a share in power. However, the existence of diverse interests in a post-uprising milieu may offer an opportune moment for democratic forces, change-seeking unemployed youth, women's rights activists, trade unions, and the poor and middle classes to regroup and reshape themselves in order to communicate to the people their alternative visions and strategies for change and stop the Islamists' ideological and political onslaught.

Both Tunisia and Egypt escaped the immediate bloody episodes of postrevolutionary Iran, which witnessed the effective slaughter of hundreds of the former regime's figures, including army generals, ministers, members of parliament, top bureaucrats, and lower-ranked army officers and security police, within the first weeks and months after the revolution. This butchery generated a lasting rage among sections of the population that were affiliated with the victims or simply hoped for fair and open trials for these individuals. Also, before his death, Khomeini ordered the massacre of several thousand political prisoners, followed by kidnappings and assassinations known as "chain murders" of prominent figures inside and outside Iran.

The consequences of the Islamists' brutality were manifold. They desensitized people to violence—a problem that has deeply infested Iranian society and is now a major social concern and source of fear for ordinary citizens. State violence and unflinching bloodshed also demoralized and frightened others who had enthusiastically participated in prerevolutionary street demonstrations and who were disappointed at the revolution's outcome but became fearful of or were paralyzed by the brutality of the new regime.

A second important factor is that, contrary to the case of Iran, the uprisings in the Arab countries did not rely on anti-Western and anti-imperialist discourse to mobilize people's support. Neither were they "Islamic revolutions," contrary to some suggestions (Fadel 2011). In fact, given that the demands of the revolutions in none of the Arab countries included the rule of the sharia or a return to more Islamic practices, one can reasonably say that they were popular uprisings of overwhelmingly Muslim populations with distinctly secular demands. Whether it was a military coup that ousted President Morsi or the continuation of the revolution expressed in the anti-Morsi twenty-two-million-signature petition, the events of July 3, 2013, in Egypt and the continued clashes in other parts of the region are about the identity of the future regimes that the people of the Arab world envision for their countries. It then follows that the governing Islamists are not able to manipulate people's religious emotions and label the opposition's challenges as anti-Islamic, as their counterparts did in Iran. Neither do they have a charismatic leader comparable to Ayatollah Khomeini, with an ideological blueprint for the kind of Islamic regime that was to replace the monarchy (*velayat-e faqih*, or supremacy of the jurist), with a remarkable talent to reach out to people, manipulate religious emotions, and get away with unimaginable forms of violence against the opposition. In addition, the relatively late entry of both Ennahda and the Muslim Brotherhood into the mass protests denies them any claim against other forces that they initiated the uprising and therefore have legitimate reasons to rule.

All these factors mean that the very issues that prompted the revolts are still there: the military dictatorships; the high unemployment of youths, who constitute 50 to 65 percent of the total population in the Arab countries; low wages; police harassment; brazen state corruption; and the concentration of wealth, businesses, and job opportunities in the hands of those individuals connected to the regime.

The leftists and liberal intellectuals who started the protests in Iran against the shah had similar grievances. However, the inability of the regime to respond to their demands effectively and promptly, coupled with the devious skill of Khomeini and his associates to rally people around the idea of foreign threat, successfully diverted attention, at least temporarily, from the original economic and political demands of the revolution. His famous words—"Economics is for donkeys, not for believers"—clearly show what we were dealing with.

What conclusion can be drawn from all this? Surely, the signs are many for the hard challenges ahead for the peoples of the Arab countries, particularly for the opposition of which women are a part. But we also see many signs that militant Islamists are losing their grip on the people in every Muslim-majority country that has tasted a dose of the Islamists' violence and illusory plans to restore Islamic traditions that have nothing to do with people's genuine concerns and urgent needs. Resistance and the gains of secular forces against the ruling Islamist party in Tunisia, the mass uprising that led to the ouster of the Islamist regime in Egypt, people storming the headquarters of the Islamist militia in Libya following the killing of the US ambassador, protest rallies in Pakistan following the shooting of Malala Yousafzai and the massacre of flu-shot technicians, massive street demonstrations against Jama'at-i Islami in Bangladesh, and several weeks of huge protest rallies against the Turkish "neo-Ottoman" Justice and Development Party all speak to one fact: that while women and men certainly number among those individuals on the side of the Islamists, there are at least as many women and men who oppose the rise of the Islamic brand of the religious Right in their countries. Surely, the case of Iran after the establishment of an Islamic regime in that country has made people in the region aware of the fact that when religious conservatism is combined with sexism, classism, and ethnic and religious discrimination, as well as neoliberal economic policies, the battle for achieving democratic rights and social justice becomes even more precarious.

I started with a rather grim outlook. But I want to end with hope and optimism. By all indications, people throughout the Middle East are determined to protect existing rights and civil legal institutions and to push for the materialization of their democratic demands. Mention can be made of the coalition of thirty-three women's rights organizations in Egypt that came together around the issues women wanted to see included in the constitution, such as a law criminalizing sexual harassment (*Ahram Online* 2012). The coalition activists have been instrumental in raising public consciousness through street demonstrations and role-playing in subways against the sexual harassment of women, which they see also as a veiled Islamist policy to drive women out of public spaces. These efforts finally led to the passage of a new law against sexual harassment of women, an endemic problem in Egypt (Mokbel 2016).

We see the same determination in Tunisia. The Coalition for Women of Tunisia, made up of fifteen registered nongovernmental organizations, was announced in September 2012, based on "the shared ideal of gender equality as a dimension of human rights" (E-Joussour Women 2012). The coalition's objective was "not only to preserve and defend Tunisian women's acquired rights [as] stipulated in the Tunisian Law since Independence (Personal Statute Code or CSP promulgated in 1956 including all amendments added until 2010)," but to make women's full citizenship status a reality. The new constitution approved in January 2014 indicates the success of their efforts: it gives all Tunisians, women and men, the right to be presidential candidates; guarantees parity between men and women in all elected assemblies; and obligates the state to ensure gender equality in the workplace (UN Women 2014). Similar steps, though on a smaller scale, were taken in Libya through launching the Libyan Women Forum, which represents eight women's rights organizations, immediately following the results of elections to the General National Congress in 2011, with the objective of advocating that Libyan women's rights be embedded in the forthcoming constitution (*Tripoli Post* 2012).

These developments are significant. Their success will have defining impacts on future political directions in the region, including in Syria and Iran. Surely, a lasting and deeper social and cultural makeover of the society, and the transformation of gender relations and sexual roles within them, requires a radical revolution in thought, to use a Gramscian concept. However, reflecting on the experiences of women in Iran during the past three decades has taught us not only the fragility of legal and social rights gained under authoritarian regimes, but also that women rise to the challenges, face gendered limitations head-on, and respond creatively to policies expressly designed to enforce domesticity and male notions of "Muslim womanhood."

Sources Cited

Abdel Kouddous, Sharif. 2012. "Will Egypt's New Constitution Take Us Backwards?" *Indypendent*, Oct. 10. http://www.indypendent.org/2012/10/10/will-egypts-new-constitution-take-country-backwards.

Abu Lughod, Lila, and Maya Midashi. 2012. "Tradition and the Anti-politics Machine: DAM Seduced by the 'Honor Crime.'" *Jadaliyya*, Nov. 23. http://www.jadaliyya.com/pages/index/8578/tradition-and-the-anti-politics-machine_dams-s . . . 1/25/2013.

Ahram Online. 2012. "Women's Rights Groups March to Presidential Palace, Thursday." Oct. 4. http://english.ahram.org.eg/NewsContent/1/64/54786/Egypt/Politics-/Womens-rights-groups-march-to-Egypt-presidential-p.aspxahramonline:.

Al-Akhbar. 2012. "Tunisia's Islamists Attack Union Activists" [in English]. Dec. 5. http://english.al-akhbar.com/node/14254.

Al Arabiya News. 2012. "Islamist, Leftist Students Clash." Mar. 8. http://english.alarabiya.net/articles/2012/03/08/199296.html.

Ali, Randa. 2012. "Egypt's Left Launches 'Democratic Revolutionary Coalition.'" *Ahram Online*, Sept. 19. http://english.ahram.org.eg/News/53304.aspx.

Al-Monitor. 2012. "Islamists, Leftists Clash at Tunisian Universities." Oct. 20. http://www.al-monitor.com/pulse/ru/politics/2012/10/tunisia-universities-turn-to-battle-ground-as-islamists-leftists-clash.html.

Arfaoui, Jamel. 2009. "Possible Polygamy Revival Raises Debate in Tunisia." *Magharebia*, Aug. 14.

Barrie, Christopher. 2012. "Tunisian Media: Al-Nahda Tightens Its Control." *Jadaliyya*, Sept. 7. http://www.jadaliyya.com/pages/index/7232/tunisian-media_al-nahda-tightens-its-control.

Bennoune, Karima. 2013. "The Taliban of Timbuktu." *New York Times*, Jan. 23. http://www.nytimes.com/2013/01/24/opinion/the-taliban-of-timbuktu.html.

Daily Star. 2017. "Tunisians Protest against Returning Militants." Jan. 9. http://www.pressreader.com/lebanon/the-daily-star-lebanon/20170109/281788513743349.

Ebadi, Shirin. 2012. "A Warning for Women of the Arab Spring." *Wall Street Journal*, Mar. 14.

Egypt Independent. 2013. "Shura Council Committee Says Female Protesters Should Take Responsibility, If Harassed." Feb. 11. http://www.egyptindependent.com/news/shura-council-committee-says-female-protesters-should-take-responsibility-if-harassed.

E-Joussour Women. 2012. "Coalition for Women of Tunisia." *E-Joussour*, Sept. 25. http://www3.e-joussour.net/en/node/11770.

Elsadda, Hoda. 2011. "Egypt: The Battle over Hope and Morale." *50.50: Inclusive Democracy*, Nov. 2. https://www.opendemocracy.net/5050/hoda-elsadda/egypt-battle-over-hope-and-morale.

Eltahawi, Mona. 2012. "Why Do They Hate Us? The Real War on Women Is in the Middle East." *Foreign Policy* (May–June). http://foreignpolicy.com/2012/04/23/why-do-they-hate-us/.

Fadel, Mohammad. 2011. "Modernist Islamic Political Thought and the Egyptian and Tunisian Revolutions of 2011." *Middle East Law and Governance* 3: 94–104.

Good, Allison. 2012. "Debating the War on Women." *Foreign Policy* (Apr. 24). http://foreignpolicy.com/2012/04/24/debating-the-war-on-women/.

Moghissi, Haideh. 2001. "Women, War and Fundamentalism in the Middle East." *After Sept. 11*, Social Science Research Council online collection of essays. http://essays.ssrc.org/sept11/essays/moghissi.htm.

Mokbel, Reham. 2016. "New Initiative Helps Egyptians Fight Back against Sexual Harassment." *Al-Monitor*, Oct. 30. http://www.al-monitor.com/pulse/originals/2016/10/egypt-sexual-harassment-aman-initiative.html.

Tripoli Post. 2012. "Libyan Women Alliance for Embedding Women's Rights in the Constitution." Nov. 19. http://www.tripolipost.com/articledetail.asp?c=1&i=9513.

UN Women. 2014. "Tunisia's New Constitution: A Breakthrough for Women's Rights." Feb. 11. http://www.unwomen.org/en/news/stories/2014/2/tunisias-new-constitution.

———. 2017. "Government Commitments." http://www.unwomen.org/en/what-we-do/ending-violence-against-women/take-action/commit/government-commitments#tunisia.

Part Four

Media and Cultural Expressions

12

State-Sponsored Media, Cultural Production, and Information Wars

The Case of Iran

NIKI AKHAVAN

Since its establishment after the 1979 Revolution, the Islamic Republic of Iran's approaches to media and cultural production have been shaped by assertions that have pulled its policies in competing directions: on the one hand, its claims of a cultural onslaught from outsiders have been used as the justification for countless repressive and regulatory measures; on the other hand, its emphasis on the importance of cultural independence has necessitated the embrace of various media forms. Similarly, the state's desire to appear technologically progressive and independent has been in tension with its concerns that advances in media technologies may be used to undermine the ruling structure. For these reasons, official approaches to the media have been inconsistent, often employing a two-pronged and seemingly contradictory approach, according to which one set of policies aims at restricting content and technologies and another focuses on expanding state-approved involvement with the same media.[1]

Attempts at unified media messaging or policy making are further complicated by Iran's highly factionalized political landscape:

1. Gholam Khiabany (2010) has led the way in closely examining the state's various proactive uses of diverse media and highlighting the Iranian state's contradictory approaches.

while there may be agreement about the necessity of promoting various forms of homegrown media productions, no such consensus exists on their nature and scope. At the same time, massive outlets sponsored by foreign states and independent media users operating in opposition to the ruling system pose additional challenges for any efforts at presenting an uncontested portrait of contemporary Iran. The confused landscape that has emerged as a result of the combination of these factors is apparent in new and traditional media arenas alike. Using two very different sites of media participation, namely, an overview of the Iranian Internet and a brief case study of state broadcasting's Documentary Channel in its early years, this chapter highlights the tactics of state organs for enhancing their influence as producers of media and culture. It also notes the inconsistencies in these tactics, as well as the obstacles the state faces in its attempts to advance itself as a major player in the country's culture wars against its external and internal opponents. The ongoing struggle for reform and improved human rights in Iran is most clearly seen against this backdrop in which a divided state counters an even more divided opposition and where cultural production is at the heart of political contestations. An analysis that reveals the ambiguities of the Iranian state's relationship to media, rather than one that focuses only on its repressive policies, allows for a fuller picture to emerge of the challenges facing advocates for social and political justice in Iran.

Perhaps more than any other medium, the Internet reflects the complexities that arise when state entities attempt to reconcile their aims of engaging various media forms with the desire to assert control over them. That is to say, the Internet clearly reflects the state's two-pronged approach to media technologies. The first prong, and the one on which most popular and scholarly attention has focused, consists of repressive tactics, strategies aimed at limiting, regulating, or surveillance of new media activities. Operating alongside are another set of tactics aimed at increasing state and state actors' presence and participation on new media sites. The latter include two main mechanisms for promoting content production that benefits state interests and counters dissenting materials: first, new spaces have been created online where state actors and those individuals sympathetic to the state can be actively engaged; second, efforts have been made to penetrate existing spaces where oppositional voices already have a presence.

The creation of new digital spaces has taken a number of forms, such as websites, online magazines, and discussion forums. During the first years of the new millennium, reformist publications and sympathies dominated the Iranian Internet. The reasons were twofold. For one, many reformist outlets took to the Internet after their print publications were banned. Furthermore, reformists had managed to attract young, urban, middle-class supporters, the same demographic that was both Internet savvy and had the resources to participate online.[2] Recognizing that proreform users had a platform to reach broader audiences, state institutions as well as other political factions developed their online presence (this early period will be further discussed below). Such sites steadily expanded through the 2000s, with a spike in the years following the disputed 2009 election.

In the aftermath of that election, governmental resources and institutions were mobilized alongside diverse media technologies in the service of what has been officially dubbed "soft war." Within months of the massive demonstrations, Ayatollah Khamenei said in a public speech to his supporters, "Today, the country's top priority is to fight against the enemy's soft war" (*Fars News* 2009). While this "soft war" is identified as something that is being done to Iran, it is also used to encompass tactics that Iran employs to combat the "cultural, literary, artistic, propaganda, linguistic, and communication" practices of its enemies.[3] Following Khamenei's speech, state organs

2. For a review of factional fighting between reformists and conservatives during the late 1990s and early 2000s and its impact on the Iranian Internet as a site of dissent, see Rahimi 2003.

3. The quote is translated from the "About Us" section of the Jang-e narm (Soft War) website (http://www.psyop.ir/?page_id=525), one of the many soft war sites that have cropped up since the announcement of the soft war project following the 2009 demonstrations.

and officials devoted much attention and resources to articulating and cultivating material related both to fighting and to carrying out soft war. It is important to note that while a wide range of officials have expressed enthusiasm about soft war, and numerous websites have cropped up to support it, there is a lack of uniformity that makes it difficult to determine whether soft war is a concept, strategy, policy, or some combination thereof. State actors are especially worried about the targeting of Iranian value and belief systems via a soft war that is part of a larger strategy of overthrowing the current ruling structure (Price 2012). And while the proliferation of digital and traditional media devoted to increasing knowledge and cultural production on the issue has been noteworthy, the most intense period of activity lasted only from 2009 to 2011.

Nonetheless, soft war marks an important point in official approaches to cultural production and explains developments in post-2009 digital and traditional media spheres that emphasize the importance of producing favorable materials and countering oppositional content. This emphasis is evident in the range of websites dedicated to soft war that cropped up in this period; some of these sites were virtual arms of offline entities, indicating the scope of the state's support for soft war projects. Examples include the website of Dabirkhane Daemei Moqabele ba Jang-e Narm-e Keshvar (the Country's Permanent Secretariat for Confronting Soft War), previously available at http://www.h-jangenarm.com; Jang-e narm (soft war), http://www.psyop.ir/; Afsaran (Soldiers), Afsaran.ir; and the blog http://jang-e-narm.ibsblog.ir/.

While the official sites of soft war are distinct in their explicit and sometimes aggressive commitment to exposing the perceived enemies' cultural onslaughts and countering them with their own content, their aims are in continuity with the state's earlier approaches to digital media. Without state support for telecommunications infrastructure and the permission it grants private Internet service providers (ISPs), the Internet could not function in Iran; the state is also a main investor in the telecommunications and information industries (Sreberny and Khiabany 2011). At the same time, concerns about new sites for foreign intervention or oppositional activism (or both) have also prompted the state to take restrictive maneuvers, such as artificially keeping Internet speeds down and setting conditions for ISPs that included filtering content. Alongside these maneuvers, however, state entities have been active in establishing a foothold in online spaces by building websites for institutions and variously encouraging the production of friendly content.

To do so, the state had to stay abreast of new media trends, so that it could attempt to control new technologies and use them as a means of cultural production. Thus, during the early 2000s, when blogging was rising to its height of popularity and oppositional and reformist content was capturing the attention of scholarly and popular audiences alike, state actors took action. In addition to repressive policies of filtering content and making an example of a few young reformist bloggers, various state entities also sought ways of catalyzing blogs that bolster officially favored narratives about the Iranian state and society. Sponsoring blogging competitions that promise prizes is one mechanism that has been apparent from the heyday of the Iranian blogosphere until the present (Akhavan 2013). Such competitions were often framed to attract only populations sympathetic to hardline elements of the ruling system. In other words, they mobilized existing supporters rather than winning converts. Nonetheless, they allow state actors both to change the landscape of the Iranian Internet and to establish a place for favorable content.

In addition to creating new sites for content production, the state's active engagement prong included promoting participation in existing spaces, such as those forums provided by popular blog-hosting sites and social media. The Twitter account of the country's supreme leader, Ayatollah Khamenei, for example, is regularly active, providing tweets in Persian, Arabic, and English. He also has an Instagram account that frequently posts pictures of Khamenei attending various meetings and events. While many of these gatherings are also covered by official news agencies, the Instagram photos create the sense that the viewer is privy to exclusive content. Other social media spaces also show the active participation of state-linked persons and institutions. The aggregate service Friendfeed, for example, which was very popular among Iranian users but often overlooked in English-language accounts, was filled with official and semiofficial news agencies with active Friendfeed accounts.[4] On Friendfeed and other social media sites, numerous users explicitly identifying with the soft war against cultural onslaughts devote their posts to producing content aimed at countering oppositional material circulated via these same services.[5]

The range of state-endorsed efforts to create new online spaces and to integrate within existing platforms has been effective in preventing oppositional or critical voices from monopolizing new media spheres. But this digital engagement has not been without its complications. While countless magazines, forums, new sites, and individuals with connections or sympathies to the state have established a place for themselves online, this presence has not translated into a unified message about the nature and identity of the state. On the contrary, many such online arenas manifest infighting. As such, they magnify rather than smooth over various splits within the country. During Mahmoud Ahmadinejad's second term, the news website Baztab, for example, which is linked to conservative former presidential candidate Mohsen Rezaee, devoted much of its coverage to vitriolic criticism of the presidential administration, often focusing on Ahmadinejad himself. Young supporters of another conservative former presidential candidate and mayor of Tehran, Mohammad Baqer Qalibaf, who have a heavy presence on social media and a range of websites, were also vocal critics of Ahmadinejad and other major players in Iran's political scene, going so far as to question funds

4. Fars News Agency and Mehr News Agency, for example, had active accounts at http://friendfeed.com/farsnews and http://friendfeed.com/mehrnews. Much to the dismay of Friendfeed users, Facebook—which had purchased the service in 2009—shut it down on April 9, 2015. Since ending the service, Facebook has not made archives of the site publicly available.

5. The account http://friendfeed.com/farmande10, whose user name translates to "Soft War Commander," was one such example.

allocated to cultural productions in the name of soft war. Other websites have also publicly questioned whether Ahmadinejad supporters have received undisclosed funding to carry out their own soft war (*Farda News* 2011).

Furthermore, contradictions between the two prongs of the state's approach to media and cultural production—the repressive arm aimed at controlling content and the proactive arm aimed at producing it—become particularly evident in social media spaces. As these sites are often blocked, the use of proxy websites and software is required to circumvent government filters. The very appearance of state actors and supporters on popular social media platforms raises questions about how they are accessing them. Perhaps they are using filter breakers or are able to use the Internet unhampered by blocks. Either way, they are participating on sites and via means that are prohibited. Ordinary users, especially those individuals who are critical of the state, have frequently taken the opportunity afforded by social media to directly confront state entities and supporters about their double standards. After Khamenei launched his Twitter account, the outcry over these apparent double standards was loud enough to capture the attention of the foreign press (Dehghan 2011).

In addition to questions of accessing blocked sites, social media participation of state actors reveals internal tensions in official discourses on new media as they appear in relation to soft war. Self-identified participants in the endeavor to fight the perceived enemies' soft war specifically identify popular social media like Facebook and Twitter, as well as various Google-owned platforms, as venues that spread anti-Iran propaganda, collect information on Iranian users, and promote "Western" lifestyles (Gerdab 2012a, 2012b; Jang-e narm 2011). Yet not only do state actors, supporters, and entities have accounts on these sites, but the same conservative outlets that warn against them also carry articles encouraging participation (for example, Teribon 2012). Thus, the new media presence of the state and its supporters reveals internal tensions that go beyond issues pertaining to their accessing forbidden aspects of the Internet: they are also about inconsistencies over the basic principle of whether to participate on these sites. While these contradictions are not unique to the state's new media policy and can be found in its media and cultural policies more broadly, they are more easily discernible in digital media spaces.

In short, the specificities of Internet technologies, such as their conduciveness to decentralized modes of content production and dissemination, have had mixed results for state efforts at deploying the Internet in the service of winning the culture wars against foreign content producers and internal critics. On the one hand, it has taken relatively modest amounts of funding and encouragement to establish a formidable presence on the Internet. At the same time, however, engagement online makes participants vulnerable to being directly questioned, especially on sites with minimal to no moderation. Even strictly monitored websites that allow no reader interaction are subject to greater scrutiny. Furthermore, their content may be easily reproduced or altered for the purposes of challenging or ridiculing the original content. For example, Internet users have variously altered Ayatollah Khamenei's Instagram photos and have set up parody accounts poking fun at his tweets and ideas. The Fars news agency was recently forced to make a rare apology for publishing as serious news an article from the satire site the *Onion* after Internet users widely circulated the mistake, taking screen captures as proof before the Fars website could take down the offending article (BBC News 2012).

In contrast to online arenas and their potential pitfalls as outlined above, traditional media structures offer state powers more control over how material is presented and how audiences, in turn, engage with that material. Television broadcasting is particularly useful in this regard. To begin with, the Islamic Republic of Iran Broadcasting, which has a monopoly on national broadcasting, allows for centralized command over programming. Long dominated by conservative factions, the head of the IRIB is directly appointed by the supreme leader, giving that office great power in determining the direction of the national broadcasting system. Furthermore, television remains a top media form in terms of domestic penetration, thus allowing the state to target a larger audience share than can be expected from the Internet.

Despite its control over national broadcasting, however, the IRIB has long struggled to attract viewers. Constitutionally mandated to keep the public well informed, the IRIB has also been tasked with a central role in the culture wars, namely, to broadcast content that rejects foreign influences and emphasizes and exalts the country's Islamic identity. Given the ideological demands placed on the IRIB, it is not surprising that it has been unable to draw a diverse, loyal audience. This is not to say that the broadcaster has not had its successes. While the IRIB has always been squarely in the camp of the conservative factions of the Iranian state, it has benefited from the slow shifts in the country's cultural and political landscapes that have expanded the limits of acceptable content. Broadly speaking, these changes were set in motion first with the conclusion of the Iran-Iraq War and the presidency of Hashemi Rafsanjani and then with the rise of the reformists in the late 1990s. As a result, the IRIB has broadcast a number of popular drama and comedy series. The various satiric serials of Mehran Modiri—which have been airing regularly since 2002—are one example of popular programming.

Such successes, however, have not fully mitigated the broadcaster's troubles. While the state is able to head off competition from private broadcasters by preventing the participation of private capital (Khiabany 2010, 181), forestalling the influence of satellite broadcasters has proved to be a bigger challenge. Since the rise of satellite broadcasting in Iran in the 1990s, the state has followed the dual tactic that it would later use in relation to the Internet. At the same time that it decried the attempts of foreign and foreign-funded channels to influence and interfere in Iranian culture and politics, it went about establishing its own satellite channels. The Arabic language al-Alam and the English Press TV are two examples of its attempts to penetrate foreign markets. The state also attempted to reach diasporic Iranian audiences via the Persian-language Jam-e-Jam satellite channels. On the domestic front, similar tactics have been at play. On the one hand, the state has attempted to disrupt access to foreign channels by physically removing satellite dishes from private homes or jamming satellite signals. At the same time, it has attempted to provide more options—in the form of both content and available channels—to its domestic audiences.

The March 2011 launch of the IRIB's Documentary Channel is one example of the effort to expand content and reach. Although the emphasis appears to be on attracting domestic audiences, it is also broadcast internationally. The channel, which is Iran's first to be digitally broadcast, began a limited broadcast in October 2009, just three months after the disputed presidential election. Reza Pourhossein, the moderator of the candidate debates in that election, was chosen as the channel's director. However, the Documentary Channel is not entirely original in its content, often rebroadcasting programs from IRIB Channel 4, which itself includes much documentary content. Nonetheless, the Documentary Channel does try to distinguish itself in claiming to cultivate Iranian filmmakers and in attempting to provide a variety of nonfiction films. This variation is reflected in the channel's programming schedule, which organizes its documentaries according to categories such as "nature," "arts and culture," "political," and "social."

The choice to focus on documentaries in providing new content may be explained by several interrelated factors. For one, nonfiction films can be made with lower budgets than works of fiction; whereas Iranian-produced fiction films may have a hard time competing with big-budget Hollywood productions, nonfiction works offer more flexibility. It is generally cheaper to produce documentary works with high production values, and, furthermore, the documentary genre is more forgiving of gritty works whose unpolished aesthetics can work well with particular subjects. In addition to considerations of cost and production, the IRIB's satellite rivals have also increasingly incorporated documentary works into their programming, and such films—which often broach social and political topics that would be taboo inside Iran—have proved popular with Iranian audiences. Therefore, it is not surprising that the IRIB would aim to counter this programming with its own documentary output. Finally, the documentary is not totally unfamiliar territory for either audiences or producers: the documentary form is well established in Iran and on IRIB in particular (Naficy 2011, vols. 2–3).

During the devastating eight-year war with Iraq, for example, Morteza Avini made a series of films on the front lines of the conflict that were broadcast as sixty-three episodes entitled *Revayat-e Fath* (Story of Victory) on IRIB Channel 1. Indeed, one of the Iranian state's major successes in the field of cultural productions is in the arena of discourses on the Iran-Iraq War, officially dubbed "the Sacred Defense." In his comments announcing the launch of the Documentary Channel, former IRIB head Ezatollah Zarghami specifically referred to these achievements in emphasizing the importance of nonfiction films: "In all these years we have seen how political and Sacred Defense documentaries fundamentally changed society's attitudes toward many political issues; they provided historical reminders and raised people's awareness" (Jam-e-Jam Online 2009). Zarghami also indicated the importance of replicating such successes in the case of other documentary genres in order to expand the IRIB's audience more generally.

Films about the Iran-Iraq War are only one genre of documentaries with a history of being broadcast on state-owned channels. Political documentaries, such as campaign films produced for presidential elections, have found eager audiences and have been circulated online after being broadcast on national television. The IRIB has also produced original political documentaries, many of which are direct attacks on dissidents and rival factions. These documentaries often receive much attention, even if only in the form of criticism from viewers who consider these films works of pure propaganda. The documentary *Fetne: Doostan-e Dirooz Doshmanan-e Emrooz* (Sedition: Yesterday's Friends, Today's Enemies), broadcast on the first anniversary of the 2009 election and the demonstrations that followed, is one such example. In addition to original and Iranian works, dubbed foreign documentaries have long been a regular staple of IRIB television. In short, the documentary format is well known and popular with Iranian audiences, but this fact alone seems not to have been enough to ensure the success of the Documentary Channel. Not surprisingly, and similar to the overall fate of the IRIB, the development of the Documentary Channel has been the focus of political wrangling.

While the IRIB's centralized structure and the control it exerts over programming allow state actors to avoid some of the aforementioned pitfalls of engaging with the Internet, the Documentary Channel has been subject to the same factionalized disputes that have long plagued the IRIB. Like the IRIB more broadly, discussions of the Documentary Channel have served as an occasion to critique the management of the broadcaster, its programming choices, as well as (often indirectly) the political interests to which they are tied (for example, Alef 2012).

Perhaps an even bigger indicator of the Documentary Channel's failures was that it was all but completely ignored by those individuals with no ties to or sympathies for the ruling power structure. Oppositional voices inside and abroad, who have been very vocal in objecting to Iranian broadcasting, especially in its news coverage and its attempts to reach broader audiences via satellite, have been largely silent on the Documentary Channel. It may be because, unlike Iran's foreign-language broadcasting services, such as the Arabic al-Alam or the English Press TV,[6] the Documentary Channel has not made significant gains in reaching new audiences. Almost all the critiques leveled against the channel have come from institutions and individuals either affiliated with state organs or who have worked with them in some capacity. Despite its inability thus far to make notable gains in attracting audiences or swaying sentiments in Iran's culture wars, the channel remains an important example of the state's ongoing attempts to amplify its reach both domestically and internationally.

6. Despite gains made by channels such as Press TV in reaching new audiences, sanctions placed on Iran by the European Union and the United States have negatively impacted the country's ability to broadcast internationally. In October 2012, French and British satellite providers Eutelsat and British Arqiva had to terminate their contracts with Iran, a move affecting nineteen Iranian channels (RT 2012).

The period under consideration in this chapter roughly spans from the rise of the Internet through 2012, but the patterns it highlights remain largely unchanged. Iran's virtual and traditional media spheres continue to reflect new efforts at expanding state-supported forms of cultural production and public participation. In both cases, state-sponsored institutions and individuals have often explicitly situated their projects as part of a broader cultural war against those identified as internal and external enemies. Facing competition from handsomely funded Persian-language outlets from abroad as well as from a range of independent and media-savvy sectors of the Iranian opposition, the state's project in this regard is further complicated by increased splintering within Iran's ruling establishment. The result has been inconsistent media policies and mediascapes that—far from allowing the state to present a unified front against entities it identifies as enemies—reflect the fissures within the ruling establishment and open spaces, however small, for critics and reform advocates to enter the fray.

Sources Cited

Akhavan, Niki. 2013. *Electronic Iran: The Cultural Politics of an Online Evolution*. New Brunswick, NJ: Rutgers Univ. Press.

Alef. 2012. "Pakhshe mosabeghe football az shabake Mostaned montafi shod" [Football Broadcasting on the Documentary Channel Canceled]. June 10. http://alef.ir/vdca0on6649nmw1.k5k4.html?159071.

BBC News. 2012. "Iran's Fars Agency Sorry for Running the Onion Spoof Story." Sept. 30. http://www.bbc.com/news/world-middle-east-19778656.

Dehghan, Saeed Kamali. 2011. "Supreme Leader Tweetings Infuriate Iran's Persecuted Bloggers: Twitter Account Apparently Run from Ayatollah Ali Khamenei's Office Draws Accusations of Hypocrisy after Online Crackdown." *Guardian*, Jan. 12. https://www.theguardian.com/world/2011/jan/12/ayatollah-ali-khamenei-twitter-row.

Farda News. 2011. "Does the Deviant Movement Have Its Own Cyber Center?" Sept. 26. http://www.fardanews.com/fa/news/162996/.

Fars News. 2009. "Today the Country's Top Priority Is to Combat the Enemy's Soft War." Nov. 29. http://www.farsnews.com/newstext.php?nn=8809041385.

Gerdab. 2012a. "Ahdaf-e Keshvarhay-e Gharbi Baray-e Gostaresh-e Site-hay-e Mostajan" [The Aims of the West for Expanding Obscene Sites]. Dec. 24. http://www.gerdab.ir/fa/news/12467.

———. 2012b. "Tashkhees Chehre ham be Abzar Jasoosi Google Ezafe Shod" [Face Recognition Has Been Added to Google's Instruments of Espionage]. Oct. 3. http://gerdab.ir/fa/news/12187/.

Jam-e-Jam Online. 2009. "The Documentary Channel Will Be among the Most Popular." Mar. 17. http://www1.jamejamonline.ir/newstext.aspx?newsnum=100838489438.

Jang-e narm. 2011. "Shabakehay-e Ejtemayee Cyberi va Zendegi Gharbi" [Cyber Social Networks and Western Lifestyles]. Aug. 8. http://www.psyop.ir/?p=8129.

Khiabany, Gholam. 2010. *Iranian Media: The Paradox of Modernity*. New York: Routledge.

Naficy, Hamid. 2011. *A Social History of Iranian Cinema*. 4 vols. Durham, NC: Duke Univ. Press.

Price, Monroe. 2012. "Iran and the Soft War." *International Journal of Communication* 6: 2397–415.

Rahimi, Babak. 2003. "Cyberdissident: The Internet in Revolutionary Iran." *Middle East Review of International Affairs* 7 (3). http://www.rubincenter.org/2003/09/rahimi-2003-09-07/.

RT. 2012. "Iran Lashes Out at EU for Blocking Its Satellite Channels." Oct. 17. https://www.rt.com/news/iran-slam-eu-channels-626/.

Sreberny, Annabelle, and Gholam Khiabany. 2011. *Blogistan: The Internet and Politics in Iran*. London: I. B. Tauris.

Teribon. 2012. "Chegoone dar Facebook Mahboob Shaveem?" [How We Can Get "Liked" on Facebook?]. Nov. 26. http://www.teribon.ir/archives/138572/.

13

The Power of Corruption and the Corruption of Power

The Arabic Historical Novel in Morocco (and Elsewhere)

ROGER ALLEN

The process of change and the means whereby it is recorded and evaluated have provoked a variety of comments over the course of the centuries. I will begin with a series of epigraphs, the relevance of which to the topic I hope to demonstrate in what follows. First, on history and the process of change:

"Change is the only constant" (Heraclitus).

"Plus ça change, plus c'est la même chose" (Jean-Baptiste Alphonse Karr).

"Those who cannot remember the past are condemned to repeat it" (George Santayana).

"The one thing we owe to history is to rewrite it" (Oscar Wilde).

And then, on power and corruption: "Power tends to corrupt, and absolute power corrupts absolutely" (Lord Acton).

This chapter explores and illustrates the ways in which Arabic novels, and in particular those works of fiction that may be designated "historical," have played a role, however apparently tangential it may seem, in the development of a social and political atmosphere that resulted in the events of 2011 in the Arabic-speaking world. As is the case regrettably often, the term used by the Western media to describe those events—the *Arab Spring*—not only fails to depict the actual phenomena involved but also actually diminishes the clear differences in the social and political fabrics and the sequences of events in each particular region. As Theodore Friend (2011) notes, first, there is no season of "spring" in most of the Arab world region; second, the analogy to the "Prague Spring" of 1968 is hardly appropriate, in that that particular social uprising ended with the arrival of Soviet tanks in the city that proceeded to crush the revolt. The major issue here is perhaps the attempt to combine all these Arab-world movements during 2011 into a single entity—mostly grouped around the perfectly valid impact of the Internet and its organs on the events in question, but utterly ignoring the enormous local differences connected to the history and social fabric of each country or region. One is reminded of the similarly inappropriate European assignation of the title "Arabian Nights" to a collection of tales, the earliest version of which is of Indo-Persian origins. As is the case with the term *renaissance* (often rendered into Arabic as *nahda*), the notion of "awakening" implies that some phenomenon has been in a kind of comatose state. While one might describe the social conditions of the Arab countries or nations involved in the events of 2011 in a variety of ways, they could hardly be depicted as "comatose."

One aspect of the events clearly involves what a session at the Middle East Studies Association conference in Washington, DC (December 2011), described as "the fall of the dictators," illustrating one aspect of the confrontation of "power" and "corruption," on the one hand, and "freedom" (*hurriyya*) and "liberation" (*tahrir*), on the other, the last concept being loudly proclaimed, particularly in the Cairo Square of that name—thus an expression of the desire to have "freedom from," in this case autocratic rule and the corruption that frequently accompanies it. However, it is when we consider the consequences of that liberation, "freedom to," that matters become that much more complex.

I would suggest that history, and fairly recent history at that, provides us with at least two appropriate illustrations: the Egyptian Revolution of 1952 and the Iranian Revolution of 1979. In each case a wide variety of different social and political groups united to rid themselves of a tyrannical and corrupt ruler and entourage—King Faruq and Shah Reza Pahlavi, who both had managed to exploit ties to Western powers to their personal advantage. In both cases, the aftermath of the revolutionary process included periods of political uncertainty, as systems and identities were explored, adopted, or abandoned; security forces were trained and empowered; and those groups that turned out to be the losers in those processes were imprisoned, eliminated, or exiled—the fate of the communists in both Egypt and Iran, whose Tudeh Party fled to Algeria, and the Muslim Brotherhood in Egypt. With regard to Egypt in particular, those processes and their aftermaths have already been the subject of any number of Arabic novels (for example, Mahfuz 1962; see Allen 1995). Such works of fiction provide ample evidence of their authors' conviction regarding what appears to be a principle in the analysis of periods subsequent to all genuinely popular revolutions, namely, that there are bound to be winners and losers. History, in another common phrase, is said to be written by the winners.

Is it then to be a primary function of fiction to depict the fate of the losers? How is such depiction to be achieved within those changing and uncertain societies and times, and what should be the nature of their resort to the past and its record in history? Harking back to the epigraphs with which I began, are we to go with Heraclitus's notion that "change is the only constant," or stick with the more cynical statement of Jean-Baptiste Karr that "Plus ça change, plus c'est la même chose"? It is into this recklessly brief and speculative survey—and by a literature scholar at that—of the events of 2011 and their consequences that I now wish to place this chapter on literature's role in "setting the stage," as it were: history and fiction, the historical novel, and examples of that genre from the modern Arabic tradition—most of them Moroccan.

The first pair of epigraphs cited above concerns the process of change, although the two well-known aphorisms clearly take a different view as to the consequences of such transformations. The latter two discuss the process of recording such movements of change, the means whereby such records are assessed over the course of time and, in the case of Oscar Wilde, the need to have regular resort to them. These records are, of course, what we term "history," although we have immediately to acknowledge—as do any number of studies on the topic—that the term *history* may refer both to "the past" in and of itself and to the process whereby that past is recorded. The discipline of "historiography" chooses to examine not only the methods that are used in creating such records, but also the validity and purpose of such methods and the resulting records. One of the great pioneers in that field of historical analysis is, of course, Ibn Khaldun (1332–1406), whose personal experiences and variegated career in North Africa, Spain, and Egypt are clearly reflected in his development of the cyclical model of historical transformation that has long been acknowledged as his pioneer contribution to the theorization of history. At this point I cannot resist the urge to insert a more specific reference to my major focus, namely, the interesting fact that Ibn Khaldun has played a role of his own in at least two modern Arabic novels. In a novel by Algerian writer Rashid Abu Jadra (Boujedra in French), *Ma'rakat al-zuqaq* (also in French as *La prise de Gibraltar*), a father with a strong interest in history names his son Tariq, after Tariq ibn Ziyad, the renowned Amazigh general who crossed the Straits in 710 CE, passing the rocky outcrop that now bears his name—and initiated the Muslim conquest of the Iberian Peninsula. Throughout the novel, reference is made to a miniature painting that shows the historical Tariq delivering a ringing address to his troops before they embark. In the novel, the father becomes outraged when his son comes home and tells his father that his history teacher declared Ibn Khaldun's record of the speech to be spurious. Thus does the recording of historical events come back to impinge upon the present. In Ben Salem Himmich's novel, *Al-'Allama*, Ibn Khaldun's later life as a Maliki judge in Cairo is the major topic, as the historian spends a series of evenings with his Moroccan amanuensis revisiting some of his earlier conclusions in the introduction to his historical work *Kitab al-'ibar*, those reworkings of his earlier ideas being substantially based on his personal experiences of power and corruption in working for a whole series of North African Muslim dynasties (Allen 1997, 2006, 2008).

There is, of course, no shortage of sardonic comment on the nature and veracity of historical records, ranging from Voltaire's "History is a pack of lies we play on the dead," to Napoleon's "History is a set of lies agreed upon," to Santayana's "History is a pack of lies about events that never happened, told by people who weren't there" (not to mention the variously attributed "History is just one damn thing after another"). The majority of these quotations seem to be mainly concerned about the *veracity* of history, and it is in that context that the works of scholars such as Hayden White become particularly useful, in that they endeavor to move the discussion away from questions of truth and falsehood—as though such absolutes could exist within the realms of human fallibility—and instead to address a variety of textual genres as being at base composed narratives, each of which has its own particular characteristics and, above all, its own "horizon of expectations," to cite the renowned expression of Hans Robert Jauss concerning reception theory (White 1973, 1978, 2010; Jauss 1982). In his manifesto *Reality Hunger*, David Shields provides a provocative yet useful statement in such a context: "The line between fact and fiction is fuzzier than most people find it convenient to admit. There is the commonsensical assertion that while the novelist is engaged on a work of the creative imagination, the duty of the journalist [historian?] is to tell what really happened, as it happened. The distinction is easy to voice but hard to sustain in logic. For imagination and memory are Siamese twins, and you cannot cut them so cleanly apart. There's a good case for arguing that any narrative account is a form of fiction" (2010, 65).

Hayden White proposes a kind of narrative spectrum, which can range from history to biography, to autobiography, and to what we term fiction. In bookstores and libraries, of course, examples of these various genres will be carefully shelved as separate entities, yet questions concerning the nature and functions of autobiography, for example, not to mention the yet more specific genre of "memoir," may suggest to us that, as narrative genres, all these categories may share just as many features—of inclusion and exclusion, for example—as they do differentiating factors. Once again, David Shields has a telling comment to offer in this particular context of "memoirs" and their reception: "The memoir rightly belongs to the imaginative world, and, once writers and readers make their peace with this, there will be less argument over the questions regarding the memoir's relation to 'the facts' and 'truth'" (ibid., 133). Shields's work is probably the most cogent recent statement of the many issues associated with assumptions about narrative genres that are seen to be relying on human memory. The fracas that erupted, mostly on the Oprah Winfrey television program, over James Frey's memoir (2004) was, it would appear, prompted by the notion that anything called a "memoir" should be "true," with "facts" that could be verified.

Within the Maghribi context that is my primary focus here, the renowned text of Moroccan author Muhammad Shukri (1935–2003), *Al-Khubz al-hafi* (1982), translated by Paul Bowles as *For Bread Alone* (1973), terms itself a "novelistic autobiography" (*sira dhatiyya riwa'iyya*), clearly desiring to play with the more "traditional" generic categories.

The healthy skepticism displayed by the composers of the epigraphs and quotations that I have cited seems to indicate, through their distrust of the notion of veracity, that they have chosen to read historical texts critically and to interpret them in their function as narratives of the past and, in the terms of Santayana's epigraph, to stress the necessity of evaluating the validity of their contents with reference to both the present and the future. Needless to say, this debate over the generic purposes, similarities, and differences of narratives that we term history and fiction becomes yet more interesting when we focus on the subgenre of fiction that is the historical novel, the category to which the Maghribi works that are my primary focus here belong. As is the case with literary genres in general, the historical novel emerges at a certain time in response to combinations of cultural phenomena and, as Walter Ong observes, as a direct response to the emergence of the press, meaning both printing and newspapers (Ong 1991). With regard to the specific genre of the historical novel, the renowned Scottish critic David Daiches is in no doubt as to its origins: "[Sir Walter] Scott not only invented the historical novel, but made it available for a great variety of new kinds of writing. Balzac in France, Manzoni in Italy, Gogol and Tolstoy in Russia, were among the many writers of fiction influenced by the man Stendhal called 'notre père, Walter Scott.' . . . What Scott did was to show history and society in motion: old ways of life being challenged by new; traditions being assailed by counterstatements; loyalties, habits, prejudices clashing with the needs of new social and economic developments" (1998, v).[1]

Daiches's mention of Tolstoy in this quotation allows me to introduce into the discussion the great Russian novelist's mighty work *War and Peace*, proverbial for its incredible length and detail, and to point out that the novel provides its readers with a powerful illustration of the linkage between history and fiction, in that a close reading of the text reveals it to be a lengthy and cogent critique of historical writing and, in particular, the ways in which the Napoleonic invasion of Russia was depicted in works penned by historians. In an extensive reflection on the topic that makes up the first chapter of book 11 of the novel ("1812"), for example, Tolstoy notes that "the first method of history is to take an arbitrarily selected series of continuous events and examine it apart from others, though there is and can be no beginning to any event, for one event always flows uninterruptedly from another. The second method is to consider the actions of some one man—a king or a commander—as equivalent to the sum of many individual wills; whereas the sum of individual wills is never expressed by the activity of a single historic personage" (1934–37, book 11, chapter 1).

As we hope to demonstrate, Tolstoy's use of fiction and the historical novel as a vehicle for criticism of historians and their modes

1. Here I might also cite Perry Anderson: "What novelists or poets can bring to an objective study of the past are cognitive instruments: techniques of estrangement as social critique in Tolstoy, free direct style as passage to a new interiority in Stendhal, ellipsis as at once suspender and accelerator of time in Flaubert, unmediated visualisation as access to fresh insight in Proust" (2012, 6).

of writing finds echoes in Arabic novels. I would like to conclude this investigation of the linkage between history and fiction and the contemporary functions of the historical novel by noting that in a recent work David Cowart identifies four subcategories of the fictional genre, the fourth of which is particularly germane to our focus here: what he terms "The Distant Mirror," "fictions whose authors project the present into the past" (Cowart 1989, 8–9). In turning now to the Arabic literary tradition and especially its modern fiction, I hope to show how, by using such projections, Arab novelists may be seen as providing ready, exemplary illustrations of power and corruption from previous eras as a means of expressing what is inexpressible through more direct and forthright means, at least until the as yet uncertain liberating effects of the uprisings of 2011.

Literature in Arab Social and Political Life

Literature has always played a central role in Arab social and political life, from the times of the tribal traditions reflected in pre-Islamic poetry to the defiant proclamation of the contemporary poet Adunis (born ca. 1930), "Hadha huwa-smi" ("This Is My Name"). While Suzanne Stetkevych has provided us with a superb study of the prevalent tradition of panegyric (*madh*) poetry in the premodern era as an example of gift exchange as theorized by Marcel Mauss (1966), Muhammad Loutfi Yousfi (2006) has more controversially seen the relationship of patron to poet in a more negative light. We can provide an illustration of the vagaries of this kind of relationship between literature and power by noting that when the renowned Hamdanid ruler of Aleppo Sayf al-Dawla (916–67) won a glorious victory against the Byzantines at the Battle of al-Hadath (954), the great Arab poet al-Mutanabbi, never known for either his modesty or his subtlety, recited a ringing ode in his patron's honor, but toward the end the poet reminds this Arab ruler of certain realities, "To you belongs the praise for the pearl that I am to pronounce / You have provided it, but I am the one to string it."

The modern Arab poet has also been called upon to sing praises of authority figures. I was in attendance at a very equivocal occasion during the 1988 Marbid Festival in Baghdad and Basra, when a succession of Arab poets, including the Sudanese Muhammad al-Fayturi (born ca. 1930), the Syrian Nizar al-Qabbani (1923–98)—who had earlier written a stinging condemnation of the Arab peoples in his poem "'Ala hamish daftar al-naksa" (On the Margins of the Notebook on the [June 1967] "Setback")—and the Kuwaiti Su'ad al-Sabah, all recited stirring poems in praise of Saddam Hussein, following the ouster of Iranian forces from the Faw Peninsula earlier in the same year. Su'ad al-Sabah presumably had reason to reconsider her stance when Iraqi forces invaded her homeland just two years later.

Within this broader context of the relationship of the Arab writer to power, its uses, and abuses, the historical novel has come to play a variety of roles, in line, one might say, with the various categories and functions illustrated by the works of Scott, Tolstoy, and others and categorized by Cowart. Thus, the pioneer series of novels by Jurji Zaydan (1861–1914), for example, aim at one and the same time to entertain and educate, part of the author's clear agenda to serve as a major participant in the arousal of a new sense of Arab identity and nationalist sentiment through his magazine, *al-Hilal*, in which he published in serial form not only his historical novels but also studies on Islamic history and Arabic language and literature.[2] These works of Zaydan, and the writings of his immediate Lebanese predecessor Salim al-Bustani (1848–84) (Holt 2009; Halevy and Zachs 2007), provided the model for a whole trend in historical novel writing, notably in Egypt but a pattern repeated in other regions of the Arab world. In the 1930s, for example, the young Najib Mahfuz (Naguib

2. A list of English translations of his novels is provided in the "Sources Cited" section. The Zaidan Foundation has also published a volume of studies devoted to his career (Zaidan and Philipp 2013).

Mahfouz [1911–2006]), already imbued with a love for ancient Egypt by his mother and their regular visits to the Egyptian Museum, first translated a work on the ancient history of his country (Baikie 1912) into Arabic (Baikie 1932) and then composed three historical novels set in the distant past. While these works may be considered contributions to what has been termed the "Pharaonism" movement in the country—a reflection of increasing national pride bolstered by the discovery of Tutankhamon's tomb in 1922—it was suggested that the second of them, *Radubis*, was a questionably subtle attack on the womanizing proclivities of King Faruq (Mahfuz 1942, 2003). However, it was the cataclysmic event of June 1967, the so-called *al-naksa* (setback), that transformed attitudes toward the past in the Arabic-speaking world and modes of engaging with it. In the 1970s, the terms *turath* (heritage) and *asala* (cultural authenticity) became almost buzzwords among those intellectuals who sought to analyze the contemporary Arab world's relationship to its past and thus the most appropriate responses to the developments and mistakes of recent decades (Boullata 1990). It was into this fraught environment that the Egyptian novelist Jamal al-Ghitani (1945–2015) inserted his pathbreaking work of historical fiction, *Al-Zayni Barakat*, a novel that, for the purposes of my current discussion, seems to mark the first unequivocally clear example of Cowart's fourth category of historical novel, "fictions whose authors project the present into the past." Like Mahfuz in his novel *Al-Karnak* (1974, 2007), al-Ghitani is using his work to "look back in anger," in this case to the atmosphere of terror during the 1960s in Egypt created by the ubiquitous presence of the secret police. However, while Mahfuz situates his narrative in the time period in question, al-Ghitani invokes history and historical texts not only by citing the work of an Egyptian historian, Ibn Iyas (1448–1524), about the period immediately before the Ottoman invasion of Egypt in 1516 and, most especially, about the spy system established by the *muhtasib* of Cairo, the upholder of public morality, who lends his name to the novel's title, but also by composing his own pastiches of official proclamations and accounts from a Venetian traveler (Mehrez 1994, chaps. 3–5).

Ben Salim Himmich, Ahmad al-Tawfiq, and the Arab Spring

And so, from revolutions and uprisings, via history, historical fiction, and the Arabic historical novel, I now come to the specific examples that I have selected from the Moroccan tradition.[3] I am focusing here on the works of two Moroccan novelists, who—typical of Moroccan contributors to the genre—are also prominent academics, intellectuals, and participants in the cultural life of the country: Bin Salim Himmish (Bensalem Himmich [b. 1948]) and Ahmad al-Tawfiq (Ahmed Toufiq [b. 1943]).[4] Al-Tawfiq's two novels are both set in premodern Morocco, although the precise time period is never defined; Himmich's scenarios are spread over a much wider geographical range, and indeed two of them—devoted to the historical figures of Ibn Khaldun (already noted) and Ibn Sab'in (1217–69), arguably one of the most controversial figures in medieval Islam[5]—are peripatetic characters forced to travel across the breadth of North Africa, as

3. It is as well for me to admit at this juncture that I have translated into English all the novels that I will be discussing.

4. Himmich is a scholar of the philosophy of history, a poet, and a novelist who has taught at the Muhammad V University in Rabat. From 2009 to 2011, he served as minister of culture in Morocco. Ahmad al-Tawfiq specializes in the premodern history of Morocco and, in particular, in the edition of significant texts in the spheres of religion and history, most noticeably the *Dala'il al-khayrat* of al-Jazuli (1404–65). Having previously served as director of the National Library in Morocco, since 2002 he has held the position of minister of religious affairs and endowments.

5. An indication of the nature of his influence may be seen in the comment of the renowned Muslim theologian Ibn Taymiyya (1263–1328), who assesses Ibn Sab'in's impact in the following terms: "Ibn Sab'in was more knowledgeable about philosophy than Ibn al-'Arabi. In theology, both of them sought information from the same source, namely al-Juwayni, the author of the *Irshad*, and his followers, such as al-Razi. Ibn Sab'in was a major heterodox figure, a polytheist and magician. He was by far the brightest and cleverest of them all, and the most knowledgeable in matters of philosophy and philosophical Sufism" (Ibn Taymiyya, *Al-Rasa'il wa-l-masa'il* [Epistles and Questions], quoted in Himmich 2007, 502; Himmich 2011, 389).

their confrontations with power and corruption, not to mention the upholders of Islamic orthodoxy who are primary supporters of both, place them in continuous jeopardy.

With the events of Tahrir Square in Cairo during 2011 and into 2012 in mind, Himmich's novel *Majnun al-hukm* (1989), the English version of which I originally wanted to call "Power Crazy," but which eventually emerged as *The Theocrat* (2005), can be easily read, as its title readily suggests, as a historical narrative passing comment on the nature and abuse of power. In this case, the ruler in question is the Fatimid caliph al-Hakim bi-Amr Allah (r. 996–1021), who governed Egypt during the century of the three caliphates—the Abbasids in Baghdad, the Fatimids in Cairo, and the Umayyads in Cordoba. The Druze community, named after Muhammad al-Durzi, a follower of al-Hakim who took his devotees from Egypt to the mountains of Syria, believes that the caliph went into occultation and will return. However, historical accounts and Himmich's novel strongly suggest that such was the oppressive nature of al-Hakim's rule—he ordered, for example, that all Egyptians should work by night and sleep by day, he banned the consumption of *mulukhiyya* (one of Egypt's most typical dishes) and the performance of the hajj pilgrimage, and he forbade women to leave the house—he was actually assassinated on the orders of his sister, Sitt al-Mulk (970–1023), who assumed power following his disappearance or demise in the name of the young successor, who, in line with Fatimid predilections for lengthy names, adopted the title "al-Zahir li-I'zaz Din Allah" (r. 1023–36). Himmich's novel gives a full account of these and other abuses of power, and indeed of the ruler's clearly bipolar or schizophrenic condition, but a large segment of the novel (and of historical accounts of his reign) is given over to the uprising against him that was led by the figure known as "Abu Rukwa," that being the nickname of a scion of the Umayyad family who succeeded in organizing the discontented tribes in the coastal region of what is now Libya and proceeded to march on Cairo, scoring a number of significant victories on the way, before being finally defeated near Giza in 1006 at the hands of an army composed largely of mercenaries, the hiring of whom substantially emptied the Egyptian treasury. Himmich's account of the gruesome death of the leader of this revolt and his followers at the hands of "the ruler in God's name" (the literal translation of the Fatimid caliph's name) concludes with the following words: "Dear children of mine . . . , take my place. . . . Turn your lives into a weapon with which to confront the enemies of love and knowledge. Never submit or throw down your arms. Keep yourselves forever alert and ready for action. Resist, and victory will be yours; resist and resist again with all your might" (1989, 181; 2005, 150).

If those ringing words pronounced in eleventh-century Cairo are not seen as having any contemporary relevance, we can point to the fact that the sardonic masterpiece by Palestinian novelist Emil Habibi (1922–96), with the improbably long title *Al-Waqa'i' al-ghariba f-ikhtifa' Sa'id Abi al-Nahs al-mutasha'il* (*The Secret Life of Saeed the Pessoptimist*), has a specific reference to this revolt: "A thousand years ago our leader Abu Rukwa . . . saw that his sultan, who bore the title Governor by Right of God, was ruling with tyranny. . . . [He] did not feel helpless and wait for the people to become fit to fight. He adopted the title Rebel by Right of God and conquered with power" (1977, 102; 1982, 77). Habibi's novel is, in fact, replete with references to history, as he makes masterful use of the events of the past, and in particular a wide variety of leadership figures, to paint his unforgettable picture of the Palestinian and wider Arab present.

I have already drawn attention to the relevance of Himmich's novel *Al-'Allama* to the question of historiography and fiction. However, in conjunction with his more recent work *Hadha l-Andalusi*, it emerges as a powerful commentary on the negative impact of a fractured Dar al-Islam (Abode of Islam) and those individuals who exercise power within it on the daily lives of people and on the multifarious ways in which the exercise of that power is in constant confrontation with values of religious belief and justice. In the thirteenth and fourteenth centuries, both Ibn Sab'in and Ibn Khaldun found themselves forced to confront the demise of Muslim control over the Iberian Peninsula, as inept rulers, moral decay, and rampant corruption allowed the encroaching Christian forces to capture more and more territory, until only Granada remained, itself to fall in 1492. In Himmich's novel, Ibn Sab'in responds in fury to the suggestion of his own brother that he cooperate with the Banu Hud, the dynasty that controls the region around his native city of Murcia:

> The symptoms are many, but the illness is one and the same: favoritism, cronyism, and dissipation at the top; grand larceny and corruption on the broadest conceivable scale, and lastly letting the culprits off scot-free, a surefire sign of support for the ongoing series of disasters we are suffering. When it comes to sheer shame, just take a look around you. You'll find politicians and notables who personify the present crisis. In return for all this, they proceed to hand over Muslim property and land to the enemy. . . . Your companions have corrupted political life by distorting it, transforming it into something cheap and nasty for barter. When it comes to warfare, any sensible person can tell that it's the populace that ends up suffering hardships. (2007, 91–92; 2011, 69–70)

Ibn Khaldun escaped from the political intrigues of the various potentates of North Africa by returning to the Andalusian domains that his ancestors had left earlier and by joining the court of the Nasrid ruler of Granada Muhammad V. From there he was sent (in 1364) on a delicate diplomatic mission to the court of Pedro "the Cruel," king of Castile, in Seville, to finalize a peace treaty. Such was his repute as a scholar and statesman that he found himself having to turn down the offer of a position at the Christian king's court. Returned once again to Granada, he soon found himself in a situation typical of what Ibn Sab'in had faced earlier, in that he fell out with another illustrious courtier and littérateur at the Nasrid court, Ibn al-Khatib (1313–74), nicknamed Lisan al-Din (Tongue of the Faith), and was sent back to North Africa.

The breakdown of authority and accompanying corruption that led to the loss of Andalusia was, of course, a calamity for both the Muslim and the Jewish communities in the Iberian Peninsula (and at the same time the beginning of a dark era in that region's history), but the issues of the abuse of power and corruption that it illustrates were symptomatic of a social and political phenomenon of a much broader kind. Himmich's novels about these two prominent intellectuals who involved themselves in the political events of their times go on to describe their travels to the east across the breadth of North Africa. Passing through the domains controlled by various dynasties, they both arrive in Cairo, where, albeit one century apart, they have to adapt themselves to situations in which governmental tyranny and the intransigence of religious authorities seem to be the norm. In Ibn Sab'in's case, his arrival in Cairo coincides with the defeat of the so-called seventh Crusade, led by King Louis IX of France (r. 1226–70), at the hands of the Mamluks of the Ayyubid ruler, Turanshah, and notably his general Baybars. Viewed by the local religious leaders in Cairo as a dire threat to Muslim orthodoxy, Ibn Sab'in is soon hounded out of the city, as he has been previously from Murcia, Sabta, Béjaïa, and Tunis, and travels to Mecca. His sojourn in Islam's holiest city, where he performs the rituals of the pilgrimage several times and gathers clusters of devotees, is punctuated by dire news of the ever-encroaching force of the Mongol armies under Genghis Khan and the threat that they pose to virtually every corrupt potentate in Islam's traditional centers of power. However, once the Mongols are thrown back after the battle of 'Ayn Jalut (Goliath's Spring) in 1260, the victorious Mamluk commander, the very same al-Zahir Baybars, is portrayed in Himmich's novel as coming to Mecca to perform the pilgrimage, at the same time eager to rid Islam of all traces of heterodoxy. Ibn Sab'in's radical and completely unusual response is, according to several historical accounts and Himmich's novel, to commit suicide inside the Ka'ba itself.

With Ibn Khaldun, the period in Cairo—more than a century later—coincides with the second period in power of the Mamluk sultan Barquq (1390–99). The polymath historian is regularly appointed as Maliki judge (*qadi*) of the city, only to be dismissed when he refuses to make compromises on the basis of political expediency; as soon as he declares his desire to return to his native Maghrib, he finds himself reappointed, and it is in Cairo that he dies in 1406. Before his death, however, the period also coincides with the threat of another invasion from the East, that of Timur Lang (Tamerlane). Barquq's successor, his son al-Nasir Faraj, leads a Mamluk force to oppose the ever-advancing Mongol army, but Ibn Khaldun's own autobiographical text, *Al-Ta'rif bi-Ibn Khaldun wa-rihlatihi gharban wa-sharqan* (Acquaintance with Ibn Khaldun and His Travels East and West), makes it clear that the Mongol leader specifically asks that the eminent historian be the one to negotiate the surrender of the city of Damascus. In Himmich's novel, the two old men meet and discuss matters of cultural confrontation, but they finish their conversation by ruing the fact that their much younger wives are so far distant. Thus does fiction at least allow a little human touch to insert its way into accounts of such momentous moments of history.

Himmich thus makes use of actual historical figures and accounts of their lives, penned by both the figures themselves and their contemporaries, to illustrate to his contemporary readers any number of aspects of power, tyranny, oppression, corruption, and, equally important, the co-optation by such rulers of one particular and reactionary notion of orthodoxy for a continuous conflict with the forces of radical change and intellectual debate. Himmich's geographical canvas regularly includes part of his native Maghrib but, as I have noted in my brief discussions of his novels, spreads far beyond that region toward the east.

His countryman Ahmad al-Tawfiq, a specialist in the philology of texts dealing with Moroccan history and religion, prefers to set his novels in the particular environment of premodern Morocco, but their message concerning authority and corruption is, I would suggest, no less cogent for this particularity. His most famous novel is *Jarat Abi Musa* (Abu Musa's Women Neighbors), a work that, in addition to its rich content of local historical and folkloric detail, focuses primarily on the utterly corrupt regime of one Jarmun, governor of the port of Salé, the ancient city that sits directly opposite the present capital city of Rabat at the mouth of the Abu Riqraq River (Tawfiq 1997, 2006). One might suggest that al-Tawfiq teases the reader, in that the title raises the interesting question as to the identity of the person named Abu Musa and indeed why, in a society like Morocco in whatever period, the narrative should be concerned with his female neighbors.[6] In another interesting narrative strategy, we learn the identity and significance of this figure only late in the novel's sequence, the earlier part being taken up by the intrigues of the governor; his passion for the beautiful and accomplished Shama, who is married to a Spanish-born Muslim artisan, 'Ali Sancho; and the extortionate taxes that the governor exacts from the merchant community of Salé, the port being a significant trading post with Andalusia and the Mediterranean during this period. From a historical perspective, if one asks "Which period?" the narrative does not tell us; it begins simply with the phrase "In those days." However, those readers familiar with the premodern history of Morocco—as, of course, al-Tawfiq himself is—may be able to glean from the account of the naval disaster that occurs during the reign of one particular sultan in Fez and his replacement by his son that we are dealing with the Marinid dynasty in the fourteenth century. Jarmun's exactions from the citizens of Salé are reported to the distant capital city, and the arrival of an official decree ordering him to desist from his unjust exactions is accompanied by a drought that is brought to an end only when the mysterious figure of Abu Musa, a Sufi hermit who has taken a number of divorced and abandoned women under his protection, leads them out of the city to perform an elaborate and highly unusual Sufi *dhikr.* Thus, quite apart from the wonderful illustration that this novel provides of patterns of mercantile trade and the special ties between Morocco, the Iberian Peninsula, and the ports of the Mediterranean Sea, the ability of central authority to control events and practices over a large area, and the tyranny and corruption that emerge from a failure to maintain that authority, is a clear object lesson from this narrative. One is reminded here of the fact that, for most of premodern Moroccan history, the regions

6. I insert this strategy into the title of my English translation, duly envious of French, which has the specific feminine form *voisines*. I should also note here that the novel was turned into a famous film of the same name, directed by Mohamed Abderrahman Tazi (2003).

beyond the capital cities (and there were more than one of them) were known as *bilad al-siba* (recalcitrant regions).

The very same issue of central authority, its modes of operation, and their efficiency or lack thereof is also the theme of another of al-Tawfiq's novels, *Shujayrat hinna' wa-qamar* (The Moon and the Henna Tree) (1998, 2013). In this novel, the capital city of Fez, where the sultan resides, is remote; we are indeed in the *bilad al-siba*, the nonurban hinterland. As part of that process, we are introduced to two stereotypically negative characters: Hmmu, the venal and gullible son of a much-beloved father and authority figure who, after journeying to Fez to curry favor with the sultan, is duly appointed as his father's successor (*caid*) of the lower mountainous regions,[7] and his Machiavellian counselor, Ibn al-Zara. The contrast between father and son as authority figures, presaging the disastrous regime that is to make up the major topic of the novel, is vividly expressed in the opening chapter: "What concerned the father specially was his son, Hmmu, who by now was middle-aged. To his father he seemed particularly fond of owning things, exerting authority, showing off, and sating his desires, even in matters of marriage and divorce. 'Ulla [the father] was his complete opposite, in that throughout his entire life the only land he had ever owned was a small enclosed garden in which he grew lucern grass for his cow" (1998, 7). With the new *caid* showing a cluster of such authoritarian instincts that are readily susceptible to manipulation, Ibn al-Zara, the former slave trader and now majordomo to Hmmu, is able to implement his schemes. The *caid*'s primary goal is to subdue

7. This example of father-son succession may be seen perhaps as an echo of recent trends in the Arab world. It produced the Egyptian joke that noted that the Arab world seemed to have two primary systems of government: the republican form, known as *jumhuriyya*, and the monarchical form, known as *mamlaka*. In recent times, however, a new form had emerged, *jam-laka*—something like "republarchy," whereby, even in an allegedly republican system, sons succeeded their fathers—as with Bashar al-Assad and, before the 2011 uprisings, Gamal Mubarak.

the tribes of the surrounding regions, the plains and the high Atlas mountains. The implementation begins with construction of an enormous prison, but Ibn al-Zara's alleged master stroke exploits one particular aspect of Hmmu's character, namely, "marriage and divorce." The rival sheikhs are forced to agree to the marriage of one of their daughters to the *caid*, the hope being that the rivalry among the wives can be manipulated to his advantage in dealing with their fathers. Matters, however, turn out otherwise: the daughter-wives become the closest of friends and visit the compounds of each other's parents; Hmmu is hauled before the authorities in Fez for illegal land grabs and is eventually assassinated by a combined force made up of the sons of both the plains and the mountains, who have come together to rid themselves of this corrupt tyrant.

Inept rulers, warring factions, co-optation of reactionary religious figures, venality, corruption, and sexual perversion—these historical novels provide their readers with instances of all these traits from previous centuries, whether based in history or folklore, traits that, along with Ibn Khaldun's cycles of social and political transformation, seem to offer, to cite an expression oft used in *Alf layla wa-layla*, *'ibrah li-man ya'tabir*, an object lesson to whoever wishes to learn from it.

It is worth mentioning that Himmich's most recent novel is in some ways historical, but not set in the remote or even near-distant past. Entitled *Mu'adhdhibati* (*My Torturess*), its primary topic is what has been termed "extraordinary rendition," using typically complex and ambiguous terminology to describe what is illegal and appalling (2010, 2015). In it, a Moroccan bookseller is "rendered" to a prison camp in an unknown location and country, where he is interrogated, brutally tortured, and detained for six years, all in the belief that he has information about his jihadist cousin. This work too, of course, involves the illegal exercise of authority, and the novel makes clear which nation it is whose policies toward the identification of so-called terrorists is behind the measures that are described in such gruesome detail.

Conclusion: The Contribution of Novels to Historical Reflection

Earlier I mentioned the novels of Walter Scott. The most famous of them is, of course, *Ivanhoe*, which is set during the time of the Crusades—a series of events in premodern times, accounts of which have until relatively recently been totally distorted by the biases of that very category of historians who are castigated by Tolstoy. Thus, while Scott's novel and the legend of the swashbuckling Robin Hood both paint a picture of King Richard as a great hero and Christian warrior, and of his brother King John as a ruthless tyrant who terrorizes the citizenry of England, a more reasoned account points out, on the one hand, that it is King John who signs the Magna Carta in 1215—imposing restrictions on the power and authority of the monarch—and, on the other hand, that it is King Richard who slaughters his Muslim prisoners at Acre, while the Muslim commander Şalah al-Din (Saladin) adheres to the pact that he thought he had made with the Christian king by releasing his Crusader prisoners to Richard. The contributions to this topic penned by Amin Maalouf (1984), Carole Hillenbrand (1999), and Paul Cobb (2014), among others, provide an entirely different picture of that centuries-long series of conflicts—duly reflected in some of the historical novels that are cited in this study—a picture that continues to resonate to this day in intracultural and intercultural confrontations. History, historians, and the historical novel are all inevitably affected by external factors, as Tolstoy reminds us at length. However, as Oscar Wilde wisely instructs us, there is always the need to rewrite and rethink in the light of subsequent historical events and the study of them. The novels that I have described here can be seen, I would suggest, as ongoing contributions to that process.

Sources Cited

Allen, Roger. 1995. "Arabic Fiction and the Quest for Freedom." Festschrift for M. M. Badawi. *Journal of Arabic Literature* 26 (1–2): 37–49.

———. 1997. "Translation Translated: Rashīd Abū Jadrah's *Ma'rakat al-Zuqāq*." *Oriente Moderno* 16 (2–3): 165–76.

———. 2006. "Lords of Misrule: History and Fiction in Two Moroccan Novels." *Middle Eastern Literatures* 9 (2): 199–209.

———. 2008. "Historiography as Novel: Bensalem Himmich's *Al-'Allamah*." In *Transforming Loss into Beauty: Essays on Arabic Literature and Culture in Honor of Magda al-Nowaihi*, edited by Marlé Hammond and Dana Sajdi, 269–80. Cairo: American Univ. in Cairo Press.

Anderson, Perry. 2012. "The Force of the Anomaly." *London Review of Books* 34 (8): 3–13.

Baikie, James. 1912. *Ancient Egypt*. London: A. and C. Black.

———. 1932. *Misr al-qadima*. Translated by Najib Mahfuz. Cairo: Maktabat Misr.

Boullata, Issa J. 1990. *Trends and Issues in Contemporary Arab Thought*. Albany: State Univ. of New York Press.

Cobb, Paul M. 2014. *The Race for Paradise: An Islamic History of the Crusades*. Oxford: Oxford Univ. Press.

Cowart, David. 1989. *History and the Contemporary Novel*. Carbondale: Southern Illinois Univ. Press.

Daiches, David. 1998. Foreword to *Ivanhoe*, by Sir Walter Scott. Edited by Graham Tulloch. Edinburgh: Edinburgh Univ. Press.

Frey, James. 2004. *A Million Little Pieces*. New York: Random House.

Friend, Theodore. 2011. "The Arab Uprisings of 2011." *Foreign Policy Research Institute* (July).

Habibi, Emil. 1977. *Al-Waqa'i' al-ghariba f-ikhtifa' Sa'id Abi 'l-Nahs al-mutasha'il*. Jerusalem: Manshurat Salah al-Din.

———. 1982. *The Secret Life of Saeed the Pessoptimist*. Translated by Salma Jayyusi and Trevor Le Gassick. New York: Vantage Press.

Halevy, Sharon, and Fruma Zachs. 2007. "*Asma* (1873): The Early Arabic Novel as a Social Compass." *Studies in the Novel* 39 (4): 416–30.

Hillenbrand, Carole. 1999. *The Crusades: Islamic Perspectives*. Chicago: Fitzroy Dearborn.

Himmich, Ben Salem. 1989. *Majnun al-hukm*. Rabat: Dar al-Aman.

———. 2005. *The Theocrat*. Translated by Roger Allen. Cairo: American Univ. in Cairo Press.

———. 2007. *Hadha l-Andalusi*. Beirut: Dar al-Adab.

———. 2010. *Muʻadhdhibati*. Cairo: Dar al-Shuruq.

———. 2011. *A Muslim Suicide*. Translated by Roger Allen. Syracuse: Syracuse Univ. Press.

———. 2015. *My Torturess*. Translated by Roger Allen. Syracuse: Syracuse Univ. Press.

Holt, Elizabeth. 2009. "Narrative and the Reading Public in 1870s Beirut." *Journal of Arabic Literature* 40 (1): 37–70.

Jauss, Robert. 1982. *Toward an Aesthetic of Reception*. Minneapolis: Univ. of Minnesota Press.

Maalouf, Amin. 1984. *The Crusades through Arab Eyes*. New York: Schocken Books.

Mahfuz, Najib. 1942. *Radubis*. Cairo: Maktabat Misr.

———. 1962. *Al-Summan wa-al-Kharif* [Autumn Quail]. Cairo: Maktabat Misr.

———. 1974 (written in 1971). *Al-Karnak*. Cairo: Maktabat Mişr.

———. 2003. *Rhadopis of Nubia*. Translated by Anthony Calderbank. Cairo: American Univ. in Cairo Press.

———. 2007. *Karnak Café*. Translated by Roger Allen. Cairo: American Univ. in Cairo Press.

Mauss, Marcel. 1966. *The Gift: Forms and Functions of Exchange in Archaic Societies*. Translated by Ian Cunnison. London: Cohen and West.

Mehrez, Samia. 1994. *Egyptian Writers between History and Fiction*. Cairo: American Univ. in Cairo Press.

Ong, Walter. 1991. *Orality and Literacy: The Technologizing of the Word*. London: Routledge.

Shields, David. 2010. *Reality Hunger: A Manifesto*. New York: Alfred A. Knopf.

Shukri, Muhammad. 1973. *For Bread Alone*. Translated by Paul Bowles. London: Peter Owen.

———. 1982. *Al-Khubz al-hafi*. Beirut and London: Dar Saqi.

Tawfiq, Ahmad al-. 1997. *Jarat Abi Musa*. Marrakesh: Dar al-Qubba al-Zarqa'.

———. 1998. *Shujayrat hinna' wa-qamar*. Marrakesh: Dar al-Qubba al-Zarqa'.

———. 2006. *Abu Musa's Women Neighbors*. Translated by Roger Allen. Sausalito, CA: Post-Apollo Press.

———. 2013. *Moon and Henna Tree*. Translated by Roger Allen. Austin: Univ. of Texas Press.

Tolstoy, Graf Leo. 1934–37. *War and Peace*. Planet PDF version.

White, Hayden. 1973. *Metahistory: The Historical Imagination in Nineteenth-Century Europe*. Baltimore: Johns Hopkins Univ. Press.

———. 1978. *Tropics of Discourse: Essays in Cultural Criticism*. Baltimore: Johns Hopkins Univ. Press.

———. 2010. *The Fiction of Narrative: Essays on History, Literature, and Theory, 1957–2007*. Baltimore: Johns Hopkins Univ. Press.

Yousfi, Muhammad Lutfi. 2006. "Poetic Creativity in the Sixteenth to Eighteenth Centuries." In *Arabic Literature in the Post-Classical Period*, edited by Roger Allen and D. S. Richards, 60–73. Cambridge History of Arabic Literature. Cambridge: Cambridge Univ. Press.

Zaidan, George C., and Thomas Philipp, eds. 2013. *Jurji Zaidan's Contributions to Modern Arab Thought and Literature*. Bethesda, MD: Zaidan Foundation.

Zaydan, Jurji. 2010. *The Conquest of Andalusia*. Translated by Roger Allen. Bethesda, MD: Zaidan Foundation.

———. 2012a. *The Battle of Poitiers: Charles Martel and 'Abd al-Rahman*. Translated by William Granara. Bethesda, MD: Zaidan Foundation.

———. 2012b. *The Caliph's Heirs: Brothers at War: The Fall of Baghdad*. Translated by Michael Cooperson. Bethesda, MD: Zaidan Foundation.

———. 2012c. *The Caliph's Sister: Harun al-Rashid and the Fall of the Persians*. Translated by Issa J. Boullata. Bethesda, MD: Zaidan Foundation.

———. 2012d. *Saladin and the Assassins*. Translated by Paul Starkey. Bethesda, MD: Zaidan Foundation.

———. 2012e. *Tree of Pearls, Queen of Egypt*. Translated by Samah Selim. Syracuse, NY: Syracuse Univ. Press.

14

From Sayed Darwish to MC Sadat

Sonic Cartographies of the Egyptian Uprising

TED SWEDENBURG

> The uprising was a golden hour of poetry and songs (both old and new) that expressed the spirit of defiance and faith in a different life.
>
> —Samuli Schielke, *Egypt in the Future Tense: Hope, Frustration, and Ambivalence before and after 2011*

"Carnivalesque" is how numerous observers and participants have described the atmosphere at Cairo's Tahrir Square during the eighteen-day occupation, from January 25 to February 11, 2011, that led to President Hosni Mubarak's ouster—besides, of course, depicting it variously as riotous, sad, inspiring, violent, and terrifying. During the second week of the protest, as demonstrators established themselves on the square, they set up stages in various locations. From these platforms, activists delivered speeches, artists performed or read their works, and loudspeakers broadcast announcements and ballads of revolution. Numerous musicians, able now to play freely

Portions of this chapter were published in Ted Swedenburg, "Egypt's Music of Protest, from Sayyid Darwish to DJ Haha," in *Middle East Research and Information Project (MERIP)*, no. 265 (Winter 2012), © Middle East Research and Information Project.

on the square for the first time in fifty years (Sanders and Visonà 2012, 216), descended there along with other protesters, to perform on stage and to wander through the crowds like minstrels, singing favorites for groups large and small. Some artists composed new tunes for the occasion. For the most part, the musicians of the insurrection were not famous or even very well known, other than within specialist scenes. Music, performed and recorded, was an essential part of the raucous Tahrir scene, and sound played a crucial role in the construction of an insurrectionary social and political space (see Revill 2000).

Tahrir participants and activists used cellphones and other devices to record major and minor artistic performances. They uploaded their footage onto mainstream media websites as well as social media platforms, particularly YouTube. Meanwhile, news media from around the world also recorded and broadcast the sounds of the occupation. In addition, during the sit-in and in its immediate wake, a number of musicians, ranging from the amateur to the highly professional, in Egypt as well as abroad, produced "revolutionary" music videos (known locally as "video clips") that were broadcast on YouTube and satellite television.

Since the unfolding of the momentous events of 2011, a number of writers—academics, bloggers, journalists, and the like—have documented and analyzed the key songs and most important artists of the Tahrir scene, as well as the musical trends that emerged post–sit-in. Here I survey and map some of the most important musical tendencies of the days of insurrection. I also discuss musical varieties that were not part of the square's sonic mix, some of which—in particular *mahraganat*—subsequently emerged into more general visibility and audibility owing to the social ruptures caused by the insurrection. I am interested, then, not just in the sonic community forged at Tahrir but also in its boundaries and in what sorts of sounds were mostly absent or excluded from the insurgent space. Finally, I briefly assess the status of Egyptian "revolutionary music" since the events of the summer of 2013 and the rise of the Sisi counterrevolution.

Recovered and Recoded Patriotic Heritage

The protest music at Tahrir was integrally tied to and embedded within the social movement. Musicians typically performed a repertoire that crowds could sing along with, choosing from a body of songs that connected the artists and their audience to a history of national struggle. The purpose of musical performance at Tahrir was to move the crowds (and the musicians themselves) into an appropriate sentimental or affective state, whether of anger, mourning, nostalgia, or patience, or to unify the crowds in the kind of group feeling that Durkheim (1995 [1912]) called "collective effervescence." The meanings of a song played on the square were not simply already inherent in the lyrics and melody or in the associated memories and resonances, but also forged in performance at charged political moments.[1]

Official patriotic songs from the "golden" days of nationalism, that is, the high point of Nasserism in the 1950s and 1960s, played an important role in fostering a sense of unity on the square. These were typically nationalistic songs recorded and performed by popular and revered singers like Abdel Halim Hafez, Umm Kulthum, and Shadia, songs that enjoyed an official imprimatur during the fifties and sixties and whose lyrics were typically penned by state-approved poets, such as Salah Jaheen (Sanders and Visonà 2012, 222; El-Saket 2011).[2] By the time of the 2011 insurgency, however, the popular currency of such songs had faded, and so performers reworked them so as to emphasize the importance of "the people" in the national struggle (Sanders and Visonà 2012, 226). Such numbers represented a culture that had gone out of style in official circles during the Mubarak era, owing to a prevailing neoliberal ethos that was critical of the revolutionary Arab socialist era that lasted from the 1950s to the early 1970s. To revive the patriotic songs of the likes

1. These observations are critically informed by Colla (n.d.).

2. Prince's diary (2014) of the Tahrir days frequently references this repertoire.

of Abdel Halim was to push against the official mind-set, as well as to assert present-day connections to an era when, at least in popular memory for many on the square, the Egyptian people had been united in opposition to the forces of colonialism and imperialism, as in the resistance to the Tripartite Aggression of 1956.

Dating from an earlier era of national mobilization, the nationalistic songs of Sayed Darwish (1892–1923) were also revived on Tahrir—sung by musicians or broadcast over loudspeakers, with the throngs enthusiastically joining in. This repertoire gave insurrectionists a sense of being actors who were part of a long, revered heritage of patriotic protest. Singer and composer Darwish is celebrated for having modernized Egyptian song in the early twentieth century and is especially remembered for tunes he wrote during the 1919 revolution against British occupation, as well as others expressing nationalist themes. (The respected poet Badi' Khayri composed the lyrics for most of these Darwish songs.) Among Sayed Darwish's most memorable patriotic compositions are "'Um Ya Masri" (Rise, O Egyptian) and "Biladi, Biladi" (My Country, My Country), which became Egypt's national anthem. Another is "Salma ya Salama" (Welcome Back to Safety), about the million-plus Egyptians recruited, often by force, to assist in Britain's war effort during World War I, many shipped off to serve outside the country. The song articulates the yearning of exiles abroad for the beloved homeland. Several Egyptian music groups present on the square that belong to the country's so-called underground scene (discussed below)—Eskenderella, Cairokee, and Wust El Balad—were notable for doing numbers from the Sayed Darwish songbook.[3] The canonically trained blind singer and *oud* (lute) virtuoso Mustafa Said, who gained fame at Tahrir for putting to music the words of Tamim al-Barghouti's famous poem "Ya Masr Hanet wa Banet" (O Egypt, It's So Close), was also known for his performance of songs by Darwish (Valassopoulos and Mostafa 2014, 656).

3. Montasser (2011) gives an account of an Eskenderella performance on the square during the occupation.

Another song from the revolutionary repertoire is Sayyid Darwish's "Ahu Da Illi Sar," variously translated as "This Is What Happened," "So It Goes," and "This Is Where We're At." "Ahu Da Illi Sar" has remained in the popular repertoire in Egypt for the same reason, and it has been recorded and performed by numerous prominent Egyptian and Arab artists since it was first composed, probably around 1919. The song was apparently not composed for any of Darwish's operettas—but it sounds like it could have been. Probably the most well-known performances of "Ahu Da Illi Sar" from the days of the Egyptian uprising were by the "alternative" rock band Massar Egbari, which originated in Sayed Darwish's hometown of Alexandria and appears in the 2010 film about Alexandria's underground art scene, *Microphone*. One can view a very moving clip on YouTube of Massar Egbari performing "Ahu Da Illi Sar" at El Sawi Culture Wheel in Cairo on January 10, 2011, just days before the Tahrir uprising was launched. They were playing at an event held in commemoration of the victims of the bombing at a Coptic church in Alexandria on December 31, 2010, which killed twenty-one and wounded ninety-six. The attack was widely thought to be the work of Egyptian intelligence, and it was one of the precipitants of the demonstration called on January 25 that launched the eighteen-day revolution. Massar Egbari performed "Ahu Da Illi Saar" at El Sawi with a great deal of emotion. The song comes across, however, as a call to self-reflection and introspection more than as a summons into the streets. The lyrics, open to a variety of readings, include the following lines:

> This is what happened, this is what was
> You don't have the right to blame me
> The wealth of our country is not in our hands
> Egypt, O mother of wonders
> Let's link hands and fight.

While there is general consensus that "Ahu Da Illi Sar" is associated with revolutionary times and traditions of resistance, there is less agreement on what, precisely, it means. Some Egyptians I consulted stress the line "Let's link hands and fight" and assert that the song argues for unity in confronting the powers that be. Others construe it as meaning "If we were unable to do what needed to be done in the past, let's leave aside our differences now and struggle to rebuild our country." Others were particularly moved by the line "The wealth of our country is not in our hands." If the nation's riches used to be held by colonialists, the song seemed to say in early 2011, today they are in the clutches of Husni Mubarak's kleptocracy.

In addition to singing numbers by Sayed Darwish and from the officially sanctioned nationalistic songbook of the fifties and sixties, several artists on the square performed patriotic numbers from the leftist opposition, most particularly those songs made famous by Sheikh Imam (1918–95), whose main lyricist was Ahmad Fouad Negm. Sheikh Imam's tunes were iconic during the heyday of the Egyptian Left, from the late sixties to the eighties (Booth 2006). One of the most prominent players of the Sheikh Imam repertoire on the square was Azza Balba', a veteran female singer well known for her opposition to Presidents Sadat and Mubarak and for her long association with Sheikh Imam and Negm. Her performances at Tahrir returned her to the public eye after many years' absence (Valassopoulos and Mostafa 2014, 653). El Hamamsy and Soliman (2013, 253) observe that the performance of this varied repertoire represented an interesting and somewhat surprising merging or blending of two quite different musical trends, that of official (Nasserist) revolutionary ideology with its dreams of national greatness, and that of the marginal, dissenting citizen. It should be noted, finally, that the songs in question, from both trends, are typically rather straightforward nationalistic hymns, played with the aim of stirring the blood, encouraging the assembled mass to sing along, and fostering feelings of mass unity. For instance, from the "committed" repertoire, Sheikh Imam's "Ya Masr 'Umi" (Egypt, Arise), with lyrics by Naguib Shihab al-Din, is as follows:

Egypt, rise and pull yourself together (*shiddi l-hayl*)
. . . .
Now they raise their noble foreheads, free

Extending their hands to fulfill holy duty
Without a caliph or a muezzin.

(Sanders and Visonà 2012, 224)[4]

One might add to this group of songs Dalida's "Hilwa Ya Baladi" (Beautiful, My Homeland). Dalida (1933–87) was born in Egypt to Italian parents, raised in the multiethnic, working-class Cairo district of Shubra; worked in the country as an actress, singer, and model; and was crowned Miss Egypt in 1954. She went on to become a major singing star in France who recorded in not just French but also Italian, Spanish, and German, among other languages, and was immensely popular throughout the Mediterranean. In the late seventies she recorded several songs in Arabic, including Sayed Darwish's "Salma Ya Salama" as well as "Hilwa Ya Baladi." The latter is a song of nostalgic love for the country from the point of view of exile or diaspora and has been much beloved in Egypt ever since its release. Its chorus is as follows:

One lovely word, two lovely words
Beautiful, my homeland
One lovely song, two lovely songs
Beautiful, my homeland.

It too was a patriotic favorite on the square during the occupation.[5]

Folklore

Egyptian folkloric music does not enjoy the same status in official discourse as the nationalistic anthems sung by beloved neoclassical

4. Among those performers known for doing the Imam repertoire are Mustafa Said and Eskenderella.

5. Kamal Sedra posted a YouTube video showing Tahrir denizens dancing to a broadcast of "Hilwa Ya Baladi" over the loudspeakers on February 5, 2011 ("Kilma hilwa wa kilmatayn min midan al-Tahrir," https://www.youtube.com/watch?v=FLWaAf0oSgk&feature=youtu.be).

singers such as Abdel Halim or Umm Kulthum; neither does it rank as high on the cultural scale as "committed" music from the likes of Sheikh Imam. Both the neoclassical and the committed genres are considered modern, performed and valued by members of Egypt's urban, educated classes, especially in Cairo and Alexandria. Folkloric music, by contrast, is produced by Egypt's lower orders, in rural areas or in second-tier regional urban centers. Yet although it is not "modern," the music of the "folk" does hold national value as the "authentic" music of "the people."[6]

Perhaps the most prominent folkloric musical presence at the square was the group El Tanbura, a collective of musicians from the city of Port Said on the Suez Canal founded in 1988 by Zakaria Ibrahim, an amateur folklorist and singer. El Tanbura, which performs often in Cairo,[7] plays a variety of local music that developed over the past 150 years, dating back to 1859 when Port Said was first settled and when Egyptian workers conscripted by corvée to dig the canal were housed in barracks and tents. The group's music is the product of a confluence of musical traditions—brought by the migrants from their villages in the Nile Valley, music typical of the ports of the Red Sea, music enjoyed by the Europeans who lived in the city's foreign quarter until 1956, and music of the entertainers on the decks of ships passing through the canal. The genre known as *damma* developed in the early twentieth century out of the influence of a new repertoire of recorded music brought by the introduction of the gramophone (known as *aghani al-'ishq*, or love songs) and based on the dominant local tradition of Sufi songs. Another strand started to develop in the late 1930s with the introduction of the *simsimiyya*,

6. See Armbrust (1996) on the dynamic relation between the modern and the folk in Egyptian national culture.

7. El Tanbura plays regularly at El Tanbura Hall in the Abdeen district and at the El Dammah Theater for Free Arts, located downtown, under the auspices of the El Mastaba Center for Egyptian Folk Music. El Tanbura has recorded four CDs, the first issued by the Institut du Monde Arabe in Paris, and the other three issued in Egypt.

a lyre with wire strings played traditionally by fishermen and by urbanites in coffeehouses in coastal towns throughout the Red Sea area. The *simsimiyya* became the dominant instrument of the Port Said musical tradition in the wake of the 1956 Suez war, when popular demand arose for new songs appropriate for new conditions. The *tanbura*, a lyre with strings made of hair and with a deeper sound than the *simsimiyya*, was originally played in the *zar* rituals practiced by residents of Port Said who were of Sudanese and Nubian origin; it began to be introduced into the music of urban cafés and taverns around the 1940s. El Tanbura is named after the type of lyre that has its origins in the Sudanese *zar*, and it performs music that it has systematically collected and revived from the various Port Said traditions (*damma*, *simsimiyya*, *tanbura*).[8]

El Tanbura was reportedly on Tahrir Square every day during the January–February 2011 occupation, performing nationalist songs such as "In Patriotic Port Said" (*Fi Bur Sa'id al-Wataniyya*) and "O Houses of Suez" (*Ya Buyut al-Suwis*) multiple times from various stages, as well as in the street (Hamza 2011).[9] The song "In Patriotic Port Said," which El Tanbura performs in a very upbeat and celebratory manner, refers to the 1956 Suez war, known in Egypt as the Tripartite Aggression, when Israel, France, and Great Britain attacked Egypt after President Gamal Abdel Nasser nationalized the Suez Canal. When war broke out on October 29, lightly armed civilians in Port Said were able to hold off the foreign invaders in house-to-house combat. Local musical groups quickly composed songs, performed on the *simsimiyya*, to commemorate the martial success. At the time, the residents of Port Said were hailed as champions of Egypt's

8. On El Tanbura and the Port Said music scene, see Chammah 2012; Dib 2006; Elkamel 2010; Eltanbura.org n.d.; Ibrahim n.d., 2005; D. Mostafa 2013, 162–63; Out Focus 2015; Poché 1999; Ramsis 2004; Reynolds 2007, 146–50; Rinne 2005; Shiloah 1972, 22; and Stokes 2002.

9. A video of El Tanbura performances at Tahrir can be found on YouTube: https://youtu.be/J5UTl3Q-53U. "El Tanbura @ 25 january revolution," posted by Mamdouh Elkady on February 15, 2011.

anti-imperialist struggle, and the *simsimiyya* came to be identified with their fight.

In the wake of the June 1967 war, when the Israeli army occupied the eastern side of the canal, Port Said's residents were evacuated and settled in refugee camps dispersed throughout the Nile Valley; El Tanbura's song "O Houses of Suez" deals with this story. Only after the 1973 war, when Egypt regained the eastern side of the canal, were the refugees returned home. During the period of evacuation, young people from Port Said formed *simsimiyya* groups and toured the refugee camps in an effort to preserve the memory of the city and its neighborhoods. "In Patriotic Port Said" is reportedly one of the songs performed during those difficult times. It includes the following lines:

> In patriotic Port Said
> Youth of the popular resistance
> defended with virtue and virility
> And fought the army of occupation
> Congratulations, O Gamal!

The "Gamal" referred to is President Nasser, but when performed on the square in 2011, *gamal* (a noun meaning "beauty") could be understood as standing for the youth of the anti-Mubarak resistance. The song is a rousing anthem, designed to mobilize feelings of militancy and of the unity of a nation and people that includes all its citizens, not just residents of Cairo. By performing such songs, El Tanbura positioned Port Said and its distinctive musical culture, not unfamiliar to Cairenes but very different from the sonic traditions of the Nile Valley, within the national revolutionary culture staged and remembered on the square. El Tanbura also located the struggles at Tahrir within the longer history of Egyptian resistance and figured Mubarak's security forces and his *baltagiyya* (thugs) as the most recent in a series of armies of occupation.

The presence on the square of the music of the *zar*, a healing ritual that includes music and dancing and whose purpose is to propitiate spirits that have taken possession of individuals, seemed somewhat startling, at first brush, by comparison with the participation of El Tanbura. In polite and official circles, *zar* is typically regarded as an un-Islamic and primitive ritual, in part because of its East African origins. *Zar* is therefore an occult practice, mostly pursued by women of the underclass and typically behind closed doors (Van Der Linden 2015). Yet *zar* made its appearance on the square, as evidenced by at least one YouTube video dated February 6, 2011,[10] as well as the account of Helmy and Frerichs (2013). A *zar* ritual is led by a female "sheikha" or male "sheikh." At Tahrir the "sheikh" of the YouTube clip ritual wore a Santa Claus cap, an allusion, perhaps, as Helmy and Frerichs (464) suggest, to a wizard's or magician's cap. The *zar* "ritual" at Tahrir, however, was a humorous spoof, a refunctioning of "folk" culture for insurrectionary purpose. A person in the crowd feigned possession, and others clapped, played drums, and chanted "Irhal!" (Leave!) to the spirit who had afflicted the possessed person. *Irhal*, of course, was the constant refrain of the masses assembled at Tahrir, shouted vehemently to Mubarak.[11]

Ramy Essam, "Irhal!"

Ramy Essam, a rock singer from Mansoura, a city of half a million in the Egyptian Delta, joined the crowd at Tahrir with his guitar on the first days of the occupation. Essam is best known for his song "Irhal" (Leave!), which he composed on the spot out of the slogans that the assembled mass was chanting nonstop on the square: "The people want the fall of the regime," "He's leaving, we aren't leaving," and so on. One of the lines, "Kullina id wahda" (We are all one

10. The video was posted by Abubakr Mohamed ("Zar fi midan al-tahrir li-rahil Mubarak," https://youtu.be/vmui6OFgZh8) on February 6, 2011.

11. It may be the case that *zar*'s public presence has become more acceptable as it is incorporated into the acceptable "folklore" category. In particular, the El Mastaba Center for Egyptian Folk Music sponsors three *zar*-related groups: Rango, Abul Gheit Dervishes, and Asyad El Zar (http://www.el-mastaba.org/bands.html).

hand), was courtesy of the "We Are All Khaled Said" (*Kullina Khalid Sa'id*) Facebook campaign, one of the precipitants of the insurrection (Sanders and Visonà 2012, 237). Essam stitched together the rallying cries and set them to a kind of grunge acoustic guitar backing; his performance of the song was an immediate sensation and quickly earned him, via YouTube clips viewed by hundreds of thousands, a global reputation.[12] El Hamamsy and Soliman (2013, 256–57) observe that when Essam sang "Irhal!" as well as other songs from his repertoire on the square, it was as though he was leading a demonstration. He typically sang a portion of the lyrics of "Irhal!" and then fell silent, leaving the crowd to finish singing and yelling the slogan.

Western observers frequently depicted Essam as the herald of a new generation of Egyptian artists who had brought something entirely novel to national culture, as an example of how the insurrection was aiding the supersession of stale tradition. Essam saw himself, however, as connected to Egypt's revolutionary cultural heritage, and he was also noted for his performances of "Al-Gahsh 'Al li-l-Himar" (The Foal Said to the Donkey). The song's words have been attributed to Ahmad Fouad Negm, the beloved lyricist of Sheikh Imam, still alive and in his eighties at the time of the insurrection. "The Foal Said to the Donkey" is a clever satire in the form of a fable about hereditary succession, composed at a time when Hosni Mubarak was grooming his son Gamal to take over as president. The issue of Mubarak's apparent plan to have his son succeed him was one of the many issues that incited the 2011 insurrection. In the fable, the son, the foal, wants to assume the burden of pulling the cart from his father. The donkey responds that he is not ready:

The foal said to the donkey
Dad, hand me the cart
Dad, you've aged and it's my turn now

12. *Time Out* (London) in 2011 named "Irhal!" number three in its list "100 Songs That Changed History."

The donkey coughed strongly, the passengers panicked
It's not about health, son, the donkey said
Even the bridle is too big for you, son
Think and don't be greedy or the passengers will rise up.

There is some doubt as to whether the poem was really Negm's, but Egyptians familiar with the genre say it is certainly Negm-like. It seems to have first seen the light of day on various Egyptian blogs in the fall of 2010, at a time when a great deal of verse attributed to Negm, in reality penned by other poets seeking to gain an audience by using the legendary artist's name, started to circulate via the Internet. The name "Negm" retained a revolutionary aura in Egypt, and Essam's "Al-Gahsh 'Al li-l-Himar" traded on that reputation. (Asked about poets who used his appellation to publish their verse online, Negm said it did not bother him.)

Humor

Humor—highly prized in everyday Egyptian culture—was also a key element of the Tahrir performance atmosphere. Humor was deployed at Tahrir to launch withering attacks on the Mubarak political system, and it therefore served, as Helmy and Frerichs (2013, 476) note, to help undo people's fears of the repressive regime and to foster mocking attitudes toward it. Essam's "Al-Gahsh 'Al li-l-Himar" and the *zar* performance discussed above are typical examples of comic regime ridicule. According to Helmy and Frerichs, one of the important forms used to express humor on the square was the *zajal*, a form of vernacular poetry that has been employed in Egypt for decades to voice political satire. Political *zajal*s circulated widely via email in the run-up to the revolution. One of the best known, *"Hamamtak ya rayyis"* (Your Pigeon, O Boss), penned by Ahmad Fouad Negm, begins as follows:

Your pigeon oh boss, your pigeon of peace
Is floppy oh boss, go ahead and ask [your wife] Suzanne

I wish, oh boss, to eat well and go to bed
And you would piss off, and so would the madam
And your son [Gamal], too, would piss off.

(ibid., 462)

The ridicule and venom aimed here at Mubarak (the *rayyis*, the president, also meaning "boss" in colloquial Egyptian), his wife, Suzanne, and son Gamal, is highly sexualized, as the colloquial for "pigeon" (*hamama*) is a euphemism for penis. Another example of derisive Tahrir wit is the couplet chanted and sung over and over on the square, "Irhal, ya'ni imshi / ya illi ma yafhimshi." That is, "*Irhal* means *imshi*, in case you don't understand," or as Colla eloquently renders it, "'Depart ye' means 'get lost' / You thick-headed idiot!" (2013, 43). The couplet pokes fun at Mubarak's lack of cultural capital, for he was known for being unable to maintain formal Arabic standards when speaking in public and frequently slipping into colloquialisms. *Irhal* (depart) is literary "high" Arabic, while *imshi* (beat it) is eminently colloquial (Zimmer 2011).

A final example of typical sarcastic witticism is Muhammad Bahgat's poem "Wahad, itnayn, al-gaysh al-'arabi fayn" (One, Two, Where Is the Arab Army?), put to music by Ramy Essam and enjoyed immensely by the crowds at Tahrir. One verse makes fun of the Egyptian army—living in the upper-class Cairo suburb of Nasr City, waking up late in the morning, and lounging around sipping tea, rather than defending its people. Another faults the Arab armies for failing to defend Bosnia or Afghanistan (Sanders and Visonà 2012, 240).

Underground and Alternative

The urban Egyptian music scene known variously as "underground" and "alternative" came into much greater public visibility during the Tahrir days of January and February 2011. During the decade leading up to the uprising, Egypt witnessed what Catherine Cornet (2013, 5) has cleverly labeled a "shy cultural renaissance," in which the "alternative" music scene, which had some links to the social and oppositional movements of this period like Kifaya, played an important role (Miller 2010; see also Schielke 2015, 167–68; and El Chazli 2013). A key institution that nurtured this trend was El Sawy Culture Wheel, founded in Cairo's Zamalek district in 2003 by entrepreneur Mohammad El Sawy. El Sawy's performance space offered "underground" artists a stage on which to perform and develop their skills and repertoire (Cornet 2013, 19). The scene also found space to grow and evolve at the theater of al-Azhar Park, a public institution that opened in 2005, and at El Cabina in Alexandria, sponsored by the Gudran Foundation, which receives support from international funding agencies such as the Ford Foundation and from the cultural affairs offices of Western embassies (El Chazli 2013, 355). The alternative music scene also developed at festivals, mostly held in summer, like the S.O.S. Festival, launched in 2006 in the upper-class Cairo district of Madinat Nasr (Nasr City), and the International Occidental Music Competition, first staged in 2006 at Alexandria's Bibliotheca Alexandrina (Miller 2010).[13] Perhaps the most prominent bands in the scene were heavy-metal ones, but there was also the development of bands playing syntheses of Western and "Oriental" music. Such hybridization, El Chazli notes (2013, 35), was not peculiar to Egypt but was found in diverse Arab countries, and many of the bands in the region developed transnational links with each other.

The three most visible "alternative" bands (Cairokee, Wust El Balad, and Eskenderella) that played a role at Tahrir emerged from this "hybridized" trend. Cairokee, a rock band whose name is formed from a combination of "Cairo" and "karaoke," was founded in 2003 and was distinctive among "alternative" bands for doing songs with socially conscious lyrics. The group was not well known, however, before it released its song or anthem of revolution, "Sawt al-Hurriyya" (Voice of Freedom), written in response to the violent

13. The 2010 film *Microphone* (directed by Ahmad Abdalla) provides a lively view of the alternative music scene in Alexandria.

attacks of January 28 (the "Day of Anger") on Tahrir demonstrators and to claims in the mainstream media that the protesters were foreign agents (Shalaby 2015, 179; Gilman 2014, 179). Also appearing on Cairokee's "Voice of Freedom" was Hani 'Adil, the lead singer for the band Wust El Balad.

Founded in 1999, Wust El Balad is often described as a "soft rock" band, but it also incorporates "Oriental," jazz, blues, reggae, and other genres in its music (ibid., 127). Wust El Balad commenced its career performing the repertoire of Sayed Darwish and eventually went on to play its own compositions. The group's name, which translates as "Downtown," represented an effort by a group of middle-class musicians to associate themselves with Cairo's downscale and increasingly decrepit city center, which has been abandoned by the well-off middle classes for the trendier districts of the city, particularly the new gated communities on the edges of the desert. Wust El Balad at first performed in pedestrian areas downtown that state agencies had recently transformed in an effort to "revive" the area in a kind of museumizing fashion, but it eventually made its reputation playing at El Sawy and at the Cairo Opera House (Soliman 2011, 401).

Eskenderella, founded in 2000 and relaunched with a new lineup in 2005, hails from Alexandria and is more "Oriental" and *oud* focused in its basis than Cairokee or Wust El Balad. The mixed-gender group was launched with the aim of reviving the repertoire of Sayed Darwish (born in Alexandria) and Sheikh Imam. Eskenderella has also adapted the verse of venerated colloquial poets Fouad Haddad and Salah Jaheen and includes among its members children and grandchildren of these two great poets (Valassopoulos and Mostafa 2014, 652; Cornet 2013, 19; Sélim 2014). Among the songs Eskenderella performed at Tahrir during the occupation were Darwish's "'Um ya Masri" (Rise, O Egyptian) and Sheikh Imam's "Yetgamaa al-'ushaq" (All Lovers Gathered) and "Ya masr 'umi washiddi l-hayl" (O Egypt, Arise and Be Strong), all stirring hymns of patriotism.

While these alternative bands, which performed both a "committed" and a "nationalist" repertoire, were notable for their ability to move the crowds at Tahrir, their base audience in Cairo (and Alexandria) is relatively circumscribed and select, and the music they play appeals to upper-middle-class tastes. The scene is rather closed and elitist, mostly limited to the relatively well-off middle classes as well as the wealthy, educated in exclusive, private foreign-language secondary schools and at private universities or at faculties charging tuition at public universities. The spaces where they typically performed, such as El Sawy or Al-Azhar Park, for the most part excluded the working and lower-middle classes, both by ticket price and by social atmosphere (Miller 2010; Gilman 2014, 139; El Chazli 2013, 258; Metwaly 2014).[14]

Videos

A number of Egyptian artists also produced videos of songs popularly sung on the square or inspired by the dramatic events and released them on YouTube during or soon after the insurrection. Stephan Procházka analyzed thirty-three of these videos and found that—with the exception of a few rap numbers—the songs' lyrics served to "create an atmosphere of solidarity, mutual understanding, and non-violence" (2013, 19). The video "Sawt al-Hurriyya" (The Voice of Freedom), by Cairokee with Wust al-Balad's Hany Adil, uses footage of the musicians filmed on the square during the sit-in. Released on February 10, 2011, "Sawt al-Hurriyya" quickly became a viral hit. One of its notable features is how it foregrounds the crowds at Tahrir and shows the artists blending into the assembled masses (Hamamsy and Soliman 2013, 255; Gilman 2014, 179). Another very popular video from this period, recorded in late 2011, Cairokee's "Ya el-Midan" (O Square), voices criticism of repression

14. One might also mention as part of this larger scene the underground artist Maryam Saleh, chiefly because her recordings of Sheikh Imam songs, set to jazz and rock melodies, contributed to making Sheikh Imam relevant and current during the "revolutionary" period (Valassopoulos and Mostafa 2014, 646; Zaatari 2011).

at the hands of Egypt's interim military government, the Supreme Council of Armed Forces, and expresses a desire for the return to the remembered peaceful and united struggles at Tahrir of January–February: "We assemble to drink tea / and we know how to achieve our rights" (Nitgamma' nishrab al-shay, il-haqq 'arifna bingibu izzay) (Procházka 2013, 19). Another notable clip, "Qillah Mondassah" (A Minority of Infiltrators), launched the reputation of guitar-slinging vocalist Yasser al-Manawahly, who could be categorized in the camp of "committed" musicians. Released shortly after Mubarak was toppled from office, the song is a satirical critique of state media coverage of the uprising, which called the protesters "the agents of 'external hands' working in the interest of a 'foreign agenda'" (Valassopoulos and Mostafa 2014, 655; Howeidy 2014).

Mohamed Mounir's video clip "Izzay" (How) represents one of the few "revolutionary" contributions from a commercially successful Egyptian musician. The lyrics of "Izzay," recorded a few months before January 2011, personify Egypt as the beloved and express disappointment in the country's inability to provide love and comfort to its people (Sanders and Visonà 2012, 226). Upon the clip's release, state censors, considering its critiques too provocative, banned it from the airwaves (Gilman 2014, 1–2). Once the occupation of Tahrir began, Mounir hired a videographer to produce a clip of the song that incorporated footage of the sit-in, and the song became an immediate sensation after it was broadcast both on YouTube and by TV journalists willing to buck directives from on high. Mounir, fifty-six years old at the time of the release of the clip, is one of the very rare artists in Egypt who is both a successful "pop" artist and at the same time respected as a "committed" and "socially conscious" singer (Miller 2010; Gilman 2014, 135).[15]

One of Egypt's best-known rap groups, Arabian Knightz, released a video clip of their prorevolution song "Rebel" on February

15. The only other pop singer of Mounir's stature who is similarly respected for his "serious-mindedness" and political and artistic integrity is Ali El Haggar.

7, 2011, a number that was recorded before the insurrection but not released owing to government warnings. The clip, featuring scenes of the struggles on the square, received attention both inside Egypt (mostly among educated middle-class youth) and abroad (Robertson 2015, 79). The appeal of the song abroad was doubtless owing in part to the fact that the second verse is rapped in English (by Sphinx, the Egyptian American member of the band), as well as the presence of a sample from famed US rapper Lauryn Hill, and an instrumental track supplied by German producer Iron Curtain (Mangialardi 2013, 41–42). The wide international circulation of this very sharp and incisive video helped feed the impression among many observers abroad that rap played a key musical role in the so-called Arab Spring.[16] But in Egypt, at least, rap music was not a strong presence on the insurrectionary square, and the genre's appeal in the country, at least at the time of the uprising, was mostly limited to relatively well-off educated urban youth.

The Limits of Sonic Community

At the square, a kind of temporary, participatory sonic public was thus created, through the sharing of songs and the sorts of affects that accompanied them—unity, nationalism, nonsectarianism, militancy, and so on. The scene of the Tahrir occupation of 2011 is a striking example of how music can serve to animate imagined communities (Born 2013, 32) and how it can be deployed to help create "affective alliances" (Straw 1991, 374). But at the same time, music can also configure spaces where social and cultural divisions are played out, because flows of affect in fact have their limits (Born 2013, 46). The sonic community created at Tahrir was based on a unity that at the same time served to exclude other sound-based groups. The varieties of music played on the square represented a particular hierarchy of

16. See, for instance, Westland 2012, which is full of unjustified or exaggerated claims about the role of rap in the "revolution."

tastes, one that valorized nationalist, neoclassical music (patriotic anthems of Abdel Halim Hafez, Sayed Darwish, Shadia), "committed" music (Sheikh Imam), underground music (Cairokee, Wust El Balad), and the national folkloric (El Tanburah). All but the folkloric fit into the category of what educated and refined middle-class standards would define as modern. The incorporation of underground or alternative music represents a recent entry of a new genre into national respectability, and the fact that alternative artists performed songs by highly regarded nationalist and committed artists, in updated, sometimes rock-ish settings, enabled their legitimation. Moreover, underground music was produced by young, educated, middle-class youth, and the alternative scene emerged from that milieu. For its part, folkloric music of the sort done by El Tanbura is unimpeachable because it is seen as representing the "authentic" values of the people. Although lower-class Egyptians participated in very large numbers at Tahrir events, the official cultural ethos of the revolution tended to be set by middle-class standards, and middle-class activists tended to control the stages and to ensure that the quality of the music broadcast was appropriate.

What sorts of music were (mostly) not incorporated into the Tahrir sonic community? First, there is the massively popular genre of Egyptian (and, more broadly, Arab) pop, which is broadcast nonstop on radio and via video clips on numerous satellite music channels. Egyptian pop, or *shababiyya*, is the most commercially successful music found on Egyptian airwaves, and it is the favored soundtrack of Egypt's youth (Gilman 2014). But, according to the standard hierarchies of taste, Egyptian pop is too commercial, unserious, "cheap," and lightweight to be considered appropriate for performance or broadcast on weighty political occasions, especially insurrectionary ones. And although many Egyptian pop musicians have at times released nationalist songs, the public typically holds these numbers in disdain and regards them as vulgar propaganda, because they have been commissioned either by the government or by satellite channels (ibid., 154). Moreover, those individuals involved in the opposition movement regarded Egyptian pop artists as compromised by their ties to the Egyptian regime (ibid., 177). The only exceptions to this rule were the handful of Egyptian pop singers considered to be more serious artists, who sang songs dealing with social issues and were considered to be part of the Egyptian progressive political wing, like Mohamed Mounir and Ali El Haggar, discussed above.

Another important Egyptian sound that was mostly absent from the Tahrir 2011 scene was religious music and, in particular, that most popular of Egyptian religious musics, the songs of the Sufi *munshidin*. Sufi *inshad*, or "hymnody," as Frishkopf renders it, are songs in praise to the Prophet, his family, and venerated saints. The *munshidin* perform most notably at *mulid*s, the numerous festivals held throughout Egypt each year that are devoted to saints and to members of the Prophet's family and are attended by millions of the country's populace. The recordings of the *munshidin* have been widely available on cassette ever since the 1970s and, more recently, online. They are rarely broadcast, however, on official media.[17] But *mulid*s are almost exclusively lower- and lower-middle-class events, and they are considered unruly, undignified, and chaotic events that the self-respecting, educated, and refined middle classes should scrupulously avoid. The music of the *munshidin* is on occasion presented and celebrated as "folklore," but only if abstracted from the context of its most popular site of performance, the *mulid*.[18] The one exception to the general absence of *inshad* from the Tahrir sit-in of which I am aware is the concert given one night on the square by the respected *munshid* Sheikh Ahmad al-Tuni (Jennifer Peterson, personal communication).

17. The *munshid* Sheikh Yasin al-Tuhami is one of the few exceptions who appears on state television. Sheikh Yasin is the superstar of Sufi singing, whose performances at major *mulid*s attract tens of thousands, and he is respected by at least some intellectuals, owing to the fact that he sings refined classical Sufi texts (Schielke 2012, 171, 173).

18. Here I am only touching on the quite elaborated objections to *mulid*s of educated Egyptians, both secular and Islamist; see Schielke 2012 for an in-depth analysis.

Sha'bi (literally, "popular") music is a commercial rival to Egyptian pop music, but unlike *shababiyya*, which is ubiquitous on Egypt's mass media, it is essentially a nonpresence on Egypt's television, radio, and satellite channels (Grippo 2010, 138). *Sha'bi* too was largely absent from the main Tahrir stages and loudspeakers. It is closely related to the *inshad* scene; both types of music appeal to roughly the same class base, and many of Egypt's renowned *sha'bi* singers developed their skills singing at *mulid*s. Egypt's mandarins of refined sensibilities consider *sha'bi* to be vulgar, in poor taste, and tacky, and they regard it as particularly offensive to the official hierarchy of tastes because *sha'bi* combines the folkloric with the commercial, thus degrading the culture of the "folk." The development of cassette technology in the 1970s, providing a very affordable means for recording and distribution of music, enabled *sha'bi* to circulate outside of official media channels. The dissemination of cassette tapes helped propel the genre, and its great star Ahmad 'Adawiyya, to mass popularity.

Sha'bi's base remains rooted firmly in Egypt's urban "popular" quarters—the run-down traditional districts of Old Cairo, the city's *'ashwiyyat* (haphazard), unplanned, or informal districts, and the shabby apartment blocks built by the state in satellite suburbs. It is in these rough slums that the majority of Cairo's poor, working, and struggling lower-middle-class population reside, and here they receive little in the way of government services other than police harassment and security crackdowns on its young men. The "respectable" middle classes fear and denigrate such neighborhoods and typically avoid them at all costs; they do not appear on the maps one purchases of the city (Shenker 2016, 92). It is conventional for the mass media to refer to the *'ashwiyyat* as spaces of disorder and poverty, as nests of criminals and drug dealers, or, more charitably, *fallahin* (peasants) who have migrated from the countryside and retained their primitive and backward folkways (ibid., 89; Deboulet 2009, 206; Singerman 2009, 111). Typically, in fact, informal neighborhoods are peopled by a heterogeneous mix, with varied incomes, including industrial workers, civil-sector employees, shopkeepers large and small, owners of workshops, and so on (Shenker 2016, 111).

Sha'bi's roots are in the "folk" improvisatory tradition of the *mawwal* (some scholars refer to *sha'bi* as "neo-*mawwal*"), but played much faster than traditional *mawwal* and with modern instruments.[19] The highly percussive *sha'bi* is especially made for dancing, is loud and infectious, and is the preferred wedding music of the Egyptian urban masses. Indeed, it is the wedding party (*farah*) scene that has provided a living for dozens of great *sha'bi* singers (Puig 2010). (Cassettes of *sha'bi* artists help gain them renown but because of massive piracy are usually a meager source of income.) *Sha'bi* singers do on occasion cross over to the mainstream, as, for instance, Hakim, Sa'd al-Sughayyar, and Shaaban Abdel-Rahim—the latter especially after his breakthrough "political" 2001 hit, "I Hate Israel" (*Ana Bakrah Isra'il*) (Grippo 2010, 155, 157; Grippo 2015; Marcus 2007, 155–74). But for the most part, *sha'bi* has remained firmly entrenched in the spaces and practices of the lower classes and is mostly disdained by Egypt's educated and sophisticated classes. The explicitly political lyrics of Shaaban Abdel-Rahim's "I Hate Israel" were quite exceptional for *sha'bi* music and in any case expressed a critique of a foreign, not a national, entity.

Crossovers

Although the sonic community forged at Tahrir served to create regimes of authorized and unauthorized sound, the creative and revolutionary cultural energies released in the wake of the 2011 insurrection served to create the possibilities for a genre of unauthorized sound, known variously as "electro-*sha'bi*," "techno-*sha'bi*," or, most commonly, *mahraganat* (festivals),[20] to break into the

19. On *mawwal*, see Cachia 1977.

20. The name for the phenomenon seems to have been in flux before finally settling on *mahraganat*. *Hip Deep* (2012) reported that the names in currency were "*mahragan*" (festival, sing.), "electro-*sha'bi*," "techno-*sha'bi*," and "*sha'bi* DJs."

mainstream and also to go international, riding on the global reputation of Egypt's "revolution." Of all Egypt's popular types of music, *mahraganat* is clearly, and somewhat ironically, given its absence from the square, the genre that probably benefited the most from the moment of global interest, excitement, and solidarity generated by the Tahrir uprising. Even though Arab rap was hailed by many outside observers as having played a key mobilizing role in the Arab Spring, and while several Egyptian rappers produced songs and videos in solidarity with the revolution, of all Egyptian musical artists it is the *mahraganat* artists who, in the wake of the uprising, have had the greatest international impact.

Mahraganat is essentially an outgrowth of a trend in *sha'bi* music that researcher Jennifer Peterson has termed "*mulid* dance" music. The *mulid* dance trend is said to developed first in 2001, in the wedding milieu of Matariyya, a popular quarter in Cairo, by deejays who played or spun variations of *sha'bi* dance tunes, and, somewhat later, began to add *mulid*-oriented lyrics (Peterson 2008b, 274). *Mulid* dance deejays started to find employment at weddings in popular neighborhoods, owing in part to the fact that it was cheaper to hire a disc jockey with his sound system than to engage a *sha'bi* band with its multiple personnel (ibid., 275). Spanish anthropologist José Sánchez García (2016, 305) posits a somewhat different but related origin for the trend, stating that in the early 2000s, informal youth associations in popular quarters began to collect donations during the year in order to afford the rental of portable sound systems to set up at *mulid*s. These associations would then hire a deejay who used mixers, computers, and turntables to create a hybrid dance music that blended *inshad* themes with *sha'bi* music and electronic instrumentation. According to Sánchez García, this musical style was known as *mahraganat*, or "festivals," in reference to the weddings, birthday celebrations, and *mulid*s where such music was

---

Wa'il (2011) used the name "*al-di ji al-sha'bi*," that is, "*sha'bi* DJ," to describe the music.

typically played. Meanwhile, Peterson observed in 2008 that *mulid* dance music—the same brand of music Sánchez García identified as *mahraganat*—was commonly being heard at weddings, engagement parties, and some *mulid*s in Cairo's popular quarters, and she also describes seeing a *mulid* dance disc jockey spinning discs at a *mulid* held in a town in the Delta that same year (2008b, 273).[21]

New forms of hybrid dancing emerged along with the music trend. Sánchez García reports that young men at these *mahraganat* events created a dance style that employed the stationary, swaying body movements known as *dhikr* that are typical of *mulid* Sufi rituals, while at the same time it involved the motion of the arms and hands in a manner resembling hip-hop dancing (2015, 353). Peterson (2008a) observes that the dance style characteristic of the *mulid* dance trend borrows from a number of traditions, in an improvised form called *tashkil* ("diversification" or "compilation"). Performed by a single person or by a pair, it includes elements of *raqs sharqi* (belly dancing) of the sort that one typically encounters at weddings in popular quarters, as well as movements variously drawn from hip-hop, voguing, martial arts, and interactive play-fighting that resemble *tahtib*, a traditional stick-fight dance that originated in Upper Egypt (the *Sa'id*) and is a typical feature of that region's *mulid*s (Biegman 1990, 16). (Many residents of Egypt's popular quarters are originally from Upper Egypt.) The novel *mahraganat* and *mulid* dance moves are often very theatrical and frequently framed by aerosol jets, lit on fire.

Mulid dance music and the bodily motions associated with it were strongly marked as rooted in local popular-quarter identity, as well as adhering to Sufi religious traditions, since the songs repeat pious formulas of love for the Prophet and the saints. These facts tended to mitigate any potential local criticism of the music and its young practitioners for their ostensible transgressions of tradition, such as singing praises to the Prophet to dance rhythms. Citing Paul Willis (1990, 21–26), Sánchez García asserts that, because of *mahraganat*'s

21. See also Schielke 2012, 32.

roots in popular neighborhoods, it represents a kind of "grounded aesthetics" (2010a, 12). Peterson (2008b), for her part, notes that a *mulid* dance disc jockey or dancer who sported bleached, gelled, or long hair, stylistic attributes that at the time would normally have been considered quite foreign to the acceptable dress aesthetics in Egypt's informal quarters, would nonetheless be considered a "neighborhood boy" if he were involved in authentically grounded local music.[22] The audiences at the *mahraganat* tents set up at *mulid*s, moreover, were not restricted to young people and the lower classes (Sánchez García 2010a, 31), and the *mahraganat* music offered up at weddings was for the enjoyment of a general audience and not simply for young people.

Peterson (2008a) observed in 2008 that remixes of *mulid* dance music, an art form previously enjoyed almost exclusively by the popular classes, had started to gain favor with broader swaths of Egyptian youth, including the middle classes. In part it was because *mulid* dance music had become widely available on bootleg cassettes and, more important, as MP3s. Digitization made it possible for young *sha'bi mulid* deejays to produce recordings cheaply and easily, as computer use, because of the decline in prices, had become common even for urban and rural families with modest incomes. Digitization also facilitated the wider circulation of compilations of *sha'bi mulid* music, via memory sticks, Internet cafes, cellphones that stored and played music, CD burning, and Internet forums with the name "*aghani mulid*" (*mulid* songs). In Cairo's public arena in 2008, it was common to hear *mulid* dance hits blaring from the motorized pleasure boats that transport merrymakers on the Nile or from the bespangled horse carriages that convey excursioners along the Corniche (Peterson 2008c, 73). Both *sha'bi* and *mulid* music have also long been commonly played on the cassette players of the private minibuses, whose share of total trips in Greater Cairo by 1998 had reached 28 percent,

22. Schielke has observed that long hair on village youth from the Delta was not uncommon in the 2000s (2015, 40).

half of all modes of public conveyance. Minibuses are an especially important means of transportation in informal neighborhoods where government buses typically do not reach, and they are particularly patronized by the urban poor (Sims 2010, 230).

The musical trend known since the days of the revolution variously as electro-*sha'bi* or *mahraganat* emerged around 2007, according to those individuals who claim to have originated the trend (see below). Although, by today, this brand of music has been hailed as a kind of brand-new, exciting, and even revolutionary artistic development in Egypt, it is important to stress that it is, in fact, an outgrowth or offshoot of *sha'bi* and *mulid* music. Its various names are testament to those roots. *Mahragan* (pl. *mahraganat*), or "festival," moreover, is essentially synonymous with *mulid* (Jennifer Peterson, personal communication). Recall as well that, according to Sánchez García, from the early 2000s the name *mahraganat* referred to the trend that Peterson has identified as *mulid* dance music. Moreover, the milieu where electro-*sha'bi/mahraganat* developed is precisely the same as the one that fostered Sufi *inshad*, *sha'bi*, and *mulid* dance: the popular quarters of Greater Cairo, where the bulk of the city's population resides.[23] But as *mahraganat* has gained national and international prominence, since 2011, its roots in other forms tend to be forgotten or effaced. The practitioners of the now-famous trend have also tended to dispense with *mulid* motifs.

The stories told about electro-*sha'bi/mahraganat*'s origins, moreover, tend to emphasize individual creation rather than emergence from a wider scene. The origin tale of well-known *mahraganat* artist disc jockey Figo, recounted to *Guardian* journalist Jack Shenker (2016, 369–70), is typical.[24] Figo hails from Madinat al-Salam (Salam City), a suburb north of downtown Cairo, a project launched in 1981

23. In 2011, out of Greater Cairo's total population of eighteen million, 66.7 percent resided in informal quarters (Sims 2013). This figure does not count the population of run-down, old, "traditional," "formal" quarters of the city.

24. Figo's father was a *sha'bi* wedding singer.

by the Cairo Governorate. Consisting of modest, poorly maintained, modernist apartment blocks and surroundings, it housed 150,000 people by the mid-2000s, together with the neighboring al-Nahda suburb. A number of its residents were relocated there from inner-city Cairo owing to urban redevelopment projects or building collapse, the latter mostly caused by the 1992 earthquake (Sims 2010, 55). Deejay Figo reports that he learned to make music by watching "How to make beats" tutorials on YouTube. Since he did not understand English, he would pause the videos and try to work out the lessons by looking at screen shots. It took him six months to figure out how to add layers of sound and to control the speed. A posse of local boys began to hang out in his bedroom, most notably a young man who had been producing his own raps under the name Alaa Fifty, and the two began producing songs, Alaa doing the vocals and Figo the mix. One day an acquaintance, who was getting married in the popular quarter of Matariya, requested a song for his wedding. Alaa, Figo, and another local singer going by the name of Sadat produced "Mahragan al-Salam." The wedding crowds loved it, recorded it on their phones, and shared it with their friends, and the song spread, mobile phone to mobile phone, throughout Cairo's *'ashwiyyat* and popular quarters. "The phenomenon of *mahraganat* music," reports Shenker, "was underway." Soon the crew was joined by another deejay/producer from 'Ain Shams known as Amr 7a7a, a computer repairman who sold personalized ringtones on the side. MC Sadat, probably the most famous of the Madinat al-Salam circle, insists that the music is *not sha'bi* and *not mulid*, but something distinct, *mahraganat*. Sadat claims that he coined the term himself (Mohsen 2013)[25] and that he and his group of friends invented the genre (Loccatelli 2013).

From this point on, I will use the term *mahraganat* to designate what is now generally considered a brand-new genre, although the

25. In Mohsen's (2013) interview with Sadat, both *mahragan* and *mahraganat* are used to describe the music.

research of Peterson and Sánchez García shows that it is an outgrowth or offshoot of *mulid* dance music, or *mahraganat*.[26] Other artists involved in practices similar to the productions of the Madinat al-Salam posse began to come into prominence as well, most notably a posse known as Eight Percent (Tamaniya bi-l-miya), led by Oka, Ortega, and Weza, from the informal Cairo quarter of Matariyya. *Mahraganat* artists begin making local reputations, and cash, by playing at weddings in popular quarters, taking advantage of the fact that it was cheaper to hire a deejay and one or two singers than the much larger *sha'bi* ensembles. In addition, they began to organize modest parties in their own neighborhoods, blocking off their narrow streets to set up improvised stages and folding chairs. The events, cobbled together with their own resources and social connections, are characteristic of the informal milieu, which requires a do-it-yourself, self-reliant, self-help (*guhud zatiyya*, in colloquial Egyptian [Shenker 2016, 94]) sense of initiative for the sake of survival. The parties are raucous, thunderous, garish, celebratory, humorous, heavily masculinized, rough-and-tumble affairs. Strings of light illuminate the alleys as crowds of young males dance intensely and aggressively to the music, shouting the names of the disc jockeys and the lines of choruses; blowing vuvuzelas; shooting off bright flares, flaming aerosol jets, and firecrackers; and pulling off their shirts in the excitement. The scene of the parties very much resembles the atmosphere of *mulid*s—also celebrated in popular quarters—and, like *mulid*s (Madoeuf 2006, 474), these events are mixed-gender affairs, although the wild and aggressive dancing mostly takes place in male space. Like the singers and disc jockeys, the youths are frequently garbed in skinny jeans, sneakers, hoodies, and baseball caps. If *mahraganat* artists are playing at a popular quarter wedding, off to the side and separated from the men are the women, some in *hijab*, many of them dancing too. *Mahraganat* music at weddings, moreover, is

26. Tomren (2015, 54) also considers *mulid* dance music as a predecessor of *mahraganat*.

not just for the sake of the youths who dance so vigorously, but is entertainment for the entire family, young and old. Like *mulid*s, and like the parties that *mahraganat* posses organize, wedding parties in popular quarters are held in the street. Anyone can attend, and it has long been customary for young men to show up at wedding parties to enjoy the music and scope out young women.

Mahraganat is, at root, *dance* music. When performed live, the beat is often delivered by the rhythms of the *darbuka*, the Egyptian goblet drum or *tabla*, and the *dohola*, a larger-sized *darbuka*, which pound out distinctive *sha'bi* rhythms, known as *maqsum*. These beats are combined with synthesized musical accompaniment, produced by electronic keyboards or synthesizers, or sounds and beats remixed or refixed or sampled from various recordings. Vocals, usually chanted, sometimes sung, or, less frequently, rapped, are most typically distorted, and enhanced, by autotune.[27] While the sound is strongly electronic and synthesized, and might be considered a version of rap, the fact that the dance beats are *sha'bi*, *maqsum*, and not hip-hop means that the seemingly novel music is, in fact, deeply rooted in the familiar dance traditions of the popular neighborhoods. Lyrics display the legendary humor, irreverence, slang-heavy language, local concerns, and pride in the neighborhood of the youth (mostly male) of Cairo's popular districts, of the sort that is typical of *sha'bi*. This identification with the neighborhood or the residential street represents a kind of movement away from an older, more traditional form of urban identification with the rural village or region of origin or religion or extended kin group (Haenni 2009, 314).

Besides being passed among friends via mobile phone, *mahraganat* songs circulated in the popular quarter milieus via what Asef Bayat has dubbed "passive networks"—the "instantaneous communications between atomized individuals that are established by tacit recognition of their commonalities and are mediated through real

27. Autotune is an audio processor technology used to alter pitch and distort the voice.

or virtual space" (2012, 120). One crucial means by which computer-created *mahraganat* tunes spread in public were via Cairo's ubiquitous *tuk-tuk*s, the three-wheel motorcycle rickshaw taxis that, since their introduction in the mid-2000s, convey tens of thousands of passengers around the city on a daily basis and are particularly in use in popular quarters, where they can maneuver easily through the narrow and congested streets and alleys. *Tuk-tuk*s are a completely informal mode of transportation that runs without license plates, because the Ministry of Interior refuses to register them, and they are tolerated as long as they remain in informal quarters and do not operate on major roads (Sims 2010, 242–43). *Tuk-tuk*s are typically outfitted with USBs, as well as inexpensive and loud sound systems. *Mahraganat* is the preferred music of the *tuk-tuk* drivers, often daredevil teenagers, who typically decorate their vehicles with bright lighting, decals, and other ornamentation. The respectable classes, of course, look on the *tuk-tuk* driver with disdain, and the stereotype held by middle-class sophisticates is that he is a hashish-smoking twelve-year-old (ibid., 243). If a passenger in the *tuk-tuk* hears a song that he or she fancies, a driver can easily send it to the rider's phone using Bluetooth technology (Niazy 2014, 74) or transfer it to a memory stick. *Tuk-tuk*s are probably the most important conveyance vehicles for broadcasting *mahraganat* music, but since the late 2000s *mahraganat* is also commonly heard in the minibuses that clog Cairo's streets and convey its citizens and goods, in taxis, on speakers mounted on motorcycles, at local food stands and ice cream carts, and on Nile party boats (Detrie 2012). The Internet, and in particular the video-sharing website YouTube, has also been of great importance in disseminating the music, especially for broadcasting *mahraganat* beyond Cairo's popular quarters. It was the fall of 2011, well before *mahraganat* had begun to receive much international attention, when I first became aware of the *mahraganat* videos posted on YouTube, and by then many of the genre's best-known songs had already registered over one or two million views. Since many of these postings were labeled only in Arabic, only Arabic speakers, and in massive numbers, were viewing these *mahraganat*

YouTube clips. The numbers are testimony to the large size of the local audience and also to the spread of computers and the Internet in Egypt's urban popular quarters, where the audience base was then mostly located. Listeners who accessed *mahraganat* songs via YouTube, of course, were clever enough to find software to convert the video clips to MP3s, which they could play on their phones, computers, and *tuk-tuk* sound systems and also share easily with friends and acquaintances.

Although the officially sanctioned sound regime at Tahrir Square during the January–February 2011 uprising seems for the most part to have excluded *sha'bi*, *mulid*, and *mahraganat* music, fans of these types of music from Cairo's popular quarters were, of course, present on Tahrir, and in significant numbers. Although on-site observers who have given accounts of the music of the revolution have not, for the most part, reported on the presence of *mahraganat* or *sha'bi*, these types of music were not completely absent. Jennifer Peterson (personal communication) recalls occasionally hearing *sha'bi* music blasting from the loudspeakers of trucks and motorcycles conveying persons on their way to join the sit-in. *Guardian* reporter Jack Shenker remembers hearing *mahraganat* music coming from pleasure boats on the Nile as he was running along the Corniche, attempting to escape the tear gas tossed at demonstrators by the security forces (2016, 371). Mona Prince (2014, 189–91), in her diary of the days she spent at Tahrir during the insurrection, recalls that on the day Mubarak was overthrown, she ran into Emad, from the popular quarter of Bulaq al-Dakrour, on Tal'at Harb Street near the square.[28] Also present were a number of *tuk-tuk* drivers, who had taken the occasion of the fall of the dictator to drive their vehicles downtown, from which they had previously been proscribed. The *tuk-tuk* drivers were blasting music with which Prince was unfamiliar. She asked, "What's this music? Where did you get it?" Her friend replied, "They

28. Shenker incorrectly identifies this incident as having taken place on January 28, the "Day of Rage" (2016, 371).

brought it from Bulaq al-Dakrour." He asked her to dance, and she joined him, and together with all the *tuk-tuk* drivers, they moved to the sounds of the outsiders. Prince never identifies the music, but Shenker, in his recounting of her story, says—and there is no doubt that he is correct—that it was *mahraganat* (2016, 371).

Shenker's and Prince's encounters with *mahraganat* in the days of the insurrection portend what was to come in the wake of the January–February 2011 insurrection—the release of tremendous amounts of creative energy, the partial unsettling of traditional class cultural barriers, and the awakening of international interest in Egyptian politics and culture. Boundaries between authorized and unauthorized sound became more fluid, in part because it is not easy to draw hard-and-fast boundaries around sound, and music can be a contagion and can circulate via nonauthorized networks. *Mahraganat* was one of the local cultural movements that has most benefited and profited from these developments. And so, while *mahraganat*/electro-*sha'bi* was not a musical presence *at* the insurrection, it has come to be indelibly associated *with* the Egyptian revolution, and often even to be regarded, especially by foreign observers, as *the* music of the revolution.

Some *Mahragan* Songs

Although there is by now a huge and variegated archive of *mahraganat* songs, for the most part they share a number of important characteristics. One of the more notorious of the *mahraganat* hits is "Aha al-shibshib da'" (Fuck, I Lost My Slipper) by 'Amr 7a7a, Sadat, and Figo. The song's use of the extremely and virtually unrepeatable vulgar expression "aha" ("fuck it" or "fuck that") created a sensation in Egypt. The emergence into public use of the hitherto taboo expression "aha" was, according to Helmy and Frerichs (2013, 462), largely a product of the 2011 uprising. "Aha," they assert, was widely employed in the humor of the insurrection, and they suggest that its use "marks the transition from a culture of self-denial (gallows humor) on the verge of self-destruction (fatalistic suicide) to a culture of self-empowerment and self-defense." According to Colla, the "appearance [of *aha*] in popular public spectacle signals a break with prior structures of politeness, a reminder (or threat) that the rules of language itself might be overturned by revolution" (2013, 44). "Aha al-shibshib da'" is also characteristically *sha'bi* in its orientation, Soraya Morayef notes (2012), owing to its focus on a mundane and supremely inexpensive object of everyday use, the *shibshib*, or plastic slipper. Tomren notes (2015, 60) that the song also underscores the extreme economic division between the popular classes, for whom the loss of a very cheap item is a cause to express regret, whereas for the middle classes the *shibshib* is a kind of throwaway item. "Fuck it, the slipper got lost," the song goes,

> Fuck, it had a toe-thong
> Fuck, the slipper got lost
> Fuck, it was still new
> Fuck, it was for the Eid [holiday].
>
> (translation adapted from ibid., 100)

Another famous *mahraganat* song of the postrevolutionary period expresses skeptical and humorous support for the revolution. Deejay Amr 7a7a, Sadat, and Figo's "Al-Sha'b Yurid Khamsa Ginih Rasid" (The People Want Five Pounds' Phone Credit) opens to the slowed-down strains of Egypt's national anthem, "Biladi, Biladi," penned by Sayed Darwish, played on a cheesy-sounding electric keyboard. The patriotic hymn quickly grinds down and then is abruptly halted by a jarring electronic crash. The beats of *sha'bi darbouka* take over, and the autotuned vocalist chants:

> The people want something new [to think about]
> The people want five pounds' phone credit
> The people want to topple the regime
> But the people are so damn tired.

"The People Want Five Pounds' Phone Credit" invokes the famous slogan of the Arab revolts ("The people want to topple the regime"), while at the same time it expresses the concerns of "the people" (especially of the popular quarters) for everyday needs (finding enough cash for a new SIM card for their cellphones); it indexes as well their exhaustion over the process of insurrection, which did not end with the exit of Mubarak (Colla 2012).

Another *mahraganat* hit, "Ana Aslan Gamid" (I'm Really Tough), focuses on everyday life in the popular quarter. Vocalists Oka, Ortega, and Weza of the group Eight Percent name-check their hood (Matariyya) and versify about religious faith, envy, and the evil eye, evoking concerns often expressed in songs of the *mulid*s:

> I walked out the front door and came to a neighbor's house
> Someone had written a spell on me, on the wall and on the ground
> I continued to walk while I was aware and played dumb
> I don't know who did it, but maybe it will bring [on] me a jinn . . .
> What do people want? What are people doing?
> The evil eye and the jealous eye
> Tell me what should I do
> O holy, O mother of Hasan, O mother of Hasan and Husayn.[29]

The subjects of *mahraganat* are also frequently women, drugs, and colloquial turns of phrase (Benchouia 2015, 7). A review suggests, finally, that they are very much in line with those songs sung by *sha'bi* superstar 'Adawiyya, who dominated the scene in the seventies and eighties. Like 'Adawiyya, they employ a number of "affective devices" in their effort to impart folk wisdom, including "double entendre, indirect metaphor . . . and popular slang to convey commonplace topics, socially charged issues, and innumerable variations of romantic and religious themes" (Grippo 2007). And, like *sha'bi*,

29. Translation and transliteration adapted from Tomren 2015, 75. The Hasan and Husayn (d. 680) referred to are among the revered family of the Prophet. Their father was the fourth caliph, 'Ali ibn Abi Talib. Their mother was Fatima Zahra, the daughter of the prophet Muhammad, and so they are the grandsons of the Prophet.

the most popular *mahraganat* involves "short songs with unforgettable refrains" (Grippo 2010, 148).

Mahraganat, Revolution, and Commerce

Of all today's Egyptian popular musical genres, it is *mahraganat* that has come to be most closely associated with the "revolution" and the one that has gained the most from the revolutionary opening. Several outside observers have asserted a hard connection, but as we have seen, *mahraganat* was *not* part of the music of insurrection on the square. There is a relation, but a complicated one.

First of all, the changed social, cultural, and political atmosphere that occurred in the wake of the revolution was essential to the emergence of *mahraganat* as a significant musical phenomenon. Although the official musical culture of the insurrectionary square was largely controlled by the educated middle class, considerable numbers of participants in the uprising came from Cairo's popular quarters—like the young men from Bulaq al-Dakrour with whom Mona Prince made friends. Class barriers on the square became, during that utopian moment, less rigid, and social and cultural hierarchies and boundaries were, if not shattered, at least shaken up. Moreover, the conditions for breakthrough had to some extent already been prepared, particularly by Mahmoud Refat, founder of 100 Copies, a downtown performance space, recording studio, and record label specializing in electronic experimental music. Refat recognized the significance of *mahraganat* prior to the uprising and began organizing concerts for *mahraganat* artists starting in 2010 (Jawad 2014). As opportunities opened up for the presentation of new and previously unheard music in early 2011, Refat was well placed to play a key role in getting concerts organized for *mahraganat* artists, so that more people, and in particular young people from beyond the popular quarters, could experience their performances live. At first, according to Jawad (2014), it was middle-class activists who became interested in *mahraganat* artists when they performed at downtown spaces like 100 Copies and the Greek Club, spaces that were formerly the exclusive province of the middle classes and of alternative or jazz artists (Detrie 2012). *Mahraganat* artists also performed at al-Azhar Park, reserved by state authorities prior to the revolution for "respectable" performers. The *mahraganat* artists' inroads into the cultural mainstream were facilitated by the fact that the insurrection had made many people more willing to listen to what was novel, full of youthful energy, and "street." In addition, the Egyptian pop or *shababiyya* produced by the major recording labels, which dominated the airwaves and had been commercially successful, now seemed irrelevant in the new "revolutionary" climate, and so opportunities were created for new artists (Nur 2014). *Mahraganat* artists seem to have been the most successful at exploiting this opening.

In the course of a couple years after the insurrection, *mahraganat* moved into the mainstream in quite remarkable ways. *Mahraganat* artist Sadat was asked to compose a song for the mainstream film *Game Over*, released in June 2012, a remake of the 2005 Hollywood release *Mother-in-Law*, starring Jane Fonda and Jennifer Lopez. In the movie, film stars Yousra (sixty-one years old) and Mai Ezzedine (thirty-five years) lip-sync the *mahraganat* song "Haqqi bi-Raqabti" (Never Again). The scene appears fairly ridiculous, especially the figure of Yousra dancing and singing to the autotuned vocals of Sadat, but it is nonetheless quite popular.[30] While Sadat's name does not appear in the movie credits (Meddeb 2013), soon thereafter it would be hard to imagine *mahraganat* artists *not* being acknowledged for their work and hard to picture anyone other than the artists themselves performing their own songs on-screen.

Oka and Ortega have been the most successful *mahraganat* stars at mainstreaming, appearing on television talk shows, in the movies, and in advertisements for ground beef (the food company Meatland), Viagra, telecom companies, and beer (Tomren 2015, 55–56; Hubbard 2013). In 2012 their music was featured in the very successful

30. As of this writing, the video clip has more than two and a half million views. https://www.youtube.com/watch?v=zMtI-UNI6J0.

film *Abdo Mota*, the story of a young man from a popular quarter who got into the drug trade after his parents died under mysterious conditions. Oka and Ortega, together with their disc jockey Shehta Karika, appear in the film performing the film's theme song in a scene set in a popular quarter, and their previously released song "Ana Aslan Gamid" is also used in the soundtrack. It was their move into the realm of commerce that caused Oka and Ortega to split with their erstwhile Eight Percent partner, Weza, as the media moguls were interested only in promoting the duo (Meddeb 2013)—possibly because Weza appears somewhat older than the pair and does not share their skinny good looks. Oka and Ortega's part in *Abdo Mota* greatly enhanced their celebrity and also helped make them the most successful of all *mahraganat* artists on the wedding circuit (Tomren 2015, 56). In 2012 Oka and Ortega, as well as other *mahraganat* stars, were performing at tourist resorts like Hurghada and Sharm al-Sheikh (Freemuse 2016). By 2014 the duo was starring in a commercial movie called *Eight Percent*, but the film turned out to be a clunker that contributed to a decline in their popularity (Jawad 2014). In February 2015, Oka married Egyptian film star and singer Mai Kassab, a union that attracted a great deal of media criticism because Kassab is from the upper-middle classes and is the possessor of high cultural and educational capital, in contrast to Oka, with his secondary education (Tomren 2015, 77). The marriage nonetheless offered increased connections to the Egyptian arts-world scene for Oka and his crew (Freemuse 2016).

The Madinat al-Salam posse of Sadat, Fifty, Figo, and their comrade from Ain Shams, Amr 7a7a, have made inroads into the mainstream as well, but have not gone as commercial as Oka and Ortega. They too are playing the resorts and at middle- and upper-middle-class weddings. By 2012 Amr 7a7a, Sadat, and Fifty were playing regular gigs at After Eight, a fancy downtown Cairo nightclub with a high cover charge and a dress code (Shenker 2016, 373). Like Oka and Ortega, Sadat and Fifty also starred in a 2014 film. *Al-Mahragan*, a fictionalized account of their own careers, was received more positively than Oka and Ortega's *Eight Percent* and served to enhance rather than detract from their reputations. Other *mahraganat* artists have succeeded as well. Al-Madfa'giya (the Artilleryman), who hail from Madinat al-Salam like Sadat and Fifty, are also big on the wedding and resort circuit, and they appear in the action thriller *Qalb al-Asad* (2013), together with star Mohamed Ramadan, performing their song "Ana Aslan Gan." The remarkable popularity of the track can be gauged by the fact that one of the many versions posted on YouTube has nearly thirty-seven million viewers.[31] "Ana Aslan Gan" is topped in views, however, by a track from the *mahraganat* outfit Shobik Lobik called "Mafish Sahib Yitsahib" (There's No Friend to Befriend Anymore), which appears in the September 2015 film *Eyal Harifa*. The official music video currently has gained an impressive eighty million views, while the video clip of the song as screened in the film currently has twenty-six million views.[32] Meanwhile, *mahraganat* is aired now on radio, on the Nile FM station, and on Saturday afternoons (Freemuse 2016), and a satellite TV station is devoted to the genre.

The 2011 revolution also galvanized a great deal of international interest in Egypt, its politics, and its culture, and this appeal too has redounded to the benefit of *mahraganat*. After an initial spate of articles asserting—mistakenly for the most part—a link between the insurrection and Egyptian hip-hop, gradually the focus shifted to *mahraganat*, and it is probably the case that over the last five years this genre has received more outside attention than any other Egyptian popular music of the past several decades. The result has been a fair amount of misinformation—in particular, assertions that *mahraganat* is the music of the revolution—but the attention has also proved a boon to some of the major performers. Sadat, Figo, and Fifty have played a number of concert events in Europe (France, Switzerland,

31. https://www.youtube.com/watch?v=qGWn3Hdxo2c&list=RDqGWn3Hdxo2c. The title of this YouTube post is Arabic, suggesting that its audience is almost entirely Arab.

32. https://www.youtube.com/watch?v=pMx5DU2fsp8; https://www.youtube.com/watch?v=GACDrZ7rvf0.

Germany, England, the Netherlands) as a result of international interest. Mahmoud Refat of 100 Copies played a central role in brokering such events, garnering support from the Cairo offices of the British Council and the French Cultural Center to fund both European and local concerts (Golia 2015). With the support of an EU grant, 100 Copies also launched a record sublabel called ReTune, to record and release *mahraganat* recordings (Nur 2014). In 2014 the London-based community radio station Rinse FM and the British Council collaborated on a cultural exchange program called Cairo Calling. Part One brought Figo and Sadat, plus Diesel and KNKA of Madfa'giya, to London in January to do studio sessions with prominent UK grime and dubstep producers Faze Miyake, Kode 9, Pinch, Mumdance, and Artwork. Part Two, in March, put Figo, Sadat, Fifty, Diesel, and KNKA onstage with British grime artists Faze Miyake, Mumdance, and Pinch at the third annual Downtown Contemporary Arts Festival (D-CAF) in Cairo (Holslin 2015; ElNabawi 2014).

The collaborations opened the *mahraganat* artists up to new sounds and techniques, and since then many have been more experimental with their own productions, mixing in some songs elements of UK electronic. Access to professional recording equipment and exposure to other performers and genres has also, according to Jawad (2014), led to the improvement of *mahraganat* productions, more "coherent" lyrics, and more professional performances. Some have found the new sounds to be quite "fresh," while others have been critical of the different direction some of the leading *mahraganat* artists have taken (ElNabawi 2014; Jawad 2014). Among the notable recorded collaborations that have occurred are Sadat's work with Egyptian rapper MC Amin, the appearance of Alaa Fifty on experimental Egyptian artist Maurice Louca's album *Benhayyi al-Baghbaghan* (Salute the Parrot, 2014), Sadat and Fifty's collaboration with the Paris electronic outfit Acid Arab on the track "Hez Hez," and the Sadat and Fifty appearance on a 2015 track by Saudi Arabian rapper Qusai, called "Umm al-Dunya." The collaboration with Qusai is, in my opinion, rather unfortunate, a tribute to Egypt in which the artists appear together with soldiers and give the impression of lending support to the current military regime. Sadat, Amr 7a7a, and Fifty even produced a quite mainstream-sounding song with only traces of *mahraganat* ("Al-Shari' Zahma"), in the manner of the "Spanish Tinge" (Frishkopf 2003) forged by 'Amr Diab's 1996 smash hit "Nur al-'Ain," for the film *El Mahragan.*

Subculture

It is important to emphasize that *mahraganat* is not just the artists but also the scene and the emergent subculture surrounding the music. According to Salem (2013), *mahraganat* partiers have developed a "new" type of dance, but it is clear from his description that the "new" styles are either an outgrowth or more recent iteration of the steps Peterson (2008a) describes in connection with "*mulid* dance music." According to Salem, the "new" *mahraganat* dance is an Egyptian version of the French dance known as *techtonik*, developed by residents of Paris's southern *banlieues* in the 2000s and connected to electro house music. The new dance is variously called *tashkil*, *al-tet*,[33] *raqs mahraganat* (*mahraganat* dance), and techno-*sha'bi*. It is more aggressive, says Salem, than French *techtonik* and involves two individuals facing each other and making moves that "entail some sort of attack and defence between the dancers with lots of ducking as well as jumping involved." It would appear, therefore, that, like the *mulid* dance steps Peterson describes, the new *mahraganat* dance was also influenced by the Upper Egyptian traditional stick dance, the *tahtib*. Jawad (2014) also considers the *mahraganat* dance steps to be something new, describing them as incorporating breakdance, hip-hop, and krump[34] moves with Egyptian styles. She observes that the *mahraganat* form of dancing serves a means by

33. Al-Tet is the name of a private Egyptian television channel devoted 24-7 to belly dancing.

34. Krump is a form of dancing connected with rap music, developed in South Compton as a competitive form of dancing that was conceived as an alternative to gang life.

which young men can express their emotion, whether frustration, rage, or joy, in a very powerful manner, and one that much more overtly celebrates the male body than do traditional Egyptian male dances. It is quite common in mass assemblages of *mahraganat* performance—and often negatively remarked upon by educated middle-class observers—for young men to dance bare-chested, their jeans hanging low and the tops of their boxer shorts exposed. According to Jawad (2014), young women fans of *mahraganat* have recently developed a specifically female version of the male dances, one that is much more assertive than traditional female dances and that they practice in the female spheres at *mahraganat* performances.

The subculture connected with *mahraganat* is, however, very much male identified. According to Benchouia (2015, 25), the term often used to describe a fan of *mahraganat* is *sarsagi* (pl. *sarsagiyya*), which denotes a certain style of fashion, a set of attitudes, and social status. The *sarsagi* "look" involves colorful and tight-fitting clothes (especially jeans), long nails, and hair gel applied in abundant quantity. The attitude, according to Benchouia, includes youthfulness, carelessness, and "hapless masculinity." *Sarsagi*, he notes, is related to the term *sabrsagi*, the name for someone who grabs a tossed-away cigarette off the ground and lights it up to smoke the tiny bit of remaining tobacco. The partisan of *mahraganat* or the *sarsagi* is seen then as a florid and fashion-conscious youth who is too poor to buy his own cigarettes. *Mahraganat* aficionados are also often called *awlad al-sis*, *awlad* meaning young men, and *sis*[35] meaning someone who dresses in a showy manner and is self-centered and egotistical, constantly monitoring his phone and communicating on social media (ibid., 25–26). According to Benchouia, *sarsagi* is associated in particular with low social and cultural status and *sis* with obsessive concern for personal appearance (27).[36]

35. Some claim that the term *sis* comes from the English "sissy."

36. A typical negative account of *sis* and *sarsagi* is found in a 2009 article in the Egyptian newspaper *al-Yawm al-Saba'*. It describes the *sis* as an egotistical

The *awlad sis* and the *sarsagiyya* also favor cruising on inexpensive motorcycles (Ryzova 2011). Benchouia describes how, especially in the wake of the 2011 insurrection, young men blasting *mahraganat* from mounted speakers on rented motorcycles or bicycles were a growing presence on public sections of Alexandria's seaside Corniche, especially the stretch that he dubs the boardwalk (2015, 16, 21). (*Mahraganat* was also heard from taxis and *tuk-tuks*.) Their presence, he adds, was often regarded as a nuisance by others trying to enjoy their stroll along the seaside. The at-times aggressive, brash, and very noisy presence of *sarsagi* lovers of *mahraganat*, according to Benchouia, invoking Lefevbre, represents a kind of claim on their part of the "right to the city" (ibid., 61), as well as a challenge to the hierarchies of cultural distinction characterized by what Ochoa Gautier (2006, 818) calls the "aural public sphere." It is a "gleeful reclamation," as Shenker puts it, "of sonic space by citizen outsiders" (2016, 371).

Counterrevolution

Since the dramatic events of 2013—the massive campaign of Tamarrod against the presidency of Mohammed Morsi of the Muslim Brotherhood, the military coup d'état against Morsi in July, the bloody massacre of Brotherhood supporters at Rabi'a Square in August—and the subsequent election of General Abdel Fattah el-Sisi as president in June 2014, the spirit of revolution in Egypt has effectively been crushed. A window into the role of "alternative" musicians in the process, and its effects on them, is provided by a documentary produced by MTV about Egyptian musicians, the Tamarrod campaign,

---

and vapid youth who sports "strange" hair (braided, spiked) and low-hung pants, whereas the *sarsagi* is a low-class youth bedecked in bright colors, spangled T-shirts, and cheap belts with gewgaws. Shenker (2009) reported an Egyptian media frenzy over so-called emos, who share a great deal in common with styles associated with the *awlad sis* discussed by Benchouia and Ryzova (2011), but are more middle class.

and the subsequent coup (MTV 2015). It recounts the involvement of Karim Adel Eissa of the rap group Arabian Knightz, Ramy Essam, and Nariman El Bakry, promoter for the Cairo Jazz Club, an important alternative music venue, in the Tamarrod-led anti-Brotherhood mobilization. All three express their strong opposition to the Morsi presidency and to the actions of the Muslim Brotherhood and the Brotherhood-led Freedom and Justice Party. Ramy Essam performs at demonstrations against the government, but then, playing at a rally the night before the massive Tamarrod-organized June 30 mobilization against Morsi, he walks off the stage, disgusted by the crowd's expressions of support for the army. Karim Adel Eissa and Nariman El Bakry, on the other hand, cheer Sisi's statement announcing the army takeover and the departure of Morsi, and they take part in the popular celebrations of the coup d'état.

Ramy Essam, who steadfastly opposed military rule, eventually went into exile in Malmö, Sweden, in October 2014, and he continues to produce music as well as, for the first time, taking formal music classes. Karim Adel Eissa is no longer a supporter of military rule (personal communication, July 2016), but the role that he and Nariman El Bakry played in the campaign that resulted in the coup against Egypt's lawfully elected president is symptomatic of the one played by many liberals. Yasser al-Manawahly, for his part, was one of the artists who came to fame in the wake of the revolution who continued, for a time, to produce important critical or "committed" music. "Al-Sunduq" (The Fund), released on YouTube in October 2012, brilliantly satirizes the notion that the International Monetary Fund and its loans would be Egypt's economic savior (Vox Populi Editors 2013; Shenker 2016, 304). Manawahly's biting humor is also present in his January 2014 release (on YouTube) of a well-crafted music video entitled "Rima," a brave, bold, and—for the postcoup era—all too rare allegorical critique of the military regime (Valassopoulos and Mostafa 2014, 640). As Howeidy (2014) explains, the song references the Arabic proverb of Rima, "who went back to her old habits," here serving as a metaphor for the return of the Mubarak-style authoritarian regime. The song also alludes to the toppling of

Morsi, "the change" that returned "Rima," and the familiar tale of the "raised whip," "censored talk," and "people dying from bullets and hunger." But Manawahly, while still able to get live gigs in early 2014, had not yet put out his much-anticipated album and seemed unlikely to. Howeidy concludes dryly that, by 2014, "popular, post-revolution songs are not a lucrative genre."

The alternative or underground scene (jazz, rock, rap) continues to function, but dissent is muted, metaphorical, or altogether absent; the spaces of performance remain quite limited; and the audiences, as before the insurrection, are primarily upper middle class.

Mahraganat Redux

Mahraganat, for its part, has continued to grow exponentially as a scene, with *mahraganat* artists, groups, and posses springing up in every town, village, and neighborhood throughout the country (Jawad 2014). Along with the increasing use of *mahraganat* bands for wedding parties, the weddings themselves, especially at the high end, have become much more detailed and complicated affairs. In addition to the *mahraganat* artists, wedding parties typically involve the hiring of dancers, stage builders, sound and lighting systems and operators, porters, drivers, and supervisors, plus even more photographers and video artists than were used in wedding parties previously. All these workers are typically part of the package hired together with the performers, and *mahraganat* stars therefore have become job creators in their popular neighborhoods (ibid.). In a remarkable turnaround, the Musicians Association, the arbiter of "appropriate" culture that was previously opposed very resolutely to the recognition of nonmusic and uncivilized "noise" from the popular milieus, has now begun to license *mahraganat* artists, but only a handful—major stars like al-Madfa'giya, Sadat and Fifty, Oka and Ortega, and Amr 7a7a. Without the license, a musician cannot perform at hotels, where performance fees are highly lucrative. Without the license, one cannot copyright one's songs. Because of the high cost of registration and the unlikelihood that lesser talents would be recognized, the licensing regime has created a large gap between the few "crossover" artists and the remainder of the *mahraganat* practitioners throughout the country. The latter cannot make money from playing hotel or resort dates and cannot afford the expenses and licenses (or bribes) to put on their own concerts, and so their incomes come only from playing weddings—and they, of course, play at less lucrative affairs than those events that feature the big stars. The fact that top-tier *mahraganat* artists are able to copyright their songs comes at a price, however, as the Musicians Association has the right to determine whether a song's lyrics are acceptable. This control, reportedly, has meant that the licensed *mahraganat* artists do not engage in the same degree of social criticism as they did before they started to cross over (Freemuse 2016). In addition, the kind of support that foreign funders have extended to *mahraganat* artists also typically redounds to the benefit of the top artists, and the interest of the British Council in strengthening the *mahraganat* scene in order to assist the musicians in "monetiz[ing] their industry" (Hall 2014) will doubtless benefit licensed artists like Sadat and Figo, but it is unlikely to aid many others, given the obstacles that the Egyptian state imposes on the normalization of many *mahraganat* musicians.

Although some *mahraganat* artists, and most notably the Figo, Sadat, and Fifty crew, did compose songs dealing with the revolution, they have never been "political" in the official sense. At times they have stated in interviews that they are not "political" when they deal with social issues that make their lyrics "political" (Kowalczyk 2014; Hip Deep 2012; Kingsley 2014). In the wake of the military coup, Jawad (2014) notes, the political climate has meant that *mahraganat* artists "prefer not to deal with politics in an explicit fashion." In December 2013, Sadat stated that he was conflicted between supporting those individuals who planned to vote yes in the referendum for a new constitution, which would mean the consolidation of military power and the election of Sisi, or to support those Egyptians opposed (Hall 2014). The referendum, of course, passed the following month, with a reported 98.1 percent of yes votes, and so Sadat's decision not to come out in favor of the opposition might be viewed as pragmatic for someone seeking to continue to pursue a successful music career.

Nonetheless, *mahraganat* artists continue to serve as important representatives of their popular neighborhood and to assert their loyalty to them and their organic relation to their populace. In a short documentary from 2014, Sadat reveals that he gets several gigs a week for weddings in fancy hotels but that he mostly lip-syncs, acting as if he were singing. But if it is an event in Madinat al-Salam, his hood, he will, of course, sing and not lip-sync (El Kaoutit 2014). And the *mahraganat* audience from the popular quarters remains active, continuing to assert its presence in public space, in the manner of what Bayat terms a "non-movement movement" (Ghandour-Demiri 2013). *Mahraganat* partisans may do so less brazenly and in fewer spaces since the coup of 2013, but they have not disappeared. According to Benchouia (2015, 67, 69), *mahraganat* fans no longer ride on bikes and motorcycles on the Corniche, but they are still a presence in popular quarters, but with the volume on their speakers turned down a bit. The fan base of the music also remains, despite *mahraganat*'s crossover appeal, under the threat of regulation and suppression. In 2014 the government imposed a one-year hold on the import of *tuk-tuk* vehicles and parts and a crackdown on unlicensed conveyances. A report by the State Commissioner's Authority prompted the move; it claimed that the vehicles posed dangers to people's health (polluting engines, unstable) and security (used for criminal activity and hard for police to trace) (Afify 2014). The recent effort to regulate *tuk-tuks* is, of course, of a piece with ongoing official views about the "chaotic" and "uncivilized" popular quarters and their unruly denizens. And despite *mahraganat*'s inroads, the state continues to regulate the music to ensure that it does not transcend official boundaries that determine what is respectable and what is not. In the spring of 2015, the Ministry of Education sent a letter to all governorate education departments, stating that only music preapproved by the ministry was to be used in classroom instruction and that *mahraganat* music was banned preemptively (Freemuse 2015a). In the fall of 2015, the state censorship board delayed the release of the film *4 Kotshena* (4 Playlands), starring Oka and Ortega, demanding that the song "Shartit 'Aynak Betjannin" (Your Eyeliner Is Astonishing) be deleted (Freemuse 2015b).

Probably the worst fate to befall the *mahraganat* scene to date, however, is the killing of Ahmad "Zo'la" Mohsen, on January 25, 2015, in Matariyya. Matariyya's name is thought to come from the Latin *mater* (mother), a reference to the "tree of the Virgin Mary" that marks the spot where the Holy Family is thought to have stopped as it fled to Egypt, taking refuge from King Herod's organized massacre of infants. Today a massive popular quarter that started to develop in the mid-1970s, Matariyya emerged as the center of Muslim Brotherhood dissent after the 2013 massacre. In 2015 partisans of the Brotherhood organized demonstrations on the anniversary of the beginning of the 2011 insurrection, and in the course of the crackdown the security forces killed at least twenty-three civilians, most of them in Matariyya. Among them was Zo'la, a disc jockey with the crew of Sadat, Fifty, and Figo and a resident of Matariyya. Zo'la was not, in fact, involved in the demonstration but was viewing it from a distance when he was struck and killed by a bullet. Egypt's Ministry of Information blamed the twenty-three deaths on the Muslim Brotherhood, but Sadat has insisted that the bullet that killed Zo'la was from the police, not the Brotherhood (*Egypt Independent* 2015; M. Mostafa 2015).

To end on a potentially hopeful note, not only has *mahraganat*, the sonic flag of the socially excluded, crossed over and gained legitimacy among an important segment of the young, liberal population, but reports also suggest that young people in the popular quarters are listening to bands like Wust al-Balad and Cairokee, previously the near-exclusive province of the upper middle classes. Perhaps such cross-class connections can be deepened and developed and help in the construction of new sorts of political ties, ties that could become significant if and when another surge of activity against Egyptian authoritarianism erupts. Although music by itself is not a vehicle for social change and social justice, a close investigation of musical practices can provide insights into the workings and limits of social movements. If we think of music as a practice that produces sonic communities and, as a consequence, draws social boundaries, it might push us to consider how one might develop sonic and music practices that create connections rather than exclude. The struggle for social justice in the Middle East would be enhanced by attention to such matters.

Sources Cited

Abdalla, Ahmad. 2010. *Microphone.* Film-Clinic. http://www.imdb.com/title/tt1684913/.

Afify, Heba. 2014. "Tuk Tuks: Tottering through Regulations." *Mada Masr,* May 7. http://www.madamasr.com/sections/politics/tuk-tuks-tottering-through-regulations.

Al-Yawm al-Saba'. 2009. "Sis wa-sarsagi . . . akhir mustalahat al-shabab [*Sis* and *Sarsagi*: The Latest Youth Nomenclature]." Apr. 15. http://www.youm7.com/story/2009/4/15/.

Armbrust, Walter. 1996. *Mass Culture and Modernism in Egypt.* Cambridge: Cambridge Univ. Press.

Bayat, Asef. 2012. "Politics in the City-Inside-Out." *City & Society* 24 (2): 110–28.

Belakhdar, Naoual, et al., eds. 2014. *Arab Revolutions and Beyond: Change and Persistence.* Proceedings of the International Conference Tunis, Nov. 12–13, 2013. Working Paper no. 11, Aug. Berlin: Center for Middle Eastern and North African Politics, Freie Univ. Berlin.

Benchouia, Tarek Adam. 2015. "Festivals: The Culture and Politics of *Mahraganat* Music in Egypt." Master's thesis, Univ. of Texas.

Biegman, Nicolaas H. 1990. *Egypt: Moulids, Saints, Sufis.* London: Gary Schwartz/SDU and Kegan Paul International.

Booth, Marilyn. 2006. "Exploding into the Seventies: Ahmad Fu'ad Nigm, Sheikh Imam, and the Aesthetics of a New Youth Politics." *Cairo Papers in Social Science* 29 (2–3): 19–44.

Born, Georgina. 2013. "Music, Sound and Place: Transformations of Public and Private Experience." Introduction to *Music, Sound and Place: Transformations of Public and Private Experience*, edited by Georgina Born, 1–69. Cambridge: Cambridge Univ. Press.

Cachia, Pierre. 1977. "The Egyptian 'Mawwal': Its Ancestry, Its Development, and Its Present Forms." *Journal of Arabic Literature* 8: 77–103.

Chammah, Maurice. 2012. "Port Said's Political House Band." *Rolling Stone Middle East*, May 20.

Colla, Elliott. N.d. "Emplotting Revolution: History and the Novel in Egypt." Unpublished paper.

———. 2012. "The People Want." *Middle East Report* 263: 8–13.

———. 2013. "In Praise of Insult." *Review of Middle East Studies* 47 (1): 37–48.

Cornet, Catherine. 2013. "Art for Social Change: Supporting Art for Community Building, New Philanthropic Orientations in Egypt." Working Paper, June. American Univ. in Cairo.

Deboulet, Agnès. 2009. "The Dictatorship of the Straight Line and the Myth of Social Disorder: Revisiting Informality in Cairo." In *Cairo Contested: Governance, Urban Space, and Global Modernity*, edited by Diane Singerman, 199–234. Cairo: American Univ. of Cairo Press.

Detrie, Megan. 2012. "Electro *Shaabi* Mixing the Parties and the Politics." *National*, Dec. 9. http://www.thenational.ae/arts-culture/music/electro-shaabi-mixing-the-parties-and-the-politics.

Dib, Philippe. 2006. *El Tanbura—Capturing a Vanishing Spirit*. Documentary posted on YouTube. https://www.youtube.com/watch?v=ZSIpuVjfQec.

Durkheim, Emile. 1995 [1912]. *The Elementary Forms of Religious Life*. Translated by Karen Fields. New York: Free Press.

Egypt Independent. 2015. "Friends of Popular DJ: Police Killed Zo'la." Jan. 28. http://www.egyptindependent.com/news/friends-popular-dj-police-killed-zo-la.

El Chazli, Youssef. 2013. "Alexandrins en fusion: Itinéraires de musiciens égyptiens des milieux alternatifs à la révolution." In *Jeunesses arabes: Du Maroc au Yémen: Loisirs, cultures et politiques*, edited by Laurent Bonnefoy and Myriam Catusse, 355–64. Paris: La Découverte.

El Hamamsy, Walid. 2012. Shooting under Fire: Filmmaking and the Aesthetics of Resistance. *Wasafiri* 27 (4): 45–49.

El Hamamsy, Walid, and Mounira Soliman. 2013. "The Aesthetics of Revolution: Popular Creativity and the Egyptian Spring." In *Popular Culture in the Middle East and North Africa: A Postcolonial Outlook*, edited by Walid El Hamamsy and Mounira Soliman, 246–59. New York: Routledge.

Elkamel, Sara. 2010. "El Tanboura: Rapturous Folk Music at a Medieval Palace." *Al-Misri al-Yawm*, Sept. 9.

El Kaoutit, Khalid. 2014. "Mahraganat: Cairo's Music Revolution | Journal Reporters." *Deutsche Welle English*. Documentary posted on YouTube, Apr. 13. https://youtu.be/wGbYG41-6wU.

ElNabawi, Maha. 2014. "Hiccups and Energy: Looking Back at This Year's D-CAF Music." *Mada Masr*, Apr. 13. http://www.madamasr.com/sections/culture/hiccups-and-energy-looking-back-years-d-caf-music.

El-Saket, Ola. 2011. "Remembering Abdel Halim Hafez, the Voice of Revolution." *Egypt Independent*, June 21. http://www.egyptindependent.com/news/remembering-abdel-halim-hafez-voice-revolution.

El-Shamy, Omar. 2014. *Mahragan—Short Documentary*. Caftvonline, YouTube, posted Nov. 10 (film made in 2012). https://www.youtube.com/watch?v=kq_M9qiybEI.

Eltanbura.org. N.d. "The Instruments." eltanbura.org/instruments/.

Freemuse. 2015a. "Egypt: Ministry of Education Bans 'Mahrajant' [*sic*] United States Music at Schools." May 27. http://freemuse.org/archives/10206.

———. 2015b. "Egypt: Move Song Banned by the Egyptian Censorship Authorities." Sept. 9. http://freemuse.org/archives/11290.

———. 2016. "Egypt: Mahraganat Artists Challenge Limits." Feb. 23. http://freemuse.org/archives/11798.

Frishkopf, Michael. 2003. "Some Meanings of the Spanish Tinge in Contemporary Egyptian Music." In *Mediterranean Mosaic: Popular Music and Global Sounds*, edited by Goffredo Plastino, 143–78. New York: Routledge.

Ghandour-Demiri, Nada. 2013. "The Urban Subalterns and the Non-movements of the Arab Uprisings: An Interview with Asef Bayat." *Jadaliyya*, Mar. 26. http://www.jadaliyya.com/pages/index/10815/the-urban-subalterns-and-the-non-movements-of-the.

Gilman, Dan. 2014. *Cairo Pop: Youth Music in Contemporary Egypt.* Minneapolis: Univ. of Minnesota Press.

Golia, Maria. 2015. "Egypt's Mahragan: Music of the Masses." *Middle East Institute*, July 7. http://www.mei.edu/content/at/egypt%E2%80%99s-mahragan-music-masses.

Gonzalez-Quijano, Yves. 2013. "Rap, an Art of the Revolution or a Revolution in Art?" *Orient-Institut Studies* 2. http://www.perspectivia.net/publikationen/orient-institut-studies/2-2013/gonzalez-quijano_rap.

Grippo, James R. 2007. "I'll Tell You Why We Hate You! Shaaban Abdel Rahim and Middle East Reactions to 9/11." In *Music in the Post-9/11 World*, edited by Jonathon Ritter and J. Martin Daughtry, 255–75. London: Routledge.

———. 2010. "What's *Not* on Egyptian Television and Radio! Locating the 'Popular' in Egyptian *Sha'bi*." In *Music and Media in the Arab World*, edited by Michael Frishkopf, 137–62. Cairo: American Univ. in Cairo Press.

———. 2015. "Sha'bi." In *Bloomsbury Encyclopedia of Popular Music of the World*. Vol. 10, *Genres: Middle East and North Africa*, edited by Richard Jankowsky. London: Bloomsbury.

Haenni, Patrick. 2009. "Cousins, Neighbors, and Citizens in Imbaba: The Genesis and Self-Mobilization of a Rebel Political Territory." In *Cairo Contested: Governance, Urban Space, and Global Modernity*, edited by Diane Singerman, 309–30. Cairo: American Univ. of Cairo Press.

Hall, Josh. 2014. "EDM (Egyptian Dance Music) Comes to London. A Full Report. The Quietus, Jan. 2. http://thequietus.com/articles/14329-electro-chaabi-knaka-sadat-diesel-figo-kode9-rinse.

Hamza, Doaa. 2011. "Life in Tahrir Square, Everywhere . . ." *Ahram Online*, Mar. 2. http://english.ahram.org.eg/NewsContent/5/35/6798/Arts--Culture/Stage--Street/Life-in-Tahrir-Square,-everywhere-.aspx.

Helmy, Mohamed M., and Sabine Frerichs. 2013. "Stripping the Boss: The Powerful Role of Humor in the Egyptian Revolution 2011." *Integrative Psychological and Behavioral Science* 47: 450–81.

Hip Deep. 2012. http://www.afropop.org/hipdeep/.

Holslin, Peter. 2015. "Pyrex Pyramids: Egyptian Rap Keeps Cooking." *Passion of the Weiss*, Apr. 14. https://www.passionweiss.com/2015/04/14/sadat-and-fifty-hez-hez-egyptian-rap-acid-arab/.

Howeidy, Amira. 2014. "Yasser El-Manawahly: Music as Political Act." *Ahram Online*, Feb. 22. http://english.ahram.org.eg/NewsContent/5/33/94665/Arts--Culture/Music/-Yasser-ElManawahly-Music-as-political-act.aspx.

———. 2015. "Matariyya, Egypt's New Theater of Dissent." *Middle East Report Online*, June 4. http://www.merip.org/mero/mero060415.

Hubbard, Ben. 2013. "Egypt's Music Revolution." *New York Times*, YouTube, posted May 13. https://www.youtube.com/watch?v=ix6v4_CpQ5o.

Ibrahim, Zakaria. N.d. "Zakaria Ibrahim." http://www.el-mastaba.org/zakaria-ibrahim.html.

———. 2005. *The Siren*. Documentary film, El Mastaba for Egyptian Folk Music, posted on YouTube, Oct. 7, 2010. https://www.youtube.com/watch?v=uhXrYUtebHw.

Jawad, Ferida. 2014. "Guest Bloggers around the World: Mahraganat—Musical Revolution in Egypt." Afropop Worldwide, June 12. http://www.afropop.org/18897/mahraganat-the-establishment-of-a-genre/.

Kingsley, Patrick. 2014. "Cairo's Street Music Mahraganat Both Divides and Unites." *Guardian*, May 9.

Kniaz, Malgorzata. N.d. "Shaaban Abdel Rahim and the Changing Stardom Culture in Egypt." https://www.inter-disciplinary.net/critical-issues/wp-content/uploads/2014/05/kniazcelpaper.pdf.

Kowalczyk, Pete. 2014. "Cairo's Underground Producers Defy Military Rule. *Dazed*, May 29. http://www.dazeddigital.com/music/article/20043/1/egypts-underground-producers-stand-against-military-rule.

Loccatelli, Giovanna. 2013. "Sadat: 'Mahraganat Is Pure Energy.'" *Guardian*, Nov. 30. https://www.theguardian.com/music/2013/dec/01/dj-sadat-mahraganat-salam-cairo.

Madoeuf, Anna. 2006. "Mulids of Cairo: Sufi Guilds, Popular Celebrations, and the 'Roller-Coaster Landscape' of the Resignified City." In *Cairo Cosmopolitan: Politics, Culture, and Urban Space in the New Globalized Middle East*, edited by Diane Singerman and Paul Amar. Cairo: American Univ. in Cairo Press.

Makar, Farida. 2011. "'Let Them Have Some Fun': Political and Artistic Forms of Expression in the Egyptian Revolution." *Mediterranean Politics* 16 (2): 307–12.

Mangialardi, Nicholas Rocco. 2013. "Egyptian Hip Hop and the January 25th Revolution." Master's thesis, Ohio State Univ.

Marcus, Scott L. 2007. *Music in Egypt: Experiencing Music, Expressing Culture*. New York: Oxford Univ. Press.

Meddeb, Hind. 2013. *Electro Chaabi*. IPS. http://www.imdb.com/title/tt2887002/.

Metwaly, Ati. 2014. "Sufi Funk." *Al-Ahram Weekly*, July 10. http://weekly.ahram.org.eg/News/6728/23/Sufi-funk.aspx.

Miller, Catherine. 2010. "'On tour' sur la scène musicale cairote 1996." https://halshs.archives-ouvertes.fr/halshs-00592456.

Mohsen, Ali Abdel. 2013. "A Q&A with Leading Mahraganat Singer Sadat." *Egypt Independent*, Apr. 18. http://www.egyptindependent.com/news/qa-leading-mahraganat-singer-sadat.

Montasser, Farah. 2011. "Eskenderella Perform to Anti-Mubarak Protestors in Tahrir." *Ahram Online*, Feb. 7. http://english.ahram.org.eg/NewsContent/5/33/5154/Arts--Culture/Music/Eskenderella-perform-to-antiMubarak-protestors-in-.aspx.

Morayef, Soraya. 2012. "'We Are the Eight Percent': Inside Egypt's Underground Shaabi Music Scene." *Jadaliyya*, May 29. http://www.jadaliyya.com/pages/index/5738/we-are-the-eight-percent_inside-egypts-underground.

Mostafa, Dalia Said. 2013. "Popular Culture and Nationalism in Egypt: 'Arab Lofti and Egyptian Popular Music." In *Arab Cultural Studies: History, Politics and the Popular*, edited by Anastasia Valassopoulos, 154–75. London: Routledge.

———. 2015. "Introduction: Egyptian Women, Revolution, and Protest Culture." *Journal for Cultural Research* 19 (2): 118–29.

Mostafa, Mohamed. 2015. "Ahmed(Zo'la) Mohsen, a Famous Pop DJ Killed Accidentally during Protests on 25 January, 2014, in Matariya." *Egypt Independent*, Jan. 26. http://www.egyptindependent.com//node/2443243.

MTV. 2015. "Rebel Music | Egypt: Bittersweet Revolution (Full Episode) | MTV." YouTube, posted Apr. 16. https://www.youtube.com/watch?v=wZeZKmn2R7g.

Niazy, Fatéma. 2014. "The Revolution of Form: Art and the Uprising." In *Revolution as a Process: The Case of the Egyptian Uprising*, edited by Adham Hamed, 48–79. Bremen: Wiener Verlag für Sozialforschung.

Nur, Yousif. 2014. "A Radical Century: Mahmoud Refat of 100 Copies Cairo Interviewed." The Quietus, Dec. 17. http://thequietus.com/articles/16831-mahmoud-refat-interview.

Ochoa Gautier, Ana María. 2006. "Sonic Transculturation, Epistemologies of Purification and the Aural Public Sphere in Latin America." *Social Identities* 12 (6): 803–25.

Out Focus. 2015. *Al-Mastaba*. Documentary film, posted on YouTube Oct. 31. https://www.youtube.com/watch?v=TH9OGLu_RL4.

Peterson, Jennifer. 2012. "Going to the Mulid: Street-Smart Spirituality in Egypt." In *Ordinary Lives and Grand Schemes: An Anthropology of Everyday Religion*, edited by Samuli Schielke and Liza Debevec, 113–30. New York: Bergahn.

———. 2008a. "Playing with Spirituality: The Adoption of Mulid Motifs in Egyptian Dance Music." *Contemporary Islam* 2 (3): 271–95.

———. 2008b. "Remixing Songs, Remaking Mulids: The Merging Spaces of Dance Music and Saint Festivals in Egypt." In *Dimensions of Locality: The Making and Remaking of Islamic Saints and Their Places*, edited by Samuli Schielke and Georg Stauth, 67–88. *Yearbook of the Sociology of Islam* 8. Bielefeld: Transcript Verlag.

———. 2008c. "Sampling Folklore: The Re-popularization of Sufi Inshad in Egyptian Dance Music." *Arab Media & Society* 4. http://www.arabmediasociety.com/?article=580.

Poché, Christian. 1999. Liner notes to *Ensemble al-Tanbûrah, la simsimiyya de Port-Saïd* [CD]. Paris: Institut du monde arabe.

Prince, Mona. 2014. *Revolution Is My Name: An Egyptian Woman's Diary from Eighteen Days in Tahrir.* Translated by Samia Mehrez. Cairo: American Univ. in Cairo Press.

Procházka, Stephan. 2013. "The Voice of Freedom: Remarks on the Language of Songs from the Egyptian Revolution 2011." *Orient-Institut Studies* 2. http://www.perspectivia.net/publikationen/orient-institut-studies/2-2013/prochazka_freedom.

Puig, Nicolas. 2010. *Farah: Musicien de noces et scènes urbaines au Caire.* Arles: Actes Sud/Sindbad.

Ramsis, Amir. 2004. *Nuh al-hamam* [Wailing of the Doves]. SEMAT for Production and Distribution. Documentary film posted on YouTube. https://www.youtube.com/watch?v=j2wDbRvEynM.

Revill, George. 2000. "Music and the Politics of Sound: Nationalism, Citizenship, and Auditory Space." *Environment and Planning D: Society and Space* 18: 597–613.

Reynolds, Dwight. 2007. *Arab Folklore: A Handbook*. Westport, CT: Greenwood Press.

Rinne, Tuija. 2005. "Sing, O Simsimiyya" [Finnish]. *Ishtar*, Jan. English translation at http://www.elhossenydance.com/layali_simsimiyya.html.

Robertson, Craig. 2015. "Whose Music, Whose Country? Music, Mobilization, and Social Change in North Africa." *African Conflict & Peacebuilding Review* 5 (1): 66–87.

Ryzova, Lucy. 2011. "The Battle of Muhammad Mahmud Street: Teargas, Hair Gel, and Tramadol." *Jadaliyya*, Nov. 28. http://www.jadaliyya.com/pages/index/3312/the-battle-of-muhammad-mahmud-street_teargas-hair-.

Salem, Mostafa. 2013. "Dancing in Cairo Streets." *Daily News Egypt*, Aug. 13. http://www.dailynewsegypt.com/2013/08/13/dancing-in-cairo-streets/.

Sánchez García, José. N.d.a. "Celebraciones para los santos: *Mahraganat*, Utopía y juventud en Egipto." From Academia.edu.

———. N.d.b. "De la resistencia cotidiana a la revolución: Baltagiya y hooligans en Tahrir." From Academia.edu.

———. N.d.c. "La 'revolución contra los jóvenes': Movimientos políticos juveniles y producciones discursivas en la insurrección Egipcia." From Academia.edu.

———. 2010a. "De las celebraciones para los santos a la mulid dance music: Utopía y juventud en Egipto." *TRANS* 14. http://www.redalyc.org/html/822/82220947018/.

———. 2010b. "Entre la modernidad y la tradición: Modos de ser joven en El Cairo." *QuAderns-e* 15 (2): 34–57.

———. 2016. "From *hara* to *midan*: Public Spaces of Youth in Cairo." In *Youth, Space and Time: Agoras and Chronotopes in the Global City*, edited by Carles Feixa, Carmen Leccardi, and Pam Nilan, 293–317. Leiden: Brill.

Sanders, Lewis, IV, and Mark Visonà. 2012. "The Soul of Tahrir: Poetics of a Revolution." In *Translating Egypt's Revolution*, edited by Samia Mehrez, 213–48. Cairo: American Univ. in Cairo Press.

Schielke, Samuli. 2012. *The Perils of Joy: Contesting Mulid Festivals in Contemporary Egypt*. Syracuse, NY: Syracuse Univ. Press.

———. 2015. *Egypt in the Future Tense: Hope, Frustration, and Ambivalence before and after 2011*. Bloomington: Indiana Univ. Press.

Sélim, May. 2014. "Eskenderella Turns the Page with Their First Album." *Ahram Online*, Sept. 9. http://english.ahram.org.eg/NewsContent/5/33/110314/Arts--Culture/Music/Eskenderella-turns-the-page-with-their-first-album.aspx.

Shalaby, Nadia A. 2015. "A Multimodal Analysis of Selected Cairokee Songs of the Egyptian Revolution and Their Representation of Women." *Journal for Cultural Research* 19 (2): 176–98.

Shenker, Jack. 2009. "Egypt's Emos, the Latest Hate Figures." *Guardian*, May 6. https://www.theguardian.com/commentisfree/2009/may/06/egypt-emo-backlash.

———. 2016. *The Egyptians: A Radical History of Egypt's Unfinished Revolution*. London: Allen Lane.

Sherief, Abdel-Rahman. 2013. "El Mastaba Preserves Egypt's Musical Heritage." *Daily News Egypt*, Jan. 21. http://www.dailynewsegypt.com/2013/01/21/el-mastaba-preserves-egypts-musical-heritage/.

Shiloah, Amnon. 1972. "The Simsimiyya: A Stringed Instrument of the Red Sea Area." *Asian Music* 4 (1): 15–26.

Sims, David. 2010. *Understanding Cairo: The Logic of a City Out of Control*. Cairo: American Univ. in Cairo Press.

———. 2013. "Les quartiers informels du Caire tirent-ils avantage de la 'révolution' égyptienne?" In *Quartiers informels d'un monde arabe en transition: Réflexions et perspectives pour l'action urbaine*, edited by Pierre-Arnaud Barthel and Sylvy Jaglin, 71–87. AFD, Coll. Conférences & Séminaire, no. 7. http://www.abhatoo.net.ma/maalama-textuelle/developpement-economique-et-social/developpement-social/urbanisme/politique-urbaine/quartiers-informels-d-un-monde-arabe-en-transition-reflexions-et-perspectives-pour-l-action-urbaine.

Singerman, Diane. 2009. "The Siege of Imbaba, Egypt's Internal 'Other,' and the Criminalization of Politics." In *Cairo Contested: Governance, Urban Space, and Global Modernity*, edited by Diane Singerman, 111–44. Cairo: American Univ. of Cairo Press.

Soliman, Mounira. 2011. "Artistic Interpretations of Downtown Cairo." *Journal of Postcolonial Writing* 47 (4): 391–403.

Srage, Nader. 2013. "The Protest Discourse: The Example of 'Irhal' (Go/ Get Out/Leave)." *Orient-Institut Studies* 2. http://www.perspectivia .net/publikationen/orient-institut-studies/2-2013/srage_protest.

Stokes, Martin. 2002. "Review of *La Simsimiyya de Port-Said.*" *Music and Anthropology* 7. http://umbc.edu/MA/index/number7/stokes/simsi .htm.

Straw, Will. 1991. "Systems of Articulation, Logics of Change: Communities and Scenes in Popular Music." *Cultural Studies* 5 (3): 369–88.

Tomren, Ingvild. 2015. "Mahragānāt i den humorløse staten (Mahraganat in the Humorless State)." Master's thesis, Univ. of Oslo.

Valassopoulos, Anastasia, and Dalia Said Mostafa. 2014. "Popular Protest Music and the 2011 Egyptian Revolution." *Popular Music and Society* 37 (5): 638–59.

Van der Linden, Neil. 2015. "Zār." In *Bloomsbury Encyclopedia of Popular Music of the World*, vol. 10, *Genres: Middle East and North Africa*, edited by Richard Jankowsky. London: Bloomsbury.

Vox Populi Editors. 2013. "Yaser El Manawahly: The Monetary Fund." *Jadaliyya*, Nov. 7. http://www.jadaliyya.com/pages/index/14965/yaser -el-manawhly_-t.

Wa'il, Ahmad. 2011. "Mas'alat al-dī jī al-sha'bī." *Masress*, Oct. 29. http:// www.masress.com/adab/3526.

Westland, Naomi. 2012. "Rappers Provide Anthems for Arab Spring." *USA Today*, May 22. http://usatoday30.usatoday.com/news/world/story /2012-05-21/arab-spring-hip-hop/55120262/1.

Willis, Paul. 1990. *Common Culture*. Boulder, CO: Westview Press.

Zaatari, Ahmad. 2011. "Maryam Saleh: Rocking Sheikh Imam's Revolutionary Songs." *Alakhbar English*, Dec. 27. http://english.al-akhbar .com/node/2855.

Zimmer, Ben. 2011. "How Mubarak Was Told to Go, in Many Languages." Language Log, Feb. 13. http://languagelog.ldc.upenn.edu/nll/?p=2964.

Contributors ✦ Index

Contributors

Niki Akhavan is assistant professor of media studies at the Catholic University of America. Her research focuses on the relationship between new media technologies and Iranian political and cultural production. She is the author of *Electronic Iran: The Cultural Politics of an Online Evolution* (2013).

Roger Allen is professor emeritus of Arabic language and comparative literature and the former Sascha Jane Patterson Harvie Professor of Social Thought and Comparative Ethics at the University of Pennsylvania. The leading expert on modern Arabic literature in North America, he is the author of *An Introduction to Arabic Literature* (2000) and many other works. He is also a translator of modern Arabic fiction into English, for which the Kingdom of Morocco awarded him a Medal of Honor at the 2010 Casablanca Book Fair.

Ramazan Erdağ is associate professor and head of the Department of International Relations at Eskişehir Osmangazi University. His areas of expertise are Turkish foreign policy, international security, international foreign aid, and regional security in the Middle East. He is the author of *Libya in the Arab Spring: From Revolution to Insecurity* (2017).

Behrooz Ghamari-Tabrizi is professor of Near Eastern studies and director of the Sharmin and Bijad Mossavar-Rahmani Center for Iran and Persian Gulf Studies at Princeton University. He is the author of *Islam and Dissent in Postrevolutionary Iran: Abdolkarim Soroush, Religious Politics and Democratic Reform* (2008), *Foucault in Iran: Islamic Revolution after the Enlightenment* (2016), and *Remembering Akbar: Inside the Iranian Revolution* (2016).

Joshua D. Hendrick is associate professor of sociology and global studies at Loyola University Maryland in Baltimore. He has conducted extensive field research in Turkey and is the author of *Gülen: The Ambiguous Politics of Market Islam in Turkey and the World* (2013) and articles on Turkish democratization and religion and politics in that country.

Valerie J. Hoffman is professor of Islamic studies and head of the Department of Religion at the University of Illinois at Urbana–Champaign. Her research interests include Islamic theology, Sufism, gender ideology, and modern Islamic thought. She is the author of *Sufism, Mystics and Saints in Modern Egypt* (1995), *The Essentials of Ibadi Islam* (2012), and numerous articles on Sufism, Islamic gender ideology, Ibadi Islam, human rights, and contemporary Islamic movements.

Gül Aldıkaçtı Marshall is associate professor in the Department of Sociology at the University of Louisville. Her research is on gender, politics, social movements, and mass media. She is the author of *Shaping Gender Policy in Turkey: Grassroots Women Activists, the European Union, and the Turkish State* (2013).

Haideh Moghissi is professor emerita and senior scholar at York University in Toronto. She was a founder of the Iranian National Union of Women and a member of its first executive and editorial boards before leaving Iran in 1984. Her publications in English include seven monographs and edited volumes, in addition to articles in books and journals. Her *Feminism and Islamic Fundamentalism: The Limits of Postmodern Analysis* (1999), winner of the Choice Outstanding Academic Book Award, has been translated into Farsi, Korean, and Indonesian. She was awarded a Pierre Elliot Trudeau Research Fellowship in 2011 and the Status of Women Award of Distinction from the Ontario Confederation of Faculty Associations in 2015.

Feisal G. Mohamed is professor of English at the Graduate Center of the City University of New York. He is the author of *In the Anteroom of Divinity: The Reformation of the Angels from Colet to Milton* (2008) and *Milton and the Post-secular Present* (2011), which received the Milton Society of America's James Holly Hanford Award. He is also coeditor with Mary Nyquist of *Milton and Questions of History: Essays by Canadians*

Past and Present (2012), which received the Milton Society of America's Irene Samuel Award; coeditor with Gordon Hutner of *A New Deal for the Humanities: Liberal Arts and the Future of Public Higher Education* (2016); and coeditor with Patrick Fadely of *Milton's Modernities* (2017). In addition to academic journals, Mohamed's work has appeared in *Dissent Magazine*, the *Huffington Post*, the *Chronicle Review*, the website of the *New Republic*, and the *New York Times* series "The Stone."

Cheryl A. Rubenberg (died June 16, 2017) was an independent analyst and former associate professor of political science at Florida International University. She is the author of several books about the Israeli-Palestinian conflict, including *The Palestinians: In Search of a Just Peace* (2003), *Palestinian Women: Patriarchy and Resistance in the West Bank* (2001), and *Israel and the American National Interest: A Critical Examination* (1989). She is also the editor of the three-volume *Encyclopedia of the Israeli-Palestinian Conflict* (2010).

Ted Swedenburg is professor of anthropology at the University of Arkansas. He is the author of *Memories of Revolt: The 1936–39 Rebellion and the Palestinian National Past* (1995) and is coeditor, with Rebecca Luna Stein, of *Palestine, Israel and the Politics of Popular Culture* (2005) and, with Smadar Lavie, of *Displacement, Diaspora, and Geographies of Identity* (1996). He is currently working on a book manuscript on Middle Eastern "border" music and Middle Eastern–inflected musical genres that have been embraced in the West.

Mariz Tadros is professor at the Institute of Development Studies at the University of Sussex, where she leads the Power and Popular Politics cluster. She specializes in the politics and human development of the Middle East. She is the author of *The Muslim Brotherhood in Contemporary Egypt: Democracy Redefined or Confined?* (2012) and *Copts at the Crossroads: The Challenges of Building an Inclusive Democracy in Contemporary Egypt* (2013) and is editor of *Women in Politics: Gender, Power and Development* (2014).

Index

Italic page numbers denote illustrations and tables.